Sustainable Resource Management in Next-Generation Computational Constrained Networks

Scrivener Publishing
100 Cummings Center, Suite 541J
Beverly, MA 01915-6106

Industry 5.0 Transformation Applications

Series Editors: Dr. S. Balamurugan (sbnbala@gmail) and Dr. Sheng-Lung Peng

The increase in technological advancements in the areas of artificial intelligence (AI), machine learning (ML) and data analytics has led to the next industrial revolution "Industry 5.0". The transformation to Industry 5.0 collaborates human intelligence with machines to customize efficient solutions. This book series covers various subjects under promising application areas of Industry 5.0 such as smart manufacturing, intelligent traffic, cloud manufacturing, real-time productivity optimization, augmented reality and virtual reality, etc., as well as titles supporting technologies for promoting potential applications of Industry 5.0, such as collaborative robots (Cobots), edge computing, Internet of Everything, big data analytics, digital twins, 6G and beyond, blockchain, quantum computing and hyper-intelligent networks.

Publishers at Scrivener
Martin Scrivener (martin@scrivenerpublishing.com)
Phillip Carmical (pcarmical@scrivenerpublishing.com)

Sustainable Resource Management in Next-Generation Computational Constrained Networks

Edited by

Subhasis Dash
School of Computer Engineering KIIT Deemed to be University, Bhubaneswar, Odisha, India

Manas Ranjan Lenka
School of Computer Engineering, KIIT Deemed to be University, Bhubaneswar, Odisha, India

S. Balamurugan
Intelligent Research Consultancy Services (IRCS), Coimbatore, Tamil Nadu, India

Ambika Prasad Tripathy
Cisco's Network Security Business, Bangalore, India

and

Amarendra Mohanty
Intel Corp, Bangalore, India

Scrivener Publishing

WILEY

This edition first published 2025 by John Wiley & Sons, Inc., 111 River Street, Hoboken, NJ 07030, USA
and Scrivener Publishing LLC, 100 Cummings Center, Suite 541J, Beverly, MA 01915, USA

For more information about Scrivener publications please visit www.scrivenerpublishing.com.

Wiley Global Headquarters
111 River Street, Hoboken, NJ 07030, USA

For details of our global editorial offices, customer services, and more information about Wiley products visit us at www.wiley.com.

The manufacturer's authorized representative according to the EU General Product Safety Regulation is Wiley-VCH GmbH, Boschstr. 12, 69469 Weinheim, Germany, e-mail: Product_Safety@wiley.com.

Library of Congress Cataloging-in-Publication Data

ISBN 978-1-394-21256-9

Cover image: Generated with AI using Adobe Firefly
Cover design by Russell Richardson

Set in size of 11pt and Minion Pro by Manila Typesetting Company, Makati, Philippines

Printed in the USA

10 9 8 7 6 5 4 3 2 1

Contents

Preface

The exponential growth of the internet and the increasing interconnectedness of devices worldwide have revolutionized our daily lives and resource management. As we navigate this technological surge, the imperative for sustainable resource management intensifies. This book provides an in-depth exploration of the latest advancements in networking technologies that meet these sustainability challenges.

The material herein explores the transformative potential of 6G and 5G technologies, which are set to overhaul our communication networks with their increased capacities, extensive connectivity, and low-latency features. These next-generation networks are crucial for enabling significant automation, thereby reducing energy demands and processing requirements. Additionally, the book examines the Internet of Things (IoT) and its industrial counterpart, Industrial IoT (IIoT), for their ability to revolutionize industrial cyber-physical systems. Despite IoT's vast potential, its adoption has been curtailed by scalability, interoperability, and security issues. The discussion extends to how robust IIoT solutions can effectively tackle these challenges.

A focal point of the book is blockchain technology, which ensures robust end-to-end security in IoT environments, safeguarding against central attacks even if individual entry points are compromised. It also covers the roles of software-defined networking (SDN) and network function virtualization (NFV) in enhancing network scalability and facilitating dynamic service configurations. Moreover, the significance of mobile edge computing is highlighted, bringing computational power closer to data sources to boost real-time application performance while reducing latency and bandwidth usage.

The value of this book lies not only in its technological insights but also in its practical applications and real-world impacts, spanning intelligent homes, data centers, e-health, and smart cities. These technologies optimize resource management in computationally constrained networks, enhancing environmental sustainability and societal well-being. Targeted at a diverse readership of researchers, academicians, and industry professionals, the book provides a comprehensive understanding of current technological trends and their potential to drive sustainable resource management. It offers a detailed analysis of challenges and solutions, aiming to inspire further research and development in sustainable and efficient networking technologies. We hope this book serves as a valuable resource and a source of inspiration for those interested in the nexus of technology and sustainability, encouraging collaborative efforts and innovative thinking to forge a more sustainable future for our globally connected world.

Chapter 1 examines the use of Neurosky Mindwave Mobile 2 (NMM2) to monitor students' cognitive activity in educational settings, enhancing learning through personalized video recommendations based on brain wave signals, with data analysis from institutions like the National Institutes of Technology Rourkela to optimize engagement and educational outcomes. Chapter 2 explores the integration of blockchain technology in supply chain management, emphasizing its role in enhancing transparency, traceability, and efficiency, addressing IoT security, and promoting sustainability through decentralized approaches and blockchain interoperability. Chapter 3 delves into the transformative impact of IoT on the aquaculture industry, using sensors, cameras, and RFID tags to collect and analyze real-time data on fish behavior and environmental conditions, significantly improving efficiency, reducing losses, and enhancing the sustainability of fish farming practices.

Chapter 4 delves into consumption optimization in Wireless Sensor Networks (WSNs), crucial for prolonging network lifetime and enhancing performance. It discusses strategies such as energy-efficient routing with protocols like LEACH and PEGASIS, data aggregation to reduce redundancy, duty cycling to save energy, and advanced methods like energy harvesting and adaptive algorithms to further optimize consumption, ensuring sustainable WSN operations.

Chapter 5 explores the significant reliance of U.S. consumers on online reviews and testimonials before making purchases, with 82% reading reviews and 40% doing so frequently. The chapter details a study that analyzed data from online airline reviews using advanced machine learning techniques like random forests and Convolutional Neural Networks (CNNs). The predictive analysis, based on over 3000 instances from www.airlinequality.com, aimed to identify the most suitable airlines from customer feedback, demonstrating how machine learning can enhance customer satisfaction and decision-making in the airline industry.

Chapter 6 discusses the accelerated shift towards online shopping and the rising need for contactless delivery solutions spurred by the COVID-19 pandemic. It provides a comprehensive overview of delivery robots, their adoption boosted by their ability to minimize human contact, reduce manpower, and decrease pollution. The chapter examines their development, functionality, and the challenges they face, highlighting their role in the Emerging Disruptive Technologies for Society 5.0 initiative and their effective use across various industries globally. It posits that as technologies evolve, delivery robots will play a crucial role in the future of logistics and transportation, enhancing goods delivery efficiency and safety, and fostering the creation of smarter, more sustainable societies.

Chapter 7 explores the integration of cloud computing with IoT, emphasizing how cloud services like SaaS, PaaS, and IaaS manage large volumes of IoT data. It discusses cloud-based IoT standards and protocols like MQTT and HTTP, and illustrates their applications in sectors like healthcare and agriculture. The chapter also highlights challenges such as security risks and presents case studies on smart home automation and industrial IoT, suggesting future research in edge computing and serverless processing.

Chapter 8 examines sensory networks within the IoT framework, focusing on their impact on industries like smart homes and healthcare. It details the role of IoT in enhancing functionalities such as home security and energy management with renewable sources. Challenges like interoperability and security are addressed, alongside the increasing role of wearable devices and edge computing in expanding IoT capabilities.

Chapter 9 discusses integrating AI with cloud security to combat data breaches, emphasizing the use of deep learning for malware detection and intrusion prevention. It outlines the importance of minimizing human error and advocates for a self-learning AI system to enhance security intelligence and protection of sensitive data. Strategies include deploying AI-operated servers and utilizing deep learning to strengthen cloud security defenses and ensure resilience against cyber threats.

Chapter 10 addresses the escalating threat of Distributed Denial of Service (DDoS) attacks and the innovative use of AI and machine learning to enhance network resilience. Researchers analyze DDoS attack patterns to develop countermeasures that improve real-time detection and mitigation, ensuring the integrity and accessibility of web infrastructures.

Chapter 11 introduces CyberEDU, a practical educational tool for simulating and preventing DDoS attacks, bridging the gap between theoretical knowledge and practical application. This tool enhances the skills of professionals and students, equipping them to effectively combat DDoS threats and contributing to a more prepared and aware cybersecurity workforce.

Chapter 12 explores effective resource management techniques in network systems constrained by limited resources. It discusses the optimization of bandwidth, buffer space, and computational assets to enhance network performance, minimize latency, and meet diverse performance objectives, providing crucial insights for practitioners and researchers navigating the complexities of network optimization.

Chapter 13 discusses the evolution of network architectures through software-defined networking (SDN), which separates network control from data forwarding to enhance flexibility and efficiency. It provides a detailed overview of SDN, including its architecture, components, and workflow, and examines its role in improving management in resource-constrained networks (RCNs). Additionally, the chapter explores SDN's integration with IoT and 5G, aiming to familiarize newcomers with its transformative impact on modern networking.

Focusing on reducing vehicle emissions to combat global warming, Chapter 14 introduces an innovative system combining IoT and a CNN-SVM hybrid machine learning model. This system analyzes emission streams to identify high-polluting vehicles and prompts regulatory actions. By enhancing real-time monitoring and alert mechanisms, it supports environmental sustainability and energy efficiency in transportation, presenting a proactive solution to control emissions and mitigate air pollution.

Addressing the rising crime rates in Malaysia, this research integrates IoT technology with biometric systems to bolster home security. It proposes a biometric door lock system using fingerprint and facial recognition to prevent unauthorized access, while considering sustainable resource management in smart home systems. Chapter 15 highlights the advantages of biometric authentication and the importance of refining these systems to enhance residential security, advocating for the integration of technology into daily living for secure and convenient environments.

We want to express our deepest appreciation to all the contributors who have dedicated their time and efforts to making this book a success. Additionally, we extend our deepest thanks for the suggestions, help, and support from Martin Scrivener and the team at Scrivener Publishing.

The Editors
May 2025

1

Enhancing Digital Learning Pedagogy for Lecture Video Recommendation Using Brain Wave Signal

Rabi Shaw[1]*, Simanjeet Kalia[2] and Sourabh Mohanty[2]

[1]Dr B R Ambedkar National Institute of Technology, Jalandhar, India
[2]School of Computer Science, Kalinga Institute of Industrial Technology, Bhubaneswar, Odisha, India

Abstract

In this study, recent research advancements, such as those involving the NeuroSky Mindwave Mobile 2 (NMM2), have been explored across areas including emotional identification, drowsiness detection in healthcare, attention analysis within educational settings, and the use of collaborative filters for interpreting brain signals. Thus, several researchers have employed a variety of sensors to record brain wave patterns [electroencephalography (EEG)] that are indicative of human cognition. However, many studies are currently employing single sensors to track students' cognitive activity in the educational setting due to the expense of sensors, the complexity of the experimental setup, and the hassles this causes for the students. A single-channel EEG headset, i.e., NMM2, is considered. The raw data of the EEG signal, attention, eye blink, mediation, and all frequency subbands are collected by this device and stored in a CSV file. The intersection of e-learning, m-learning, t-learning, and sustainable networking in the educational domain highlights the potential of 5G and 4G networks to transform educational experiences while emphasizing the importance of green Internet and Communication Technology, digital inclusion, scalability, security, and privacy. By incorporating sustainable networking practices, this study aims to enhance the effectiveness and longevity of educational initiatives. After systematically searching online bibliographic databases, over 40 pertinent publications were found and included in the study. These studies have made several attempts to enhance students' educational opportunities in a variety of settings.

**Corresponding author*: shawr@nitj.ac.in

Subhasis Dash, Manas Ranjan Lenka, S. Balamurugan, Ambika Prasad Tripathy and Amarendra Mohanty (eds.) Sustainable Resource Management in Next-Generation Computational Constrained Networks, (1–30) © 2025 Scrivener Publishing LLC

The investigations dealing with brainwave signals (EEG), together with attention and concentration analyses, aim to affect e-learning situations in a positive way.

Keywords: Classification, cognitive-aware, EEG signal, pedagogy, recommendation

1.1 Introduction

In the modern era, people can access various types of data on many topics. The development of the internet has changed mortal existence in many ways. The experimenters and analysts from various universities and institutions across the world offered several proposals for improved recommendation discovery for academics because of the fast growth of ICT (Internet and Communication Technology).

The education sector has been transformed by advancements in technology, leading to the emergence of innovative learning approaches such as e-learning, m-learning, and t-learning. However, it is essential to consider the role of networking technologies in supporting and sustaining these educational initiatives.

The advent of 5G networks, with their higher bandwidth, lower latency, and increased capacity, enables seamless streaming of multimedia content, immersive virtual reality experiences, and real-time collaboration. Meanwhile, 4G networks have played a significant role in supporting e-learning and m-learning initiatives by providing learners access to online courses, educational apps, and multimedia content on their mobile devices.

However, sustainable networking practices in the educational domain go beyond the scope of high-speed connections. The literature reveals that sustainable networking encompasses several key aspects. First, it includes the adoption of green ICT and energy-efficient networking infrastructures to reduce environmental impact.

Second, sustainable networking aims to address the digital divide and ensure inclusion for all learners. Efforts such as community networks, public Wi-Fi initiatives, and partnerships with telecommunication providers can bridge the connectivity gap and promote digital inclusion. Equitable access to broadband connectivity and affordable internet services are crucial considerations.

In similar correspond of a set of questions, donations, e-books, and assignments scholars can pierce them anytime anywhere. This is aimed to study the minds of scholars who are not confident, knowledgeable, and mature enough to prefer working in a particular career field.

Electroencephalography (EEG) signals are autographs of neural activities. Generally, they are the integrals of active capabilities, which evoke from the brain with different domains and populations around each time moment.

Here, the signal output effort of the brain neurons is measured using EEG signals or brain signals. Because they are non-invasive and often used in tests like those measuring emotion [1], alertness [2], and sleepiness [3], EEG headsets are used to read the EEG signal. In order to develop an optimal response to the many problems in the educational sphere, such as [4–6], a lot of research has been conducted on EEG signals. They accomplish this by wearing an EEG headpiece with numerous efficient channels and electrodes connected to various parts of the brain. But, it has a negative impact on students' innate attention spans.

The electroencephalogram (EEG) data captured from the T-learning system can be analyzed in this research employing unsupervised literacy (clusters), a variety of approaches to group emotion, alertness, doziness, or any sort of triggers indicated by a pupil during the course of the check. Brain surge is seen using a low-cost EEG headset. In each cluster, the dominating frequency band is grounded. Afterward, a non-attentive approach is used for proposing careers based on the independent applicants' attentiveness indicators. On the basis of conventional assessment standards, experimental analyses are estimated in recommendations. Two congenital distinct strategies have been outperformed by the suggested model. The section below shows the results that are appropriate for this approach. The following best exemplifies the extras and benefits:

- Using unsupervised literacy (clusters) approaches for grouping to equivalent behaviors demonstrated by a pupil during the course of the check, the brain waves (EEG) signal is anatomized.
- A method of guidance that seeks to retrieve the check and searches for indications of the non-attentional surge has been presented by the authors. The Recommendation System (RS) measures each participant's attention to suggestions using a scale, which forms the foundation of the system.
- The efficiency of their suggested career suggestion system on data collected at their research center for exploration has been estimated based on the analysis of experimental outcomes using convectional performance criteria. The suggested model has outshined the two congenital nascence approaches.

1.2 Related Work

In this module, different approaches for bringing reforms to educational domains have been mentioned.

1.2.1 E-Learning, M-Learning, and T-Learning

E-learning: E-learning has gained significant attention in K-12 education, with studies exploring its effectiveness. Author [7] conducted a systematic review, highlighting its positive impact on student learning outcomes. However, Means [8] emphasized the importance of evidence-based practices in online learning, underscoring the need for rigorous evaluation. To advance the field, San-Martín *et al.* [9] called for future research directions in e-learning. Learning analytics and educational data mining were also identified as promising areas [10].

M-learning: In the realm of M-learning, Kukulska-Hulme *et al.* [11] provided a comprehensive handbook for educators, emphasizing the unique characteristics of mobile learning. In a research paper, Sharples *et al.* [12] promoted the mobile age learning, emphasizing learner-centered education. The historical overview by [13] traced the evolution of mobile learning and its transformative potential. Author [14] investigated how mobile learning has influenced the way education and training are delivered.

T-learning: T-learning encompasses a broader integration of technology in education. Dillenbourg and Tchounikine [15] discussed the flexibility of macro-scripts for computer-supported collaborative learning. The NMC Horizon Report [16] outlined emerging trends and technologies in the field. A research paper highlighted the value of student-generated content in creating technology-enhanced learning experiences. Author [17] introduced technological pedagogical content knowledge (TPACK), promoting the need to productively integrate technology for educators.

This study aims to build upon and extend the current knowledge for e-learning, m-learning, and t-learning by exploring the benefits, challenges, and potential future directions of these technologies. It looks at their effectiveness, pedagogical approaches, mobile technologies, collaborative learning, and integration of technology in education.

Combining e-learning, m-learning, and t-learning, the concept of sustainable networking in the educational domain has gained importance. Here are some key points related to sustainable networking. *Green ICT and Energy Efficiency:* Researchers have explored the potential of green ICTs to reduce the environmental impact of networking infrastructures in the educational domain. The use of energy-efficient hardware, data centers, and cloud computing technologies can minimize energy consumption and carbon footprint.

Digital Divide and Inclusion: Sustainable networking in the educational domain also emphasizes bridging the digital divide and ensuring inclusion for all learners [18]. Efforts such as community networks, public Wi-Fi initiatives, and partnerships with telecommunication providers can address the connectivity gap and promote digital inclusion. Sustainable networking initiatives should prioritize providing access to marginalized communities, rural areas, and underserved populations.

Scalability and Future-Proofing: Sustainable networking in the educational domain considers scalability and future-proofing as crucial factors. As e-learning, m-learning, and t-learning continue to evolve, networking infrastructures need to accommodate increasing user demands and emerging technologies. Literature has explored the scalability of networking solutions, such as cloud-based learning platforms and software-defined networking architectures [19]. Flexible and scalable networking infrastructures ensure the adaptability and longevity of educational initiatives.

Security and Privacy: Security and privacy are essential for sustainable networking for education, as sensitive educational data is transmitted and stored on networks. Robust security measures, encryption protocols, and privacy frameworks are necessary to address concerns related to data breaches and cyber threats [20]. Sustainable networking practices contribute to reducing the environmental impact, promoting equitable access to education, accommodating future needs, and ensuring data security and privacy. Addressing these aspects supports the overall sustainability and effectiveness of e-learning, m-learning, and t-learning initiatives. With 150 million total Internet users in India, the Internet penetration is merely 12% [21] as compared to TV penetration at 65% [22] and that of mobile at 26% [23]. For an average-income family in India, the upfront infrastructure costs for a computer and internet are exorbitant, but television is affordable and available in every corner of the nation. Furthermore, for web-based learning, a student must be computer proficient, but there are no such restrictions for television-based learning. On the other hand, M-learning learners confront a number of technological obstacles including connection, battery life, multiple material formats, numerous mobile operating systems, and restricted memory.

1.2.2 Involvement of Networking Reforms in Education

In addition to exploring e-learning, m-learning, and t-learning, it is essential to consider the role of networking technologies in enhancing these learning approaches. Here are some key points regarding networking technologies, such as 5G and 4G, in the context of the reviewed literature: Firstly, 5G networks have the potential to revolutionize educational experiences by enabling seamless streaming of multimedia content, immersive virtual reality experiences, and real-time collaboration. This allows learners to access rich and interactive educational resources anytime and anywhere, enabling personalized and engaging learning experiences. Secondly, even though the 5G network holds enough advantages, the existing 4G networks have already played a significant role in supporting e-learning and m-learning initiatives. With 4G, learners can access online courses, educational apps, and multimedia content on their mobile devices. The relatively fast connection speeds and widespread coverage of 4G networks have facilitated remote learning and bridged the digital divide to some extent [24]. The availability of 4G networks has enabled learners in remote areas or underprivileged communities to access educational resources and participate in online learning activities.

Connectivity and Infrastructure: It emphasizes the importance of a robust networking infrastructure to support e-learning, m-learning, and t-learning initiatives effectively. Adequate connectivity, whether through 5G or 4G networks, is crucial for learners to access online learning materials, participate in virtual classrooms, and engage in collaborative activities. Researchers have stressed the need for reliable and high-speed internet connections, especially for learners in under-served areas. Efforts to enhance networking infrastructure and expand connectivity are critical to ensure equitable access to educational opportunities.

1.2.3 Literature Review for Use of NeuroSky Headset in Education Domain

A similar approach was used in studying students' attention and learning performance using the questionnaire survey and analysis of EEG signals [25].

Both studies using the pre-test and post-test technique and "EEG analysis" used the criteria of flow experiences, including joy, telepresence, focused attention, and temporal distortion, to analyze the impact of flow experiences on learning performance. The EEG study involved the usage of NeuroSky's MindSet EEG headset, which captured the attentive value, ranging from 0 to 100.

Chen Lin [26] used EEG signals to determine the attention, comprehensibility, and cognitive load of users reading different texts with different modes of activities. The user's brain signals were captured while reading static/dynamic or a combination of both in various contexts like sitting, standing, and walking. The NeuroSky gadget was used to assess attention and cognitive stress. Chen *et al.* [27] implemented the support vector machine (SVM)–Genetic Algorithm (GA) methodology in which EEG data captured the attentiveness of students. To categorize kids based on high or low attention rates, a unique method using GA is used to choose seven desirable qualities that were then passed through SVM model. The system identifies times of video lectures when the least students pay attention. Similar to this, Chen and Wu [28] examined sustained attention, mood, cognitive burden, and learning performance for several types of video lectures. Three different varieties of films were evaluated: the picture-in-picture technique, voice-over presentation design, and lecture capture format. NeuroSky MindSet headset and EM-Wave Stress Detector measure sustained attention and stress levels. Illustrating the impact of positive stimuli during video lectures, Huang *et al.* [29] used the analysis of the Learners's reaction with the infusion of humorous images in lectures as against the absence of the same. The experimental group received humorous images as positive reinforcement, brainwaves, attention levels, and facial responses were analyzed. The findings showed a connection between the test outcomes and the usage of humorous visuals in lectures. The study lacked thorough examinations of brain waves. A similar technique was experimented by Lai *et al.* [30], where the students were rewarded with funny images for correct answers. NeuroSky was used for brainwave (EEG) analysis, and the photographs collected were used for facial recognition. The experiment has been summarized in Figures 1.1 & 1.2. The emotional labeling of the facial expression was done based on the valence values. Lin *et al.* [31] developed an effective learning system to enhance the experience of the students while watching video lectures. The system made use of emotion recognition and attention studies for this purpose [32]. Yildirim *et al.* [33] proposed an application, where students can play such games while, at the end, their attention and meditation level scores are displayed. The association between attention levels and performance has been explored in higher educational scenarios like engineering courses [34]. A similar experiment has been undertaken by [35] with university students in English Course. The amount of attention was measured using the NeuroSky Mindset. The performances were evaluated using the pre- and post-test outcomes, and they were validated using the ANOVA test. A ubiquitous use of EEG signals has been used in measuring attention levels.

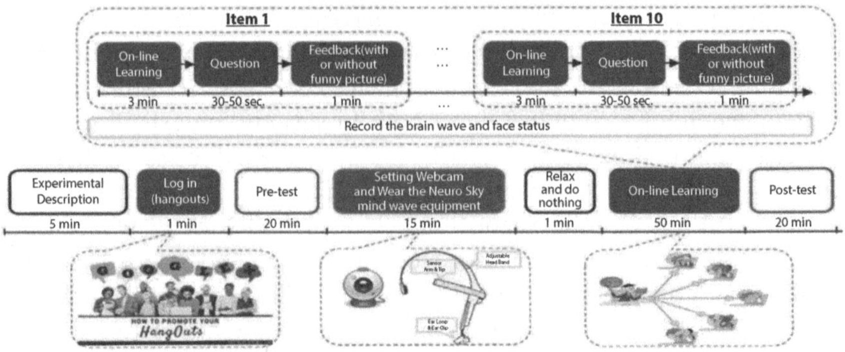

Figure 1.1 Attention-promoted mechanism architecture [30].

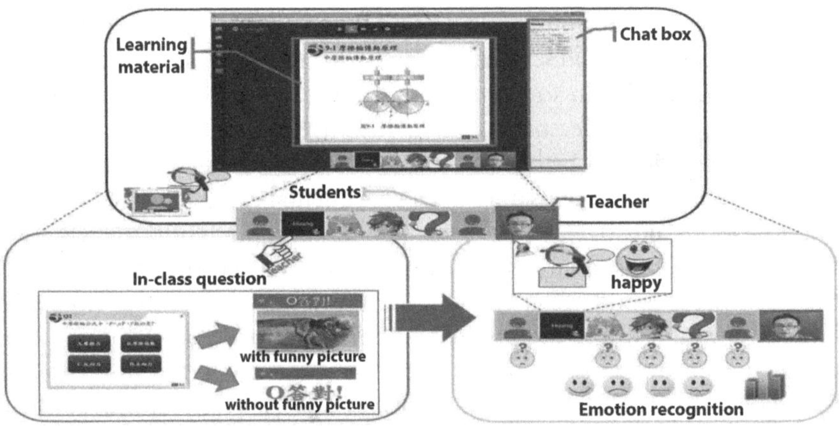

Figure 1.2 Experimental environment [30].

Attention is a key feature of a focused and concentrated brain. It is essential for learning as well as memorizing things. Katona [36] used computer-based tests such as the CPT (Continuous Performance Test) and TOAV (Test of Attentional Vigilance) to examine the student's level of attention in high and low mental states. The work stated that attention levels are higher for active minds than for tired minds. CPT has also been used by [37] to assess students using an Attention Aware System. A very handy warning system is proposed by Yildirim and Varol [38], where the attention levels of drivers are monitored to prevent accidents. Nakao *et al.* [39] developed an Arduino-based application that recognizes brain activity from EEG signals and classified the sleep stage from wakefulness and listening to music.

Morshad *et al.* [40] presented differences in brain activities of people of different age groups in attention, meditation and eye-blinking conditions. The outcome is that attention levels increase during brain activities while meditation levels remained unchanged. In order to forecast a powerhouse from a MOOCs course, a study [41, 42] at the University of California, Berkeley, United States, involved a Markov model armature that used machine learning techniques to analyze the liability of powerhouse, a succession pattern in those who volunteered in it.

A flipped literacy script with an adaptive material review was the foundation of [43] experimental technique for analyzing student attentiveness by evaluating students' recall skills in both flipped literacy and birth systems in order to increase students' recall abilities better than that in conventional methods. The use of flipped classroom strategies is currently receiving attention [44–46]. The importance of flipped literacy in the development of reading abilities was emphasized by the authors of [44], even though no experimental data have been presented to support the assertion. Xu and Zhou [47] established a link between three different types of engagement: applicants' behavioral, cognitive, and emotional involvement in a lecture video.

In his study, Seery [48] has examined the flipped literacy workshop that has been published. They came up with the conclusion that using flipped literacy is a key strategy for improving students' learning capacities. The cognitive apprehensive recommender system [49], a novel concept in the realm of recommender systems, has recently come to light. This highlights the advantages of videotaped courses using flipped literacy scripts. Lee *et al.* [4] used heart rate, camera, microphones, and other information sources with EEG signals to gather data on the students in order to evaluate their behavior. The attention and cognitive cargo in [5] were evaluated. A fuzzy set and relative qualitative analysis were used to evaluate the performance of the 32 undergraduate participants in this trial. The face videography also included gaze-tracking and EEG signals in addition to wristband data [6]. These traits were used to forecast academics' behavior and performance. To keep students' attention during a flipped literacy script, researchers [50] devised an experiment in which EEG signals were monitored as students took an exam. In [51], for internal work categorization, Liang *et al.* have utilized an extreme learning machine with EEG input. Lee *et al.* [4] classified six-word imagined speech using EEG data and a Siamese Neural Network. A lecture videotape RS was proposed by Dias [52] using the two tasks of reflection and similarity analysis. As a result, Dias *et al.* [52] used the textbook that was on the videotape, using similar captions, titles, etc. Lei *et al.* [46] displayed a 3D interactive literacy environment based on an online trial and demonstration in the classroom [53]. Yet, these studies fail to take into account the students' fundamental comprehension. The usage of recommendations in the educational environment is undoubtedly advantageous.

1.3 Background

Mel Frequency Cepstral Coefficient (MFCC): The Mel frequency, created by [54, 55], is a helpful scale of assessment being non-cognitive in nature. The theory of visceral pitch and human perception holds that some lower frequencies are more apparent and are simpler to distinguish from higher frequencies, served as its inspiration. Logarithmic gives the perceived lower end of the spectrum more weight. These are the steps: First, prior to conversion to Mel frequencies, the highest and lowest frequencies are measured. "Central frequencies" are the number of filters generated that are uniformly spaced away from the lowest and highest Mel-frequency range. In line with the sampling rate, the produced center frequencies are calculated, assessed, and then converted back to the Hz scale. The signals are scaled using Fast Fourier transform (FFT) bins, and then triangle filter banks are created. The signal is transmitted through a filter bank with a discrete Fourier transform and monitored coefficient amplitudes to avoid imaginary values. Frames yield the same amount of coefficients regardless of filtering.

Discrete Wavelet Packet Transform (WPT): The Wavelet Packet Transform has devised a mechanism for decomposing signals into fundamental building components known as wavelets, as explained in [56]. Discrete and continuous are derivable from WPT. The wavelet transform was used to extract important information from the time and frequency domain, resulting in estimation coefficients and detailed coefficients. As the final stage in the construction of the standard Discrete Wavelet Transform (DWT), DPT involves the final decomposition of both approximate coefficients and detailed coefficients.

1.4 Dataset

NeuroSky Mindwave Mobile1 (NMM2) headsets, which produce EEG waves, can be linked to a computer through Bluetooth or an adapter. The same brain neurons that produce the EEG signals also produce the stimuli.

The brain wave EEG time series data is collected and saved in a CSV file at 512 data points per second. Time series EEG data is saved in a CSV file at 512 samples per second (512-Hz sampling rate). The EEG raw data was collected by the Data Analysis Lab at the National Institutes of Technology Rourkela. In this trial, 44 students comprising 31 males and 13 women were signed up to take part in this experiment. These participants ranged from 17 to 20 years of age. Five surveys, aggregating 220 data samples, were captured from each student (44 × 5). For categorization, labeling for the collected data is necessary for which students completed two exams: a pre-test and a post-test, each of which directed them to respond to a series of questions. The Pearson association between pre and post test scores for one youngster demonstrates the connection between passing tests and attending lectures. Equation 1.1 can be used to identify a student's degrees of attentiveness. The student's progress from the pre-test is shown here (Impx).

$$V(x,y) = \begin{cases} \text{Discarded} & if(x >= \{80\%\}) \\ Non\,Understood & if(y < 50\%)\,\text{or}\,(Impx < 30\%) \\ Understood & Otherwise. \end{cases} \tag{1.1}$$

1.5 Proposed Method and Result

1.5.1 Collaborative Filtering Using Brain Signal–Induced Preferences

This section uses preferences inferred from human brains to calculate preferences for samples that haven't been seen yet.

1.5.1.1 Neurophysiological Experiment

In this section, an experiment is conducted based on neuropsychology in which volunteers were shown artificially created facial photographs and their computed brain responses were recorded using an EEG, and the recorded EEG data were compared to the volunteer's personal preference ratings.

Participants: Around 31 participants from Helsinki University were chosen. Absolute readings were acquired out of whom 18 self-identified as men and 13 as women. The average age was calculated to be 28 years (SD = 7.14, range 18 to 45). A tribute of two local movie tickets was given to each for their service.

Stimuli: Finding stimuli was one of the main obstacles in designing a subjective preference trial. Finding stimuli that will enable numerous preference tests to be performed within the time limits of a typical EEG session is especially important (between 30 and 90 min, including setup). The operation was designed as a human facial beauty experiment aimed to accurately reflect visual judgements for users of online dating services when they see a face that naturally ranges ranging from higher to a low preference. It is necessary that they do not know any face stimuli when choosing them so that their evaluations of each stimulus are only based on their perceived preferences and not on their potentially conflicting knowledge of the contents of the image.

The generation of stimuli required a 512-dimensional multivariate normal distribution, a GAN architecture trained on 30,000 images of well-known faces, and a random operation involving the selection of 70k latent vectors. To guarantee that the output images were error-free, a human assessor carefully examined each stimulus for any artefacts. No further physical characteristics were checked on the generated photos. In order to create a total of 240 distinct images, the first 120 photos in each group of men's and women's photographs were then used. Following a 512 × 512 pixel resolution, an elliptic grayish frame was applied to the photographs after pixel down-scaling to hide the background and any non-facial characteristics.

Apparatus: The stimuli were displayed on a 1,680 × 1,050 resolution LCD panel with a viewing distance of roughly 60 cm. The time of the display was then set using the psychology program Tool E-Prime 3.0.3.60 stimulus presentation program utilized for adjusting the EEG amplifier trigger. The EEG data was then captured using 32 Ag/AgCl electrodes that were placed at similarly spaced points on the 10–20 system. The data was processed and converted to digital format using a Brain Products GmbH QuickAmp USB amplifier operating at a 2,000-Hz frequency. To record the electrooculogram (EOG), which is used to eliminate artefacts during the data processing stage, two sets of bipolar electrodes were positioned 1cm laterally to the outer canthi of each eye, 2cm under and above the right pupil, and 3 cm beneath and above the left pupil.

Task: Volunteers were instructed to concentrate on the faces on the screen and judge the personal beauty of each face. Each of the three blocks in the study had eight rapid serial visual presentation (RSVP) trials. With 60 photos in each RSVP trial, there were 480 stimulus presentations in each block. Volunteers were instructed to look at the faces before each RSVP trial and to mentally comment on any faces they found appealing.

The RSVP then started, with 60 images shown over a gray backdrop at a frequency of 2 Hz (stimulus onset asynchrony: 500 ms). The software then requested an estimate of how frequently the volunteers had taken a mental note after watching the final stimulus. The volunteers were split into groups of 60 and shown smaller versions of each image that had been shown during the RSVP trials. They were then instructed to choose which photos they thought were most attractive by clicking on them. The experiment lasted approximately 25 min.

Data Cleaning and Labeling: To support the paradigm of a realistic BCI application, simple heuristics were applied to pre-process the data hence enhancing signal-to-noise ratio in order to use EEG data in real-time while disregarding human input. When the EEG data was originally digitized, it was assigned a common average value. Then, to reduce line noise and sluggish signal, a band-pass filter (frequency range: 0.2 Hz to 35 Hz) was applied. The data was then time-locked for the beginning of the shock and divided into 1100-ms chunks (also known as "epochs"), each with 200 ms of baseline electrical activity. The remaining epoch was reduced by the estimated mean of this baseline activity. They applied some preprocessing techniques and finally dataset was made.

Neurophysiological Results: The grading averages of the voltages of the epoch data among participants, organized by individual ratings, were used to produce the ERP plots. At the Fz and Pz electrodes, there was a discernible, rationally ordered reaction. To determine the outcome of attractiveness, ERPs were analyzed, and the estimated average utilized by pictures was looked at. Optical analysis of the results of attractiveness over the scalp identified two key elements. An increased frontal element was found over the Fz a little early, and, then, an increased prefrontal element was found over the Pz. To determine whether beauty had distinct results between these two places, distinct frequent measures ANOVAs were conducted. The first frequent measures ANOVA used attractiveness (0, 1, 2, or 3), with means ranging from 250 to 350. An outcome $F (3, 90) = 15.13$, $p < 0.0001$, $\eta^2 = 0.34$ attractiveness resulted in a tight linear impact of mean amplitude spanning between 0.23 μV and 1.22 μV, with attractiveness one and two lying between 0.80 μV and 1.11 μV). Bonferroni examined and rectified post differentiation and proposed almost every comparison presented variation, $ts < 0.005$, apart from 3 vs. 2, 0 vs. 2, and 0 vs. 1. A second frequent measure ANOVA utilized a mean magnitude of (350–500) as means and attractiveness (3 vs. 2 vs. 1 vs. 0) as a factor to examine the upcoming, prefrontal outcome. Attractiveness had a further important outcome, $G (3, 90) = 34.931$, $p < 0.0001$, $\eta^2 = 0.54$, distinguished by a monotomous ascending amplitude promoting higher image ratings. Post-hoc differentiation led to notable outcomes (ps < 0.01) between every combination of attractiveness ratings (except for 1 vs. 2).

1.5.1.2 Deducing Preferences from Brain Signals

Information from the issue in the preceding section is retrieved here. They learn a mapping $F(B, U) = Y$, where predicted preferences Y of users U and brain signal B for computing preferences of a specific user, using brain signal sets X is from diverse users and validated preference interactions (unseen items). This challenge may be broken down into two smaller ones, which are described below.

Preference Approximation: First, it is looked at how a user's brain signal and their declared preferences for various items relate to one another. A mapping between participants' recorded brain responses and self-reported preferences was looked at in order to determine new preferences for previously viewed content that lacked preference information. A mapping $F(B, U) = Y$ was investigated so that for fresh brain signals $\hat{Y}x$, they could determine from 32 channel brain wave signal B_i. With this, they were able to get associated preference rating Y_i for an item X_i. Possibly, this type of complication appears to be a supervised classification task.

User-Item Collaboration: After that, the links between users and products are studied such that, even if a particular user's brain signals are not caught for a certain item, their preference responses may still be inferred from the readily accessible preferences acquired from other users. Given the projected preferences $\hat{Y}$ of U (users) for I (items), mapping between U (users) and I (items) is investigated $F(B, U) = \hat{Y}$ such that for a given I (item) unseen by U (user), they might approximately respond to their preference y_{u_i}. This procedure may be viewed as a matrix factorization problem in which knowledge about the relationships between users and things is sought through an estimate of latent representations.

Machine Learning Tests: The neural architecture detailing the combination of a neural EEG classifier and a neural collaborative filtering (NCF) technique is built for the brain signals. For instance, 3 depicts this architecture graphically. The development of a multi-layer perception (MLP) system that uses vectorized epochs and labeling information as inputs and estimates class probabilities were considered as an output to decode individual preferences. Three closely linked layers of 256, 128, and 64 neurons each make up the MLP architecture (using ReLU activations). In between these layers, batch normalization is used along with 25% dropout. The last layer contains four neurons that stand in for various preference levels and a softmax activation. With the aid of Adam optimization, leave-one-out cross-validation for each contributor, and sparse categorical cross entropy as the loss function, a multi-layered model accommodating 10 epochs was created. NCF step has been redesigned for the architecture that is now in use. The root mean square error was used as the loss function, and 10 epochs of leave-one-out cross-validation for each contributor were supported by the NCF model.

Data Processing: A demonstration was conducted on how highly each contributor prioritized the stimulus picture corresponding to that epoch, given that the dataset for each epoch consists of time series data with lengths of 1100ms, 32 channels, and integer labels ranging from 0 to 3. These epochs were reduced from 1,100-ms extended chunks to 900-ms extended chunks by removing the 200 ms of pre-stimulus baseline activity.

A sliding window of 750 ms length was used, with a starting position of 0 ms and a maximum position of 150 ms in increments of 2 ms, and a total of 75 re-sampled epochs were formed from each of these. Down-sampling was used to fix class imbalances for each participant. The measured voltages were then averaged over all time frames and channels, and each epoch was divided into 25 time intervals of equal length. As a result of this procedure, the EEG data were vectorized. As a result, each n response had a data matrix of $X^{n \times m.t'}$, with $m = 32$ channels and $t' = 25$ time windows. This yielded a total of 800 in data points.

Prediction Structure and Control Order: To acquire the output of brain input for collaborative filtering, they modified the experiment to incorporate controls for rating data distributions, collaborative filtering, upper-bound performance and explicit categorization. It is crucial to keep in mind that the experiment's objective was to determine if the brain's input might serve as a dependable replacement for clear feedback while excluding the possibility that the effect was brought on by a particular computational design choice [57]. (Refer Figure 1.3 for a visual representation of the experimental setup.)

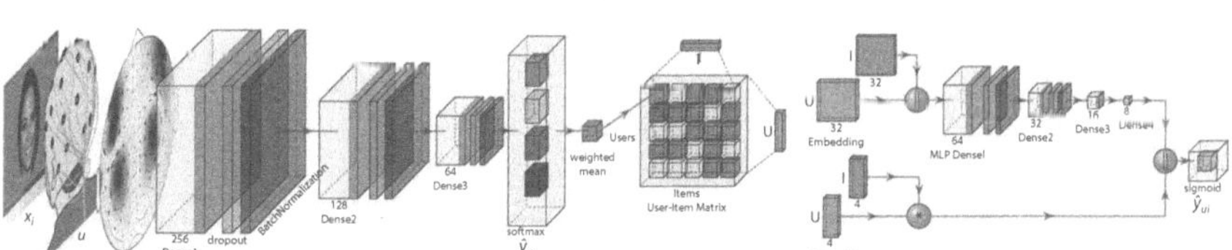

Figure 1.3 Design of collaborative filtering with preferences inferred using brain signals [57].

1.5.2 Proposed Methodology for FlipRec Model

Two processes are performed in order to execute the procedure. First, two distinct pre-processing techniques (MFCC and WPT) are used in the first phase. Both were employed to obtain a favorable performance review. Second, considerable feature extraction from EEG data is done to develop a cognitively aware lecture video recommendation engine as well as for various classification approaches. Figure 1.4 displays the entire categorization system as well as FlipRec.

1.5.2.1 Module for Data Preparation

There were 44 students who participated in the work. Each of them had to view five lectures through video. A total of 220 samples were, therefore, recorded in total. The beginning and last 6 s of data are eliminated during pre-processing. Each sample's D size is $((X - 12) \times Y)$, where X stands for the video's total running length in seconds and Y for the feature points, which correspond to the sampling rate of the EEG headset utilized in this study (Y = 512).

Pre-processing using MFCC: MFCC, a well-known frequency computation method, is thought to be more perceptually meaningful and has been used widely in voice recognition. To give the lower frequencies a greater value, a logarithm was used. The D was given the STFT (Short Term Fourier Transform) to calculate the MFCC. The coefficients' value was specified to prevent illogical values. It is discovered that the outcome is a magnitude

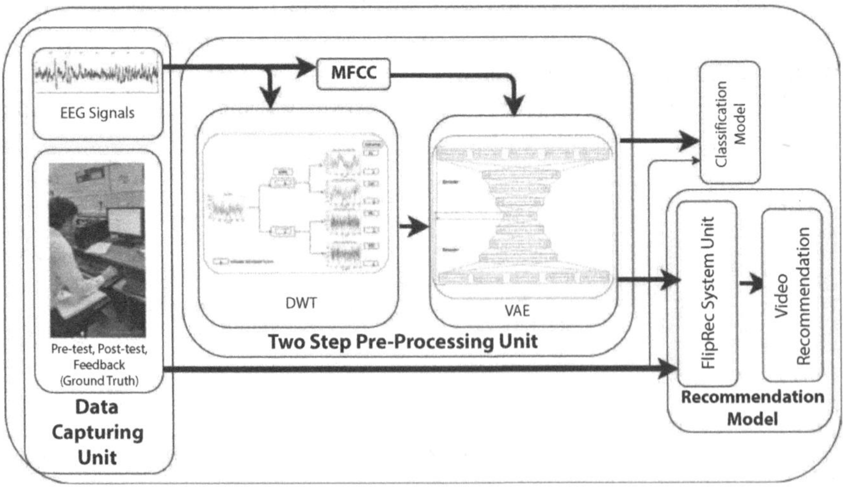

Figure 1.4 Proposed framework [58].

matrix with the same dimensions as the initial data D. They set the minimum frequency (*fmin*) and maximum frequency (*fmax*) at 1 Hz and 128 Hz, respectively, and the number of filters (F) at 64, with the parameters (F) to be determined by trial and error. The f_{min} and f_{max} are converted to Mel frequency using $\Theta_f = c_1 \times ln\left(1+\frac{f}{c_2}\right)$. In this study, c_1 and c_2 were fixed at 1125 and 700 [59]. Let the entire frequencies of f_{min} and f_{max} be (Θf_{min} Θf_{min}) and ($\Theta_{f_{max}}$), respectively. Next, they compute for each filter of central frequencies (Θ_{fcs}) using $\Theta_{fcs}(n) = \times\delta_\theta$, where n = 1, 2,.., F, and δ is computed using $\delta_\theta = \frac{\theta_{f_{max}} - \theta_{f_{min}}}{F+1}$. The inverse Mel transform is then used to convert the center frequencies back to the Mel spectrum. The center frequencies are referred to as *fcs* once they have been scaled down to Hz. They investigate WPT, another pre-processing method, and evaluate its effectiveness against MFCC. The WPT is discussed below.

Pre-processing with WPT: In this case, two DPT levels are used to make use of the higher-dimensional (dimension, 512) data. Following that, db4 wavelet processing is employed to generate low-frequency (approximation) and high-frequency (detailed) sub-bands. Because all movies vary in length, as is well known, they were altered to be as brief as possible. Each video sample's resultant attributes are altered for the remainder of the experiment after DPT-related work. After applying DPT, the dimensions of dataset is (220 × (x – 12) × Q), where Q = 128 resulted to be a total number of pre-processing features. Following the use of both pre-processing techniques, the z-score normalization function is used to produce normalized data. The final resultant vector was not uniform since the lengths of all videos were different. Valuable characteristics are extracted from higher dimensions to pre-processed data ((X – 12) × 64) for MFCC and ((X – 12) × 128) for WPT.

Variational auto-encoders: Variational auto-encoders is very popular to use for reduce the dimension of data from high-dimension to low dimension data. Compared to a linear PCA, this makes modeling non-linear functions simpler. It is, therefore, an effective technique for restricting the dimension of data. EEG data with five various lengths of coefficients that were recovered using MFCC and WPT, respectively, are required as input for the suggested model. Assuming the length of the videos to be Θ_i, where $i \in [1, 5]$. Because the five video's duration times differ from each other, the decoder's output was attached to five distinct output layers, corresponding to the different Θ_i. The loss L (p_β, q_α) between output sample Θ_{yi} and input sample Θ_{xi} is calculated using Equation 1.2. (Refer Figure 1.5 for a visual representation of the experimental setup.)

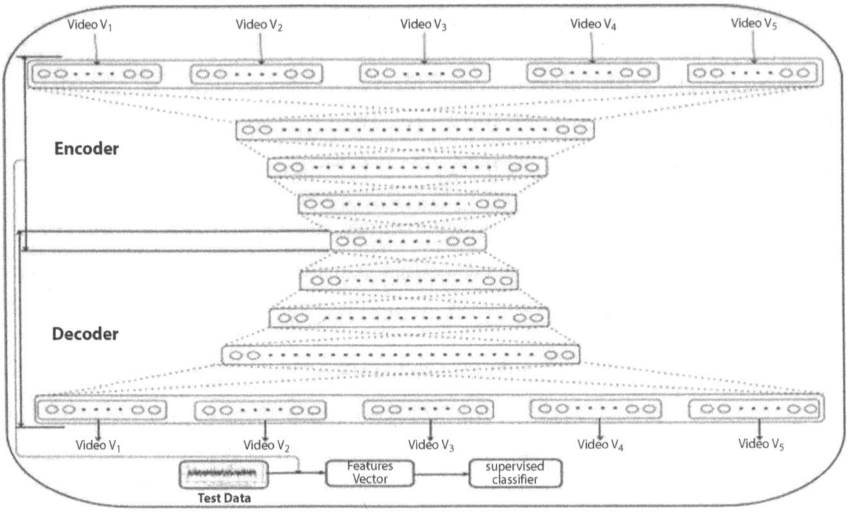

Figure 1.5 Proposed model architecture of autoencoder [58].

$$L(p_\beta, q_\alpha) = -D_{KL}[q_\alpha(\theta_{zi} \mid \theta_{xi}) \,||\, p_\beta(\theta_{zi})] + E_{q\alpha}(\theta_{zi} \mid \theta_{xi})[\log(p_\beta(\theta_{yi} \mid \theta_{zi}))] \tag{1.2}$$

The first part on the right-hand side (RHS) of Equation 1.3

$$D_{KL}[q_\alpha(\theta_{zi} \mid \theta_{xi}) \,||\, p_\beta(\theta_{zi})] \tag{1.3}$$

is the Kullback–Leibler (KL) divergence while another part is the reconstruction loss. RELU (Rectifier Linear Unit) activation function was used in the layers to demonstrate non-linearity. Backpropagation was then used

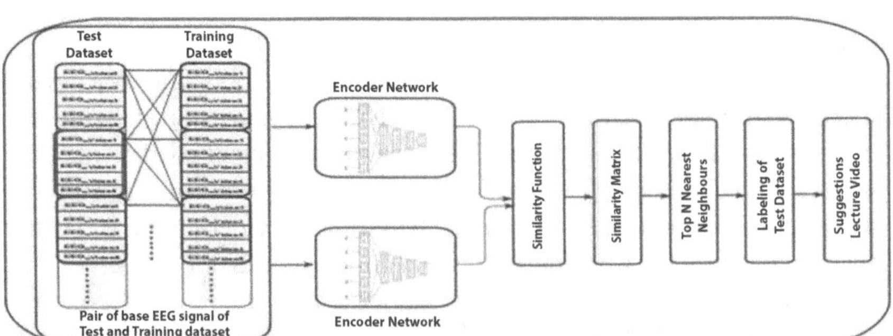

Figure 1.6 Proposed model architecture of autoencoder [58].

to change the value of the various layers. Videos of different lengths were simply included in the model because there were separate input and output layers. The model training was completed successfully with an 8-person batch size. After hyper-parameter adjustment, the parameters that produced the smallest loss were generated. For each epoch, all of the flattened coefficients for h2 were utilized first, then all of the compressed coefficients for h1, and so on until h5. After the training, the encoder was the sole device utilized. To explore the categorization each student was randomly chosen and used for testing, while the other signals were retained for training. This set of data was considered as dataset A. Second, eight people were randomly selected to serve as test subjects exclusively. They used the extracted feature sets and cutting-edge approach to classify this dataset as dataset B. The proposed recommender system, which is detailed in the next part, is developed using the same set of extracted features. (Refer Figure 1.6 for a visual representation of the experimental setup.)

1.5.2.2 FlipRec: Preferred Recommendation Model

Using a VAE and keeping in mind the preceding section, the high-dimensional feature vector was coded. The suggested recommendation model is created using these programmed properties, as demonstrated in 6. As a consequence, this model offers recommendations. These are the recommendations to which a student should pay close attention while they watch the lecture video. It operates in the manner listed below. Students who saw every video must be included in a training set that includes their EEG data. The students categorized these films as "Non-Understood" or "Understood" by them. The K-nearest Neighbors (K-NN) calculation of each student from the training set is made possible by identifying similarities between feature vector t1 and feature vectors of each student's EEG data. Each student is given the first video in the sequence they observed (outside of the training set), and t1 is the features vector produced from the training encoder for that video. The first video of each student was mostly used to generate the feature vector. For measuring similarity, Dynamic Time Warping (DTW) and the Pearson Correlation Coefficient (PCC) were both helpful. Examining the second video's class title helped determine whether a student should exercise caution when watching it in order. According to the study, the student should pay great attention while watching this one if the majority of these movies or their nearby neighbors are labeled as "Non-Understood". Utilizing the same process, related concepts might be developed for further videos. A hypothetical report that uses this method was created. FlipRec is a model that consists of two variants called

FlipRecS and *FlipRecP*. Individual EEG signal properties are considered in this model as pairs of EEG signals from a test sample student and from video, respectively. This model is based on the EEG signal combination of test sample videos considered for achieving the nearest neighbors.

1.5.3 Using Brain Signal Technology, a Cognitively Aware Lecture Video Recommendation System in Flipped Learning

An unsupervised machine-learning approach was used to assess the number of active cognitive states of a student watching a lecture video (i.e., clustering). Finally, a recommendation technique based on the cognitive states of flipped-learning students is proposed. The suggested paradigm is divided into three stages. Initially, a clustering method is used to seek beneficial cognitive states. In the second stage, feature extraction is recommended for determining attentiveness. Instructors link students to lecture videos in the third phase.

1.5.3.1 Finding Successful Cognitive States with a Clustering Method

The condition of the human mind is very unstable. A state can change in response to any external stimuli, no matter how slight the distraction can be. A student could behave in a variety of ways while taking a lecture in a manner similar to this. A clustering method is applied to group similar student behaviors while watching a lecture video. In each resultant cluster, attention analysis is performed while taking into consideration the clustered lecture video. The whole film's worth of time series data is then extracted from each video. Thus, they received a total of 200 samples (20 participants × 10 videos). There were numerous challenges in using EEG technology. The main challenges are the artefacts. With NMM2 EEG headgear, certain artefacts may still be disregarded. During collection, EEG data may contain internal or external/non-physiological artefacts. External objects such as filthy hairy leather, electrode placement, and electrode impedance affect the EEG headwear. Several processes in the body, such as the heartbeat, eye blink, muscular action, and ocular movement, generate physiological signals. An extremely amplitude-rich, low-frequency signal (< 4 Hz) is used to represent eye blinks and movements. The front electrodes (FP1) with modest propagation are often used [61]. An ear clip (A1) and sensor electrodes (FP1) are included with the Mindwave headset.

The EEG signals for learning, mind state, and attention were provided by the FP1 area of the brain. Instead, the signal was grounded in the A1 area and filtered with common-mode (CM) rejection, notch filters to convert between analog and digital, low-pass and high-pass filters, and proprietary algorithms to remove additional noise and EMG (electromyogram) distortions. It is crucial to highlight that the EEG data in section 4 were obtained using the NMM2 EEG Headset. Raw data, eSense meters (meditation and attention), eye blink, and EEG power spectra (Low, Mid, High, Delta, Theta, and Low Gamma) are among the NMM2 outputs. In the experiment, ocular artefacts were reduced using independent component analysis (ICA). After that, the data was normalized by applying the min-max method. In order to identify behaviors that are often featured in films, the K-means clustering was implemented which divided the whole dataset into time segments by distinguishing between 512 data points of one second (i.e., 512 Hz per second is the sampling rate) and another second 512 data points (1, 2, and 3 s). In the meanwhile, each second's data values were accepted as a series (single entity). Data that filled one window size was treated as one row, resulting in a matrix. The data received during those 2 and 3 s will be shown in each row if the window sizes are 2 and 3, respectively. The value of K must be clearly mentioned because the number of groups (behaviors) in the K-means clustering method is unanticipated. The silhouette score [62] is used to find the optimal number of clusters (behaviors) (2 to 5) for various values of K. The silhouette value is used to determine how similar a freshly allocated data item can be to its own cluster when compared to other clusters. It was discovered that the magnitudes ranged from [−1, 1]. Strong correspondence between the attributes of the data object and the cluster to which it is assigned—and vice versa—occurs at values close to 1. To guarantee that the silhouette score achieves the maximum score throughout that specific movie, clustering methods require similarity measurements between the two data points being compared. DTW [63] was used as a measure to determine how far apart two-time series signals are from one another. DTW is a frequently used productivity measure for distinguishing time series data [64]. If a two-time series is non-linearly deformed by stretching or contracting along the time plane, then a two-time series is chosen to identify the ideal global alignment inside the two-time series. It replaces the one-to-one point comparison used in the Euclidean distance and other related distances like the Cosine and PCC with a many-to-one point comparison. Furthermore, Euclidean distance cannot be applied to unequal lengths in two different time series data (Figure 1.7).

A K-means clustering variant known as bisecting K-means is gaining preference [65]. The Kt value generated by the silhouette coefficient is also employed when bisecting K-means. When bisecting K-means, all data points

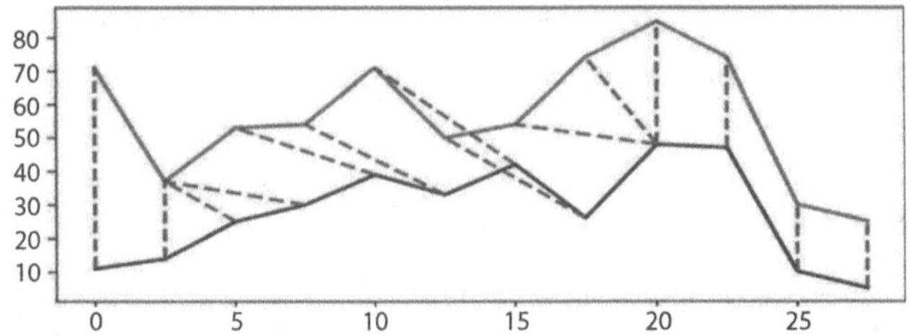

Figure 1.7 Toy example of dynamic time warping [60].

were initially thought to be in a single cluster. K-means clustering was used to split the original cluster into two. Until the necessary number of clusters has been reached, this process is repeated. Each iteration chose a cluster based on the approach with the highest SSE (sum of squared errors) for bisection.

1.5.3.2 Feature Derivation for Estimating Attention

The clusters in the movie looked to contain the information for which the student demonstrated a certain behavior. Brain wave characteristics were extracted from EEG data for 1, 2, and 3-s time frames in a cluster. The spatial domain format of EEG data from numerous trials was used to get signal amplitude values. Attention levels cannot be determined from raw data. FFT is used to convert the raw data into the frequency domain [66]. The FFT technique usually produces complicated numbers as its output.

The real piece is the only component of the convoluted word that is acceptable for scrutiny. Based on the frequency ranges, five different types of brain waves were developed. The alpha and beta values that were obtained for a particular time frame were utilized to assess the importance of attention in a cluster. The amplitude of relaxation is represented by alpha, whereas the degree of attention is represented by beta. The ratio $\frac{alpha}{beta}$ is used to measure a learner's level of attentiveness [67]. For a learner, the value of $A = \frac{alpha}{beta}$ should be less than 1 within a fixed time window for being attentive. Video clusters are assessed to identify whether a student paid attention during the lesson or not. The range of activities students did while watching the film is reflected in the number of clusters. Each cluster's size represents how long a pupil maintains a specific behavior pattern. To establish whether or not a video j was comprehended by a learner t_j, they compute the average attentive index, i.e., the attention value of each cluster. Let $\{C_1, C_2..C_k\}$ denote the clusters derived from a certain video V. Let L be the cluster size C_i. The cluster C_k average attentive value A_{Ck} is determined as follows:

$$A_{C_k} = \frac{1}{L} L_i \; a_i / \beta_i \tag{1.4}$$

If the value of A_{Ck} is < 1.0, then they deduce that the learner t_j was attentive for L seconds, and the whole cluster C_k is referred to regarded as the attentive cluster. This procedure is carried out for all V clusters. Finally, we find all of the attentive clusters and calculate their overall area. If the overall size of attentive clusters in video j reaches the pre-specified threshold t`(in their experiment, 60% of the video duration), then it is marked as attentive; otherwise, it is classed as non-attentive. After each film was marked, the attentive index for each non-attentive movie of a pupil was calculated using Equation 1.4. These non-attentive videos were ordered by attentive index, with the video with the lowest attentive value shown first.

1.6 Result Analysis

We reported a comparative analysis of the state of the art in this part. Baseline IntRec results recommended lecture video recommendation in flipped learning (LRFL) K and LRFL B utilizing a 1-s window size. They presented the experimental findings for a 1-s window size in Table 1.1. In the research paper [60], Shaw and Patra presented that *LRFL B* outperformed all other models INTREC, UserBased collaborative filtering (CF), and ItemBased CF. The Research paper [58] presented that with their MFCC the multimodal factor variational auto-encoder (MFVAE) SVM model outperformed decision tree (DT), K-Nearest Neighbour (KNN), and artificial neural network (ANN). On the other hand, the weighted probabilistic variational autoencoder (WPVAE) trained in ANN outperformed all

Table 1.1 Results of baseline *LRFL B*, MFVAE, and WPVAE using a 1-s window.

Approach	Precision	Recall	F1
ARTFuL [43]	50.00	33.25	39.94
LRFL B [60]	66.65	65.95	66.30
MFVAE [58]	93.30	73.68	82.34
WPVAE [58]	93.33	77.77	84.84

others including KNN, DT, SVM, and random forest (RF). They presented the experimental findings for a 2-s window size in Table 1.2. The weakest performance is user-based CF (accuracy = 45.00, recall = 50.00, and F1 = 47.00). The IntRec methodology outperforms the user-based collaborative filtering method. In all of these metrics, the proposed LRFL B beats IntRec, item-based CF, user-based CF, and LRFL K.

The user-based collaborative filtering method is outperformed by the IntRec methodology. The proposed LRFL B outperforms IntRec, item-based CF, user-based CF, and LRFL K in all of these criteria.

User-based CF and item-based CF generate comparable precision outcomes, as illustrated in Table 1.3. However, in terms of recall and F1 metrics, user-based CF surpasses item-based CF. When they utilized a window size of 3 s (Table 1.3), both variations of LRFL outperformed IntRec in

Table 1.2 Results of baseline IntRec, *LRFL K*, and *LRFL B* using a 2-s window.

Approach	Precision	Recall	F1
User-based CF	45.00	50.00	47.00
IntRec [60]	64.75	53.95	58.86
Item-based CF	50.00	75.00	60.00
LRFL K [60]	63.20	58.55	60.79
LRFL B [60]	67.55	64.70	66.09

Table 1.3 Results of baseline IntRec, $LRFL_K$, and $LRFL_B$ using a 3-s window.

Approach	Precision	Recall	F1
User-based CF	50.00	75.00	60.00
Item-based CF	50.00	50.00	50.00
IntRec [60]	61.75	58.70	60.19
LRFL K [60]	71.85	58.50	64.49
LRFL B [60]	74.35	58.50	65.48

accuracy measurements. However, the claimed recall values for all three techniques are quite close.

1.7 Conclusion and Future Research

This paper explored the use of EEG data for lecture video classification and recommendation in pedagogy, specifically in the context of E-learning, M-learning, and T-learning. By analyzing the brainwave patterns of learners, valuable insights can be gained regarding their engagement, attention, and cognitive load during educational video consumption.

The application of EEG data in lecture video classification allows for the automatic categorization of videos based on their effectiveness in facilitating learning. Additionally, the RS utilizing EEG data enables personalized learning experiences by suggesting videos tailored to each individual's learning preferences and cognitive abilities.

The integration of EEG data with E-learning, M-learning, and T-learning platforms opens up new avenues for enhancing educational experiences. Despite challenges in data collection and privacy, the integration of EEG data in pedagogy offers exciting prospects for improving digital learning experiences.

References

1. Sharma, R., Pachori, R.B., Sircar, P., Automated emotion recognition based on higher order statistics and deep learning algorithm. *Biomed. Signal Process. Control*, 58, 101867, 2020.
2. Andrzejewski, J.A. and Carlson, J.M., Electrocortical responses associated with attention bias to fearful facial expressions and auditory distress signals. *Int. J. Psychophysiol.*, 151, 94–102, 2020.
3. L.-l. Chen, Y., Zhang, J., Zou, J.-., Automatic detection of alertness/drowsiness from physiological signals using wavelet-based nonlinear features and machine learning. *Expert Syst. Appl.*, 42, 7344–7355, 2015.
4. Lee, D.-Y., Lee, M., Lee, S.-W., Classification of imagined speech using siamese neural network, in: *Proceedings 2020 IEEE International Conference on Systems, Man, and Cybernetics (SMC)*, pp. 2979–2984, 2020.
5. Papamitsiou, Z., Pappas, I.O., Sharma, K., Giannakos, M.N., Utilizing multimodal data through fsqca to explain engagement in adaptive learning. *IEEE Trans. Learn. Technol.*, 13, 689–703, 2020.
6. Sharma, K., Dillenbourg, P., Giannakos, M., Stimuli-based gaze analytics to enhance motivation and learning in moocs, in: *Proceedings of the 2019 IEEE*

19th International Conference on Advanced Learning Technologies (ICALT), pp. 199–203, 2019.
7. McMaughan, D.J., Rhoads, K.E., Davis, C., Chen, X., Han, H., Jones, R.A., Mahaffey, C.C., Miller, B.M., Covid-19 related experiences among college students with and without disabilities: Psychosocial impacts, supports, and virtual learning environments. *Front. Public Health*, 9, 782-793, 1972, 2021.
8. Means, B., Technology and education change: Focus on student learning. *J. Res. Technol. Educ.*, 42, 285–307, 2010.
9. San-Martìn, S., Jiménez, N., Rodríguez-Torrico, P., Pinẽiro-Ibarra, I., The determinants of teachers' continuance commitment to e-learning in higher education. *Educ. Inf. Technol.*, 25, 3205–3225, 2020.
10. Siemens, G. and d. Baker, R.S., Learning analytics and educational data mining: towards communication and collaboration, in: *Proceedings of the 2nd international conference on learning analytics and knowledge*, pp. 252–254, 2012.
11. Kukulska-Hulme, A. and Traxler, J., *Mobile learning: A handbook for educators and trainers*, Routledge, UK, 2005.
12. Sharples, M., Taylor, J., Vavoula, G., A theory of learning for the mobile age: Learning through conversation and exploration across contexts, in: *Medienbildung in neuen Kulturr¨aumen: die deutschprachige und britis-che Diskussion*, pp. 87–99, 2010.
13. Crompton, H., A historical overview of m-learning: Toward learner- centered education, in: *Handbook of mobile learning*, pp. 3–14, Routledge, UK, 2013.
14. Ally, M., *Mobile learning: Transforming the delivery of education and training*, Athabasca University, Edmonton, AB, 2009.
15. Dillenbourg, P. and Tchounikine, P., Flexibility in macro-scripts for computer-supported collaborative learning. *J. Comput. Assisted Learn.*, 23, 1–13, 2007.
16. Johnson, L., Becker, S.A., Estrada, V., Freeman, A., NMC horizon report: 2015 library edition. *The New Media Consortium*, 2015.
17. Koehler, M. and Mishra, P., What is technological pedagogical content knowledge (tpack)? *Contemp. Issues Technol. Teacher Educ.*, 9, 60–70, 2009.
18. Warschauer, M. and Matuchniak, T., New technology and digital worlds: Analyzing evidence of equity in access, use, and outcomes. *Rev. Res. Educ.*, 34, 179–225, 2010.
19. Bhardwaj, A. and Goundar, S., A framework to define the relationship between cyber security and cloud performance. *Comput. Fraud Secur.*, 2019, 12–19, 2019.
20. Almorsy, M., Grundy, J., Müller, I., An analysis of the cloud computing security problem, 2016. arXiv preprint arXiv:1609.01107.
21. Aggarwal, S., *2013 India Internet Outlook*, 2013.
22. Mathur, M.K. and Loonker, S., Interactive tv: A step ahead for imparting education in india. *Int. J. Comput. Sci. Eng. Technol. (IJCSET)*, 2, 6, 139–145, June 2011.
23. Gupta, S., Godbole, S., Angadi, Y., Desai, T-learning: Empowering india through interactive digital television (????).

24. Chen, Q., Lin, H., Wang, J., Ge, L., Li, Y., Pei, T., *et al.*, Single ring slot-based antennas for metal-rimmed 4G/5G smartphones. *IEEE Trans. Antennas Propag.*, 67, 1476–1487, 2018.
25. Wang, C.-C. and Hsu, M.-C., An exploratory study using inexpensive electroencephalography (EEG) to understand flow experience in computer-based instruction. *Inf. Manage.*, 51, 912–923, 2014.
26. Chen, C.-M. and Lin, Y.-J., Effects of different text display types on reading comprehension, sustained attention and cognitive load in mobile reading contexts. *Interact. Learn. Environ.*, 24, 553–571, 2016.
27. Chen, C.-M., Wang, J.-Y., Yu, C.-M., Assessing the attention levels of students by using a novel attention aware system based on brainwave signals. *Br. J. Educ. Technol.*, 48, 348–369, 2017.
28. Chen, C.-M. and Wu, C.-H., Effects of different video lecture types on sustained attention, emotion, cognitive load, and learning performance. *Comput. Educ.*, 80, 108–121, 2015.
29. Huang, Y.-M., Liu, M.-C., Lai, C.-H., Liu, C.-J., Using humorous images to lighten the learning experience through questioning in class. *Br. J. Educ. Technol.*, 48, 878–896, 2017.
30. Lai, C.-H., Liu, M.-C., Liu, C.-J., Huang, Y.-M., Using positive visual stimuli to lighten the online learning experience through in class questioning. *Int. Rev. Res. Open Distrib. Learn.*, 17, 23–41, 2016.
31. Lin, H.-C.K., Su, S.-H., Chao, C.-J., Hsieh, C.-Y., Tsai, S.-C., Construction of multi-mode affective learning system: taking affective design as an example. *J. Educ. Technol. Soc.*, 19, 132–147, 2016.
32. Chen, C.-M. and Wang, J.-Y., Effects of online synchronous instruction with an attention monitoring and alarm mechanism on sustained attention and learning performance. *Interact. Learn. Environ.*, 26, 427–443, 2018.
33. Yildirim, N. and Varol, A., Developing educational game software which measures attention and meditation with brainwaves: matching mind math, in: *ICEE ICIT Conference*, pp. 325–332, 2013.
34. U¨ lker, B., Tabakcıo˘glu, M.B., C¸ izmeci, H., Ayberkin, D., Relations of attention and meditation level with learning in engineering education, in: *2017 9th International Conference on Electronics, Computers and Artificial Intelligence (ECAI)*, IEEE, pp. 1–4, 2017.
35. Kuo, Y.-C., Chu, H.-C., Tsai, M.-C., Effects of an integrated physiological signal-based attention-promoting and english listening system on students' learning performance and behavioral patterns. *Comput. Hum. Behav.*, 75, 218–227, 2017.
36. Katona, J., Examination and comparison of the EEG based attention test with cpt and tova, in: *2014 IEEE 15th International Symposium on Computational Intelligence and Informatics (CINTI)*, IEEE, pp. 117–120, 2014.
37. Yang, S.-M., Chen, C.-M., Yu, C.-M., Assessing the attention levels of students by using a novel attention aware system based on brainwave signals, in:

2015 IIAI 4th International Congress on Advanced Applied Informatics, IEEE, pp. 379–384, 2015.

38. Yildirim, N. and Varol, A., Warning system for drivers according to attention and meditation status using brain computer interface, 2016.
39. Nakao, T., Hanaoka, S., Nomura, Y., Murata, M., Takenaga, T., Miki, S., Watadani, T., Yoshikawa, T., Hayashi, N., Abe, O., Unsupervised deep anomaly detection in chest radiographs. *J. Digital Imaging*, 34, 418–427, 2021.
40. Morshad, S., Mazumder, M.R., Ahmed, F., Analysis of brain wave data using neurosky mindwave mobile ii, in: *Proceedings of the International Conference on Computing Advancements*, pp. 1–4, 2020.
41. Balakrishnan, G. and Coetzee, D., Predicting student retention in massive open online courses using hidden markov models. *Electr. Eng. Comput. Sci. Univ. Calif. Berkeley*, 53, 57–58, 2013.
42. Yang, T.-Y., Brinton, C.G., Joe-Wong, C., Chiang, M., Behavior-based grade prediction for moocs via time series neural networks. *IEEE J. Sel. Top. Signal Process.*, 11, 716–728, 2017.
43. Szafir, D. and Mutlu, B., Artful: adaptive review technology for flipped learning, in: *Proceedings of the SIGCHI Conference on Human Factors in Computing Systems*, pp. 1001–1010, 2013.
44. Abeysekera, L. and Dawson, P., Motivation and cognitive load in the flipped classroom: definition, rationale and a call for research. *Higher Educ. Res. Dev.*, 34, 1–14, 2015.
45. Bergmann, J. and Sams, A., Flipped learning: Gateway to student engagement. *Int. Soc. Technol. Educ.*, 6, 5–14, 2014.
46. Lei, Z., Zhou, H., Hu, W., Deng, Q., Zhou, D., Liu, Z.-W., Gao, X., 3-d interactive control laboratory for classroom demonstration and online experimentation in engineering education. *IEEE Trans. Educ.*, 64, 276–282, 2020.
47. Xu, W. and Zhou, Y., Course video recommendation with multimodal information in online learning platforms: A deep learning framework. *Br. J. Educ. Technol.*, 51, 1734–1747, 2020.
48. Seery, M.K., Flipped learning in higher education chemistry: emerging trends and potential directions. *Chem. Educ. Res. Pract.*, 16, 758–768, 2015.
49. Shi, F., Marini, J.-L., Audry, E., Towards a psycho-cognitive recommender system. *Proceedings of the International Workshop on Emotion Representations and Modelling for Companion Technologies*, pp. 25–31, 2015.
50. Szafir, D. and Mutlu, B., Pay attention designing adaptive agents that monitor and improve user engagement, in: *Proceedings of the SIGCHI Conference on Human Factors in Computing Systems*, pp. 11–20, 2012.
51. Liang, N.-Y., Saratchandran, P., Huang, G.-B., Sundararajan, N., Classification of mental tasks from EEG signals using extreme learning machine. *Int. J. Neural Syst.*, 16, 29–38, 2006.
52. Dias, L.L., Barrére, E., de Souza, J.F., The impact of semantic annotation techniques on content-based video lecture recommendation. *J. Inf. Sci.*, 47, 740–752, 2021.

53. Yan, Y., Hara, K., Kazuma, T., He, A., A method for personalized c programming learning contents recommendation to enhance traditional instruction, in: *Proceedings of the 2017 IEEE 31st International Conference on Advanced Information Networking and Applications (AINA)*, pp. 320–327, 2017.
54. Gnana Rajesh, D., Analysis of mfcc features for EEG signal classification. *Int. J. Adv. Sig. Img. Sci.*, 2, 14–20, 2016.
55. Ibrahim, N.J., Razak, Z., Yakub, M., Yusoff, Z.M., Idris, M.Y., II, Tamil, E., Quranic verse recitation feature extraction using mel-frequency cepstral coefficients (mfcc), in: *Proc. of the 4th IEEE Int. Colloquium on Signal Processing and its Application (CSPA)*, Kuala Lumpur, Malaysia, Citeseer, 2008.
56. Kumar, N., Alam, K., Siddiqi, A.H., Wavelet transform for classification of EEG signal using svm and ann. *Biomed. Pharmacol. J.*, 10, 2061–2069, 2017.
57. Davis III, K.M., Spapé, M., Ruotsalo, T., Collaborative filtering with preferences inferred from brain signals, in: *Proceedings of the Web Conference 2021*, pp. 602–611, 2021.
58. Shaw, R., Patra, B.K., Pradhan, A., Mishra, S.P., Attention classification and lecture video recommendation based on captured EEG signal in flipped learning pedagogy. *Int. J. Human–Computer Interact.*, 0, 1–14, 2022. doi:10.1080/10447318.2022.2091561.
59. Kopparapu, S.K. and Laxminarayana, M., Choice of mel filter bank in computing mfcc of a resampled speech, in: *Proceedings of the 10th International Conference on Information Science, Signal Processing and their Applications (ISSPA 2010)*, pp. 121–124, 2010.
60. Shaw, R. and Patra, B.K., Cognitive-aware lecture video recommendation system using brain signal in flipped learning pedagogy. *Expert Syst. Appl.*, 207, 118057, 2022.
61. Aydemir, O., Pourzare, S., Kayikcioglu, T., Classifying various emg and eog artifacts in EEG signals. *Przeglad Elektrotechniczny*, 88, 218–22, 2012.
62. Rousseeuw, P.J., Silhouettes: a graphical aid to the interpretation and validation of cluster analysis. *J. Comput. Appl. Math.*, 20, 53–65, 1987.
63. Salvador, S. and Chan, P., Toward accurate dynamic time warping in linear time and space. *Intell. Data Anal.*, 11, 561–580, 2007.
64. Senin, P., Dynamic time warping algorithm review, in: *Information and Computer Science*, vol. 855, p. 40, Department University of Hawaii at Manoa, Honolulu, USA, 2008.
65. Caron, A., Redon, N., Coddeville, P., Hanoune, B., Identification of indoor air quality events using a k-means clustering analysis of gas sensors data. *Sens. Actuators B*, 297, 126709, 2019.
66. Teplan, M., *et al.*, Fundamentals of EEG measurement. *Meas. Sci. Rev.*, 2, 1–11, 2002.
67. Freeman, F.G., Mikulka, P.J., Prinzel, L.J., Scerbo, M.W., Evaluation of an adaptive automation system using three EEG indices with a visual tracking task. *Biol. Psychol.*, 50, 61–76, 1999.

2

Blockchain-Based Sustainable Supply Chain Management

Anuja Ajay[1]*, Saji M. S.[2] and Subhasis Dash[3]

[1]Computer Science, The Somaiya School, Mumbai, India
[2]Commercial Excellence, PPG Asian Paints Pvt. Ltd., Mumbai, India
[3]School of Computer Engineering, KIIT Deemed to be University, Bhubaneswar, Odisha, India

Abstract

Blockchain technology is an interesting and significant research area that has received huge attention in recent times. Blockchain technology has the potential to revolutionize supply chain management (SCM) and sustainability through its decentralized architecture and other factors such as transparency, data provenance, and trustworthiness. It provides robust security for all the transactions carried out and ensures the data integrity and privacy of the user. Conventional supply chains fail to satisfy the demand and requirements of the customers in terms of providing high-quality services with reasonable prices. The current trend is to integrate the SCM with blockchain technologies and transform the existing system into smart, automated, resilient, and sustainable. Various existing literary works related to technology, requirements of supply chain, access control, trust management, and sustainability are reviewed. This chapter intends to express the scope of improving the SCM frameworks using blockchain with an emphasis on blockchain interoperability. Although interoperability aspects are studied extensively, the research is still in its infancy stage of development. The need for a comprehensive analysis on interoperability techniques is still defiant. Hence, there is a great demand for the research related to blockchain interoperability in SCM, which can enable the blockchain platforms to be completely interoperable and allow secure communication between different blockchain platforms without depending on any trusted third party or a centralized entity. This chapter also focuses on interoperability aspects, different blockchain interoperability approaches and briefs about the design requirements, and challenges associated with it.

**Corresponding author*: anujaajay@gmail.com

Subhasis Dash, Manas Ranjan Lenka, S. Balamurugan, Ambika Prasad Tripathy and Amarendra Mohanty (eds.) Sustainable Resource Management in Next-Generation Computational Constrained Networks, (31–58) © 2025 Scrivener Publishing LLC

***Keywords*:** Blockchain, interoperability, supply chain management, sustainability, design considerations

2.1 Introduction

Blockchain is one of the advanced technologies that enable secure data sharing across different platforms. Recently, blockchain technologies have gained immense popularity as a disruptive technology. It offers several advantages that have motivated the organizations to shift their centralized process into decentralized architecture using blockchain. Blockchain is basically a distributed ledger architecture that can record the transactions and protect them from being tampered. Some of the prominent advantages of implementing blockchain are transparency, reliability, traceability, accountability, security, immutability, and sustainability (Park and Li, 2021) [1]. Blockchain can be used to develop a secured, trusted, and decentralized autonomous framework that can enhance the reliability, stability, and security of the applications. These characteristics of blockchain have increased the implementation of trusted environments without depending on any intermediaries (Perera *et al.*, 2021) [2]. Blockchain is extensively implemented in various applications such as banking and finance, Internet of Things (IoT), cloud computing, supply chain sustainability, and other smart applications. Supply chain management (SCM) is one of the most important applications that leverage blockchain technology for securing their transactions and documenting it (Saberi *et al.*, 2019) [3]. Blockchain can cope with the increasing complexity of SCM that is mainly due to global supply chain (SC) networks (Lambert and Enz, 2017) [4]. The complexity restricts the SCM frameworks to effectively carry out the transactions, document and secure the information, and manage the SC (Ivanov *et al.*, 2019) [5]. Blockchain has a distributed ledger technology (DLT) that consists of multiple immutable ledgers that are more susceptible to unauthorized access. The distributed architecture allows the formation of a peer-to-peer (P2P) network to secure the transactions using a chain of blocks. Based on the characteristics, blockchain is categorized into public, private, and permissioned blockchain (Patel *et al.*, 2020) [6]. Public blockchain networks allow only selected entities to participate in the transaction after verifying their authenticity (Yang *et al.*, 2020) [7] (Oliveira *et al.*, 2019) [8]. On the other hand, permissioned blockchain incorporates the characteristics of both private and public blockchain networks and are usually preferred in industrial applications for SCM (Dasaklis *et al.*, 2021) [9]

(Zafar *et al.*, 2022) [10]. Most of the blockchain models are programmable through which their operation can be customized according to the requirements. These programs are mainly programmed using smart contracts (Wang *et al.*, 2019) [11], and they are executed for performing application specific transactions.

Blockchain stores the data in the blocks, and these blocks are linked to each other to form a chain. The data recorded in these blocks cannot be altered or modified without modifying all other blocks in the chain. Each time a new block is added into the chain, it is connected with its predecessor (Dinh *et al.*, 2018) [12]. In addition to smart contracts, blockchain uses consensus algorithms to reach a common agreement in distributed systems. They create an agreement among the peers between the network and the ledger states to define the behavior of blockchain nodes and their ability to carry out the transactions effectively. These characteristics motivate the organizations including tech giants Walmart, FedEx, and KPMG to integrate blockchain technology for SCM and achieve better performance and efficiency. As per a recent survey conducted by Deloitte, the implementation of blockchain has increased by 18% over the last year and has attracted most of the top decision makers in the organization. This tremendous increase validates the efficacy of the blockchain technology (Insights, 2019) [13]. These facts motivate and prompt this research to identify prominent aspects of blockchain in SCM frameworks (including challenges and advantages) that augment blockchain adoption. Both challenges and benefits of blockchain solutions for SCM have been extensively studied in various existing works, which helps to understand the technical aspects of blockchain. Technical challenges in blockchain technology include high complexity, bandwidth requirements, high latency, scalability, and legal issues, lack of trust and standards, and interoperability. These challenges prevent the implementation of blockchain across various industrial sectors (Chang *et al.*, 2020) [14]. An empirical analysis of technical barriers that curtail the adoption of blockchain for SCM is one of the foremost research gaps (Queiroz *et al.*, 2019) [15]. Few research works have provided substantial evidence that highlight the significance of blockchain technology in improving the sustainability of SCM applications (Kouhizadeh *et al.*, 2021) [16] (Bai and Sarkis, 2020) [17] (Khan *et al.*, 2021) [18] (Khan *et al.*, 2022) [19]. However, the barriers faced by the SCM while integrating blockchain to support sustainability is rather under-investigated and needs a deeper investigation with an emphasis on interoperability in blockchain-based SCM applications. This chapter focuses on the intersection of blockchain technology, sustainable SCM (SSCM), and interoperability as shown in Figure 2.1.

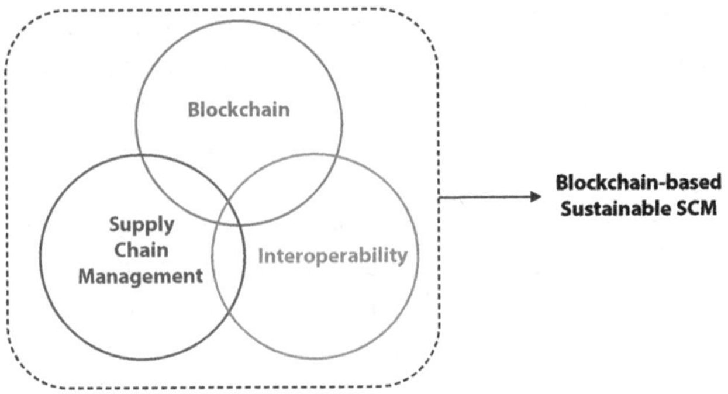

Figure 2.1 Blockchain-based SSCM.

2.1.1 Significance of Blockchain for SCM

Existing studies that have analyzed technical barriers in blockchain-based SSCMs lack theoretical support or validation. Few research works have utilized theories to investigate the objectives to implement blockchain technology for SSCM instead of understanding the challenges and limitations that are affecting the adoption. Theories mentioned in (Schmidt and Wagner, 2019) [20] examine the impact of blockchain on SCM based on transaction cost theory and highlight the reduction in transaction costs, uncertainties, and opportunistic behavior. Implementing a transparent and immutable operational infrastructure using DLT technology is practically advantageous to the business processes because it provides enormous opportunities for experimentation. The adoption of blockchain for SCM requires robust information technology (IT) architecture, and most of the existing SC companies have sophisticated and technologically advanced IT architecture to handle their business processes. This allows the SCM companies to leverage the advantages in terms of automating their documentation process including payments and purchasing, providing transparent services, reducing errors and disputes between the entities, improving traceability and accountability, proving a tamper-proof distributed ledger for protecting SC transactions, and improving the regulatory compliances. These facts clearly define the advantages of integrating blockchain technology with SCM. However, it is still crucial to understand the concept of achieving sustainability and interoperability in blockchain-based SCM and how all these elements can be combined seamlessly to extract maximum benefits.

2.1.2 Introduction to Blockchain Interoperability

Interoperability is defined as the capacity of an enterprise system to allow interoperation between different entities of the systems such as business components, software, and processes. The main challenges in performing interoperability are related to the communication, cooperation, and coordination among different entities of the system. In blockchain technology, interoperability refers to the ability of the blockchain platforms to share and communicate with other blockchain models (Schulte *et al.*, 2019) [21]. This will allow the blockchain networks to gain or access the data and create new products leveraging the advantages of multiple blockchain networks simultaneously.

Recently, SCM networks are employing a decentralized infrastructure to protect the SC data. The heterogeneous and distributed data sharing process of the SC requires blockchain technology to achieve effective interoperability while exchanging the information between stakeholders. Among different solutions available for SCs for data sharing, interoperability plays an important role in regulating the compliances for data sharing purposes (Wang *et al.*, 2020) [22]. The solutions are different for different applications and are designed based on the preference of stakeholders such as choice of blockchain platform (private or public), sensitivity of the data shared, scalability, reliability, and access control. Interoperability is also required because both blockchain and SCM solutions exist on an enterprise level. It allows the utilization of multiple blockchain systems in a SC for accomplishing different tasks. For instance, a public blockchain platform can execute digital transactions and a consortium blockchain can be used for recording the SCM transactions by providing access control and trust management services (Malik *et al.*, 2021) [23]. Blockchain solutions allow a seamless communication between two or more platforms without being concerned about the technical design challenges in each ecosystem, and interoperability approaches help to realize this aspect with better reliability and stability.

2.2 Blockchain for Supply Chain Management

The significance of blockchain in SCM has been a hot topic of research in recent times. Blockchain connects several SC participants such as suppliers, manufacturers, and retailers and provides automated services to the users. However, the potential of existing SCM theories and business processes are not contributing enough to the adoption of blockchain technology in SCM applications (Paliwal *et al.*, 2020) [24]. As a disruptive technology, blockchain has left a considerable impact on the service providers with respect to governance, societal relevance, connectivity, and trustworthiness. The positive notion of blockchain is that it is not just a single network and consists of multiple networks with different platforms, characteristics, consensus protocols, and system specifications. In certain cases, blockchain uses tokenization for asserting the ownership of a valuable asset. Tokenization helps in increasing the adoption of blockchain technology in risk-aware applications. In SCM, tokenization offers advantages to all participants and sellers by increasing the speed of transaction, improving the accessibility, reducing the cost of transaction, and enhancing transparency. Along with tokenization, deployment of smart contracts and energy-aware consensus protocols has enhanced the efficacy of blockchain technology in SCM.

For SSCM, it is essential to achieve better economic, social, and environmental performance as shown in Figure 2.2.

As shown in Figure 2.2, the social, economic, and environmental performance are considered as three main pillars to achieve SSCM. It involves a lot of complexity for business organizations to deploy sustainability policies while balancing between economic and environmental performance. The social performance signifies the democratic aspects wherein the rights and requirements of all stakeholders must be protected. Achieving sustainable objectives can have long-term advantages that motivate the researchers to focus more on the deployment of SSCM. Considering the benefits offered by the SSCM, a business organization can implement processes which can have a positive impact on the social and environmental performance (Paliwal *et al.*, 2020) [24]. In the view of these aspects, the collaboration of different SC activities must be considered, which has a greater role to play in optimizing the flow of information and increasing the rate of transactions.

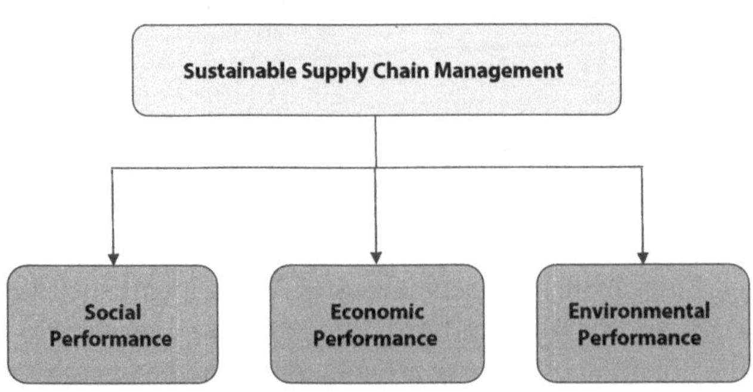

Figure 2.2 Sustainable supply chain management.

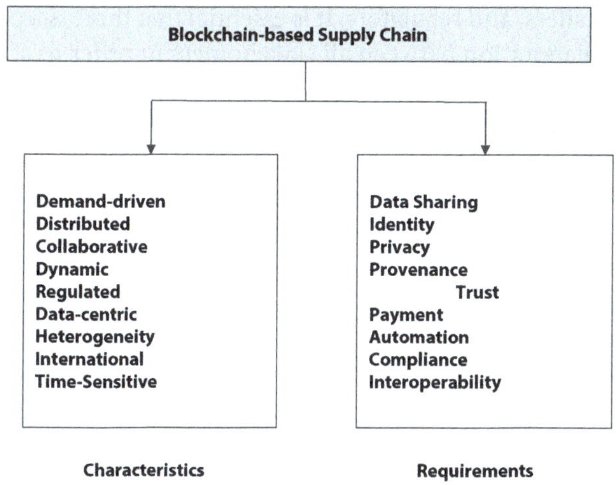

Figure 2.3 Characteristics and requirements of blockchain-based supply chain.

Most commonly, the entities participating in the SC networks have different priorities and demands. In addition, there are certain technical barriers that make the system incompatible to monitor the performance. These challenges can be addressed by integrating sustainability in all the SC networks and thereby make a positive impact on the overall social, economic, and environmental performance and inclusion of blockchain interoperability can be an added advantage. The characteristics of SC and different aspects of blockchain for SC are illustrated in Figure 2.3 and are discussed in the sections below.

2.2.1 Characteristics and Requirements of Blockchain-Based Supply Chain

In general, a SC is a sequential process for manufacturing and delivering products and services to the customers by acquiring raw materials. The SCM process contains multiple stakeholders and has a diversified set of characteristics and requirements as shown in Figure 2.3. A brief overview of the requirements and characteristics is discussed in this section.

2.2.1.1 Characteristics of Supply Chain

The prominent characteristics of SC applications are as follows:

(i) ***Collaborative:*** Most of the SC processes incorporate multiple stakeholders such as producers, transporters, auditors, retailers, and regulators. It is essential that there is a proper collaboration between all stakeholders in order to achieve operational stability and provide better services to the customers while earning financial incentives. However, it is a difficult task to collaborate between multiple stakeholders due to the difference in the trust levels and lack of transparency among stakeholders.

(ii) ***International:*** The effect of globalization has expanded the horizon of manufacturing and delivering processes across the globe. This geographic distribution of the SC involves the investors and stakeholders from different countries with different legal regulations. In global SCM applications, the raw materials will be obtained from the suppliers that are synthesized and manufactured by the manufacturers and the products are delivered to the prospective customers located at different locations. This poses potential risks and complications in the delivery process. It must be noted that all the stakeholders must agree to the regulations and compliances of all the jurisdictions involved in the process.

(iii) ***Time-Sensitive:*** Time is the most important factor in SC applications. The processes involved in the SC are time-sensitive, and stakeholders are highly concerned with respect to the timely delivery of products and information to make appropriate decisions. The delay in the process might disrupt the SC operations and can affect the overall process in terms of service quality, reduced incentives, quality degradation of goods, and high losses.

(iv) ***Distributed:*** Supply chain architecture involves both the IT and operation technology (OT) for managing the transfer of manufactured products, documents, and information that is shared between the stakeholders. The IT and OT infrastructure are basically interconnected with each other through data sharing platforms and enterprise systems.

(v) ***Regulated:*** There are several rules and regulations that the SC networks must comply with. These regulations are subjected to national and international regulations for importing and exporting the goods and information. Stakeholders must abide by the regulations of their respective jurisdiction,

and, in some cases, they must follow the regulations of the manufacturer and consumer's jurisdictions. This can be sometimes complicated, especially for cases when the SCs have to operate from multiple jurisdictions.

(vi) ***Heterogeneity:*** Due to the involvement of multiple stakeholders, SCs must deal with heterogeneous standards and systems. The difference in the standards might increase the compatibility problems and can have a negative impact on the collaboration between stakeholders.

(vii) ***Demand-Driven:*** The stochastic behavior of the end-users can be handled by incorporating a resilient SC process which can handle the varying consumer demands. In other words, the SC process must be demand-driven, which can analyze the demand or requirements and predict the operational process for optimizing the delivery of manufactured products and provide quality services to the customers. Designing a robust SC process that can respond to the varying demands of the stakeholders requires huge investment and advanced technologies that can acquire data across different entities and respond to real-time demands.

(viii) ***Dynamic and Unpredictable:*** The dynamic nature of the SC process is due to the constant changes in the regulations, service requirements, product-related changes, technological advancements, and unpredictable market dynamics. There can be unprecedented activities that can disrupt the SC networks and massively damage the business processes. It requires flexible and buoyant SC models that can respond to such real-time unpredictable instances.

(ix) ***Data-Centric:*** In order to maximize the performance of the SC process, the operation should be data-centric. It is important to make data-driven decisions based on real-time analysis to make the process more consumer-centric. Digitization of SC processes, big data analytics, trust mechanisms, secure data sharing platforms, and data provenance can help the stakeholders in making accurate yet reliable decisions about the business process and improve the efficacy of the SC process.

2.2.1.2 Requirements of Supply Chain

The prominent characteristics of SC are as follows:

(i) ***Trust:*** Trust is one of the decisive factors in the collaboration among stakeholders in the SC process. Due to the complex nature of SC networks, it is challenging to maintain the trust and integrity of the participants in the SC.

(ii) ***Payment:*** The transactions in a SC process involve the buyer and seller wherein the seller delivers the products or services to the buyer and, in turn, receives the payment. A transparent payment system must be deployed, which enables direct business payments without depending on any third-party entity. This reduces the transaction costs, lowers the possibility of financial frauds, and improves the efficiency and sustainability of the SC process.

(iii) ***Compliance:*** As discussed previously, the stakeholders must follow the standards and regulations before participating in the SC process. Non-compliance can cause huge financial losses and affects the entire process. In addition, non-compliance can also result in the disruption of the SC process which affects the reputation of the organization. Hence, it is essential to implement mechanisms such as regulatory technology (RegTech) to ensure regulatory compliance.

(iv) ***Provenance:*** The increasing consumer demand for product-related details such as origin, manufacturing process, transfer of ownership, custody necessitates the need for provenance mechanisms. It strengthens the confidence and trust of the consumer about the originality of the products and improves the accountability among stakeholders.

(v) ***Privacy:*** Privacy is the most critical aspect that affects the effectiveness of the SCs. While sharing the data, the stakeholders must be aware of the privacy standards and must share their data in the closed network. Because the SC data is highly confidential, the SC networks must incorporate robust privacy preservation mechanisms which can secure the sensitive information.

(vi) ***Automation:*** Conventional processes that are error-prone, redundant, tedious, and time-consuming can be automated to reduce time and resource consumption. Processes such as payment processing, inventory management, and product documentation can be automated using advanced technologies such as artificial intelligence (AI), IoT, and big data. This can improve the efficiency by reducing the operations costs and increasing the productivity.

(vii) ***Data Sharing:*** The sharing of information builds trust and improves the collaboration among stakeholders and also reduces the risk of non-compliance. Hence, there is a need to establish an end-to-end provenance wherein the data can be shared with the participants and the consumers. Lack of incentives might affect the data sharing process, and, hence, incentive can be provided to motivate the stakeholders to share the data.

(viii) ***Identity Management:*** The SC network is heterogeneous and distributed in nature, and, hence, it is essential to verify the identity of the stakeholders to authenticate the operation of the SC. However, in some cases, stakeholders might not reveal their identity due to certain complications, and, in such cases, the process lacks transparency, which is a critical issue. Conventional identity management techniques are based on centralized platforms for establishing trust between stakeholders, which poses security challenges. Hence, decentralized techniques must be deployed to control the data while sharing with other stakeholders.

(ix) ***Interoperability:*** The interdependence of the SC networks demands interoperability to collaborate between the stakeholders. Interoperability allows a smooth and flexible data sharing among different SC networks.

The above-mentioned requirements must be satisfied in order to make the SC applications more efficient, transparent, and trustworthy. Although most of the existing SC systems meet these requirements, they majorly depend on centralized infrastructure which increases the risk of data tampering and single point of failure. Integration of blockchain can overcome this problem and make the SC process more effective.

2.2.2 Blockchain-Based Data Sharing for Supply Chain

In the SCM process, the participating entities have to share their information with other consortiums within the SC network. The data includes details about product requirements, regulatory compliances, invoices, and customer feedback. Data sharing can be realized through both digital and manual processes wherein the information is collected and forwarded to respective stakeholders through their enterprise systems. Multiple data sharing mechanisms such as publish subscribe messaging (PSM) model, streaming data payment protocol (SDPP), and other application programming interfaces (APIs) have been implemented for SC applications. Because of its effectiveness, reliability, resource efficiency, and lightweight design, the PSM model is extensively used in the SC networks. Despite the advantages, the PSM model relies on a centralized architecture for exchanging the data through a centralized third-party entity such as Trinity. Here, Trinity is responsible for receiving the data and forwarding it to the respective end-users. This means that Trinity is crucial for data sharing. It cannot be ensured that the third-party entity is not trustworthy in all cases. Trinity is designed for multiple stakeholder applications wherein each stakeholder considered as a third-party entity and a consensus node is responsible for distributing the information across the network (Ramachandran *et al.*, 2019) [25]. All nodes are connected through a consensus layer that validates the data shared through them. All the information that is shared must be validated by one-third of the consensus nodes before sharing it to the consumers. Another important blockchain-based data sharing protocol is the SDPP, which provides incentives to the data producers. In SCM applications, SDPP handles the payments whenever it is related to the SC. Besides, the SDPP protocol enables the information provider and consumer to connect with others using payment streaming platforms (Radhakrishnan *et al.*, 2019) [26], as shown in Figure 2.4.

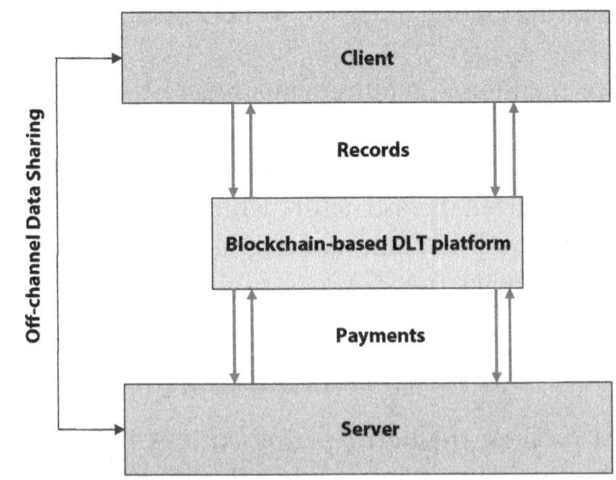

Figure 2.4 Data sharing through SDPP protocol.

In addition to these protocols, blockchain-based SCMs also use third-party blockchain service platforms such as IBM's FoodTrust and TradeLens. For effective data sharing, SCM applications must be integrated with blockchain technologies through APIs. However, the integration of SCM with blockchain becomes challenging when the data sharing protocols and platforms are not compatible with blockchain APIs. Although protocols such as Trinity, FoodTrust, and TradeLens allow seamless data sharing, there is a need for efficient interoperable APIs and protocols that can increase the implementation of blockchain in SCM applications.

2.2.3 Access Control and Trust Management in Blockchain-Based SCM

The security of SCM transactions demands robust trust management and access control approaches. Because the SC process involves data sharing across multiple organizations, it is suggested to control the access to the data using different access control mechanisms and thereby build trust.

2.2.3.1 Access Control Mechanisms in SCM

A SCM organization has several employees and systems that record the SC data. The access to the data must be provided to the right entity with a specific permissible limit. Any breach in the security might have lethal consequences on the entire SC process. Considering the significance, it is crucial to design an effective access control mechanism for SCM (Liu *et al.*, 2022) [27] (Li *et al.*, 2021) [28]. Access control is a technique that is implemented to ensure the safety of the data shared by verified entities. This technique restricts the access to only selected and trusted entities. These restrictions are managed by a set of policies that are controlled and regulated by the organizations (Pal *et al.*, 2018a) [29]. The access control process in the SCM applications must consider several attributes of the SC system such as time-sensitive, data-centric, and collaboration, considering the views of multiple stakeholders. Conventional access control techniques such as Role-based Access Control (RBAC), Attribute-based Access Control (ABAC), Organization-based Access Control (OrBAC), and Capability-based Access Control (CapBAC) are implemented for providing a fine-grained access control for SCM (Pal, 2021) [30]. In RBAC techniques, access is provided to employees based on their role and level in the organization. Only those users who belong to that level can access the data. However, RBAC is a centralized mechanism and is distributed in nature which is not suitable for blockchain-based SCM. On the other hand,

ABAC employs features such as data, location, and time for setting up access control regulations. Compared to RBAC, ABAC mechanism is flexible in controlling the identities of the users. In addition the ABAC mechanism considers common features and does not use any unique identity of a user. This attribute of ABAC makes it feasible for SCM applications to employ it for securing the data, and it can maintain the anonymity of the stakeholder. However, ABAC mechanisms are also centralized similar to RBAC and fail to achieve better control when the number of users increase beyond a specified limit within the SC (Pal *et al.*, 2018b) [31]. The OrBAC access control mechanism uses object, subject, and action for controlling the access to the SC data. This mechanism enables the access controller to explicitly define the security policies. However, the OrBAC mechanism is not flexible in its architecture because of its centralized nature. The CapBAC mechanism grants access to the users based on their capacity, which is in the form of unforgeable tokens of authority. This mechanism consists of access control policies for certain resources. The capability tokens are evaluated at the time of granting access. However, the CapBAC cannot manage a large number of capabilities and in such cases, their implementation can be difficult. It can be inferred from these techniques that access control mechanisms for SCM should be simple, energy efficient, reliable, flexible, scalable, trustworthy, and decentralized in nature. In addition, the access control techniques should be able to preserve the confidentiality, integrity, authenticity, and privacy of the SC data (Pal *et al.*, 2019) [32].

2.2.3.2 Trust Management in Supply Chain

Although there is no fixed or ubiquitous definition of trust, it is one of the intangible concepts that do have a clear understanding. This makes it difficult to design an appropriate trust management for blockchain-based SCM especially for complex systems. Trust management in SCM applications must be designed by considering multiple stakeholders (including sellers, buyers, and partners) and their functioning. In such dynamic environments, it is sometimes necessary to trust the decisions made by the stakeholders. Hence, the management of trust in SCM applications plays a greater role in enhancing the privacy and integrity of the SC systems. There are various factors that are responsible for managing the trust in SCM such as (i) data shared among multiple entities, which raises mutual expectations; (ii) commitment between the stakeholders to maintain a trusted relationship; (iii) establishing effective communication between the service providers and customers and allow customer feedback; (iv) maintaining the reputation of the SC, which is highly significant in building trust by observing the behavior of the suppliers; (v) maintaining the social behavior by highlighting the trust related concerns; (vi) implementing ethical considerations that define the responsibility of corporate social entities; and (vii) satisfying the customers by ensuring timely delivery of the products and services.

2.3 Interoperability in Blockchain

Interoperability is commonly defined as an ability of blockchain systems to share the transactional information and digital assets across different networks, without depending on any third-party entity. Because multiple platforms are involved within a single SC system, interoperability becomes important for data sharing. Interoperability solutions depend on the mutual interest of the stakeholders and are formulated based on specific requirements. A brief overview of different blockchain interoperability approaches and interoperability challenges is discussed in below sections.

2.3.1 Overview of Blockchain Interoperability Approaches

Blockchain interoperability approaches can be broadly categorized into three types, namely, public connectors, blockchain of blockchains, and hybrid connectors.

2.3.1.1 Public Connectors

Public connectors define different interoperability techniques for public blockchain that support the transactions of digital currencies. Public connectors include side-chain approaches, notary schemes, and hash time hash locks.

- ***Side Chains and Relays:*** A side chain is also defined as a secondary chain, which is implemented for two or more blockchain to interoperate (Gazi *et al.*, 2019) [33], wherein one blockchain is the main chain and the other is called the side chain, which is an extension of the main chain. The main chain maintains the ledger of transactions and is interconnected with the side chain that uses a cross-chain communication protocol for sharing the data (Garoffolo *et al.*, 2020) [34].
- ***Notary Schemes:*** The notary schemes employ a notary that is responsible for monitoring the operation of multiple chains, which executes the transactions on another chain using

smart contract (Scheid *et al.*, 2021) [35]. In practical, notary schemes can be deployed as centralized exchanges (EXs) or decentralized exchanges (DEXs).

- ***Hashed Time-Lock Contracts (HTLCs):*** The HTLCs are developed as an alternative to the centralized approaches because they can perform cross-chain atomic operations (Bhatia *et al.*, 2022) [36]. HTLCs use hash locks and time-clocks for enforcing the atomicity of operation between one or more entities.

2.3.1.2 Blockchain of Blockchains (BoB)

The BoB is an interoperability approach that reuses the data and incorporates consensus protocols, network protocols, and contract layers for creating application-specific or customizing blockchains according to the requirement, which can interoperate between each other. The BoB approaches include two main schemes, namely, Polkadot (Burdges *et al.*, 2020) [37] and Cosmos (Bhatia, 2020) [38], which are the most extensively used BoB schemes. Polkadot allows interoperability between two parties based on the validated transactions using chain relay validators. These chains communicate using a queuing approach based on the Merkel tree (Polkadot, 2019) [39] and a Cross-chain Message Passing Protocol (XCMP). On the other hand, Cosmos is defined as a decentralized platform that consists of multiple parallel blockchains called zones that are independent of each other. These zones transfer the information to other zones either directly or through hubs. The hubs reduce the number of connections between the zones and reduce the communication delay. For instance, zone 1 can connect with zone 2 through hub 3 and receive a token from zone 2. Zone 1 must trust the tokens received by zone 2 and hub 3. This mechanism allows the zones to reduce the number of connections and carry out transactions using an inter-blockchain communication protocol. This protocol is similar to the network layer in the communication system that transfers data packets to a target blockchain network. A target blockchain trusts the data packet received from another blockchain and enables cross-zone transactions.

2.3.1.3 Hybrid Connectors

Hybrid connectors belong to the class of different interoperability solutions, which cannot be solved using public connectors of BoB-based solutions. Hybrid connectors integrate the characteristics and functionalities of both private and public blockchain that aims to deliver a "blockchain abstraction layer" (Nazarov *et al.*, 2020) [40]. These connectors can expose a set of similar operations that allow the decentralized applications to communicate with blockchain without depending on additional APIs (Falazi *et al.*, 2020) [41]. Different types of hybrid connectors are deployed for achieving effective interoperability such as Trusted Relays, Blockchain Agnostic Protocols (including BOB), and Blockchain Migrators.

- ***Trusted Relays (TR):*** TRs are termed as the trusted parties that transfer the information from a source to the target blockchain by enabling the users to formulate application specific business logic. The interoperability solution is based on trusted relays, which can manage different APIs and allows a cross-chain consensus. One of the important forms of trusted relays is the Hyperledger Cactus that employs an interoperability validating module which verifies and authenticates cross-chain transactions using a trusted escrow party (Hart Montgomery *et al.*, 2020) [42]. This process validates the decentralized transactions and redirects the transactions toward a decentralized trusted relay. Cactus allows multiple entities to carry out transactions based on the ledger data, which is similar to the mechanism of notary schemes (Scheid *et al.*, 2019) [43]. The interoperability solutions are developed through interoperability validation mechanisms wherein the participating entities are the source and target blockchain.
- ***Blockchain Agnostic Protocols:*** These protocols enable cross-chain communication between two independent DLT frameworks by incorporating a blockchain abstraction layer. The solutions obtained through these protocols enable blockchain of blockchains wherein a consensus protocol is used to organize the blocks in a chain which contains the transaction data belonging to the cross chained applications distributed across different blockchain platforms. The system accompanying agnostic protocols provides accountability for the entities carrying out the transactions across different blockchain platforms and provides a holistic approach for each blockchain. An Interledger Protocol (ILP) is a decentralized P2P network that incorporates a fundamental hash locking system for allowing secure asset transfers (currently used in the transaction of cryptocurrencies). The ILP

platform is used extensively in payment transfers across different networks. The ILP framework uses a packet switching consensus protocol (ILPv4), which analyzes the behavior of participants participating in the transactions such as senders, receivers, and routers (connectors or nodes) and monitors their interaction.

- ***Blockchain Migrators:*** The blockchain migrators assist the users to migrate one blockchain state to another state. Presently, it is practically feasible to migrate the information across blockchain platforms incorporating smart contracts. The process involved in the blockchain platform locks the smart contracts on the source blockchain and then the protocol is migrated to recreate the smart contract in the target blockchain. This mechanism enables the random transaction between two blockchain platforms.

2.3.2 Gateways for Interoperability and Manageability

The future of blockchain interoperability can be analyzed with respect to the network of multiple blockchain incorporated with different consensus protocols, permission requirements, security techniques, and incentive mechanisms. The main element to the interconnection is the concept of blockchain gateways. This section discusses some of the prominent aspects of blockchain gateways for interoperability and managing the transaction exchanges across different blockchain platforms. Achieving interoperability can be a challenging task when the data in permission less blockchain interact with permissioned or private blockchain platforms. This is due to the realization of the transactions on the ledger that can reveal sensitive and private information and, hence, are regarded as private. Three main gateway concepts are identified for achieving interoperability, which are as follows:

- ***Intradomain and Interdomain Nodes***
  Similar to the routing mechanism in communication systems consisting of multiple routing paths, it can be considered as a blockchain platform with one or more ledger managing systems. Hence, the intradomain and interdomain nodes are termed as routers that are responsible for operating more routing protocols to identify optimized routes through the path. These nodes help in maintaining a distributed ledger by executing multiple protocols such as consensus protocols to improve the convergence speed and stability of the blockchain system.

- ***Defining the Perimeter for Blockchain***
  Considering different blockchain owners and network operators, it is essential to determine the physical perimeter of the network and implement system controlling techniques over the networks. By evaluating the perimeter for blockchain, one can productively understand the requirements and possibilities of the business processes. This mechanism allows the operators to design the transaction routing mechanisms based on their application requirements by employing consensus protocols and incentive mechanics in each domain.

- ***Interdomain Trust Establishment (ITE)***
  An important aspect of blockchain gateways for achieving interoperability is the potential utilization of gateways for supporting the trust establishment in the networks for different blockchain systems. It is anticipated that there is a considerable amount of significance of ITE gateways in terms of improving the interoperability. For establishing the trust, all nodes in the blockchain network must approve the transactions using trusted hardware and software elements.

2.3.3 Interoperability Approaches

Several researchers have studied the interoperability approaches. The authors (Latourcade and Lombard-Platet, 2020) [44] discussed the feasibility of achieving interoperability between two blockchain platforms. Based on their study, it can be said that two public blockchains are considered to be interoperable only if they execute the same transaction using similar consensus protocols and system architectures. The need for the blockchain interoperability was investigated by Schulte *et al.* (2019) [21] along with its ability to stimulate the pattern shift from current blockchain technologies into an open system that allows the interaction between the users and multiple devices across the diversified architecture of blockchain. A comprehensive survey on different types of public connector based approaches, which includes notary techniques, side chains, and hash-time locking frameworks, is presented by Pang (2020) [45]. Correspondingly, other works (Koens and Poll, 2019) [46] (Singh *et al.*, 2020) [47] focused on public connectors with an emphasis on side chains and hash lock time contracts. On the other hand Vo *et al.* (2018) [48] focused on designing block interoperability using blockchain (BoB) and hybrid connectors framework. Qasse *et al.* (2019) [49] presented the solutions for side chains, smart contracts, blockchain routers, and industrial solutions, whereas different categories of solutions were proposed by Johnson *et al.* (2019) [50], Siris *et al.* (2019) [51], and Monika and Rajesh (2020) [52], wherein they provided a wide range of solutions for the problems related to interoperability frameworks.

2.4 Design Considerations and Open Challenges

The main challenges in designing interoperability solutions are mainly related to the communication, cooperation, and coordination among different entities of the system. This section reviews some of the prominent challenges that are observed while implementing the interoperability solutions for blockchain-based SCMs.

- As discussed previously, one of the prominent considerations of SCM applications is the regulatory compliance, which depends from one country to another and has different legal jurisdictions. In particular, the compliances related to auditing and regulation depend on the stakeholders and their interest in sharing the data across different parts of the world. Considering the complexities associated with the collaboration of stakeholders, achieving regulatory compliance with an emphasis on data privacy remains as a big challenge, which can affect the interoperability as well as traceability. Hence, it is important to consider this issue while designing interoperability solutions for blockchain-based SCMs.
- The heterogeneity of the blockchain platform has increased the difficulties to develop interoperability mechanisms within the SCM systems. There should be high compatibility between two blockchain platforms for establishing stable communication between using consensus protocols and smart contracts. Because blockchain can record transactions with different forms of data such as raw data formats, hashed data, and encrypted data, the challenges related to heterogeneity can be more difficult to solve.
- Blockchain for SCMs requires technologically advanced and sophisticated system architecture. The elements that allow blockchain services include cloud servers for data storage, back end oracles, IT and OT infrastructure, and intra- and inter-domain network nodes. Allowing disparate blockchain systems proprietary to communicate with each other and operate

effectively is one of the major challenges related to interoperability and needs significant attention to overcome this.

2.5 Summary

The objective of this chapter is to compile the advancements in the next generation blockchain-based SCM technologies contributing toward resource management in computationally constrained networks, which can be of great aid to researchers, academicians, and industry people to have a good understanding of the current stand of the technology and carry out further developments to the technologies for the benefit of Society. This chapter discusses the integration of blockchain technologies with SCM and highlights the requirements and characteristics of SCM applications. The chapter also focuses on the interoperability aspects that play an important role in improving the sustainability of blockchain-based SCM models. The study briefs about how multiple SC stakeholders can share and access the data with better trust management using blockchain technology. Furthermore, the study defines the significance of blockchain for SCM to handle the throughputs, scalability, and latency demands of practical SCM applications with an aim to achieve sustainability. The interoperability requirements in blockchain are highlighted with a brief overview of different interoperability approaches such as public connectors, BOBs, and hybrid connectors. In addition, the interoperability challenges are discussed which can benefit the organizations to overcome the technical barriers and increase the adaptability of blockchain approaches. The chapter is concluded with design considerations, challenges, and scope of future work.

2.5.1 Advantages of Blockchain for SSCM

Blockchain has several advantages when implemented for SSCM such as better accessibility, secure data storage, data management, stringent laws and policy, decentralized architecture, and better quality (Yadav and Singh, 2020) [53]. These advantages increase the adaptability of blockchain in SCM and promote sustainability. There is a need for a comprehensive analysis of sustainability in blockchain-based transactions (Phang *et al.*, 2019) [54]. Considering its potential, blockchain can be used to design an effective approach, which can improve the sustainability of SCM and other applications by accurately providing provenance information and accomplishing transaction details through blockchain-based smart contracts (Nikolakis *et al.*,

2018) [55]. Consequently, blockchain can be used to develop a SSCM model for small and medium enterprises (Nayak and Dhaigude, 2019) [56]. By emphasizing blockchain technologies, the objectives of SSCM such as quality, computational speed, cost-effectiveness, flexibility, reliability, reduced risk factors, and sustainability can be analyzed (Kshetri, 2018) [57]. Various research works have validated the effectiveness of blockchain in terms of improving transparency, and accountability of SCM frameworks (Kshetri, 2018) [57]. It can be inferred from these studies that blockchain technology can adequately address the challenges related to SSCM (Gurzawska, 2020) [58]. In addition, blockchain can improve the integration with other technologies and improve the performance to maximize the economic benefits and achieve sustainable goals. Transparency is the most crucial factor in smart and sustainable applications because it adds value to the performance of SSCM (Freudenreich and Schaltegger, 2020) [59]. The integration of blockchain with smart city applications such as smart transformation, smart management, smart homes, and smart healthcare management is highly recommended to improve their sustainability (Filimonau and Naumova, 2020) [60].

2.6 Scope of Future Work Emphasis

Most blockchains are programmable and the programs are usually designed using smart contracts, and the execution of these smart contracts is done using designated transactions. The emergence of smart contracts has extended the application of blockchain beyond token creation and management. Blockchain platforms such as Corda, Quorum, and Hyperledger Fabric are extensively used in the several blockchain applications that use smart contracts for improving the security of transactions. However, the role of smart contracts in interconnecting blockchains is not addressed in most of the previous works. Hence, investigating the role of smart contracts in improving interoperability can be significantly increased (Khan *et al.*, 2021) [61]. The existing works also state that the diversity in the blockchain technologies and their architects makes it difficult to categorize them and their interoperability solutions due to the fact that there is a lack of blockchain interoperability techniques and supporting architecture (Bhatia, 2020) [38]. Nazarov *et al.* (2020) [40] stated that majority of the existing solutions for blockchain interoperability are developed using public and private blockchain platforms. However, the application of hybrid platforms that integrate private and public blockchain platforms needs more attention. Despite the availability of plenty of solutions for blockchain interoperability, there is a huge gap between the theoretical analysis and practical implementation. Furthermore, there is no universal framework that can solve these issues once, and this increases the need for blockchain interoperability solutions. There is a gap between theoretical analysis and practical implementation, including the lack of standardization and implementations, which adds to the existing research gaps related to interoperability.

References

1. Park, A. and Li, H., The effect of blockchain technology on supply chain sustainability performances. *Sustainability*, *13*, 4, 1726, 2021.
2. Perera, S., Hijazi, A.A., Weerasuriya, G.T., Nanayakkara, S., Rodrigo, M.N.N., Blockchain-based trusted property transactions in the built environment: Development of an incubation-ready prototype. *Buildings*, *11*, 11, 560, 2021.
3. Saberi, S., Kouhizadeh, M., Sarkis, J., Shen, L., Blockchain technology and its relationships to sustainable supply chain management. *Int. J. Prod. Res.*, *57*, 7, 2117–2135, 2019.
4. Lambert, D.M. and Enz, M.G., Issues in supply chain management: Progress and potential. *Ind. Marketing Manage.*, *62*, 1–16, 2017.
5. Ivanov, D., Dolgui, A., Sokolov, B., The impact of digital technology and Industry 4.0 on the ripple effect and supply chain risk analytics. *Int. J. Prod. Res.*, *57*, 3, 829–846, 2019.
6. Patel, V., Khatiwala, F., Shah, K., Choksi, Y., A review on blockchain technology: Components, issues and challenges, in: *ICDSMLA 2019: Proceedings of the 1st International Conference on Data Science, Machine Learning and Applications*, Springer Singapore, pp. 1257–1262, 2020.
7. Yang, R., Wakefield, R., Lyu, S., Jayasuriya, S., Han, F., Yi, X., Chen, S., Public and private blockchain in construction business process and information integration. *Autom. Constr.*, *118*, 103276, 2020.
8. Oliveira, M.T., Carrara, G.R., Fernandes, N.C., Albuquerque, C.V., Carrano, R.C., Medeiros, D.S., Mattos, D.M., Towards a performance evaluation of private blockchain frameworks using a realistic workload, in: *2019 22nd conference on innovation in clouds, internet and networks and workshops (ICIN)*, IEEE, pp. 180–187, 2019, February.
9. Dasaklis, T.K., Casino, F., Patsakis, C., Douligeris, C., A framework for supply chain traceability based on blockchain tokens, in: *Business Process Management Workshops: BPM 2019 International Workshops, Vienna, Austria, September 1–6, 2019, Revised Selected Papers 17*, Springer International Publishing, pp. 704–716, 2019.
10. Zafar, S., Hassan, S.F.U., Mohammad, A., Al-Ahmadi, A.A., Ullah, N., Implementation of a Distributed Framework for Permissioned

Blockchain-Based Secure Automotive Supply Chain Management. *Sensors, 22*, 19, 7367, 2022.
11. Wang, S., Ouyang, L., Yuan, Y., Ni, X., Han, X., Wang, F.Y., Blockchain-enabled smart contracts: architecture, applications, and future trends. *IEEE Trans. Syst. Man Cybern.: Syst., 49*, 11, 2266–2277, 2019.
12. Dinh, T.T.A., Liu, R., Zhang, M., Chen, G., Ooi, B.C., Wang, J., Untangling blockchain: A data processing view of blockchain systems. *IEEE Trans. Knowl. Data Eng., 30*, 7, 1366–1385, 2018.
13. Linda Pawczuk, Rob Massey, and Jonathan Holdowsky, Deloitte's 2019 Global Blockchain Survey, in: *Blockchain Gets Down to Business*, Deloitte, 2019.
14. Chang, Y., Iakovou, E., Shi, W., Blockchain in global supply chains and cross border trade: a critical synthesis of the state-of-the-art, challenges and opportunities. *Int. J. Prod. Res., 58*, 7, 2082–2099, 2020.
15. Queiroz, M.M. and Wamba, S.F., Blockchain adoption challenges in supply chain: An empirical investigation of the main drivers in India and the USA. *Int. J. Inf. Manage., 46*, 70–82, 2019.
16. Kouhizadeh, M., Saberi, S., Sarkis, J., Blockchain technology and the sustainable supply chain: Theoretically exploring adoption barriers. *Int. J. Prod. Econ., 231*, 107831, 2021.
17. Bai, C. and Sarkis, J., A supply chain transparency and sustainability technology appraisal model for blockchain technology. *Int. J. Prod. Res., 58*, 7, 2142–2162, 2020.
18. Khan, S.A.R., Godil, D.I., Jabbour, C.J.C. *et al.*, Green data analytics, blockchain technology for sustainable development, and sustainable supply chain practices: evidence from small and medium enterprises. *Ann. Oper. Res.*, 2021. https://doi.org/10.1007/s10479-021-04275-x.
19. Khan, S.A., Mubarik, M.S., Kusi-Sarpong, S., Gupta, H., Zaman, S.I., Mubarik, M., Blockchain technologies as enablers of supply chain mapping for sustainable supply chains. *Bus. Strategy Environ.*, 31, 8, 3742–3756, 2022. doi:10.1002/bse.3029.
20. Schmidt, C.G. and Wagner, S.M., Blockchain and supply chain relations: A transaction cost theory perspective. *J. Purchasing Supply Manage., 25*, 4, 100552, 2019.
21. Schulte, S., Sigwart, M., Frauenthaler, P., Borkowski, M., Towards blockchain interoperability, in: *Business Process Management: Blockchain and Central and Eastern Europe Forum: BPM 2019 Blockchain and CEE Forum, Vienna, Austria, September 1–6, 2019, Proceedings 17*, Springer International Publishing, pp. 3–10, 2019.
22. Wang, Z., Wang, T., Hu, H., Gong, J., Ren, X., Xiao, Q., Blockchain-based framework for improving supply chain traceability and information sharing in precast construction. *Autom. Constr., 111*, 103063, 2020.
23. Malik, S., Gupta, N., Dedeoglu, V., Kanhere, S.S., Jurdak, R., TradeChain: Decoupling Traceability and Identity in Blockchain enabled Supply Chains, *2021 IEEE 20th International Conference on Trust, Security and Privacy in*

Computing and Communications (TrustCom), pp. 1141–1152, Shenyang, China, 2021, doi: 10.1109/TrustCom53373.2021.00155.
24. Paliwal, V., Chandra, S., Sharma, S., Blockchain technology for sustainable supply chain management: A systematic literature review and a classification framework. *Sustainability*, *12*, 18, 7638, 2020.
25. Ramachandran, G.S., Wright, K.L., Zheng, L., Navaney, P., Naveed, M., Krishnamachari, B., Dhaliwal, J., Trinity: A byzantine fault-tolerant distributed publish-subscribe system with immutable blockchain-based persistence, in: *2019 IEEE International Conference on Blockchain and Cryptocurrency (ICBC)*, IEEE, pp. 227–235, 2019, May.
26. Radhakrishnan, R., Ramachandran, G.S., Krishnamachari, B., Sdpp: Streaming data payment protocol for data economy, in: *2019 IEEE International Conference on Blockchain and Cryptocurrency (ICBC)*, IEEE, pp. 17–18, 2019, May.
27. Liu, C., Xiang, F., Sun, Z., Multiauthority attribute-based access control for supply chain information sharing in blockchain. *Secur. Commun. Netw.*, *2022*, 1–18, 2022.
28. Li, D., Han, D., Crespi, N., Minerva, R., Sun, Z., Fabric-scf: A blockchain-based secure storage and access control scheme for supply chain finance, 2021, arXiv preprint arXiv:2111.13538.
29. Pal, S., Hitchens, M., Varadharajan, V., Rabehaja, T., Policy-based access control for constrained healthcare resources, in: *2018 IEEE 19th International Symposium on" A World of Wireless, Mobile and Multimedia Networks" (WoWMoM)*, IEEE, pp. 588–599, 2018a, June.
30. Pal, S., Internet of Things and Access Control: Sensing, Monitoring and Controlling Access in IoT-Enabled Healthcare Systems, vol. 37, Springer: Cham, Switzerland, 2021.
31. Pal, S., Hitchens, M., Varadharajan, V., Rabehaja, T., Fine-Grained Access Control for Smart Healthcare Systems in the Internet of Things. EAI Endorsed Transactions on Industrial Networks and Intelligent Systems, 4, 13, 154370, 2018. https://doi.org/10.4108/eai.20-3-2018.154370.
32. Pal, S., Rabehaja, T., Hill, A., Hitchens, M., Varadharajan, V., On the integration of blockchain to the internet of things for enabling access right delegation. *IEEE Internet Things J.*, *7*, 4, 2630–2639, 2019.
33. Gaži, P., Kiayias, A., Zindros, D., Proof-of-stake sidechains, in: *2019 IEEE Symposium on Security and Privacy (SP)*, 139–156, IEEE, 2019, May.
34. Garoffolo, A., Kaidalov, D., Oliynykov, R., Zendoo: A zk-SNARK verifiable cross-chain transfer protocol enabling decoupled and decentralized sidechains, in: *2020 IEEE 40th International Conference on Distributed Computing Systems (ICDCS)*, IEEE, pp. 1257–1262, 2020, November.
35. Scheid, E.J., Kiechl, P., Franco, M., Rodrigues, B., Killer, C., Stiller, B., Security and Standardization of a Notary-based Blockchain Interoperability API, in: *2021 Third International Conference on Blockchain Computing and Applications (BCCA)*, IEEE, pp. 42–48, 2021, November.

36. Bhatia, R., Jain, A., Singh, B., Hash time locked contract based asset exchange solution for probabilistic public blockchains. *Cluster Comput.*, *25*, 6, 4189–4201, 2022.
37. Burdges, J., Cevallos, A., Czaban, P., Habermeier, R., Hosseini, S., Lama, F., Wood, G., Overview of polkadot and its design considerations, 2020. arXiv preprint arXiv:2005.13456.
38. Bhatia, R., Interoperability solutions for blockchain, in: *2020 international conference on smart technologies in computing, electrical and electronics (ICSTCEE)*, IEEE, pp. 381–385, 2020, October.
39. Polkadot, Cross-chain Message Passing (XCMP) Polkadot Wiki, 2019, https://wiki.polkadot.network/docs/en/learn-crosschain.
40. Nazarov, S., Shukla, P., Erwin, A., Rajput, A., Bridging the governance gap: Interoperability for blockchain and legacy systems, in: *World Economic Forum whitepaper*, 2020, December, https://www.weforum.org/whitepapers/bridging-the-governance-gap-interoperability-for-blockchain-and-legacy-systems.
41. Falazi, G., Breitenbücher, U., Daniel, F., Lamparelli, A., Leymann, F., Yussupov, V., Smart contract invocation protocol (SCIP): A protocol for the uniform integration of heterogeneous blockchain smart contracts, in: *Advanced Information Systems Engineering: 32nd International Conference, CAiSE 2020, Grenoble, France, June 8–12, 2020, Proceedings*, vol. *32*, Springer International Publishing, pp. 134–149, 2020.
42. Montgomery, H., Borne-Pons, H., Hamilton, J., Bowman, M., Somogyvari, P., Fujimoto, S., Takeuchi, T., Kuhrt, T., Belchior, R., Hyperledger Cactus Whitepaper, 2020, https://github.com/hyperledger/cactus/blob/master/docs/whitepaper/whitepaper.md.
43. Scheid, E.J., Hegnauer, T., Rodrigues, B., Stiller, B., Bifröst: a modular blockchain interoperability API, in: *2019 IEEE 44th Conference on Local Computer Networks (LCN)*, IEEE, pp. 332–339, 2019, October.
44. Lafourcade, P. and Lombard-Platet, M., About blockchain interoperability. *Inf. Process. Lett.*, *161*, 105976, 2020.
45. Pang, Y., A new consensus protocol for blockchain interoperability architecture. *IEEE Access*, *8*, 153719–153730, 2020.
46. Koens, T. and Poll, E., Assessing interoperability solutions for distributed ledgers. *Pervasive Mob. Comput.*, *59*, 101079, 2019.
47. Singh, A., Click, K., Parizi, R.M., Zhang, Q., Dehghantanha, A., Choo, K.K.R., Sidechain technologies in blockchain networks: An examination and state-of-the-art review. *J. Network Comput. Appl.*, *149*, 102471, 2020.
48. Vo, H.T., Wang, Z., Karunamoorthy, D., Wagner, J., Abebe, E., Mohania, M., Internet of blockchains: Techniques and challenges ahead, in: *2018 IEEE international conference on internet of things (iThings) and IEEE green computing and communications (GreenCom) and IEEE cyber, physical and social computing (CPSCom) and IEEE smart data (SmartData)*, IEEE, pp. 1574–1581, 2018, July.

49. Qasse, I.A., Abu Talib, M., Nasir, Q., Inter blockchain communication: A survey, in: *Proceedings of the ArabWIC 6th Annual International Conference Research Track*, pp. 1–6, 2019, March.
50. Johnson, S., Robinson, P., Brainard, J., Sidechains and interoperability, 2019, arXiv preprint arXiv:1903.04077.
51. Siris, V.A., Nikander, P., Voulgaris, S., Fotiou, N., Lagutin, D., Polyzos, G.C., Interledger approaches. *IEEE Access*, *7*, 89948–89966, 2019.
52. Bishnoi, M. and Bhatia, R., Interoperability solutions for blockchain. *Proceedings of the International Conference on Smart Technologies in Computing, Electrical and Electronics, ICSTCEE*, vol. 2020, pp. 381–385, 2020.
53. Yadav, S. and Singh, S.P., Blockchain critical success factors for sustainable supply chain. *Resour. Conserv. Recycl.*, *152*, 104505, 2020.
54. Phang, D.C., Wang, K., Wang, Q., Kauffman, R.J., Naldi, M., How to derive causal insights for digital commerce in China? A research commentary on computational social science methods. *Electron. Commerce Res. Appl.*, *35*, 100837, 2019.
55. Nikolakis, W., John, L., Krishnan, H., How blockchain can shape sustainable global value chains: an evidence, verifiability, and enforceability (EVE) framework. *Sustainability*, *10*, 11, 3926, 2018.
56. Nayak, G. and Dhaigude, A.S., A conceptual model of sustainable supply chain management in small and medium enterprises using blockchain technology. *Cogent Econ. Finance*, *7*, 1, 1667184, 2019.
57. Kshetri, N., Blockchain's roles in meeting key supply chain management objectives. *Int. J. Inf. Manage.*, *39*, 80–89, 2018.
58. Gurzawska, A., Towards responsible and sustainable supply chains–innovation, multi-stakeholder approach and governance. *Philos. Manage.*, *19*, 3, 267–295, 2020.
59. Freudenreich, B. and Schaltegger, S., Developing sufficiency-oriented offerings for clothing users: Business approaches to support consumption reduction. *J. Clean. Prod.*, *247*, 119589, 2020.
60. Filimonau, V. and Naumova, E., The blockchain technology and the scope of its application in hospitality operations. *Int. J. Hospitality Manage.*, *87*, 102383, 2020.
61. Khan, S., Amin, M.B., Azar, A.T., Aslam, S., Towards interoperable blockchains: A survey on the role of smart contracts in blockchain interoperability. *IEEE Access*, *9*, 116672–116691, 2021.

3

Revolutionizing Aquaculture With the Internet of Things (IoT): An Insightful Learning

Arpita Nayak[1]*, Atmika Patnaik[2], Ipseeta Satpathy[3], Veena Goswami[4] and B.C.M. Patnaik[5]

[1]*KIIT School of Liberal Studies, KIIT DU, Bhubaneswar, India*
[2]*Master's in Law, King's College London, London, United Kingdom*
[3]*School of Management, KIIT University, Bhubaneswar, India*
[4]*School of Computer Applications, KIIT University, Bhubaneswar, India*
[5]*KIIT School of Management, KIIT DU, Bhubaneswar, India*

Abstract

The Internet of Things (IoT) is a collection of objects in the real world outfitted with sensors, apps, and other devices that allow them to communicate data via the internet. Temperature, pH, oxygen, and other water characteristics may be checked using devices that can be programmed. IoT technology has transformed fish farming procedures in several ways, including getting real-time data on water quality and aqua life. Data acquired by devices is stored in a data hub or repository so that users may access them through their computers or phones. IoT has been used in aquaculture to gather data, monitor fish and their environment, and anticipate illnesses and infestation. The capacity to keep a track of pond characteristics in actual time has led to more ecological environment variables, which has resulted in decreased yield losses. It has the ability to completely transform the aquaculture business by enhancing operating efficiency, lowering costs, and raising yields. The study aims to give an overview of the different use of IoT in essential components like environmental monitoring, fish health monitoring, and water quality management, all of these help in enhancing the aquaculture industry.

**Corresponding author*: 2181158@ksom.ac.in

Subhasis Dash, Manas Ranjan Lenka, S. Balamurugan, Ambika Prasad Tripathy and Amarendra Mohanty (eds.) Sustainable Resource Management in Next-Generation Computational Constrained Networks, (59–86) © 2025 Scrivener Publishing LLC

***Keywords*:** Aquaculture, environmental monitoring, farm management, water management, fish health monitoring

3.1 Introduction

Aquaculture is the economic, cultural, and scientific reproduction and husbandry of aquatic plants, creatures, and other species. It is also known as fish farming, fish culture, or mariculture. Aquaculture is a type of aquatic agriculture in which some marine and freshwater creatures are raised to augment the natural supply. Other aquaculture operations, food and industrial products, stock management in the sport fisheries sector, supplying underwater bait animals, stocking fee-fishing operations, offering aquatic organisms for aesthetic purposes, and supplying fuel sources to the pharmaceutical and chemical industries are all covered. These activities can take place everywhere in the globe. Aquaculture has existed for at least 500 years. Yet, it has only been commercially significant since the mid-20th century. Aquaculture's rapid growth has been driven mostly by the production of a surprising number of species that are commonly consumed fresh. Shrimp, crayfish, prawns, trout, salmon, and oysters are among the examples. Nevertheless, the output of catfish, carp, and tilapia generated in vast low-energy systems is also expanding. Catfish farming in the United States, for example, has more than quintupled its output since it began to expand in the 1960s. Several of these freshwater fish are also employed in aquaponics, which is a hybrid arrangement that combines aquaculture with hydroponic plant production; fish waste is used to feed the crops [1, 2]. As demand for seafood has expanded, technology has enabled food to be produced in both shallow coastal and open ocean ecosystems. Aquaculture is a technique for producing food and other economic demands while also restoring habitat, replenishing natural resources, and rebuilding vulnerable and endangered wild populations. There are two forms of aquaculture: marine and freshwater [3]. Aquaculture is the organization of activities, knowledge, and procedures for the cultivation of underwater plants and a few aquatic animal species. This initiative is essential to growing the economy and food security. The World Wildlife Fund (WWF) estimates that 85% of the world's marine stocks are either completely exploited or overfished. Our planet's population is predicted to increase by more than 2 billion people by 2050, resulting in a significantly increased need for food, particularly seafood. Because capture fisheries have little space to improve yields, aquaculture must meet the long-term supply and demand imbalance while also doing all necessary to reduce pressure on marine stocks. There are several reasons to be positive about aquaculture's growing significance in the world food supply. In accordance with the Food and Agricultural Organization (FAO), the State of World Fisheries and Aquaculture reports any future increase in fish productivity and consumption will primarily come from aquaculture. As a result, the business is rising to the occasion: from 2005 to 2014, farmed seafood output increased at a robust 5.8% annual rate, which was more than four times the annual global population growth rate between 2010 and 2014 [4, 5]. Aquaculture is a thriving business that has witnessed fast growth over the years as an alternate location for seafood production to meet global food demand and counteract overfishing. Several indicators, including air temperatures, production elements such as water bodies, and biological features, must be checked on a regular basis in order to reduce output losses and improve efficiency. IoT is a fascinating new idea that has the potential to turn almost everything into a "smart" device. It is a physical device network that may be linked to any service or network. The Internet of Things (IoT) is a collection of software and hardware technologies, as well as communications technologies, that are used to gather, extract, and analyze data. It allows for remote operation or monitoring of any device from anywhere on the planet over the current network. The IoT has transformed the aquaculture business by enabling real-time remote management with minimum human intervention. IoT aquaculture solutions often employ a local server to store massive amounts of data gathered in an Excel file or a website. Therefore, the internet infrastructure bears a heavy burden. Cloud computing complements IoT by offering a virtual hard drive space as well as a way to store and retrieve enormous amounts of data and applications. It not only enhances operational efficiency and flexibility, but it also allows for improved collaboration among programmers in different places [6]. India is the world's largest seventh-largest country by land area and the second-most populated. In the aquaculture industry. India ranks first in agricultural output but third in agricultural output. Aquaculture accounts for around 1.07% of the country's gross domestic product (GDP). India is anticipated to devour 16 million tons of fish by 2025. IoT describes a network of physical objects that include sensors, software, and other technologies that allow them to communicate with one another over the internet. Temperature, pH, oxygen, and other water characteristics may be checked using devices that can be controlled. IoT technology has transformed fish farming procedures in several ways, including getting real-time data on water quality and aqua life. Data acquired by devices is stored in a data center or database so that users may access them via a phone or computer [7, 8]. There are several instances of how IoT may assist aquaculturists in improving their working

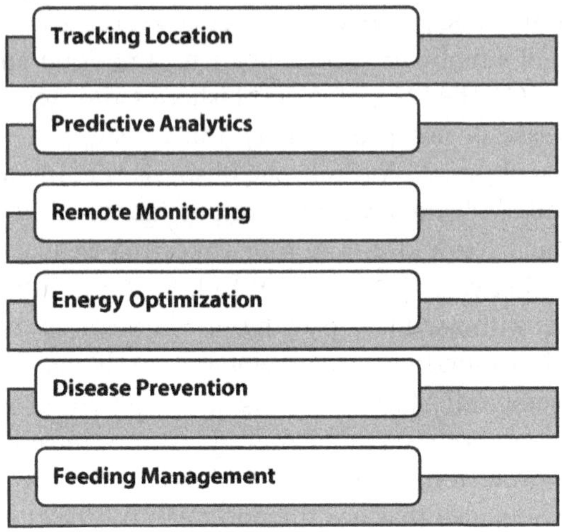

Figure 3.1 Different benefits of IoT in aquaculture. Source: Author's framework.

circumstances. In fact, some fish farms are positioned far from the land, and using IoT to monitor various water sources might assist them to save money. Because water quality changes can occur quickly and at anytime, monitoring the water in real-time with alerts can help guarantee that no specific incident is overlooked. There are other benefits of IoT in aquaculture as described below as shown in Figure 3.1 [9].

- Tracking Location: Aquaculture equipment including as nets, buoys, and cages may be tracked using IoT devices. This can aid in the prevention of equipment loss owing to high currents or other environmental characteristics.
- Predictive Analytics: IoT devices collect data on a variety of characteristics, including water quality, feeding rates, and rates of growth. Machine learning algorithms may be used to examine this data in order to forecast future trends and enhance the entire process.
- Remote Monitoring: Aquaculturists may monitor and operate their activities from any place with an internet connection because IoT devices can be accessed remotely. This can assist to lessen the necessity for physical presence while also improving overall operating efficiency.
- Energy Optimization: IoT devices are used to track energy usage and improve the operation of energy-intensive

equipment like pumps and aerators. This can assist to lower total energy expenses and increase the operation's resilience.

- Disease Prevention: IoT devices may be used to monitor aquatic species' health and identify illness symptoms. This can aid in the prevention of disease outbreaks and the reduction of the use of medications and other toxins.
- Feeding Management: IoT devices may be used to feed aquatic species automatically depending on their weight and eating patterns. This can assist to optimize feeding and decrease feed waste.

Aquaculture is critical to India's economic development and food supply, and the IoT is a new innovation that will connect individuals digitally. Water pretreatment before stocking is one area where aqua farmers in India fall short, and the use of high-quality prebiotics and probiotics in pond water aids in the establishment of beneficial bacteria. The agricultural system may be controlled remotely by employing various sensors for water parameters, saving time, money, and danger [10]. With aquaculture on the rise, IoT might be the market's future. Fish farming has been practiced for millennia but only lately has the sector reached such a large scale. Because overfishing and climate change threaten wild fish populations, aquaculture is increasingly being portrayed as a low-carbon, nutritious protein supply. But, as the world's population expands, the seafood sector has the tremendous burden of fulfilling rising demand. It is turning to the IoT to give increased yields in an economically and socially sustainable manner. IoT-enabled devices may offer a comprehensive traceability history of the fish, through hatching to harvest, including their genetic heritage, nutritional history, and health condition. Farmers may use this to assure the quality and safety of their goods while also meeting regulatory standards. Several common aquaculture chores, including water exchange, cleaning, and grading, may be automated using IoT, eliminating the need for manual labor and increasing farm efficiency and output [11].

3.2 Environmental Monitoring via IoT for Sustainable Aquaculture

The process of constantly measuring and analyzing various physical, chemical, and physiological parameters of the water habitats, such as water quality, silt character traits, and weather, is called environmental monitoring in aquaculture. Aquaculture operations depend heavily on a stable and environmentally friendly environment to ensure that the aquatic species being cultivated grow and survive. Any changes in the environment have the potential to impact aquaculture farm production and profitability. As a result, monitoring and maintaining the aquatic environment's quality is critical for a successful aquaculture industry. Aquaculture operations depend heavily on a stable and environmentally friendly environment to ensure that the aquatic species being cultured grow and survive. Any modifications to the environment have the potential to impact aquaculture farm production and profitability. As a result, monitoring and maintaining the aquatic environment's quality is critical for a successful aquaculture industry. Due to the use of novel communication and information technologies, highly intelligent video surveillance technology has been acquired in agricultural systems in recent years. ZigBee has implied the incorporation of communications networks to sensors, allowing them to track environmental parameters in real-time [12, 13]. The ecological cost of aquaculture production is a critical issue for the industry's future development. It is critical that the environmental impacts of marine aquaculture be managed in a way that is acceptable to the general public. To manage the environmental effects of marine aquaculture, a suitable environmental monitoring regime and corrective actions are essential. [14]. Among the Sustainable Development Goals (SDGs) are water resource protection and pollution prevention for water used by humans, sanitary uses, agricultural usage, industrial uses, or other reasons. The condition of the water is essential to accomplishing Agenda 2030's goals for sustainable development. Preserving excellent water quality is essential to the wellness and growth of cultivated aquatic species. Any environmental alterations can create discomfort, disease, and death rates in fish and shellfish, resulting in financial losses for the grower. As an outcome, continual monitoring of water quality factors such as the level of oxygen in the water, pH, temperature, salinity, and nutrients is required to ensure optimal conditions for aquatic species' growth and survival [15]. Environmental monitoring is critical to the long-term viability of aquaculture operations. Overuse of resources like water and feed can result in pollution of the environment. Farmers can make educated choices about the amount of feed and water required for successful growth and minimize the environmental impact of what they do by monitoring environmental parameters [16]. Environmental monitoring is critical to the long-term viability of aquaculture operations. Overuse of resources like water and feed can result in pollution of the environment. Farmers can make educated choices about the quantity of feed and water required for successful growth and minimize the environmental impact of what they do by monitoring environmental parameters. Farmers can benefit from environmental monitoring by identifying potential hazards to the environment and preventing or mitigating environmental disasters. Monitoring weather and water levels, for example, can alert farmers to prospective floods or droughts, so they can take the necessary steps to safeguard their fish [17]. Oysters are bivalve mollusks with hard calcified shells that filter feed. These organisms can survive in the inter-tidal and many river systems' intertidal zones, attempting to feed on phytoplankton currents in the upper surrounding water where the sun's rays are accessible for photosynthesis. Oysters are farmed all over the world, primarily for human usage, and account for a significant component of the global aquaculture industry. The aquaculture industry in Australia is growing and is expected to be worth $1.5 billion by 2021. Increasing consumer incomes and growing knowledge of the benefits of held-to-account aquaculture practices are driving this growth. Oyster farming is a significant aspect of Australia's aquaculture business, notably in New South Wales (NSW) [18]. Coupled with the fast expansion of the domestic aquaculture business, the area of aquaculture has grown year by year, becoming one of China's important industries for agricultural economic growth. Yet, in terms of monitoring aquaculture water quality and security, the majority of farmers continue to use conventional farming methods that depend too much on experience and are incapable of making scientific judgments about water quality and environmental changes. The EM500-UDL ultrasonic level sensor uses LoRaWAN technology. The pond water level data may be sent immediately to the gateway through LoRaWAN. The low-power aquacul ture monitoring and control system is based on LoRa, which implies that it can reach up to 10 to 20 km in a rural setting with an outside gateway, while it can go beyond 2 km to 3 km in urban areas [19]. Because they are frequently utilized for agricultural applications, remote sensor networks (WSN) provide clear precedence. IoT has successfully proven a wide range of applications in recent years. However, few fish farms today have modern equipment capable of real-time and networked water monitoring. IoT can help aquaculturists improve their working circumstances in a variety of ways. Some fish farms, for example, are located far from the land, and using IoT to screen wastewater from a remote might assist them to save money. Another school of thought says that, just because modifications to the quality of water can occur at any time and in any location, meticulous water monitoring cannot miss a specific event. The following are some of the advantages of IoT in environmental monitoring [20].

- Improved accessibility: IoT devices allow farmers to receive real-time data on environmental factors from anywhere, helping them to stay informed and make educated decisions about the aquaculture systems regardless of whether they are present physically on the farm.
- Data collection accuracy: IoT sensors capture precise data on a variety of environmental conditions, guaranteeing that the data obtained is dependable and consistent. Environmental characteristics such as temperature and IoT sensors can track pH, dissolved oxygen concentration, and water level. These data may be studied to get insights into the operation of the aquaculture system and to identify possible problems before they become serious. Reliable data collecting also allows farmers to optimize their aquaculture systems for greater efficiency and yield. Farmers can improve feed management, water quality, and stocking density by monitoring environmental conditions in real time and collecting precise data, resulting in greater fish growth rates and increased profitability.
- Automatic warnings: When environmental conditions depart from established criteria, IoT devices may be configured to transmit automated alerts, allowing farmers to respond swiftly to possible concerns.
- Enhanced decision-making: IoT devices provide farmers with a greater knowledge of their aquaculture systems, which allows them to make more educated decisions regarding stocking density, feeding management, and water quality.
- Improved efficiency: By monitoring the environmental data in real time, farmers may optimize their aquaculture operations for improved productivity, cost reduction, and profit maximization.
- Reduced environmental effect: IoT devices assist farmers in reducing the environmental impacts of their aquaculture systems by maintaining optimal water quality.
- Improved productivity: IoT devices can help farmers enhance their production and yield by improving climatic conditions for fish growth. Farmers may use IoT sensors to immediately identify environmental conditions that could impair fish health, such as low dissolved oxygen levels or excessive ammonia concentrations. Farmers may lower death rates and guarantee that more fish reach market

size by taking timely corrective action, resulting in higher output.

The IoT innovation has been utilized to manage the business performance of the system, including massive environmental monitoring, navigation system, over-limit alarm, surveillance cameras, and other newly planted functional areas, which significantly decreased worker intensity, reduced administrative expenditures, and increased production efficiency [21]. In a regulated environment, the harmonic interaction of fish, plants, and microscopic life is dependent on ideal conditions for water quality. This necessitates the implementation of regular water quality monitoring processes that rely on stringent data protection, distribution, and management. Internet of Things (IoT) technology is used to screen and regulate parameters related to water quality using sensors that provide remote, durable, and data analysis procedures that provide water quality indicators via a graphical user interface [22].

3.3 The Primacy of IoT in Enhancing Fish Health Monitoring

Fish health monitoring in aquaculture is the method of evaluating the health and well-being of fish in a farmed setting on a regular basis. It consists of a sequence of actions aimed at avoiding, diagnosing, and treating illnesses and other health issues in farmed fishery resources. The technique of periodically monitoring the health condition of fish in aquaculture or natural habitats is known as fish health monitoring. This entails gathering and evaluating the information on a variety of criteria such as fish behavior, growth rates, eating preferences, and illness prevalence. The fish monitoring system is critical for ensuring the health and well-being of fish populations. Fish farmers or fishery managers can discover and resolve health concerns early by frequently monitoring the fish, limiting illness spread, and lowering fatality rates. It can also aid in the detection of changes in water quality or environmental factors that may have an impact on the health of fish populations. Fish have emerged as major study models in the 21st century, owing to the introduction of advanced scientific surveillance and genetic manipulation tools, as well as a heightened awareness of environmental issues and toxins [23]. Fish health surveillance is essential in aquaculture to ensure the health of the fish and the company's long-term profitability. Frequent fish health monitoring can assist farmers in detecting early symptoms of sickness or stress and taking corrective action before it is a big issue. IoT is a fast-expanding technology with boundless potential as data streams have grown over time. As organizations globally adapt to cloud-based work procedures, which have been heavily helped by the COVID-19 pandemonium, future markets will transfer from conventional information processing techniques to Big Data Analytics and Cloud technology. Farmers may obtain precise and reliable data on aspects such as fish behavior, eating habits, growth rates, and water quality by employing IoT sensors to monitor fish health. This information may be studied to learn more about the general health of the species and the aquaculture business. One of the key advantages of fish health monitoring in aquaculture is the early diagnosis of sickness [24, 25]. In recent years, advances in the realm of the IoT have helped to enhance traditional farming operations. Previous fish farming systems required a significant amount of effort to watch the animals, which raised the expense of production. As the average lifespan of agricultural workers in various regions of the world grows, aquaculture production will confront a staff shortage; to address this issue, considerable modifications must be implemented, and operations must always be automated and controlled remotely. Individuals will have the opportunity to save labor and enhance output by embracing IoT. It will be crucial in the future of tracking and analytics. Organizations may combine a plethora of IoT devices to acquire massive data streams of information. Changes in fish behavior or physical indicators of sickness, like lesions or irregular swimming patterns, can be detected by IoT devices. This early diagnosis allows farmers to take immediate action to avoid disease transmission, such as altering water quality parameters, delivering treatments, or isolating ill fish. Monitoring fish health also contributes to better fish welfare. Farmers may improve feed management, population density, and environmental conditions to ensure optimal development and well-being by assuring that fish is healthy and comfortable. This can boost farmer productivity and profitability while also enhancing the integrity of the aquatic business [26]. On the other hand, climate change and increased resource exploitation have put a strain on the fish supply, particularly in the wild. In comparison to terrestrial animal proteins, fish and fishery products are high in protein, minerals, and essential fatty acids, particularly long-chain polyunsaturated fatty acids, which are important. In accordance with the FAO, more than a billion people worldwide rely on fish as their principal source of animal protein, although consuming just 20.5 kg per capita in 2018. Aquaculture is the reproduction and development of aquatic animals and plants, such as fish and shellfish, for both food and non-food reasons. The vast majority of aquaculture production takes place in regulated or semi-regulated environments. As a result, technical solutions that enable population density management or culture improvement are the only realistic alternative for assuring production efficiency at the moment. Yet, the share of worldwide fish output contributed by aquaculture has grown over time, exceeding 46% in 2016–2018, up from 40.1%, 42.6%, 43.7%, 44.7%, and 45.1% in the prior 5 years [27]. The development of aquafarming with new having to cut technologies such as IoT is very sustainable and compatible with numerous benefits. Researchers can follow the movement and position of aquatic animals, as well as their foraging patterns, using geo-tagging. Conventional sighting surveys have various benefits that the IoT, machine learning, and satellite tagging do not. The first is that tracking species at specified locations is a non-intrusive method that does not degrade the habitat. IoT connects physical items to network infrastructure through sensors deployed in their surroundings. The temperature, pH value, and oxygen rate in the fishpond are measured using a water temperature meter, a water level device, a pH motion sensor, and a dissolved pressure sensor. The integration of Zigbee, Wi-Fi, LoRa, and Sigfox modulation schemes with sensors and protocols is required for remote access. A sensor for vision-based field observations will be placed [28]. Hundreds of millions of people keep depending on aquaculture for food, nutrition, money, and a living. The worldwide fish supply in 2016 reached 171 million tons, The Status of World Fisheries and Aquaculture 2018, with China responsible for 88 percent. Regardless of the available water or the species, all fish require water to survive, consume, grow, and conduct other biological processes. As a corollary, it is not unexpected that a fish farming operation's effectiveness is mostly governed by the quality of its water. Temperature and pH are two critical elements in aquaculture. IoT is a revolutionary new concept that has the possibility of transforming practically everything into a "smart" gadget. It allows objects to be connected at any time, any location, with anything and anybody through any route, network, or application. IoT is a collection of software and hardware innovations that are used to preserve, retrieve, and analyze data as well as transmit. It enables remote control or monitoring of every object from anywhere in the world [29, 30]. As a result of usually stable capture fisheries productivity, resource efficiency, and continued aquaculture expansion, more fish are being caught for direct human consumption. Fisheries are a key SDG 14 that aims to conserve oceans, seas, and coastal habitats while also providing significant biological services to mankind. All fish require water to exist, consume, develop, and perform other biological activities, regardless of the available water or the species. Hence, using IoT as current technology, we can assist fish farmers in solving various types of fish-related problems, such as determining whether water is ideal for fish. They can detect using IoT technologies. Farmers may also learn about fish by visiting this webpage. Aquaculture research is an input to increasing stable output [31]. Bangladesh has one of the best fisheries conditions behind India and China, has the world's largest flooded marshland, and has Asia's third-highest marine diversity. Fishing has had substantial economic implications for the country. Because the quantity of oxygen in each segment of the water is not the same, the IoT-based sensor gadget will be moveable, enabling it to detect the oxygen level or even other variables in water at any location in a pond, river, or lake. This technique will be extremely beneficial to our country's fish farmers, and the country will eventually gain from exporting fish to other countries and earning foreign money, which will aid in the development of the country's economy. Aquaculture producers may take proactive actions to avoid disease transmission and enhance the development and production of their fish by tracking the well-being of farmed fish populations. This can assist to enhance the aquaculture industry's competitive sustainability and profitability while also improving animal welfare or environmental responsibility [32]. Fish health monitoring using IoT entails collecting real-time data on fish activity, water quality, and other environmental elements that might affect their health. The data is sent to a virtualized platform for processing, where algorithms and machine learning models may be utilized to spot trends and abnormalities in fish behavior or water quality. This data may then be used to alert fish farmers or aquaculture operators to any health concerns or environmental dangers that may affect the fish, so they can take proactive steps to address these issues. IoT-enabled fish health monitoring can assist enhance the effectiveness and long-term sustainability of aquaculture systems while also enhancing fish health and lowering the danger of disease outbreaks [33].

3.4 Delving Into IoT: Improving Agricultural Water Quality Management

Water is a one-of-a-kind resource that is crucial to the biosphere's sustainability. Water, as a habitat, not only sustains human life and activities but also contributes to the preservation of the environmental structure, ecosystem networks, and geographical ecosystems. Water quality control in aquaculture refers to the process of maintaining ideal water quality conditions for aquatic creatures such as fish, shellfish, and aquatic plants' development, health, and preservation. Owing to rising worldwide demand for fish as a food source, almost half of the world's fish supply is now farmed unnaturally rather than taken in natural habitats through catch fisheries. Since the 1970s, aquaculture has been the fastest-expanding sector of the global food economy, with most of it taking place in the Asia-Pacific area [34]. Because farmed fish are especially susceptible to changes in factors such as harmful chemicals, pH, humidity, and gas concentrations, aquaculture water quality management is crucial. Water quality must be examined and maintained on a regular basis in order for the fish to retain optimal health, productivity, and quality. In order for fish to maintain maximum health, production, and quality, water quality must be regularly checked and maintained. Aquaculture systems frequently include the cultivation of vast numbers of aquatic species in tiny, contained habitats like ponds, tanks, or raceways. Water quality factors in such situations can rapidly vary, resulting in stress, illness, and mortality of cultured organisms if not maintained effectively. To maintain optimal conditions for cultured organisms, aquaculture water quality management comprises monitoring and changing many water quality factors such as temperature, chemical oxygen demand (DO), pH, ammonia, nitrate, and nitrite levels. Treatment process, aeration, and fertilizer control are examples of such approaches [9]. Aquaculture is a type of fishing that aims to preserve and increase natural biodiversity by reconstructing untainted water habitats for fish and aquatic creatures. Water quality is a significant issue in fish farming, causing illness and increased mortality. Water management is an essential part of global environmental preservation because climate change is changing the quality of water. The IoT has enabled future real-time monitoring systems in aquaculture systems. The IoT may help aquaculture firms bridge the divide between rural and urban people by conserving time and energy. The evolution of network aquaculture technology, which began with mobile phones, has had a significant impact on the fishery industry by allowing for more precision in the management of farms. Only technology, such as IoT and internet programs like websites, mobile applications, radars, artificial intelligence (AI), machine learning, processing of digital pictures, and geospatial tools, can reach distant locations [35]. IoT technology has the potential to revolutionize aquaculture water management by offering real-time monitoring, and temperature, pH, dissolved oxygen, chloride, and micronutrient intake are among the water quality parameters examined. IoT sensors might be used to continuously monitor a variety of water quality measures in real time, allowing fish farms to notice water quality changes as soon as they occur. This enables immediate action to be done to address any concerns prior to becoming concerned [36]. Water quality is the most important factor impacting fish health and productivity in aquaculture production sites. Good water quality refers to what the fish want, not what people believe the fish want. This implies that we must properly understand the farmed fish's water quality requirements. Fish live in the water and rely entirely on it for existence. Many fish species require a unique set of water quality characteristics in order to survive, develop, and reproduce (temperature, pH, oxygen concentration, salinity, hardness, and so on). Pond water composition varies on a regular basis due to meteorological and cyclical variations, as well as how a pond is used. Water quality is the most important factor impacting fish well-being and efficiency in aquaculture production systems. Good water quality refers to what the fish want, not what people believe the fish want. This implies that we must completely understand the water quality requirements of farmed fish. Fish live in water and rely solely on it for survival. Several fish species require certain water quality parameters to survive, thrive, and reproduce (temperature, pH, oxygen content, salinity, roughness, and so forth are all factors to consider). Pond water content fluctuates on a routine basis due to meteorological and seasonal differences, and how a pond is used [36]. Aquaculture is a major source of human food and an important industry for many countries. Preserving water quality in aquaculture systems, on the other hand, is critical for the survival and growth of aquatic creatures, and it may be difficult and costly. This is when the IoT can be utilized to transform aquaculture water quality management. IoT equipment, like pumps, filters, and aerators, may be utilized to streamline the management of different aquaculture systems. This enables accurate management of water quality parameters while reducing the danger of human mistakes. Here are some of the reasons why IoT is significant in aquaculture water quality management [37, 38]:

- Data analysis: IoT sensor data may be evaluated to find trends, patterns, and abnormalities in water quality. This can give useful information about the general health of the aquaculture system and aid in the optimization of water quality management measures.
- Automation: Using real-time data acquired by sensors, IoT devices can automate numerous water quality management processes like feeding, aeration, and water exchange. This can assist to cut labor expenses and increase the aquaculture process performance.
- Sustainability: Proper water quality assurance in aquaculture is crucial to the industry's long-term viability. The IoT

can assist to lessen the environmental effect of aquaculture by lowering the usage of pesticides and antibiotics, as well as the danger of infectious diseases.

With the fast expansion of the aquaculture business in many nations, air temperature, pH, and chemical DO are becoming more important water quality components. They are not only necessary for aquatic animal existence, but they are also important variables influencing water quality. As a result, prompt monitoring of water quality is critical to aquaculture for optimum output, health, and protection. Aquaculture is the practice of cultivating aquatic creatures including fish, shellfish, and crustaceans in controlled conditions like ponds, tanks, and cages. The water's overall quality in these settings is crucial for these species' survival and growth. As a corollary, water quality monitoring is a vital aspect of aquaculture. Water quality is affected by several factors, including oxygen concentration, pH, temperature, and ammonia levels [39]. These characteristics can change owing to factors, such as diet, waste, and wind patterns, and can have a substantial influence on aquatic animal health and growth. Low amounts of dissolved oxygen, for example, can induce stress and even death in fish, whereas high levels of ammonia can harm gills and other organs. Too high or too low pH levels can also be hazardous to aquatic species. As a result, monitoring and managing these factors is critical for the animals' development and continued existence. Aquaculture water quality management includes a variety of measures such as oxygenation, purification, and water exchanges to ensure ideal conditions for aquatic animals. To combat infections and preserve water quality, chemicals such as bleach and hydrogen peroxide can be used. Proper water quality control in aquaculture is critical not only for the health and development of the animals but also for the industry's long-term viability. Bad water quality can lead to disease outbreaks, pollution, and economic losses [9]. Numerous contemporary remote monitoring and detection system applications enhance water quality and boost fish farm output. One of the applications JSN-SR04T waterproof ultrasonic sensor detects fish and the existence of an entity underneath. This project's main performance management system is Arduino, with an additional HC-05 Bluetooth Shield that permits Arduino to communicate with Android cellphones. Water characteristics that affect fish productivity may be monitored remotely using wireless communication protocols such as cellular, LoRaWAN, Wi-Fi, or satellite connections. One of the initiatives is an automatic IoT solution for autonomous fish farming, in which they monitor the temperature, pH, and level of the water via a Wi-Fi internet connection [40]. Monitoring the quality of water is described as the collection of data at certain locations and intervals in order to provide data that can be used to investigate current conditions, spot trends, and so on. Monitoring of water quality and forecast are required in aquaculture buildings to ensure healthy aquatic creature growth. The most important elements are oxygen saturation, pH, and humidity. The practice of monitoring these will help an aquaculture company to remain sustainable while also achieving industry and regulatory regulations [41].

3.5 Connecting the Dots: Using IoT Fish Behavior Monitoring to Improve Aquaculture Practices

The behaviors, activities, and responses displayed by fish in their natural or confined habitats are referred to as fish behavior. Swimming patterns, eating behavior, social interactions, mating behaviors, predator avoidance, and reactions to environmental cues are all part of it [42]. In recent years, the intelligent fish farm has undergone tremendous development. In addition, emerging information technologies such as IoT, big data, 5G, and edge computing have been used to increase fish welfare and productivity. Behavior analysis is a research hotspot among all the study fields of intelligent fish farms because it includes a lot of information about living conditions and is considered as a direct representation of fish welfare. A migratory drive, for example, may be represented by a clockwise or anticlockwise swimming pattern. Analyzing this swimming condition is a fantastic approach to determine whether or not the breeding environment fits the needs of fish growth; continuous swimming activity is more directly tied to physiological needs such as buoyant storage, muscle tone, fat:protein ratios, or circulatory return. Furthermore, the aberrant swimming condition demonstrates the ability to adjust to environmental changes. Thus, utilizing fish behavior analysis to monitor the health of farmed fish is an important aspect of fish farm management [43, 44]. The importance of the IoT in studying fish behavior is as described below [45]:

- Monitoring fish behavior can reveal information about the fish's health and well-being. Stress, sickness, or inadequate environmental factors can all cause abnormal behavior patterns. Aquaculturists can notice early indicators of health concerns and take required steps to prevent or treat illnesses, optimize feeding practices, and provide a healthy environment for fish well-being by studying fish behavior.

- Fish behavior may be used to predict overall environmental conditions in an aquaculture system. Changes in swimming patterns, for example, may indicate poor water quality, insufficient oxygen levels, or incorrect temperature swings. Aquaculture operators can discover possible problems in water quality, oxygenation, or other environmental aspects by monitoring fish behavior and taking remedial actions to preserve ideal circumstances.
- Fish behavior is critical in feed management tactics. Aquaculture practitioners can optimize feed efficiency, decrease waste, and guarantee sufficient nutrition for the fish by monitoring feeding behavior such as feeding rates, feed acceptance, and feeding preferences. Observing feeding behavior can also assist in identifying any irregularities or changes in appetite that may suggest health difficulties or feed-related disorders.
- Understanding fish behavior aids in predicting stocking density and controlling social interactions in aquaculture systems. Overcrowding can cause stress, hostility, and slowed growth. Aquaculture operators may set ideal stocking levels while avoiding detrimental impacts on fish welfare by taking into account the social behavior of fish species, their hierarchies, and compatibility.
- Fish behavior is important in reproduction and breeding programs. Monitoring mating behaviors, wooing rituals, and nest-building activities can help with population management, optimizing breeding circumstances, and increasing reproductive success rates. Understanding fish behavior at different stages of the reproductive cycle can assist aquaculturists to execute optimal breeding tactics.

The IoT is revolutionizing the monitoring of fish behavior in aquaculture. Aquaculturists may gather and analyze real-time data on fish behavior using IoT-enabled sensors and technology, allowing for a better understanding of their reactions and interactions within the aquaculture system. Underwater cameras, sensors, and acoustic monitoring systems, for example, may collect precise data on fish behavior, such as swimming patterns, schooling behavior, and predator–prey interactions. These gadgets collect high-resolution data in real time, allowing for accurate behavioral analysis and surveillance [46]. To analyze the massive amounts of data acquired from fish behavior monitoring, IoT platforms can use powerful analytics and machine learning algorithms. These approaches aid in the detection of patterns, abnormalities, and correlations in fish behavior, providing significant insights and prediction skills. Aquaculturists may spot possible difficulties, optimize management practices, and enhance overall fish health by analyzing data. Fish behavior monitoring IoT devices may be linked with other environmental sensors such as water quality sensors and ecological monitoring systems. This integration enables a thorough knowledge of how fish behavior responds to environmental changes. Aquaculturists, for example, may establish ideal environmental conditions for fish health by comparing fish behavior with characteristics such as water temperature, dissolved oxygen levels, and light intensity [47, 48]. The fish farming industry needs instruments that can objectively assess fish health and well-being in real time without killing, disturbing, or interfering with everyday operations. The primary goal of using the IoT potential is to contribute to the development of sustainable and resilient aquaculture systems that maintain profitability, safeguard healthy aquatic habitats, and increase capacity for climate change adaption. Enhanced sustainable and physiological sensor data (e.g., behavior, activity, energy, and feeding physiology) collected by a network of linked electronic sensors can offer precise fine-scale measures of the surrounding environment, fish health, well-being, and ecosystem use, average fish size, and biomass, which facilitates predictive modelling of rearing displays and consequences [49, 50]. Changes in fish behavior might be an early warning sign of sickness or health problems. IoT systems are capable of detecting anomalous behaviors or deviations from usual patterns, allowing for early disease diagnoses and proactive interventions such as targeted treatments or confinement procedures to avoid disease transmission inside the aquaculture complex [49]. Aquaculture fish display a variety of social behaviors, including shoaling, dominance hierarchies, and mating rituals. These social interactions may be tracked and analyzed using IoT-enabled software, yielding significant information about fish habits, compatibility, and social stress. This information may be used to improve fish well-being by optimizing stocking levels and controlling social dynamics. Here is a simple illustration of the process of how IoT helps in analyzing fish behavior as shown in Figure 3.2 [51].

- Data Collection: In aquaculture facilities, IoT-enabled equipment such as underwater cameras, sensors, acoustic monitoring systems, and radio frequency identification tags are used to collect data on fish behavior. Swimming patterns, eating activities, social connections, water temperature,

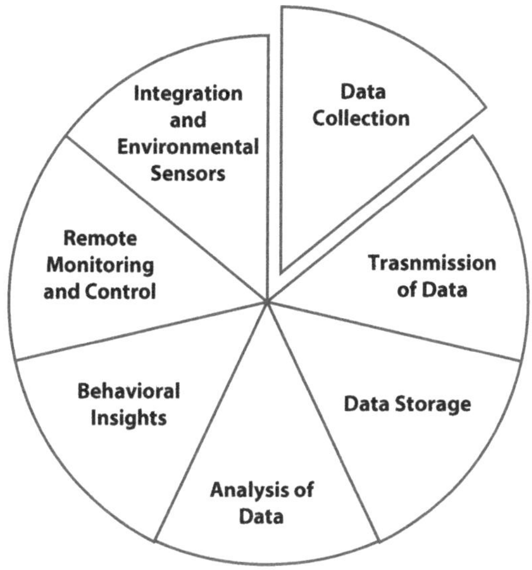

Figure 3.2 The mechanism of the IoT procedure in analyzing fish behavior. Source: Author's framework.

dissolved oxygen levels, and light intensity are all captured by these sensors.

- Transmission of Data: Using protocols for wireless communication such as Wi-Fi, Bluetooth, or cellular networks, the gathered data is transferred in real-time to a central data hub or cloud-based platform. This enables instant data access from any place with an internet connection.
- Data Storage and Management: Data about fish behavior is collected and kept in databases or cloud-based storage systems. These systems enable safe data storage, rapid retrieval, and data organization for subsequent studies.
- Analysis of Data: To analyze fish behavior data, IoT systems, and software employ advanced analytics, machine learning, and AI approaches. To uncover behavioral patterns, correlations, anomalies, and trends in gathered data, statistical algorithms, and pattern recognition approaches are used.
- Behavioral Insights: Data analysis results in significant insights and visual representations such as charts, graphs, and heatmaps. These visualizations aid researchers and aquaculturists in gaining a better knowledge of fish behavior, identifying patterns, and making sound judgments.

- Remote Monitoring and Control: IoT solutions allow for remote monitoring and control of fish behavior. Users can gain real-time data access, receive messages or alerts for aberrant behavior patterns, and remotely modify environmental conditions or management practices to assure fish welfare and production.
- Integration and Environmental Sensors: Monitoring fish behavior via IoT is frequently combined with sensors that monitor the environment such as water quality sensors and environmental monitoring systems. This integration enables the connection of fish behavior with environmental data, revealing how fish behavior responds to shifts in environmental variables.

Monitoring fish behavior via IoT is frequently combined with sensors that monitor the environment such as water quality sensors and environmental monitoring systems. This integration enables the connection of fish behavior with environmental data, revealing how fish behavior responds to shifts in environmental variables. It can be readily scaled and adapted to various aquaculture setups, whether small-scale or large-scale commercial operations. Because IoT devices are modular, they may be placed and integrated in a variety of ways, guaranteeing complete coverage of the aquaculture complex and varied fish species. Researchers can examine seasonal fluctuations, growth patterns, reproductive behaviors, and the long-term influence of environmental changes on fish behavior by collecting data over long periods of time. These studies shed light on species-specific behaviors, migratory patterns, and the impact of environmental conditions on fish behavior. Such information improves scientific understanding of fish behavior and aids in the creation of tailored management measures [52]. The integration of IoT-based fish behavior monitoring with aquaculture management systems improves overall efficiency and automation. Fish behavior data in real-time may be smoothly connected with other management systems such as feeding control systems or environmental control systems. This connection permits automated modifications depending on patterns of fish behavior. If anomalous behavior is observed, for example, the system can change feeding rates, optimize water quality parameters, or trigger warnings requiring user action. This connection simplifies operations, lowers labor-intensive chores, and guarantees that changes in fish behavior are responded to in a timely manner [53]. Fish behavior monitoring solutions based on IoT enables industrial collaboration and data exchange. Aquaculture operations may exchange anonymized and aggregated behavior data, helping to advance industry insights and best practices. Collaboration and data sharing enable benchmarking, information exchange, and the creation of standardized techniques for monitoring and managing fish behavior. The aquaculture business benefits from this collaborative approach to continual development, innovation, and sustainability [54].

3.6 The Worldwide Deployment of IoT in Aquaculture: Advantages and Success Factors

Various countries across the world have begun to use IoT in aquaculture for a variety of reasons. These are some instances mentioned below of nations throughout the world that are utilizing IoT in aquaculture and the privileges they have realized as shown in Figure 3.3

- Norway: Norway is a world leader in aquaculture and has been utilizing IoT to enhance fish farming. Water temperature, oxygen levels, and fish activity are among the characteristics monitored by IoT sensors. As a consequence, fish farmers have been able to improve feeding and eliminate waste, resulting in increased productivity and cheaper expenses. Moreover, IoT has aided in the early diagnosis of illnesses and parasites, allowing for prompt treatment and epidemic avoidance.

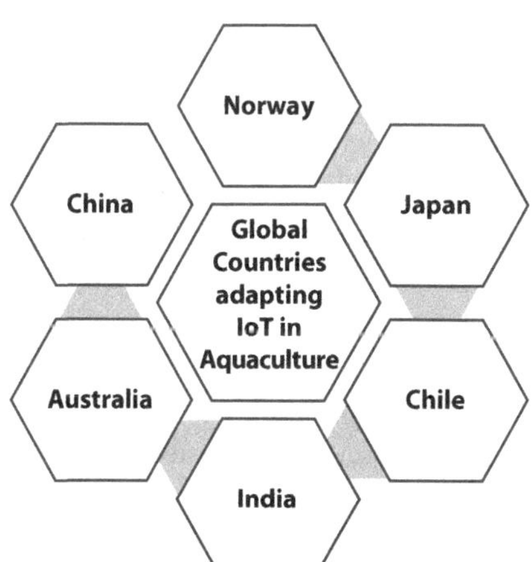

Figure 3.3 Global nations adopting IoT in aquaculture. Source: Author's framework.

- Japan: Another nation that has been in the leading of using IoT in aquaculture is Japan. IoT sensors are used to detect fish movements and eating habits, as well as to monitor water quality indicators such as pH, temperature, and salinity. This has allowed fish farmers to optimize feeding, use less water, and increase fish growth rates. Moreover, IoT has aided in the early diagnosis of illnesses and parasites, allowing for prompt treatment and epidemic avoidance.
- Chile: Chile, one of the world's major salmon producers, has started adopting IoT to improve fish farming operations of sensors detect fish activities and feeding patterns, as well as monitor water quality metrics such as oxygen content and temperature. Fish farmers have been able to optimize feeding, minimize waste, and increase fish growth rates as a result of this. Moreover, IoT has aided in the early diagnosis of illnesses and parasites, allowing for prompt treatment and epidemic avoidance.
- India: Shrimp farming is an important industry in India, and IoT has been used to enhance shrimp farming techniques. IoT sensors are used to track shrimp movements and feeding habits, as well as to monitor water quality indicators such as pH, temperature, and dissolved oxygen. Shrimp farmers have been able to optimize feeding, decrease waste, and increase shrimp growth rates as a result of this. Moreover, IoT has aided in the early diagnosis of illnesses and parasites, allowing for prompt treatment and epidemic avoidance.
- Australia: Australia has been utilizing IoT to enhance the environmental sustainability of its aquaculture business. IoT detectors detect fish movements and eating patterns while simultaneously monitoring water quality indicators such as dissolved oxygen, pH, and humidity. Fish farmers have been able to optimize feeding, minimize waste, and increase fish growth rates as a result of this. Moreover, IoT has aided in the early diagnosis of illnesses and parasites, allowing for prompt treatment and epidemic avoidance. In Australia, the use of IoT in aquaculture has also helped to improve the industry's environmental effects by reducing the usage of antibiotics and other chemicals.

- China: China, the biggest exporter of aquaculture goods, has been experimenting with IoT to improve fish and shrimp farming techniques. IoT sensors are used to detect fish and shrimp movements and eating habits, as well as to monitor oxygen concentration, pH, and temperatures are examples of water quality parameters. Farmers have been able to optimize feeding, decrease waste, and increase animal health as a result of this. Moreover, IoT has aided in the early diagnosis of illnesses and parasites, allowing for prompt treatment and epidemic avoidance.

3.7 Conclusion

The application of IoT technology in aquaculture is a game changer for fish breeders worldwide. Fish producers can better handle and track fish health, quality of water, and environmental sustainability by adding smart sensors, big data, and other IoT capabilities. The use of IoT technologies has resulted in several gains for countries throughout the world, including higher productivity, lower prices, and an enhanced resource economy. Real-time data collection and analysis will enable fish farmers to make better-informed decisions and optimize their operations. The aquaculture industry is poised to be more ecological, efficient, and lucrative with the aid of IoT. The application of IoT in aquaculture is an intriguing discovery that has the potential to change the sector. We should expect a more sustainable, efficient, and successful aquaculture business as more fish farmers across the world use IoT technology.

Acknowledgment

I would like to render my heartfelt gratitude to all my co-authors Ms. Atmika Patnaik, Dr. Ipseeta Satpathy, Dr. Veena Goswami, and Dr. B.C.M. Patnaik for their valuable contribution to their study.

References

1. Baganz, G.F., Junge, R., Portella, M.C., Goddek, S., Keesman, K.J., Baganz, D., Kloas, W., The aquaponic principle—It is all about coupling. *Rev. Aquacult.*, 14, 1, 252–264, 2022.

2. Amundson, C.H. and Petruzzello, M., Aquaculture, in: *Encyclopædia Britannica*, 2022, February 1, Retrieved February 1, 2022, from https://www.britannica.com/topic/aquaculture.
3. US Department of Commerce, N. O. and A. A., What is aquaculture? NOAA's National Ocean Service, 2019, April 2. Retrieved April 2, 2019, from https://oceanservice.noaa.gov/facts/aquaculture.html.
4. Ytrestøyl, T., Takle, H., Kolarevic, J., Calabrese, S., Timmerhaus, G., Rosseland, B.O., Terjesen, B.F., , Performance and welfare of Atlantic salmon L. post-smolts in recirculating aquaculture systems: Importance of salinity and water velocity. *J. World Aquacult. Soc.*, 51, 2, 373–392, 2020.
5. Dawood, M.A., Nutritional immunity of fish intestines: Important insights for sustainable aquaculture. *Rev. Aquacult.*, 13, 1, 642–663, 2021.
6. Gupta, S., Gupta, A., Hasija, Y., Transforming IoT in aquaculture: a cloud solution, in: *AI, Edge and IoT-based Smart Agriculture*, pp. 517–531, Academic Press, Cambridge, MA, USA 2022.
7. Using IoT (Internet of Things) in measuring water quality parameters in fish farming. *Home*, 2021, May 1. Retrieved May 1, 2021, from https://www.fao.org/teca/en/technologies/10102#:~:text=IoT%20technologies%20have%20revolutionized%20fish,using%20a%20phone%20or%20computer.
8. Javvaji, K.S.S. and Hussain, M.A., Prototype of aquaculture using iot technologies, in: *2020 11th International Conference on Computing, Communication and Networking Technologies (ICCCNT)*, pp. 1–4, IEEE, 2020, July.
9. Dupont, C., Cousin, P., Dupont, S., IoT for aquaculture 4.0 smart and easy-to-deploy real-time water monitoring with IoT, in: *2018 global internet of things summit (GIoTS)*, pp. 1–5, IEEE, 2018, June.
10. Rosaline, N. and Sathyalakshimi, S., IoT based aquaculture monitoring and control system, in: *Journal of Physics: Conference Series*, vol. 1362, pp. 012071, IOP Publishing, 2019, November.
11. Wang, C., Li, Z., Wang, T., Xu, X., Zhang, X., Li, D., Intelligent fish farm-the future of aquaculture. *Aquac. Int.*, 29, 6, 2681–2711, 2021. https://doi.org/10.1007/s10499-021-00773-8.
12. Zhang, S., Guo, Y., Li, S., Ke, Z., Zhao, H., Yang, J., Zhang, Z., Investigation on environment monitoring system for a combination of hydroponics and aquaculture in greenhouse. *Inf. Process. Agric.*, 9, 1, 123–134, 2022.
13. Hsiao, S.J. and Sung, W.T., Building a fish–vegetable coexistence system based on a wireless sensor network. *IEEE Access*, 8, 192119–192131, 2020.
14. Zhao, Y., Ma, Z., Han, H., Chen, G., Study on Fish and Vegetable Co-existing System Based on Wireless Sensor Network, in: *2016 6th International Conference on Mechatronics, Computer and Education Informationization (MCEI 2016)*, pp. 572–575, Atlantis Press, 2016, December.
15. Alexakis, D.E., Linking DPSIR model and water quality indices to achieve sustainable development goals in groundwater resources. *Hydrology*, 8, 2, 90, 2021.

16. Weitzman, J. and Filgueira, R., The evolution and application of carrying capacity in aquaculture: towards a research agenda. *Rev. Aquacult.*, 12, 3, 1297–1322, 2020.
17. Azadi, H., Barati, A.A., Nazari Nooghabi, S., Scheffran, J., Climate-related disasters and agricultural land conversion: towards prevention policies. *Clim. Dev.*, 14, 9, 814–828, 2022.
18. Bates, H., Pierce, M., Benter, A., Real-time environmental monitoring for aquaculture using a LoRaWAN-based IoT sensor network. *Sensors*, 21, 23, 7963, 2021.
19. Aquaculture: Water quality and security: Iot solution. *Milesight IoT-IoT Solution Provider*, 2022, October 8. Retrieved October 8, 2022, from https://www.milesight-iot.com/blog/iot-aquaculture-solution/.
20. Balakrishnan, S., Rani, S.S., Ramya, K.C., Design and development of IoT based smart aquaculture system in a cloud environment. *Int. J. Oceans Oceanogr.*, 13, 1, 121–127, 2019.
21. Bergland, H., Burlakov, E., Pedersen, P.A., Wyller, J., Aquaculture, pollution and fishery-dynamics of marine industrial interactions. *Ecol. Complexity*, 43, 100853, 2020.
22. Preetham, K., Mallikarjun, B. C., Umesha, K., Mahesh, F. M., Neethan, S., Aquaculture monitoring and control system: An IoT based approach. *Int. J. Adv. Res.*, 5, 2, 2019.
23. Mocho, J.P. and von Krogh, K., A FELASA Working Group Survey on Fish Species Used for Research, Methods of Euthanasia, Health Monitoring, and Biosecurity in Europe, North America, and Oceania. *Biology*, 11, 9, 1259, 2022.
24. Kodali, R.K. and Sabu, A.C., Aqua monitoring system using aws, in: *2022 International Conference on Computer Communication and Informatics (ICCCI)*, pp. 1–5, IEEE, 2022, January.
25. Alselek, M., Alcaraz-Calero, J.M., Segura-Garcia, J., Wang, Q., Water IoT Monitoring System for Aquaponics Health and Fishery Applications. *Sensors*, 22, 19, 7679, 2022.
26. Anani, O.A., Adetunji, C.O., Olugbemi, O.T., Hefft, D., II, Wilson, N., Olayinka, A.S., IoT-based monitoring system for freshwater fish farming: Analysis and design, in: *AI, Edge and IoT-based Smart Agriculture*, pp. 505–515, Academic Press, 2022.
27. Mustapha, U.F., Alhassan, A.W., Jiang, D.N., Li, G.L., Sustainable aquaculture development: a review on the roles of cloud computing, internet of things and artificial intelligence (CIA). *Rev. Aquacult.*, 13, 4, 2076–2091, 2021.
28. Kimothi, S., Thapliyal, A., Singh, R., Rashid, M., Gehlot, A., Akram, S.V., Javed, A.R., Comprehensive Database Creation for Potential Fish Zones Using IoT and ML with Assimilation of Geospatial Techniques. *Sustainability*, 15, 2, 1062, 2023.
29. Ya'acob, N., Dzulkefli, N.N.S.N., Yusof, A.L., Kassim, M., Naim, N.F., Aris, S.S.M., Water Quality Monitoring System for Fisheries using Internet of

Things (IoT), in: *IOP Conference Series: Materials Science and Engineering*, vol. 1176, pp. 012016, IOP Publishing, 2021, August.

30. Manoj, M., Dhilip Kumar, V., Arif, M., Bulai, E.R., Bulai, P., Geman, O., State of the art techniques for water quality monitoring systems for fish ponds using iot and underwater sensors: A review. *Sensors*, 22, 6, 2088, 2022.
31. Islam, M.M., Kashem, M.A., Jui, F., Aqua fishing monitoring system using IoT devices. *Int. J. Innov. Sci. Eng. Technol.*, 6, 11, 109–114, 2019.
32. Khan, M.M., An IoT Based Smart Water Monitoring System for Fish Firming in Bangladesh, 2020.
33. Abinaya, T., Ishwarya, J., Maheswari, M., A novel methodology for monitoring and controlling of water quality in aquaculture using Internet of Things (IoT), in: *2019 International Conference on Computer Communication and Informatics (ICCCI)*, pp. 1–4, IEEE, 2019, January.
34. Saha, S., Rajib, R.H., Kabir, S., IoT based automated fish farm aquaculture monitoring system, in: *2018 International Conference on Innovations in Science, Engineering and Technology (ICISET)*, pp. 201–206, IEEE, 2018, October.
35. Prapti, D.R., Mohamed Shariff, A.R., Che Man, H., Ramli, N.M., Perumal, T., Shariff, M., Internet of Things (IoT)-based aquaculture: An overview of IoT application on water quality monitoring. *Rev. Aquacult.*, 14, 2, 979–992, 2022.
36. Encinas, C., Ruiz, E., Cortez, J., Espinoza, A., Design and implementation of a distributed IoT system for the monitoring of water quality in aquaculture, in: *2017 Wireless telecommunications symposium (WTS)*, pp. 1–7, IEEE, 2017, April.
37. Rajurkar, C., Prabaharan, S.R.S., Muthulakshmi, S., IoT based water management, in: *2017 International Conference on Nextgen Electronic Technologies: Silicon to Software (ICNETS2)*, pp. 255–259, IEEE, 2017, March.
38. Haq, K.R.A. and Harigovindan, V.P., Water quality prediction for smart aquaculture using hybrid deep learning models. *IEEE Access*, 10, 60078–60098, 2022.
39. Huan, J., Li, H., Wu, F., Cao, W., Design of water quality monitoring system for aquaculture ponds based on NB-IoT. *Aquacult. Eng.*, 90, 102088, 2020.
40. FAO, E., Meeting the sustainable development goals, in: *The State of World Fisheries and Aquaculture 2018*, 2018.
41. Blancaflor, E. and Baccay, M., Design of a solar powered IoT (internet of things) remote water quality management system for a biofloc aquaculture technology, in: *Proceedings of the 2021 3rd Blockchain and Internet of Things Conference*, pp. 24–31, 2021, July.
42. Browning, H., Improving welfare assessment in aquaculture. *Front. Vet. Sci.*, 10, 2023. (N.d.-b). Fao.org. Retrieved October 29, 2024, from https://openknowledge.fao.org/server/api/core/bitstreams/6fb91ab9-6cb2-4d43-8a34-a680f65e82bd/content.

43. Huang, J., Yu, X., Chen, X., An, D., Zhou, Y., Wei, Y., Recognizing fish behavior in aquaculture with graph convolutional network. *Aquacult. Eng.*, 98, 102246, 2022.
44. Zhou, C., Xu, D., Chen, L., Zhang, S., Sun, C., Yang, X., Wang, Y., Evaluation of fish feeding intensity in aquaculture using a convolutional neural network and machine vision. *Aquaculture*, 507, 457–465, 2019.
45. Vijayabaskar, V., Development of IoT Based Fish Monitoring System for Aquaculture.
46. O'Donncha, F., Stockwell, C.L., Planellas, S.R., Micallef, G., Palmes, P., Webb, C., Grant, J., Data driven insight into fish behaviour and their use for precision aquaculture. *Front. Anim. Sci.*, 2, 695054, 2021.
47. Li, D., Wang, G., Du, L., Zheng, Y., Wang, Z., Recent advances in intelligent recognition methods for fish stress behavior. *Aquacult. Eng.*, 96, 102222, 2022.
48. O'Donncha, F., Stockwell, C. L., Planellas, S. R., Micallef, G., Palmes, P., Webb, C., Filgueira, R., Grant, J., Data driven insight into fish behaviour and their use for Precision Aquaculture. *Front. Anim. Sci.*, 2, 2021, https://doi.org/10.3389/fanim.2021.69505.
49. Sivanathan, A., IoT behavioral monitoring via network traffic analysis, 2020, arXiv preprint arXiv:2001.10632.
50. Samha, A.K., Alshelaly, E.E., Alswaigh, N.Y., Alshammri, G.H., Applied Internet of Things in Saudi Arabia Aquaculture System, in: *2021 10th IEEE International Conference on Communication Systems and Network Technologies (CSNT)*, pp. 442–447, IEEE, 2021, June.
51. Prabhakar, P.K., Vatsa, S., Srivastav, P.P., Pathak, S.S., A comprehensive review on freshness of fish and assessment: Analytical methods and recent innovations. *Food Res. Int.*, 133, 109157, 2020.
52. Bailey, L.A., Childs, A.R., James, N.C., Winkler, A., Potts, W.M., Links between behaviour and metabolic physiology in fishes in the Anthropocene. *Rev. Fish Biol. Fish.*, 32, 2, 555–579, 2022.
53. Maesano, G., Di Vita, G., Chinnici, G., Pappalardo, G., D'Amico, M., The role of credence attributes in consumer choices of sustainable fish products: A review. *Sustainability*, 12, 23, 10008, 2020.
54. Giacomarra, M., Crescimanno, M., Vrontis, D., Pastor, L.M., Galati, A., The ability of fish ecolabels to promote a change in the sustainability awareness. *Mar. Policy*, 123, 104292, 2021.

4

Energy Consumption Optimization in Wireless Sensor Networks

Avik Das, Shatyaki Ghosh and Arindam Basak*

School of Electronics Engineering, KIIT-Deemed to be University, Bhubaneswar, Odisha, India

Abstract

Wireless Sensor Networks (WSNs) have become ubiquitous in recent years, with a decade of growth across diverse sectors such as healthcare, medicine, environment, industry, and home automation. A WSN comprises a network of sensor nodes monitoring a specific area for events. Powering these nodes is critical for WSN efficiency. Prolonging WSN lifespan hinges on optimal energy management. Given the limited battery capacity of sensor nodes, energy optimization is imperative. This article explores various techniques to maximize power efficiecny within constrained power budgets. We delve into the critical role of energy efficiency in WSN applications and review existing energy optimization strategies.

Keywords: Wireless sensor network, energy optimization, energy consumption, sensor node

4.1 Introduction

The phrase "wireless sensor network" (WSN) refers to a variety of deployment methods and configurations. Nodes make up a typical sensor network. Nodes are a lot of widely dispersed, inexpensive, and low-power devices. The environment that has to be sensed and managed has these nodes placed. To put it another way, this kind of network may be used to monitor dangerous and inaccessible locations because it is made up of a

**Corresponding author*: abasakfet@kiit.ac.in

Subhasis Dash, Manas Ranjan Lenka, S. Balamurugan, Ambika Prasad Tripathy and Amarendra Mohanty (eds.) Sustainable Resource Management in Next-Generation Computational Constrained Networks, (87–114) © 2025 Scrivener Publishing LLC

lot of tiny nodes that can communicate with one another. Along with the sensor itself, each node has a processor, memory, wireless antenna, and battery. In addition to being detected by nodes, temperature, sound, and light scalars may also be processed and sent through radio.

WSNs differ from conventional *ad hoc* wireless networks owing to qualities listed above as well as the ability to interact with the environment. WSNs are application-driven because of limited software and hardware resources; hence, WSN applications are created with a specific problem in mind. Collaboration between nodes is required to properly utilize the WSN resource, and the effort may also extend WSN's lifetime [1, 2].

Figure 4.1 shows the map of a WRSN system with different MCVs. WSNs have a lot of environmental interaction, and there are both implicit and explicit timing constraints depending on where the sensor nodes are installed.

- Because WSNs require physical environment contact, they differ significantly from regular *ad hoc* networks, and traditional distributed system approaches do not apply to them. Real-time needs, noise, a high incidence of faults, and no determinism provide a new set of limitations that must be addressed [4].
- WSNs are subject to severe resource limitations, as was before mentioned. The main resource limitations include a restricted energy budget, a limited CPU frequency, a limited amount of memory, and a limited amount of network bandwidth. New approaches are required to address these traits. A new problem that has not been addressed in conventional *ad hoc* networks is the reason that WSNs contain a significant number of different nodes. For instance, balancing

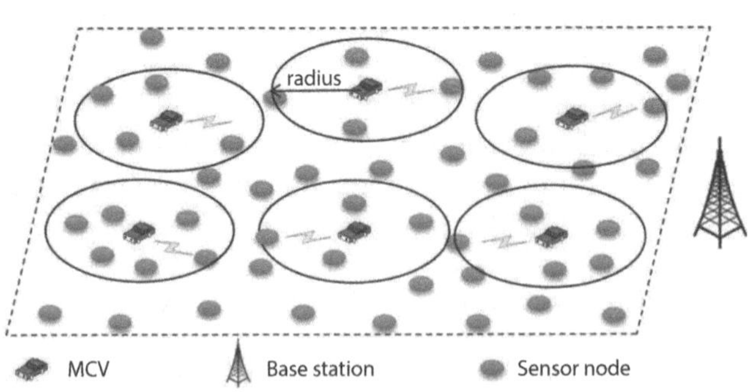

Figure 4.1 Sketch diagram of WRSN along with MCVs [3].

real-time features with trade-off tactics to ensure an active economy has grown in significance [5].

- Unpredictability: There are several unknowns that might have an impact on a WSN. For starters, WSNs are used in situations where there are a lot of uncontrolled events. Finally, nodes are not trustworthy on their own. Furthermore, it is not always feasible to fully calibrate the nodes prior to their use; routing components such as pathways and connections might be dynamically added or removed throughout the WSN's operational period. Permanent defects or battery depletion may necessitate the installation or removal of nodes. Furthermore, even during the first deployment, the energy level in some nodes might change dramatically. Finally, nodes may be physically removed owing to environmental factors or purposeful control, necessitating network redesign.
- Self: Developing the WSN's perspective at network application layers is one of the most difficult tasks. Because WSNs are designed to function with little to no human interaction, self-features like organization, optimization, and healing become essential [6, 7]. Although they are very tough to obtain, these qualities are easily mentioned as challenges.
- Real-time: Different WSNs actually operate in the actual world, which necessitates the use of real-time characteristics to ensure proper operation. Implicit real-time limitations exist in these systems. Its tasks' reaction times are also crucial; therefore, system activities must be completed as quickly as feasible. A number of WSNs have explicit real-time limitations. A structural monitoring application, for example, sets specific data sensing deadlines [8]. However, owing to the enormous types of nodes, no determinism as well as noise, ensuring real-time qualities may be exceedingly difficult.
- Security: Because WSNs might be employed in several safety applications, their ultimate security is an important consideration. Denial-of-service attacks are simple to carry out via a WSN. Furthermore, approaches to co-ordinate and real time communication actually do not take security into account. As a result, an attacker can readily take advantage of the WSN based security flaws. The big question lies on how to apply security procedures that actually need a lot

of computing power in a system that has a lot of hardware limits.

The power conservation is the most essential challenge of the networks in this situation, as nodes are to function on restricted resources, and different tactics and protocols must be devised to cope with it [9]. More specifically, network lifespan may be increased if the software associated to system, which includes many layers along with protocols, is built in different way that reduces energy usage [10]. In the order to reduce the power consumption of different WSNs, several strategies have been presented in the literature. These strategies apply to a variety of features of sensor networks, including hardware platforms, MAC protocol, routing, and topology management.

4.1.1 WSN Application and Hardware Characteristics

WSN is regarded as an application based technology. They are mainly developed with different applications in mind; hence, they cannot be used for different uses. To ensure that a node is suitable for a given application, it is crucial to take important hardware-related factors into account. When defining the nodes for a given application, considerations on the kind of critical processing unit, and communication, power supply, sensing devices, it must be made exhaustively.

Generally, a microcontroller or a microprocessor is used as the processing unit. The designer should take the intended performance gradient into account when selecting the best microprocessor for the system because high-performance microcontrollers consume more power. Another significant factor is related to this fact that microcontroller often supports many operating modes, like active-idle, along with sleep mode, which mainly impact the node's power consumption. Another intriguing design alternative recommends dividing the burden between two low-power microcontrollers, with one microcontroller handling the sensing controller and the other handling network related activities such as managing the radio-frequency link and executing the algorithms [11]. Lastly, it is possible to use techniques like dynamic voltage scaling (DVS) [12]. DVS trades off performances along with power supplies for energy saving by dynamically adjusting the power supply of microcontroller and operating frequency to fit the processing need.

To communicate data between nodes, a variety of communication devices employing media like radio-frequency and optical communications can be used. The sensor nodes need both a transmitter and a receiver to communicate. The primary function of these gadgets is to transform a microcontroller bit stream into radio signals and vice versa. More specifically, the transceiver is typically seen to be the biggest power needing equipment. Optimization the power consumption can have a substantial positive impact on the whole system [13]. The kind of modulation curricula, data transfer rate, and transmission power along with operating duty cycle of a transceiver are some of the elements that influence its power consumption characteristics [14]. The user may usually be able to adjust the power level on many transceivers. Transceivers typically have four different operating modes: transmit, receive, idle, and sleep. By changing between these modes, energy can be saved. Be aware that managing the transition between operational modes is necessary because rousing a transceiver from sleep mode along with forcing it into transmitting involves some start-up time with energy. So, putting a node into sleeping mode only makes sense when this energy saved during sleep mode outweighs the energy required to put the node back into activation mode, which means that a time until a next event should be long enough.

Most often, a battery is utilized as the power supply device, which significantly affects the lifespan of the sensor node. The capacity impact, which is associated with discharge-rate, or the total amount of current drawn from the set battery, is therefore one of the most crucial elements that a designer must take into account. Drawing more current than the recommended value significantly reduces battery life. It was crucial to note that the majority of WSN applications require placing sensor nodes in challenging and distant environments, making it challenging to employ conventional battery charging methods. Utilizing external energy sources like sunshine or wind is a viable alternative in some situations.

Figure 4.2 shows the distribution of energy intensity. Finally, depending on the type of output they provide, sensors in WSNs can be categorized as analog or digital devices. Sensors convert physical events into electrical signals. In a nutshell, there are a number of causes related to power consumption in sensors, including signal-sampling, signal conditioning, and analog to digital conversion [16]. When compared to active sensors, as like as sonar, which require energy to propagate out a signal to probe the item being viewed, passive sensors, like temperature sensors, use less electricity. Indeed, the sample rate is crucial because greater frequency associated to sampling demands many more energy. In the current situation, sensors must only obtain a single measurement sample if, when-where, and at the appropriate degree of fidelity [17]. This tactic lowers the subsystem's energy requirements and, in some cases, the processing and communication burden as well. Therefore, using mechanisms that can alter the bit resolution and sampling rate of measurement samples, as well as adaptive sampling, utilizing correlation, and redundancy models used to predict the

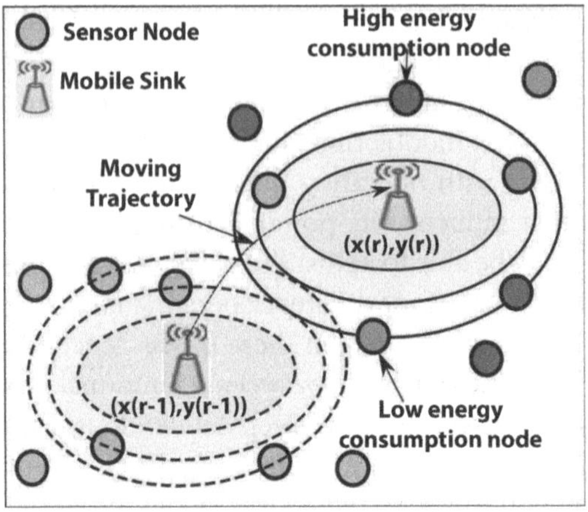

Figure 4.2 Distribution of energy intensity [15].

measurement rather than actually taking one, and lastly, the hierarchical sensing that can result in a reduction in power consumption.

Several WSN applications will be briefly introduced in the paragraphs that follow. The applicable algorithmic solutions may change significantly depending on the time requirements of the applications. In contrast to a military application, which has considerably shorter temporal validity, an environment monitoring application may have minute-long deadlines. While some applications require event-driven approaches, others require regular sensing and transmission.

Finally, the following list of further WSNs' uses:

- Intelligent housing: Other examples of WSN application in building automation include pressure sensors in chairs and microphones for voice activation. WSNs enable homes to be outfitted with temperature, light, and movement sensors. As a result, the air temperature, natural and artificial lighting, and other elements may be adjusted to meet the demands of each individual user.
- Precision agriculture: WSN use in farmlands makes it feasible to regulate irrigation and apply pesticides precisely.
- Harsh areas monitoring: Through the usage of WSNs, difficult locations might potentially be explored and monitored.

- Freshwater-quality monitoring: The WSNs can be utilized for freshwater quality monitoring because they are compact and non-intrusive.
- Military application: Examples of prospective WSN uses for military purposes include target identification, non-human combat area monitoring, troop and vehicle position and movement management, landmine clearance, and building investigation.

To sum up, WSNs may be used for a variety of purposes, and the choice of hardware for those purposes relies on the systems' needs, the resources that are available, and the setting in which the network will be used.

4.2 MAC Layer Approaches

As mentioned earlier, one of the most crucial issues when discussing the usage of WSNs is lifespan maximizing of WSNs. This is mostly because sensor nodes are regarded as inaccessible when the battery level is low. It is crucial to remember that, in WSNs, node communication is the main energy-consuming operation. The node uses a large amount of its energy for radio broadcasts and for listening to the medium in anticipation of packet receipt [18]. In other words, exchanging messaging consumes a lot more energy than processing the data or acquiring the data by the sensors. Furthermore, the nodes share a single communication channel, and the efficiency and fairness with which they distribute it greatly affects the performance of the network.

- Packet collision: A packet collision occurs when one node receives several packets simultaneously. As a result, every packet needs to be deleted and sent again.
- Overhearing: Overhearing occurs when a node gets transmitted packets that actually are intended for another different sensor node.
- Control-packet overhead: It is necessary to reduce the use of control packets while coordinating the WSN.
- Idle listening: This is the practice of a node being in the listening mode on an unused channel.
- Over emitting: When a message cannot be sent because the target node is inactive, over emitting occurs.

It is crucial to stress that message collisions are regarded as the most essential factor because they compel the network to retransmit, using more energy, and necessitate the discarding of all associated messages. As a result, the energy-efficient MAC-based protocol must prevent actual collisions and minimize energy-rated dissipation associated with overhead, overhearing, and idle channel sensing [19].

We can identify four unique types of communication patterns [20]. These are as follows:

- Broadcast: To send specific information to every node under its control, base station subsystem (BSS) often employ the broadcast communication pattern (sink). A control packet, software updates, or consultations must be included in the broadcast information. Only when all the destination receiver nodes are within the transmitter node's radio based coverage can the broadcast pattern be employed.
- Local gossip: This pattern occurs when nodes detect an event and transmit it to other nodes in the vicinity (same cluster). Within the same service area, this type of communication takes place when the one node delivers messages to its distanced neighbours.
- Converge cast: When the number of different sensors delivers their intended packets to a single node, this pattern is known as converge cast. The final node might be a BS, fusion center, or cluster head.
- Multicast: According to some situations, messages must be transmitted to a specific set of sensor nodes, and only the sensors in this added group will receive this message.

The IEEE 802.15.4 communication Standard, ZigBee technology, and primary MAC strategies that can lower power consumption are all summarized in the following sections. A subsequent paragraph will describe other MAC strategies aimed toward MSN optimization.

4.2.1 IEEE 802.15.4 Standard along with the ZigBee Technology

A major objective of ZigBee-based technology is mainly to enable WSNs made up of several operating nodes to operate with less energy usage. To increase the lifetime of their WSN applications, the majority of WSN technologies, including Mica Motes, utilize ZigBee.

Open Systems Interconnection (OSI) is the foundation of the ZigBee network design; however, only the more crucial layers have been implemented. The physical layer along with the MAC layer is the only level of the IEEE 802.15.4–based standard that ZigBee adopts [21].

The physical layer may function at either 2.4 GHz or 868/915 MHz, with a maximum transmission rate of 250 Kbps over 16 channels. The carrier sense multiple access with collision avoidance (CSMA-CA) mechanism is the foundation of the IEEE 802.15.4 MAC layer. ZigBee technology is distinct from other wireless technologies for a number of reasons; it has lower processed data transmission rate, very lower energy consumption, cheaper price, higher level of self-based organization, along with more adaptable network based topologies.

A *de facto* standard for transmission networks with minimal energy consumption and slow data rates is IEEE 802.15.4, which was first suggested in 2003. The IEEE 802.15.4 MAC-based protocol has two distinct operating modes that should be selected by a selected central node known as the personal area network (PAN)–based coordinator. These are what they are:

- Beaconless mode, in which a CSMA/CA packet without a beacon is used to carry out MAC protocol operations.
- Beacon mode: In this mode, the PAN coordinator transmits beacons on a regular basis to establish a super frame and synchronize linked nodes. The super frame time must be used for every node communication. Furthermore, during the contention phase of this frame, the time framed slotted CSMA/CA is in charge for the MAC protocol. IEEE 802.15.4 with beacon mode allows for communication through synchronization, and this contention-free window is based on predefined specified slot-based time.

4.2.2 Different Other MAC Approaches

Different other MAC strategies have been put out in the literature in an effort to lower WSN power usage. The key solutions that investigate the actual optimization of MAC protocols are outlined in the following paragraphs.

Time division multiple access (TDMA) and duty cycles are two common methods utilized in the MAC layer of WSNs (DC).

The primary concept behind the TDMA approach is mainly to split the time that devices spend on channel accesses into different time slots, each of which is used by just one device. As a result, any device using this method must reserve such a time slot in advance before sending any messages. A TDMA MAC [22] protocol is mainly based on different cross-layer optimization incorporating the MAC and physical layers serves as the foundation for this method. The major objective of the method that is being discussed is to lower total energy usage by using TDMA scheduling for clustered WSNs and the smallest frame length possible.

To reduce the energy consumed by the TDMA MAC protocol [23], the major goal is actually to schedule the different sensor nodes with successive time slots in different radio state, like transmitting, receiving, listening, sleeping, and idle, in order to decrease energy usage. The best scheduling of these stages might result in a reduction in energy usage because sensor nodes use varying amounts of energy at each selected state.

FlexiTP is a TDMA MAC protocol that uses sleep scheduling approach to schedule node messages [24]. The sensor nodes must solely transmit and receive packets within their designated time slots under the sleeping scheduling scheme before going to sleep until their designated time slot is available again. Additionally, FlexiTP offers routing, different time synchronization tasks, and sensor node capabilities for both sensing and routing data.

Another TDMA MAC protocol mainly designed for multichip WSNs is PEDAMACS [25]. When actually compared to different MAC protocols like random access protocols, which might only extend the network's lifetime by a few days or a few months, it can increase network lifetime by many years. However, because dynamic topologies are typical in hostile settings, this TDMA protocol does not function well when used with WSNs.

Complementarily, the DC techniques separate the running time of the device into two sections. In addition, the DC approach separates a device's running time into two sections: an active section and an inactive section, commonly known as sleeping time. The gadgets remain idle for longer and, as a result, use less energy. This is true when the activity period is less than the inactivity period. The network's maximum transmission rate will, therefore, decrease, which is a drawback.

These methods often help protocols handle collision, idle listening, and over emitting issues, but they come with extra costs for sending and handling control messages. In applications with low network density and few simultaneous transmissions, these extra expenditures may not be essential. All contention-based protocols like CSMA-CA appear mainly appropriate in this situation. Keep in mind that big networks cannot benefit from the CSMA/CA MAC protocol found in the IEEE 802.15.4 standard [26].

Another kind of WBN application [27] describes the MAC-based protocol that is implemented through hardware using a 0.13-m CMOS technology. A common listen-before-transmit strategy is being employed in a wireless body network (WBN) to prevent collisions with neighboring transmitters. Based on a wakeup-fallback strategy, the management of time slot overlaps was scaled back.

Another WBN, MAC protocol, was proposed with the major objective to extend each body sensor's battery life to the maximum possible extent while keeping the same degree of transmission reliability and message delay. This MAC protocol does this by utilizing energy-dependent radio activation strategy practical medical applications, as well as cross-layer fuzzy occupied scheduling method.

In asynchronous MAC-based WSNs, an energy-aware hybrid data aggregation [28] approach seeks to reduce the energy issue. The nodes closest to the WSN's sink use more energy than other nodes because they send and receive more data to the sink than nodes farther away. The system is designed to adaptively manage the volume of data transfers in order to eliminate the disadvantage described earlier.

The MAC of nodes in the game-theoretic MAC method for WSNs [29] is based on an insufficiently cooperative game mode. Time is split into super frames using this technique, known as game-theory-based MAC protocol (GMAC), and each super frame includes two segments: an active phase and a sleeping portion. During the sleeping phase, all nodes turn off their radios to save energy, and, during the active phase, any nodes that have packets to send will do so in accordance with the partially cooperative game by passing them on the channel.

Several cross-layer protocols that merge the network layers of the MAC and WSN include Contention-Based MAC and Routing (CSBF), LEACH-MAC, Geographic Routing with MAC adaptation, Cluster-based protocols with dynamic cluster head selection, and protocols utilizing SNR-based link quality information for routing decisions [30]. All of these MAC protocols are cost conscious with regard to residual energy, connection circumstances, and queue state. The routing layer chooses the most appropriate relay candidates based on the information from the MAC protocol. Because fewer in-range devices are competing for a single channel, interference is decreased.

4.3 Routing Approaches

WSNs can be used for a wide range of purposes, but nodes in all of them have the basic responsibility of detecting and gathering data, processing it, and sending it elsewhere so that the monitored parameters can be analyzed. To do this duty effectively, an energy-efficient routing protocol must be developed to establish pathways between the nodes and the data sink [31]. Because sensor nodes are energy bound, a large portion of a WSN's protocol try to reduce an amount of energy required mainly for communications. Essentially, the routing problem is made more difficult by the environment's features, which are combined with limited resources and energy. As a result, path selection should be made in such a way that a network's lifetime is maximized. Different techniques can be used in this situation to deal with the problem. One easy solution is to avoid low-quality routes, as wireless networks' instability has a negative impact on their performance. Many retransmissions are required as a result of link failures and packet losses, which result in greater power consumption.

Robust energy-aware clustering architecture (REACA) is a clustering protocol [32]. The first cycle of REACA's operation is mainly dedicated to network setting, whereas this second cycle is responsible for message transmission. The battery level of each cluster node affects which cluster head will be chosen. The node with the highest battery energy level is chosen as the cluster head as a result. Additionally, a routing technique is offered, and REACA is mathematically confirmed.

Energy aware routing for real-time and reliable communication (EARQ) is a routing protocol that is based on the energy level of a WSN [33]. EARQ is capable of ensuring reliability, time limitations, and energy efficiency. Utilizing the path with the highest energy level inside a WSN is the main goal of EARQ. Simulations show that EARQ can be integrated into a WSN for industrial use. EARQ, on the other hand, has not been verified for any WSN prototype [34].

MMSPEED is a routing technology that can ensure probabilistic quality-of-service (QoS) metrics in WSNs. It takes into account several possibilities for rapid delivery in the temporal domain and ensures package arrival [35]. There are several dependability specifications offered, each of which is based on a distinct methodology. Geographically dispersed end-to-end delivery of demands is helpful for scalability and flexibility in dynamic and dense WSNs. On the other side, geographic routing necessitates that nodes be aware of their position. As a result, the concept's creators believed that every node would be equipped with GPS or other distributed localization methods. Due to the fact that GPS devices do not work properly indoors and the additional package exchange required by distributed localization techniques for the nodes to regularly broadcast their geographic location, this poses serious problems.

The witch is a routing mechanism that supports a non-uniform node of distribution approach that is used to address the energy problem in WSNs [36]. Along with non-uniform node distribution and continuous data transmission, it has been demonstrated that the circular multi-hop WSN is also unable to avoid imbalanced energy consumption.

Energy-efficient broadcast problem (EEBP) is a technique used in *ad hoc* wireless networks [37]. The EEBP's concept may be summarized as follows:

We identify the broadcast tree with the lowest energy cost in an *ad hoc* wireless network. The network's nodes are thought to all have the same level of transmission power. Three routing algorithms aimed at minimizing network usage are given as a solution.

4.4 Transmission Power Control Approaches

Because sensor nodes rely on batteries, saving energy is crucial for WSNs. As mentioned earlier, communication is the most energy-draining activity in WSNs. Here are two main approaches to tackling this challenge:

MAC Protocol Optimization: These protocols manage data transmission, allowing nodes to conserve energy by going into sleep mode when not communicating.
Dynamic Power Control: This approach adjusts the transmission power of each node. Lower power translates to lower energy consumption and potentially a longer network lifespan. However, there is a trade-off:
Benefit: Lower power saves energy.
Drawback: Very low power signals are more susceptible to interference, potentially leading to data loss [38]. The answer to the challenges of dynamic signal quality lies in online transmit power control (TPC) strategies. These techniques adjust transmission power based on real-time environmental conditions, ensuring reliable communication while minimizing energy consumption.

Several TPC approaches have been developed:
Fixed Network-Level Power: This basic approach assigns the same power level to all nodes, sacrificing some efficiency for simplicity.

Neighbor-Level Power: This method allows nodes to adjust power based on individual neighbors, offering some improvement over fixed power.

However, most modern WSNs leverage per-packet TPC. This allows for the most granular control, optimizing power usage for each data transmission.

Extensive research has shown that TPC techniques effectively reduce energy consumption in WSNs, making them a critical tool for extending network lifetime [39, 40]. While research confirms the benefits of TPC for WSNs, real-world deployments face an additional challenge: interference.

The Problem of Interference:
Many WSNs operate in the 2.4-GHz band, commonly used by Wi-Fi (IEEE 802.11 WLAN) and Bluetooth (IEEE 802.15.1) devices.

These devices typically have stronger transmission power compared to sensor nodes, causing interference and potentially disrupting communication.

Standard TPC limitations:
Existing TPC methods often overlook interference from other wireless networks. This can significantly degrade performance in real-world scenarios.
The Solution: Interference-aware transmission power control (I-TPC)

I-TPC is a promising TPC algorithm designed specifically for WSNs.

It takes into account the presence of other wireless devices in the environment.

By dynamically adjusting transmission power based on both signal strength and interference levels, I-TPC aims to:

- reduce energy consumption and
- maintain reliable communication [41].

Here is a deeper dive into how I-TPC tackles interference:

Identifying Interference: When the I-TPC algorithm detects interference, it takes action to maintain a good connection.

Adjusting Received Signal Strength (RSS) Goal: I-TPC does not directly target the transmission power. Instead, it focuses on the received signal strength (RSS) at the receiver.

The algorithm first determines the optimal RSS level that guarantees an acceptable packet reception ratio, a measure of successful data reception.

Two-Tier Transmission Power Control: Once the target RSS is identified, each node adjusts its transmission power to achieve this target.

This control happens in two stages:

- The first stage makes coarse adjustments to bring the RSS close to the target range.
- The second stage fine-tunes the power to maintain the RSS within a narrow range around the target.

Responding to Sudden Interference:
When I-TPC detects a surge in interference, it quickly reacts by:

- Increasing the target RSS level: This effectively boosts the signal strength to overcome interference and maintain a good signal-to-interference-plus-noise ratio.
- Raising the transmission power accordingly to achieve the new target RSS.

Overall, I-TPC employs two independent local algorithms at each node to dynamically adjust transmission power and achieve a reliable connection even in the presence of interference [42]. Unlike some routing protocols, local mobility anchor (LMA) is a local technique that does not rely on specific communication protocols.

Periodic "Life Messages": Each sensor node broadcasts a special message called a "life message" at regular intervals. This message essentially announces the node's presence and availability.
Receiving Nodes Respond: Neighboring nodes within range hear these life messages and respond with an "acknowledgement message." This confirms they received the life message.
Evaluating Neighbors: Before sending any data, a node analyzes the number of acknowledgement messages it received. This gives it an idea of how many neighbors are within range and potentially reachable.
Threshold-Based Decisions: Each node has pre-defined thresholds for the number of expected acknowledgements. By comparing the actual received acknowledgements to these thresholds, the node decides:

- If enough neighbors are reachable, then it can proceed with sending data.
- If not enough neighbors are reachable, then it might need to adjust its routing strategy or wait for network conditions to improve.

In essence, LMA uses a simple exchange of messages to estimate the health and connectivity of the local network environment, aiding in route selection for data transmission. If a node receives fewer messages than the lower limit, then the transmission power is raised by factor A_{inc} for each node that falls short of the lower threshold.

Transmission Power Adjustments in LMN: LMN only adjusts transmission power when the calculated NodeResp value falls outside a pre-defined acceptable range. This helps conserve energy when communication conditions are good.

LMN vs. Other Routing Approaches:
Fixed/Global Algorithms vs. LMN: LMN outperforms fixed-power algorithms that waste energy by constantly transmitting at high power. However, LMN's network lifetime is roughly half that of some global algorithms like equal transmission power (ETP).
LMN vs. ETP: While ETP might achieve a longer network lifespan, LMN offers strong competition in terms of reliability (trust level). Here is where LMN shines:

- Scalability: LMN is easier to implement and manage in large-scale deployments compared to complex global algorithms.
- Implementation Simplicity: Due to its localized nature, LMN requires less configuration and is simpler to set up.

In summary, LMN prioritizes energy efficiency by adjusting power only when necessary. While it may not achieve the absolute longest network lifetime, its scalability, ease of use, and competitive reliability make it a compelling choice for many WSN applications.

4.5 Autonomic Approaches

In order to define computer systems that can govern themselves, IBM coined the phrase "autonomic computing" in 2001 [43].

Simple definitions are given below [44] :

- Self-configuring: The capability of the system to arrange itself in accordance with high level aims.

- Self-optimizing: In order to improve performance or service quality, the system may decide to initiate a change as a proactive measure.

Despite the fact that dense WSNs have many benefits, managing a plenty of nodes requires self-management capabilities. Autonomic computing strategies, which may well be used to handle WSNs with competing aims (energy efficiency, self-organization, time limitations, and fault tolerance), include self-management techniques.

The creation of a computing platform that does not require human input is the primary objective of self-management. When computer systems adhere to the global objectives set by a system administrator, they can self-organize and optimize themselves in this fashion [45]. For instance, the traditional IEEE 802.15.4 protocol does not appear to be able to handle the complexities in dense WSNs made up of numerous sensor devices in a star network topology when the network presents conflicting objectives (increase reliability and energy efficiency while meeting time constraints).

For instance, as the number of nodes in a network rises, the WPAN may get crowded in an effort to improve dependability, and fewer messages arrived, reach the base station on time. Using the True Time simulator 1, tests were carried out to show how the WSNs would behave in this circumstance. Eff (efficiency) and QoF ("quality of service") are two measures that have been embraced. In WSNs, a key measure of data quality is QoF. This reflects the proportion of messages successfully received by the base station compared to the total number sent.

The genetic machine learning algorithm (GMLA) is a powerful tool for optimizing performance in situations with multiple competing factors. In WSNs, GMLA excels at improving communication efficiency, especially when the base station lacks detailed network information (like the layout of sensor nodes).

Therefore, GMLA appears well-suited for balancing QoF and communication efficiency (Eff) in WSNs. It can potentially outperform the standard IEEE 802.15.4 protocol in terms of energy consumption. However, it is important to note that GMLA is most effective when the signal strength is consistent across the entire monitored area.

A variable offset algorithm (VOA) is one that seeks to maximize communication effectiveness in heavy WSNs with star topology. The VOA is a light middleware that is used at the application layer, making it simple to integrate into IEEE 802.15.4 devices.

With the use of an experimental procedure based on actual circumstances, the VOA method was evaluated, and one of the trials involved changing the quantity of slave nodes. The objective was to assess how the number of nodes affected the Eff and QoF parameters. For just one scenario—a network with four slaves—IEEE 802.15.4 exhibits findings that are comparable to those of VOA. The disparity among VOA and IEEE 802.15.4 widens as the number of slaves rises. When 29 slaves are taken into account, the efficiency gap among VOA and IEEE 802.15.4 is greater than 100%. These findings demonstrate that VOA performs satisfactorily and keeps the minimal QoS level even when there are a lot of slaves.

The major objective of the decentralized power-aware WSN (DPAWSN) strategy is to maintain a minimal QoF while enhancing the Eff and conserving energy. Because nodes have the freedom to choose whether or not to deliver messages, this method may be viewed as concentrated. A specific QoF level is mandated by the network administrator on the one hand, and the WSN's lifespan is extended by the power consciousness choice made in each node on the other.

DPAWSN tackles a key challenge in WSNs: balancing network lifetime with data quality.

Dynamic Transmission Rate Adjustment: The base station monitors a metric called "quality of service" (QoS), which reflects data quality. If the QoS falls outside a desired range (higher or lower than specified), then the base station instructs individual sensor nodes to adjust their transmission rate.

Energy Efficiency Based on Battery Life: Importantly, the adjustment considers each node's remaining battery power (residual voltage). Nodes with lower battery life can reduce their transmission rate to save energy.

By dynamically adjusting transmission rates, DPAWSN aims the following:

Maintain Desired Data Quality: Ensure data received meets the required quality standards.

Extend Network Lifetime: Nodes with lower transmission rates consume less energy, ultimately extending the overall network lifespan.

The effectiveness of DPAWSN was tested in a noisy environment with an unspecified number of computers communicating using the IEEE 802.11 Wi-Fi standard. The transmission rate can also be automatically adjusted by DPAWSN based on the nodes' voltage levels. Additionally, it can fulfill a specified QoF that system administrators have set.

4.6 Application of ZigBee in a WSN

ZigBee, built upon the IEEE 802.15.4 standard, establishes guidelines for low-rate wireless personal area networks (LR-WPAN) suitable for energy-efficient devices operating within a personal operating space (POS) of approximately 10 m. ZigBee offers self-organizing capabilities, reliable mesh networking, and the ability to transmit data across multiple hops, all while maintaining extended battery life for connected devices. As explained earlier, a full-function device and a reduced-function device participate in a LR-WPAN network. Over 65,000 nodes can be present in a ZigBee star network [46]. A regular ZigBee architecture consists of ZigBee Devices, Coordinators, and Routers. Such features make it a good fit for being used for agricultural monitoring.

Zhou *et al.* [47] proposed a greenhouse monitoring system using IEEE 802.15.4-compliant devices. They have used the JN5121 as the main microcontroller and leaf nodes with TSL2550 light sensor and SHT1x relative humidity and temperature sensor.

Let us discuss the setup of a WSN for intelligent irrigation and agricultural crop monitoring, using ZigBee as a communication protocol.

Annually, a huge amount of losses is incurred due to improper irrigation and inaccurate monitoring of crops. Therefore, setting up a WSN to remotely monitor the crop and take action based on the sensor data is crucial. This not only saves the farmer from manually surveying the fields, which is very laborious but also boosts yield and productivity.

Firstly, we will be dividing the field into various sectors. Each sector will consist of a few leaf nodes and a router. As our node, we will use JN5121-MO00X module that has the JN5121 chip. It is an 802.15.4 ZigBee-compliant microcontroller. Alternatively, an Arduino board can be paired with an XBee shield. This combination allows the Arduino board to establish connectivity and exchange data wirelessly using ZigBee technology.

Various sensors will be attached to the leaf nodes, like soil moisture (YL-69), relative humidity and temperature sensor (SHT1x), soil nutrient NPK sensor (RS485), and light sensor (TSL2550). The major benefit of using the JN5121-MO00X module is that the humidity and temperature sensor and light sensor are already present inside the sensor module; this not only helps in reducing the complexity of wiring many components but also helps in power management. The sensors can be interfaced with the input-output pins of the device. The nodes will be powered by an 18650 battery and a solar panel will be attached for continuous power supply.

These leaf nodes will be placed at a fixed distance apart. One node in the cluster will be the router node. This node is the cluster head and will gather all the data from the other cluster members. The role of the router is to forward this data through the subsequent routers to the root node in the control room. Each of the cluster heads will be having a unique MAC address. When the nodes are initially deployed, each cluster head's location is noted. As the nodes are static, we can find out the location of the cluster head nodes in each sector, using the MAC address of the nodes.

Using this information, we can create a map and accurately monitor the characteristics of the soil like soil moisture, relative humidity, temperature, and light intensity in every sector of the field. This will assist the farmer to better manage his crops. We can additionally incorporate an actuator system including pumps and values to make an intelligent irrigation. Whenever the soil moisture drops below a certain threshold level, the water sprinkler will automatically switch ON. In the instance of a rainy day when the soil moisture is above the threshold, the sprinklers will be in the OFF state.

One of the primary characteristics of a WSN is its long battery life. Transmitting and receiving signals consume the most amount of energy. In order to minimize the energy consumed in transmitting and receiving signals, we will schedule sleep cycles for each of the nodes. The cluster head will determine a sleep schedule for the cluster and the leaf nodes present in that cluster will follow that schedule. Each node will wake up after every 30 min and report its sensor data to the cluster head. The cluster head will then forward this data through the routers to the root node.

Currently, with the advent of agricultural robotics, there is a rise in vertical farming. Vertical farming makes it easier for robots to operate and autonomously tend the plants. Using the data from the sensor networks the robot will detect the locations where there is nutrient deficiency and tend the plants. Additionally, we can also incorporate camera and color sensors on the robot for detecting weeds and plant diseases. The robot can then apply pesticides and weedicides.

4.7 WSN with Cloud Computing

Integration of WSNs with cloud computing is an emerging trend that offers numerous benefits in terms of scalability, storage, processing power, and data analysis. This integration allows WSNs to leverage the capabilities of cloud infrastructure to handle the massive amounts of data generated by sensor nodes and perform complex computations on that data. Here are some key aspects of integrating WSNs with the cloud:

Data Collection and Transmission: WSNs consist of a large number of sensor nodes that collect data from the physical environment. These nodes communicate with each other using wireless communication protocols and transmit the collected data to the cloud. The cloud acts as a central repository for receiving and storing the data.

Cloud Storage: Cloud platforms provide scale-able and reliable storage capabilities for WSN data. Collected sensor data can be stored in cloud-based databases or object storage systems. Cloud storage offers advantages such as data redundancy, fault tolerance, and the ability to handle large volumes of data.

Data Processing and Analysis: Cloud computing provides powerful computational resources for processing and analyzing WSN data. Complex algorithms and machine learning techniques can be applied to the data in the cloud to extract meaningful insights, detect patterns, and make predictions. The cloud's computational capabilities enable real-time or near-real-time analysis of WSN data.

Scalability and Flexibility: Cloud infrastructure allows for easy scalability of WSN applications. As the number of sensor nodes or the amount of data increases, the cloud resources can be dynamically allocated or provisioned to handle the additional workload. This scalability ensures that the system can adapt to changing requirements and handle varying levels of traffic.

Remote Monitoring and Control: By integrating WSNs with the cloud, users can remotely monitor and control the sensor nodes and the data they collect. Through a cloud-based interface, users can access and manage the WSN, configure sensor parameters, deploy software updates, and monitor the network's performance in real time.

Cost Efficiency: Cloud-based integration of WSNs can offer cost advantages. Instead of investing in expensive infrastructure and resources to handle data storage and processing locally, organizations can leverage the pay-as-you-go model of cloud computing. They can scale resources based on demand and avoid upfront infrastructure costs.

Security and Privacy: Integrating WSNs with the cloud raises concerns about data security and privacy. Encryption techniques and secure communication protocols should be implemented to protect the data during transmission and storage. Access control mechanisms and authentication mechanisms should also be in place to ensure that only authorized entities can access the WSN data.

In the proposed setup, we have a system that includes WSNs, a cloud infrastructure, and clients. The clients are the users who want to access services from the system.

Wireless sensor networks (WSNs) are made up of tiny, battery-powered sensors that collect data for various purposes, like traffic monitoring, weather forecasting, and even military applications. Each sensor is programmed for a specific task.

These sensors are not just simple data collectors; they have built-in operating systems and network management tools to keep things running smoothly.

The data that these sensors gather was sent to the cloud. It can travel directly through a base station or take a multi-hop route, bouncing from sensor to sensor until it reaches its destination.

The cloud acts like a giant storage locker and processing center, always available to users over the internet. This is especially handy when the network needs a sudden burst of processing power or extra storage space.

In simple terms, we have a system with WSNs, a cloud, and clients. The sensor nodes in the networks sense different things like transportation, weather, and military activities. They send the collected data to the cloud for storage and processing. The cloud provides services and storage to the clients when they need them, and they can access these resources over the internet. This setup allows for efficient data collection, analysis, and resource allocation.

This framework bridges the gap between WSNs and cloud computing. It allows us to unlock the full potential of sensor data by seamlessly transferring it to the cloud for further analysis and use.

Data Collection and Processing: Sensor data travels through a gateway to the data processing unit (DPU). The DPU cleans and prepares the data for storage in the cloud.
Secure Access and User Requests: Users securely connect to the cloud through the identity and access management unit (IAMU). Based on their user permissions, they can submit requests to access specific data.
Subscription and Data Delivery: The request subscriber (RS) translates user requests into subscriptions and sends them to the Pub/Sub Broker, which acts as a central message hub. When new sensor data arrives in the cloud, the DPU identifies it and sends a notification to the Pub/Sub Broker.
Matching and Delivery: The Pub/Sub Broker's event matcher compares the notification with existing subscriptions. If a match is found, then the requested data is delivered to the user, potentially after additional processing if needed.

To summarize, the integration framework includes components such as DPU, Pub/Sub Broker, RS, IAMU, and DR. Data from the WSN is processed by the DPU, stored in the DR, and accessed by users through the IAMU. Requests are handled by the RS and Pub/Sub Broker, ensuring that users receive relevant data from the cloud after matching the requested criteria.

Overall, the integration of WSNs with the cloud brings together the benefits of both technologies, enabling scale-able, flexible, and efficient management of WSN data and applications. It opens up new possibilities for leveraging the power of cloud computing to enhance the capabilities and performance of WSN-based systems.

4.8 Final Considerations and Future Directions

WSNs are among the most intriguing technologies for monitoring and sensing data in dangerous or unreachable environments. This chapter discussed a variety of ways that designers may take to create an energy-efficient WSN. Because these networks can be employed in such a wide range of situations, there are several obstacles and limits to consider when choosing an optimization strategy. Furthermore, different objectives and applications require different targets, which may or may not all be satisfied at the same time. This chapter explores various solutions to tackle the well-known energy consumption issues in WSNs. These solutions leverage different aspects of WSN design to improve network lifetime, enhance QoS, or optimize other factors depending on the designer's needs.

Future research focuses on developing improved protocols and interaction algorithms. This is crucial because extending network lifetime is a key goal for WSNs, and data transmission/reception consumes significantly more energy than processing, sensing, or data storage.

The recent trend toward adaptable solutions that dynamically modify node behavior or balance several restrictions reflects academics' recognition of the intricate and unpredictable nature of WSN.

However, due to the current technological progress of these networks, several established study topics are becoming more significant. As a result, the hardware evolution pattern encourages researchers to use multi-objective optimization methodologies to build more complex and resilient approaches in an autonomous and distributed manner, with minimum power usage as a primary aim.

The trend is moving away from costly, centralized sensor setups. Instead, researchers are favoring networks of collaborating wireless sensor nodes.

These nodes operate independently (with self-management and self-repair capabilities) and together form a robust system. This shift has led to a rise in multi-agent and lightweight optimization techniques, perfectly suited for these distributed and efficient networks.

Furthermore, the employment of WSN data mules has been prompted by the increasing expansion in the motes' local storage capacity. The study focuses on the creation of architectures and methods in which nodes must store their sensed data locally until mobile nodes collect it.

Finally, it should be noted that the diversity of issues has resulted in an even larger range of techniques in dealing with the problems that WSNs encounter in today's harsh and loud surroundings. Now, it is up to the designers to determine the ideal match or combination for optimizing the network based on its environment, jobs, and most critical needs and restrictions. Because there is not one solution that can solve all difficulties at once, one of the most significant aspects of today's designers' job is the accurate assessment of issues to be expected.

References

1. Stankovic, J.A., Abdelzaher, T.E., Lu, C., Sha, L., Hou, J.C., Real-time communication and coordination in embedded sensor networks. *Proc. IEEE*, 91, 7, 1002–1022, 2003.
2. Hadim, S. and Mohamed, N., Middleware: Middleware challenges and approaches for wireless sensor networks. *IEEE Distrib. Syst. Online*, 7, 3, 1–1, 2006.
3. Li, J., Sun, G., Wang, A., Lei, M., Liang, S., Kang, H., Liu, Y., A many-objective optimization charging scheme for wireless rechargeable sensor networks via mobile charging vehicles. *Comput. Netw.*, 215, 109196, 2022.
4. Molla, M.M. and Ahamed, S., II, A survey of middleware for sensor network and challenges, in: *2006 International Conference on Parallel Processing Workshops (ICPPW'06)*, IEEE, pp. 6, 2006, August.
5. Yick, J., Mukherjee, B., Ghosal, D., Wireless sensor network survey. *Comput. Netw.*, 52, 12, 2292–2330, 2008.
6. Huebscher, M.C. and McCann, J.A., A survey of autonomic computing—degrees, models, and applications. *ACM Comput. Surv. (CSUR)*, 40, 3, 1–28, 2008.
7. Oliver, R.S. and Fohler, G., Timeliness in wireless sensor networks: Common misconceptions, in: *Proceedings of the 9th International Workshop on Real-Time Networks (RTN)*, vol. 6, 2010, July.
8. Kim, S., Pakzad, S., Culler, D., Demmel, J., Fenves, G., Glaser, S., Turon, M., Health monitoring of civil infrastructures using wireless sensor networks, in:

Proceedings of the 6th international conference on Information processing in sensor networks, pp. 254–263, 2007, April.

9. Gholamzadeh, B. and Nabovati, H., Concepts for designing low power wireless sensor network. *Int. J. Electron. Commun. Eng.*, 2, 9, 1869–1875, 2008.
10. Chou, P.H. and Park, C., Energy-efficient platform designs for real-world wireless sensing applications, in: *ICCAD-2005. IEEE/ACM International Conference on Computer-Aided Design*, IEEE, pp. 913–920, 2005, November 2005.
11. Karl, H. and Willig, A., *Protocols and architectures for wireless sensor networks*, John Wiley & Sons, Hoboken, New Jersey, 2007.
12. Amutha, J., Sharma, S., Sharma, S.K., An energy efficient cluster based hybrid optimization algorithm with static sink and mobile sink node for Wireless Sensor Networks. *Expert Syst. Appl.*, 203, 117334, 2022.
13. Raghunathan, V., Ganeriwal, S., Srivastava, M., Emerging techniques for long lived wireless sensor networks. *IEEE Commun. Mag.*, 44, 4, 108–114, 2006.
14. Ilyas, M. and Mahgoub, I. (Eds.), *Handbook of sensor networks: compact wireless and wired sensing systems*, CRC press, Boca Raton, FL, 2004.
15. Demirkol, I., Ersoy, C., Alagoz, F., MAC protocols for wireless sensor networks: a survey. *IEEE Commun. Mag.*, 44, 4, 115–121, 2006.
16. Moridi, M.A., Kawamura, Y., Sharifzadeh, M., Chanda, E.K., Wagner, M., Okawa, H., Performance analysis of ZigBee network topologies for underground space monitoring and communication systems. *Tunnelling Underground Space Technol.*, 71, 201–209, 2018.
17. Shi, L. and Fapojuwo, A.O., TDMA scheduling with optimized energy efficiency and minimum delay in clustered wireless sensor networks. *IEEE Trans. Mob. Comput.*, 9, 7, 927 940, 2010.
18. Wu, Y., Xiang-Yang, L., YunHao, L., Wei, L., Energy-Efficient Wake-Up Scheduling for Data Collection and Aggregation. *IEEE Trans. Parallel Distrib. Syst.*, 21, 2, 275–287, 2010.
19. Lee, W.L., Datta, A., Cardell-Oliver, R., FlexiTP: a flexible-schedule-based TDMA protocol for fault-tolerant and energy-efficient wireless sensor networks. *IEEE Trans. Parallel Distrib. Syst.*, 19, 6, 851–864, 2008.
20. Ergen, S.C. and Varaiya, P., PEDAMACS: Power efficient and delay aware medium access protocol for sensor networks. *IEEE Trans. Mob. Comput.*, 5, 7, 920–930, 2006.
21. Pinto, A., Poehls, L.B., Montez, C., Vargas, F.L., Power optimization for wireless sensor networks. *Wireless Sens. Networks/Book 2*, 2, 2012.
22. Omeni, O., Wong, A.C.W., Burdett, A.J., Toumazou, C., Energy efficient medium access protocol for wireless medical body area sensor networks. *IEEE Trans. Biomed. Circuits Syst.*, 2, 4, 251–259, 2008.
23. Kim, M.G., Han, Y.T., Park, H.S., Energy-aware hybrid data aggregation mechanism considering the energy hole problem in asynchronous MAC-based WSNs. *IEEE Commun. Lett.*, 15, 11, 1169–1171, 2011.

24. Zhao, L., Guo, L., Zhang, J., Zhang, H., Game-theoretic medium access control protocol for wireless sensor networks. *IET Commun.*, 3, 8, 1274–1283, 2009.
25. Rossi, M. and Zorzi, M., Integrated cost-based MAC and routing techniques for hop count forwarding in wireless sensor networks. *IEEE Trans. Mob. Comput.*, 6, 4, 434–448, 2007.
26. Sohraby, K., Minoli, D., Znati, T., *Wireless sensor networks: technology, protocols, and applications*, John Wiley & Sons, Hoboken, New Jersey, 2007.
27. Quan, Z., Subramanian, A., Sayed, A.H., REACA: an efficient protocol architecture for large scale sensor networks (corrected). *IEEE Trans. Wireless Commun.*, 6, 10, 3846–3855, 2007.
28. Fischmeister, S., Trausmuth, R., Lee, I., Hardware acceleration for conditional state-based communication scheduling on real-time Ethernet. *IEEE Trans. Ind. Inf.*, 5, 3, 325–337, 2009.
29. Alippi, C. and Galperti, C., An adaptive system for optimal solar energy harvesting in wireless sensor network nodes. *IEEE Trans. Circuits Syst. I Regul. Pap.*, 55, 6, 1742–1750, 2008.
30. Felemban, E., Lee, C.G., Ekici, E., MMSPEED: multipath Multi-SPEED protocol for QoS guarantee of reliability and Timeliness wireless sensor networks. *IEEE Trans. Mob. Comput.*, 5, 6, 738–754, 2006.
31. Wu, X., Chen, G., Das, S.K., Avoiding energy holes in wireless sensor networks with nonuniform node distribution. *IEEE Trans. Parallel Distrib. Syst.*, 19, 5, 710–720, 2008.
32. Li, D., Jia, X., Liu, H., Energy efficient broadcast routing in static ad hoc wireless networks. *IEEE Trans. Mob. Comput.*, 3, 2, 144–151, 2004.
33. Lin, S., Miao, F., Zhang, J., Zhou, G., Gu, L., He, T., Pappas, G.J., ATPC: Adaptive transmission power control for wireless sensor networks. *ACM Trans. Sens. Netw. (TOSN)*, 12, 1, 1–31, 2016.
34. Monks, J.P., Bharghavan, V., Hwu, W.M., A power controlled multiple access protocol for wireless packet networks, in: *Proceedings IEEE INFOCOM 2001. Conference on Computer Communications. Twentieth Annual Joint Conference of the IEEE Computer and Communications Society (Cat. No. 01CH37213)*, vol. 1, IEEE, pp. 219–228, 2001, April.
35. Ho, I.W.H. and Liew, S.C., Impact of power control on performance of IEEE 802.11 wireless networks. *IEEE Trans. Mob. Comput.*, 6, 11, 1245–1258, 2007.
36. Kim, J. and Kwon, Y., Interference-aware transmission power control for wireless sensor networks. *IEICE Trans. Commun.*, 91, 11, 3434–3441, 2008.
37. Kubisch, M., Karl, H., Wolisz, A., Zhong, L.C., Rabaey, J., Distributed algorithms for transmission power control in wireless sensor networks. *2003 IEEE Wireless Communications and Networking*, vol. 1, IEEE, pp. 558–563, 2003, March2003.
38. Kephart, J.O. and Chess, D.M., The vision of autonomic computing. *Computer*, 36, 1, 41–50, 2003.

39. Pinto, A.R. and Montez, C., Autonomic approaches for enhancing communication qos in dense wireless sensor networks with real time requirements. *2010 IEEE International Test Conference*, vol. 1-10, IEEE, 2010, November.
40. Habib, M.K., Watanabe, K., Izumi, K., Biomimetics robots from bio-inspiration to implementation, in: *IECON 2007-33rd annual conference of the IEEE Industrial Electronics Society*, IEEE, pp. 143–148, 2007, November.
41. Zhou, Y., Yang, X., Guo, X., Zhou, M., Wang, L., A design of greenhouse monitoring & control system based on ZigBee wireless sensor network, in: *2007 International Conference on wireless communications, networking and Mobile computing*, IEEE, pp. 2563–2567, 2007, September.

5

Airline Prediction Using Customer Feedback and Rating Using Machine Learning and Deep Learning

Ch Sambasiva Rao[1*], Pabbathi Manobhi Ram[2], Viswanadhapalli Siva[2] and Motakatla Satya Sai Krishna Reddy[2]

[1]Department of Information Technology, Lakireddy Bali Reddy College of Engineering, Mylavaram, Andhra Pradesh, India
[2]Lakireddy Bali Reddy College of Engineering, Mylavaram, Andhra Pradesh, India

Abstract

Internet resources are constant source of reliance for consumers while making purchases. Also, online tools help organization learn from customer evaluations, such as how different customer types have varying interests, and the way each decision of the consumer influences their feedback. Eighty-two percent of respondents in the United States say that they have read online reviews and customer testimonials before making their first purchase of a product; of these, 40% say that they have done so frequently or mostly always. In the aforementioned study that we carried out, using information acquired from online airline sites with a variety of sources and destinations, predictive analysis was performed for qualitative evaluations and ratings. The proposed system used random forest and convolutional neural networks on customer review and rating for predicting the suitable airline. The data web scrapped from www.airlinequality.com is used as dataset with more than 3,000 instances.

Keywords: Convolutional, neural network, random forest, AdaBoost

**Corresponding author*: shivachindam538@gmail.com

Subhasis Dash, Manas Ranjan Lenka, S. Balamurugan, Ambika Prasad Tripathy and Amarendra Mohanty (eds.) Sustainable Resource Management in Next-Generation Computational Constrained Networks, (115–132) © 2025 Scrivener Publishing LLC

5.1 Introduction

Internet comments have opened up a new channel for communication and marketing that connects conventional word of mouth with an expanding type of opinion destination [1]. Analyzing customerfeedback gives businesses overview into what customers really want and keeps them informed about customer satisfaction. By swiftly and effectively resolving customer complaints, businesses that use this knowledge as input can enhance customer service by encouraging a positive customer experience and concentrating attention on their wants [2]. Positive internet customer evaluations are incredibly useful and can provide more benefits than any other marketing strategy [3]. Online analyses give potential customersa consistent good opinion of a good or service and maintain brand awareness, which is advantageous to businesses both now and in the future [3, 4]. Before making a first-time purchase of any product, 82% of American adults read online customer reviews or ratings, according to Pew Research Center [4]. The proportion of people who use internet reviews for their purchases drops as people get older, with 34% of individuals in the 50–64 category and 23% of individuals in the 65+ age group engaging in this practice.

It comes to providing feedback, there is just a minor difference in age, although Americans under the age of 50 are more inclined than other people to do so [5]. It is challenging to manually analyze review data due to its unstructured nature, abnormalities, and quantity [6]. In our proposed work, we explored the data using machine learning (ML) techniques to gain insights. We used natural language processing (NLP) to the analyses by stemming, normalizing, and computing n gram information [6]. To ascertain whether a user will recommend it or not, we employed predictive analysis with various models.

5.1.1 Customer Ratings and Recommendation

One of the quantifiable measurements of consumer happiness is the ratings they provide. It is essential for assessing performance and improving customer satisfaction [7]. For input on whether customers are likely to buy a product, businesses rely on ratings. One of the most trustworthy ways to assess a company's potential for expansion is through its Net Promoter Score (NPS) [7]. Net Promoter Score represents the distinction between promoters and critics. NPS is a measure of the success of promotional operations, according to several other experts [8]. The ability to maintain a customer's interest in a productcan be offered by offering a satisfactory purchasing experience that can result in repeated purchases. Several scholars are interested in comprehending consumer purchasing behavior due to the significance of client happiness [8].

The quantity and quality of the product contribute to the consumer's decision to purchase it. Customers will be more inclined to buy the goods if it has a higher percentage of favorable reviews.

Customers now rely on reviews for their decision-making in this quickly evolving internet era and increasingly reliant on online services to alleviate any doubt around the purchasing process [9]. You can find online travel gateways on Facebook and Twitter profiles, which are both full of consumer reviews [9]. Because it attracts people who could end up buying the services being evaluated, a favorable review can act as a free advertising, which is extremely useful to online retailers. If review ratings rise by more than 5%, then there will be a 10% boost in hotel reservations made online. Hence, internet reviews have an influence on the services being examined [10]. Many factors, such as the author's emotional state at the time of writing, can have an impact. We only need to know what consumers say to their friends—word of mouth—in order to gauge client retention or happiness. One of the finest ways to gauge consumer happiness is through word of mouth. Travelers primarily use social media to communicate and arrange vacations. They can alsoassist service providers to the tourism industry (by offering pertinent information, for example), overcoming the limitations of conventional information sources. According to polls on the topic of tourism, reviews are used by travelers for 20%–45% of their decision-making, and 5%–30% of them share their experiences through reviews [10].

Unstructured text data are very granular and information-rich [11]. The automated process of extracting knowledge using textual information, such as email, tweeting, and product evaluations, is known as text analysis [11]. By text analysis, text is divided into data that computers can understand. In this study, data is extracted from text via text mining, and algorithms based on ML then process the data [12]. The amount of times a word shows up in a document directly affects the term fequency-inverse document frequency (TF-IDF), which is then balanced with the number of papers in the corpus that use that expression. Sentiment analysis is an automated method for ascertaining a person's viewpoint [12].

5.2 Literature Survey

The literature review is summarized in this chapter. This chapter highlights some of the researchers' relevant work. Numerous current strategies on airline pricing prediction and delay prediction have been examined by academics; however, our study is the first suggestion on airline review based prediction problem using social media material; a few of them are given below.

For an airline to become more successful, accurate forecasting of flight delays is essential [13]. Recent studies have concentrated on using ML methods to forecast aircraft delays. The majority of earlier prediction systems are restricted to a certain route or endpoint. The specified prediction challenges include several categorization tasks as well as a regression test. The recommended random forest (RF)–based model outperforms prior systems in regards to prediction precision (90.2% for binary classification), and it also avoids overfitting [13].

The framework developed in this study makes use of supervised data mining as well as ML approaches to forecast aircraft delays caused by bad weather [14]. From 2005 to 2015, budget airline data and American meteorological data were acquired and utilized to train the model. The effects of imbalanced training data are lessened by sampling techniques [14]. Afterward, the receiver operating characteristic curves and fp rate of each approach were contrasted [15]. At the prediction step, the model was fed the flight schedule and weather predictions. The trained model generated a binary prediction regarding whether a scheduled aircraft will arrive late or on time using these data [15].

Flight delays are often a source of annoyance in poorly organized airports [16]. Scientists and researchers are motivated to address current research challenges as ML models continue to advance [16]. In establishing air traffic with the least amount of delay possible, a robust choice process is needed due to increasing customer satisfaction with the air transportation system [17]. Nineteen percent of internal flights in the US reachat their target with a latency of 15 min, according to research [17]. Additionally, the accessibility of accurate forecast models is constrained by the aviation industry's complexity [18]. The performance of the decision tree technique and logistic regression is empirically compared in the suggested study [18].

The costing approach converts classifiers that are cost-insensitive to classifiers that are cost-sensitive by done to remove items from the original testing set based on their loss or damage suffered [19]. The effectiveness of the model has been evaluated while taking the costs of misclassification into consideration using a weighted error function [20]. Moreover, the real numbers of the two types of errors is used to assess the function [21]. In compared to the on-time class, the cost ratio shows the importance of the delayed class. When the relative cost is 10, the model could possess a reduced weighted error rate because the weighting error rate fluctuates with the cost [22].

Predicting airline ticket pricing and demand is difficult because they are affected by a variety of internal and external factors that can change rapidly [23]. In order to help passengers predict ticket prices or help airlinespredict demand, researchers have created a wide variety of airline price/demand prediction models [24]. When using current ML algorithms, external factors like publicly available data and queries from search engines are not taken into account [25].

5.3 System Design

The suggested work is implemented in Python 3.6.4 using the necessary libraries, including Keras, TensorFlow, scikit-learn, Flask, and Matlab. Datasets were acquired from airlinequality.com. The uploaded data includes discrete categories of recommendations that can be predicted as "yes" or "no" by agiven attribute. Convolutional neural network (CNN) uses a deep learning algorithm, whereas RF uses a ML method. This section offers a review of the layout of the structure, the dataset that will be used, the method, and unified modeling language (UML) designs. This section offers a review of the layout of the system architecture shown in Figure 5.1, the dataset that will be used, the method, and unified modeling language (UML) designs.

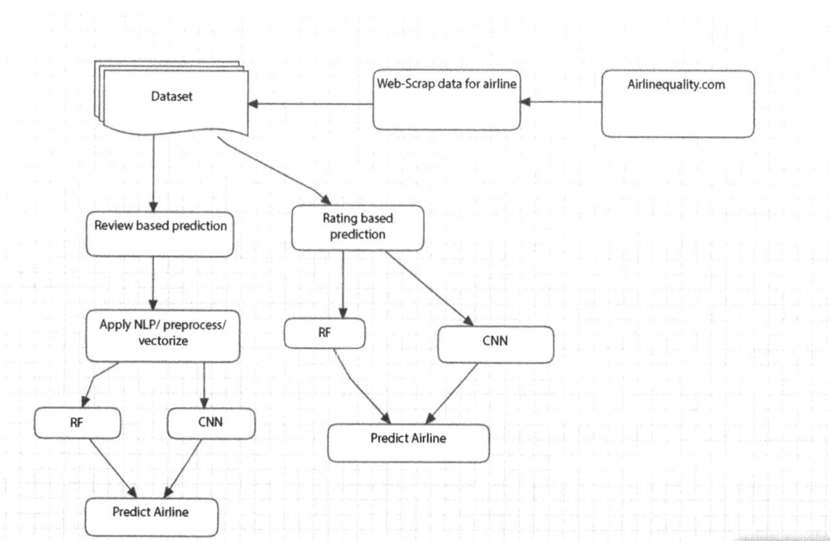

Figure 5.1 System architecture.

5.4 Methodology

Our planned research employs the modules. Support vector machines (svm, TensorFlow, scikit-learn, Flask, graphx, and others) and is built in Python 3.6.4. Our data source was airlinequality.com. Binary suggestion classes are supplied as characteristics to predict as "yes" or "no" in the downloaded data. The ML technique utilized is RF, whereas the deep learning algorithm employed is CNN. From the live dataset of airlines at www.airlinequality.com, more than 3,800 items are online scraped in real time. The dataset contained information about the type of aircraft, passengers, seats, routes, dates of travel, ratings for seat comfort, recommendations, ground services, pricing ratings, food and beverage ratings, in-flight entertainment ratings, sources, and destinations, and airlines. Text from customer reviews is used to forecast airlines. A vectorization approach is used for text input.

5.4.1 Modules

The modules included in our implementation Figure 5.1 are as follows:

1. Dataset collection
2. Review-based airline prediction
3. Rating-based airline prediction
4. Predict airline-based on source and destination

5.4.1.1 Data Collection

More than 3,800 entries are online scraped in real time from the live dataset of airlines at www.airlinequality.com. The dataset had variables for the type of aircraft, the type of seat, the route taken, the date of travel, the rating for seat comfort, the cabin crew, the rating for food and beverages, the rating for in-flight entertainment, the rating for ground service, the rating for value for money, the recommendation, the place of origin and destination, and the airlines.

5.4.1.2 Review-Based Airline Prediction

Text from customer reviews is used to forecast airlines. A vectorization approach is used for text input.

The recommendation variable is the goal or prediction variable. The value is specified as a binary value of yes or no. The following code sample demonstrates the application of the TF-IDF algorithm to evaluate text.

```
vectorizer = TfidfVectorizer(use_idf=True)
x_dataset = vectorizer.fit_transform(reviews['review_text'].values.astype('U')).toarray()
y = reviews['recommendation']
```

RF and CN algorithms are utilized in this project as ML and deep learning models.

5.4.1.3 Rating-Based Airline Prediction

Customer ratings for things like reviews, seating, cabin personnel assistance, meals and beverages, in-flight entertainment, ground service, and price effectiveness are used as learning attributes. A prediction attribute is the suggestion property. The code may be found below.

```
x_dataset=reviews.drop(columns=['title', 'reviewer_name','date_of_review','review_text','aircraft','traveller_type','seat_type',

reviews['recommendation'] = reviews['recommendation'].replace(['no','yes'],[0,1])
y=reviews['recommendation']
print(x_dataset)


x_train, x_test, y_train, y_test = train_test_split(x_dataset, y, test_size=0.2, random_state=42)
```

5.5 Algorithm Used: Random Forest, Convolutional Neural Network, and AdaBoost

5.5.1 Random Forest System

1. Random Forest shown in Figure 5.2 assuming there are n examples in the training dataset. Sub-samples are randomly chosen using replacement from these n examples. Individual trees are built using these arbitrary samples from the initial dataset.
2. A number m is chosen such that, k on the assumption that there are k variables that are input. At each node, m variables are randomly chosen from a set of k variables. The node is split using the split with the best combination of these m variables.
3. Each tree is given the freedom to enlarge as much as possible without being pruned.

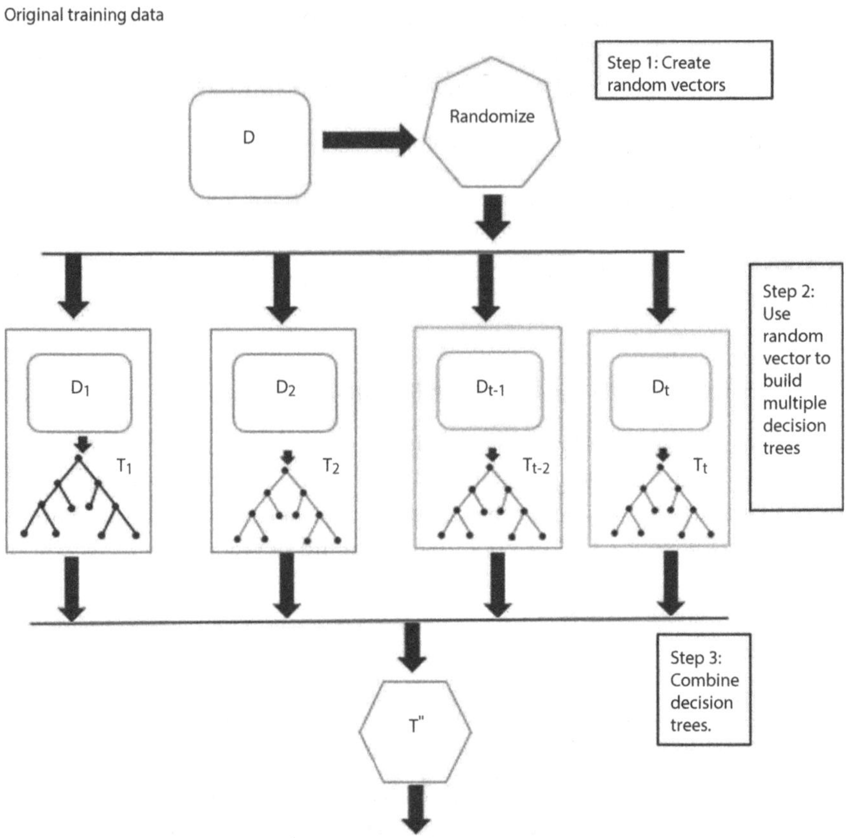

Figure 5.2 Random forest.

5.5.2 Convolutional 1D Neural Network-Based Training

We used a convolutional one-dimensional (1D) neural network from Keras for training and testing. The architecture consists of Conv1D is displayed below.

Ordered Model.

5.5.2.1 Sequential Model

Using the sequential paradigm makes it simple to stack sequential layers of the network—and even recurrent layers—from input to outcome. The model type is declared as sequential in the first line ().

5.5.2.2 *Add 1D Convolutional Layer*

Include a 1D convolutional layer to handle vectorized data. Filters and kernel size are covered in this tier. The commonly used filter sizes are 250 and 3, respectively.

We must then provide the model the size of the input for the layer because the activation function is a rectified linear unit. The input shape only needs to come from the first layer; beyond that, Keras is able to determine the amount of the tensors passing through the system.

5.5.2.3 *Adding 1D Max Pooling Layer*

Add a layer of 1D max pooling. We merely mention the pooling layer.

5.5.2.4 *Adding Dense Layer*

The next two lines declare that all of our levels are interconnected. We provide the amount using Keras' Dense () layer and, in keeping with our design, 250 nodes, each of which is triggered by a ReLU function. The second is our output layer, also known as sigmoid activation.

5.5.2.5 *Neural Network Training*

```
model = Sequential()

model.add(Embedding(max_features,embedding_dims,input_length=maxlen))
model.add(Conv1D(filters,kernel_size,padding='valid',activation='relu',strides=1))
# we use max pooling:
model.add(GlobalMaxPooling1D())

# We add a vanilla hidden layer:
model.add(Dense(hidden_dims))
model.add(Dropout(0.2))
model.add(Activation('relu'))

# We project onto a single unit output layer, and squash it with a sigmoid:
model.add(Dense(1))
model.add(Activation('sigmoid'))

model.compile(loss='binary_crossentropy',optimizer='adam',metrics=['accuracy'])
```

In order to tell the framework which sort of optimizer to employ, we must either define the loss function in the training model (i.e., gradient descent and Adam optimizer).

5.5.3 AdaBoost Algorithm

The ensemble learning technique used by ML is called AdaBoost, which is also known as adaptive boosting. Distributing the proportions to each instance while giving instances that were mistakenly recognized a bigger weight is known as adaptive boosting. In supervised learning, boosting is used to lessen bias and variation. It is predicated on the notion that infants develop gradually. Every student after the first is derived from a prior learner, with the exception of the first. It is a good idea to have a backup strategy in case the backup fails. Boosting is conceptually similar to the AdaBoost approach; however, it is slightly different. Below is a list of this algorithm's fundamental steps.

Using an ensemble approach called "boosting," weak classifiers are combined to try to produce stronger classifiers. Compared to many AI models that focus on great prediction achieved using a single model, boosting algorithms try to increase prediction power by training a sequence of weak designs, each of which corrects the flaws of its predecessors. Machine learning models can improve their prediction accuracy thanks to boosting.

A model of decision trees with a depth of one guides the AdaBoost approach. AdaBoost is nothing more than a wilderness of treeless stumps. AdaBoost functions by giving cases that are challenging to categorize more weight and cases that have been treated well less weight. The AdaBoost method was developed to address classification and regression problems.

Stumps, which consist of one node and two leaves, are only weak learners and poor classifiers because they have trouble making precise classifications. The AdaBoost algorithm is based on the idea that, by combining many weak classifiers, a powerful classifier can be produced.

Step 1: Assign each observation an equal weight
Initially assign same weights to each record in the dataset.
Sample weight = 1/N
Where N = Number of records

Step 2: Sort arbitrary samples using stumps
Draw replacement samples at random from the original data with probability equal to the weights of the samples and then fit the model. Here, decision trees are the model (base learning) that AdaBoost uses. One depth decision trees are produced, consisting of two leaves (also known as stumps)

and one node. Predict the categories for the initial information by fitting a model to the samples at random.

Step 3: Determine the total error
Total error is nothing but the sum of weights of misclassified record.
Total Error = Weights of misclassified records
Total error will be always between 0 and 1, where 0 represents perfect stump (correct classification) and 1 representsweak stump (misclassification).

Step 4: Calculate the stump's performance
Using the total error, determine the performance of the base learner. The weights are updated in subsequent iterations using the determined stump () value, which is also used to produce the final prediction. Performance of the stump(α) = ½ ln (1 – total error/total error).

Step 5: Revise the weights
Adjust the weights based on the stump's performance. By increasing the appropriate sample weight and lowering the average value of the correctly classified records, the next cycle must appropriately categorize the incorrectly classified record.

Step 6: Update weights in iteration
Make the second tree in the forest using the normalized weight. Using the recently updated sample weight, create a new dataset with repetition that is the same size as the original dataset.

5.6 Experimental Results and Evaluations

The suggested outcomes may be evaluated by classifying the output as Fake or Genuine Jobs. The proposed work is written in Python 3 and uses the libraries Keras, Tensorflow, Matplotlib, and other required libraries. CNN

CNN algorithm classification accuracy for providing epoch.

Epoch	Accuracy (%)
2	82
5	88

Performance of machine learning models.

Algorithm	Metrics	Values
Random forest	Accuracy	86%
AdaBoost	Accuracy	89%

is the deep learning algorithm used. The decision tree algorithm is used in ML. For the implementation, we trained with two types of jobs: fake and genuine. The figure below depicts the training and validation accuracy for job categorization.

5.7 Screenshots

Figure 5.3 shows the evaluation metric computed for RF-based on reviews. The plot indicates that the system's accuracy is 82%; other error metrics, such as the mean absolute error (MAE), mean squared error (MSE), R-squared error (RSE), and root mean square error (RMSE), are computed, and their corresponding values are 0.182, 0.182, 0.2, and 0.421, respectively.

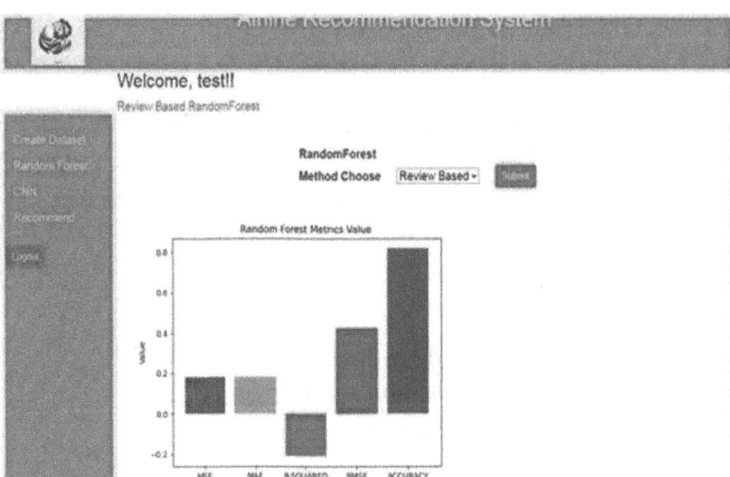

Figure 5.3 Accuracy and error analysis of random forest model in airline recommendation system.

Figure 5.4 shows the evaluation metric computed for RF-based on rating. The plot shows that the accuracy of the system is 89% and other The MAE, MSE, RSE, and RMSE metrics are computed, and the results are 0.08, 0.08, 0.45, and 0.321, accordingly.

Figure 5.5 shows the evaluation metric computed for CNN algorithm on review. The plot shows that the accuracy of training and validation dataset. The highest accuracy achieved for training dataset is 84.5%, and the highest validation accuracy achieved is 81.5%.

Figure 5.6 shows the evaluation metric computed for CNN algorithm based on reviews. The plot shows that the accuracy of the system is 82%, and other MAE, MSE, RSE, and RMSE are examples of error measures and are computed, and the values are 0.182, 0.182, 0.2, and 0.421, respectively.

Figure 5.7 shows the evaluation metric computed for CNN algorithm on rating. The plot shows that the accuracy of training and validation dataset. The highest accuracyachieved for training dataset is 97%, and the highest validation accuracy achieved is 95%.

Figure 5.8 shows the loss metric computed for CNN algorithm on review. The plot shows that the loss of training and validation dataset. The loss is 0.24 for training data and 0.16 for validation dataset.

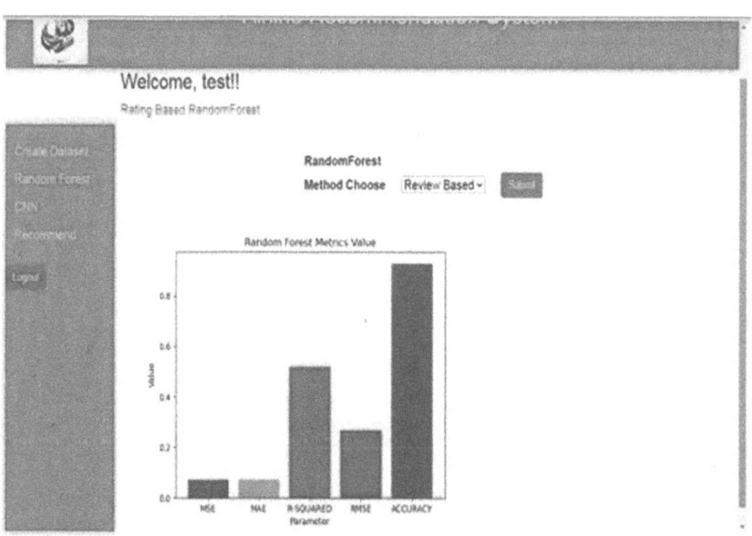

Figure 5.4 Performance metrics for airline recommendation system using random forest based on rating.

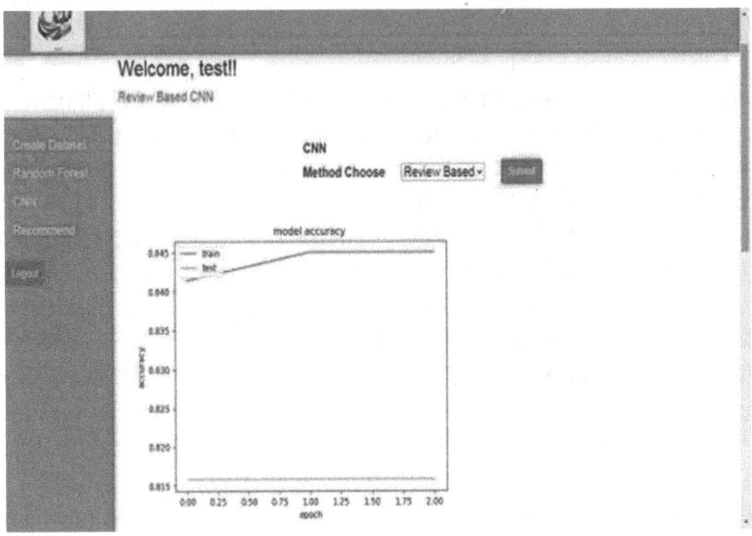

Figure 5.5 Training vs testing accuracy for CNN in airline recommendation system.

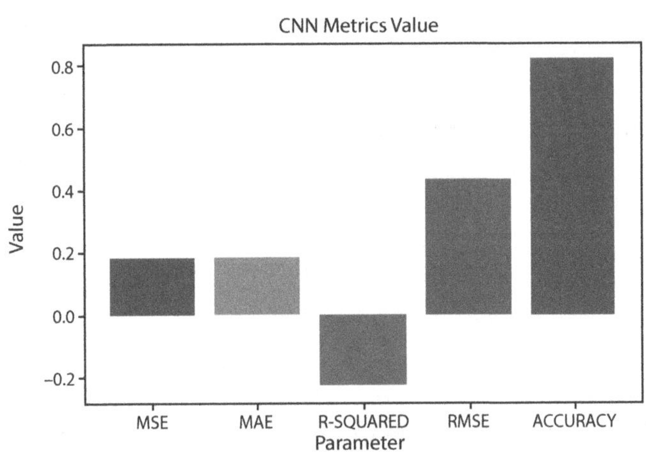

Figure 5.6 Comparison of CNN metrics: MSE, MAE, R-squared, RMSE, and accuracy.

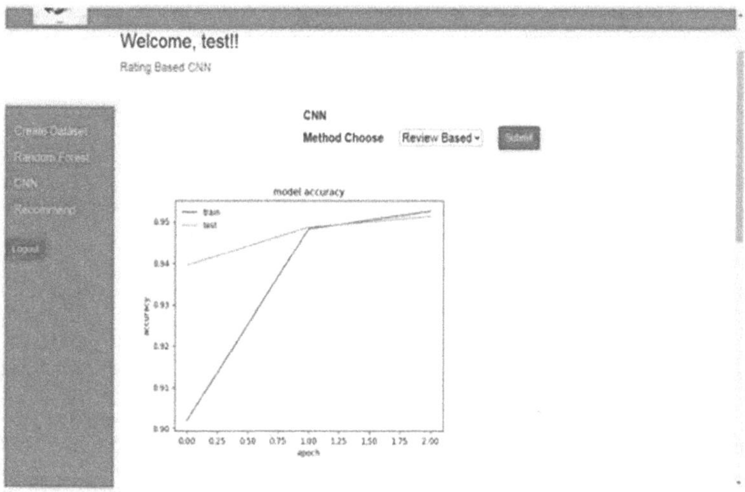

Figure 5.7 Training vs testing accuracy for CNN in airline recommendation system based training, validation dataset.

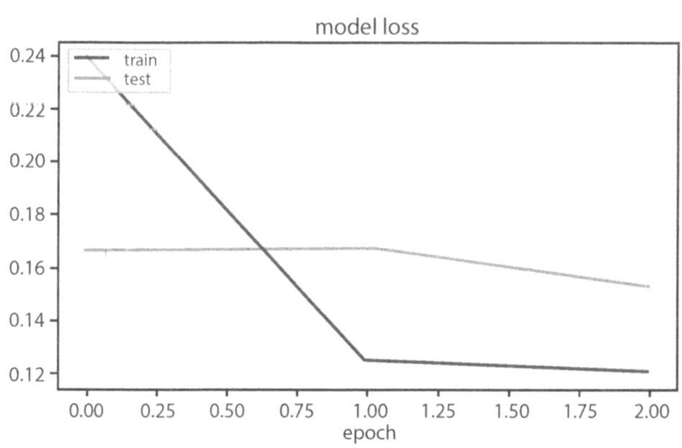

Figure 5.8 Loss metric computed for CNN algorithm based on review.

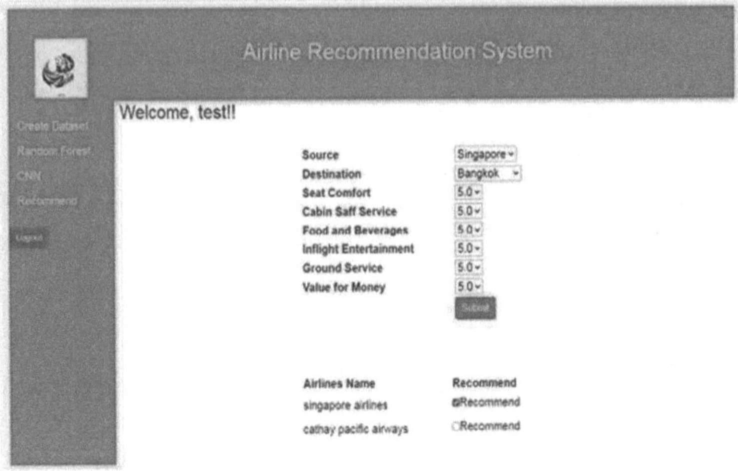

Figure 5.9 User page related to source and destination recommendation results.

The above Figure 5.9 shows the user page, where user can input source and destination, to get the results of recommended airlines are results based on the given rating. The recommended results are based on RF algorithm to get the recommended airlines; the result gives the top selected airlines based on the rating score computed.

5.8 Conclusion

The proposed study uses ML and NLP to forecast airlines based on customer evaluations and ratings.The reviews and ratings are categorized as either a "yes" or a "no" in terms of airline recommendation. CNN and RF algorithms were utilized in this research for deep learning classification. Real-time, live data from www.airlinequality.com is the dataset utilized. The application, which uses Flask Python, allows users to submit rating values to choose the best airline by prediction. According to experimental findings, rating-based RF has the best accuracy.

References

1. Gui, G., Liu, F., Sun, J., Yang, J., Zhou, Z., Zhao, D., *IEEE Transactions on Vehicular Technology*, vol. 69, pp. 140–150, Jan. 2020, doi: 10.1109/TVT.2019.2954094.

2. Choi, S., Kim, Y.J., Briceno, S., Mavris, D., *2016 IEEE/AIAA 35th Digital Avionics Systems Conference (DASC)*, pp. 1–6, 2016, doi: 10.1109/DASC.2016.7777956.
3. Natarajan, V., Meenakshisundaram, S., Balasubramanian, G., Sinha, S., *2018 International Conference on Computational Science and Computational Intelligence (CSCI)*, pp. 1081–1086, 2018, doi: 10.1109/CSCI46756.2018.00210.
4. Choi, S., Kim, Y.J., Briceno, S., Mavris, D., *2017 IEEE/AIAA 36th Digital Avionics Systems Conference (DASC)*, pp. 1–8, 2017, doi: 10.1109/DASC.2017.8102035.
5. Abdella, J.A., Zaki, N., Shuaib, K., *2018 International Conference on Innovations in Information Technology (IIT)*, pp. 169–174, 2018, doi: 10.1109/INNOVATIONS.2018.8606022.
6. Reichheld, F.F., The one number you need to grow, in: *Harvard business review*, vol. 81.12, pp. 46–55, 2003.
7. Keiningham, T.L., *et al.*, A longitudinal examination of net promoter and firm revenue growth. *J. Marketing*, 71.3, 39–51, 2007.
8. Oliver, R.L., Cognitive, affective, and attribute bases of the satisfaction response. *J. Consumer Res.*, 20.3, 418–430, 1993.
9. Jang, S., Ashutosh, P., Ratchford, B.T., How consumers use product reviews in the purchase decision process. *Marketing Lett.*, 23.3, 825–838, 2012.
10. Mudambi, S.M. and Schuff, D., What makes a helpful review? A study of customer reviews on Amazon.com. *MIS Q.*, 34.1, 185–200, 2010.
11. Ye, Q., *et al.*, The influence of user-generated content on traveler behavior: An empirical investigation on the effects of e-word-of-mouth to hotel online bookings. *Comput. Hum. Behav.*, 27.2, 634–639, 2011.
12. Chung, N., Han, H., Koo, C., Adoption of travel information in user generated content on social media: the moderating effect of social presence. *Behav. Inf. Technol.*, 34.9, 902–919, 2015.
13. Stavins, J., Price discrimination in the airline market: The effect of market concentration. *Rev. Econ. Stat.*, 83, 1, 200–202, 2001.
14. Tziridis, K., Kalampokas, T., Papakostas, G.A., Diamantaras, K.I., Airfare prices prediction using machine learning techniques, *2017 25th European Signal Processing Conference (EUSIPCO)*, pp. 1036–1039, Kos, Greece, 2017, doi: 10.23919/EUSIPCO.2017.8081365.
15. Groves, W. and Gini, M., An agent for optimizing airline ticket purchasing, in: *Proceedings of the 2013 international conference on autonomous agents and multi-agent systems.*
16. Santos Dominguez-Menchero, J., Rivera, J., Torres Manzanera, E., Concepts for designing low power wireless sensor network. *Optimal purchase timing in the airline market.*
17. Supriya Rajankar, Neha Sakharkar, A Survey on Flight Pricing Prediction using Machine Learning. *Int. J. Eng. Res. Technol. (IJERT)*, 8, 6, 1281–1284, June 2019.

18. Wang, I., Pouyanfar, S., Tian, H., Tao, Y., A Framework for airline price prediction: A machine learning approach.
19. Janssen, T., A linear quantile mixed regression model for prediction of airline ticket prices.
20. Wang, T., *et al.*, A framework for airfare price prediction: A machine learning approach. *2019 IEEE 20th International Conference on Information Reuse and Integration for Data Science (IRI)*, IEEE, 2019.
21. Abdella, J.A., *et al.*, Airline ticket price and demand prediction: A survey. *J. King Saud Univ. Comput. Inf. Sci.*, 33.4, 375–391, 2021.
22. Zhao-Jun, G., Shuang, W., Yi, Z., Flight ticket fare prediction model based on timeserial. *J. Civ. Aviat. Univ. China*, 31.2, 80, 2013.
23. Huang, T., Chen, C.-C., Schwartz, Z., Do I book at exactly the right time? Airfare forecast accuracy across three price-prediction platforms. *J. Revenue Pricing Manage.*, 18.4, 281–290, 2019.
24. Chakravarty, S., Mohapatra, P., Dash, P.K., Evolutionary Extreme Learning Machine for Energy Price Forecasting. *Int. J. Knowledge-Based Intell. Eng. Syst.*, 20, 75–96, 2016.
25. https://www.kaggle.com/datasets/nikhilmittal/flight-fare-prediction-mh.

6

The Breakthrough of Future Delivery: Delivery Robots

Ayushi Gupta

School of Computer Engineering, KIIT, Deemed to be University, Bhubaneshwar, India

Abstract

In the past few years, owing to the COVID-19 pandemic, there has been a significant shift toward online mode. Amid this highly infectious pandemic, the need for contactless exchange of goods with the outside market arose. Delivery robots emerged as a solution to this need. While delivery robots were in use before the pandemic, their usage saw a surge during this period due to their advantages, including contactless delivery, reduced need for manpower, and lower pollution levels. Additionally, they have the potential to save many lives, as road accidents claimed the lives of several delivery personnel each month. The primary aim of this paper is to provide an overview of delivery robots, including their evolution, functioning, applications, and benefits, as well as the challenges they face. It also explores the potential of delivery robots in achieving the goals of the Emerging Disruptive Technologies for Society 5.0 initiative, and it provides examples of how delivery robots are already being used in various industries worldwide.

***Keywords*:** Delivery robots, future delivery, service delivery, autonomous delivery robot

6.1 Introduction

In today's era of digitization, every industry is trying to make its operations more digital, so why should the field of delivery lag behind? We have all heard of cases where delivery personnel have met with accidents

Email: ayushigupta.9901@gmail.com

Subhasis Dash, Manas Ranjan Lenka, S. Balamurugan, Ambika Prasad Tripathy and Amarendra Mohanty (eds.) Sustainable Resource Management in Next-Generation Computational Constrained Networks, (133–168) © 2025 Scrivener Publishing LLC

while delivering orders on time and, sometimes, even lost their lives. In fact, the risk of such situations could be reduced if delivery robots were used instead.

Also, over the past few years, the world has undergone a significant transformation due to the COVID-19 pandemic. To minimize physical contact and curb the spread of the virus, people have increasingly relied on online platforms for their daily needs. This shift has also affected the way that we exchange goods with the outside world. In this scenario, delivery robots have emerged as a viable solution that enables contactless delivery of goods to customers' doorsteps. These robots have revolutionized the traditional delivery mechanism by eliminating the need for human contact and offering a safer and more efficient way to deliver goods during this challenging time. As a result, the use of delivery robots has become increasingly popular and has paved the way for a new era of contactless delivery.

Emerging Disruptive Technologies for Society 5.0 aims to create a futuristic society where new services are developed to make people's lives more comfortable and sustainable. This includes 17 goals and 169 targets, including environmental, social, and human developmental objectives. Delivery robots are one such technology that could revolutionize the way we deliver products, offering numerous advantages over traditional methods.

Delivery robots are already being used in different industries around the world, from food delivery in restaurants to guidance in hotels and nursing homes. These robots are automated and bring deliveries directly to customers' doorsteps, without requiring any human intervention in the process. They can navigate around people and public spaces without a human driver, making them safe and efficient.

With the rise of e-commerce and the increased demand for online purchasing, companies are adopting various delivery methods to ensure their products reach customers in a better and more efficient way. Delivery robots are one of the most promising methods in this regard.

Starship Technologies, a company founded in Estonia by the co-founder and chief architect of Skype, Ahti Heinla, and Janus Friis, is one of the pioneers in the delivery robot industry. Since its inception in 2014, the company has completed over 3.5 million commercial deliveries, covering a distance of more than 7 million km globally, making it one of the most successful in the field. By using delivery robots, companies like Starship Technologies are revolutionizing the way we shop and receive deliveries, making our lives more convenient and sustainable.

Delivery by robots provides several advantages over traditional delivery methods. These benefits are summarized in the following Table 6.1.

Table 6.1 Difference between traditional robots and delivery by robots.

	Traditional delivery	**Delivery by robot**
I)	Human being required for delivery purpose	Robots required for delivery purpose
II)	Higher cost due to personnel and vehicle expenses (refer Figure 6.1 for the detailed cost analysis)	Lower cost comparatively
III)	Limited delivery hours as a particular person would not be available for 24/7	Robots can be made available for 24/7
IV)	High risk for life.	No such risk for life
V)	Limited delivery distance based on personnel availability	Greater delivery distance and coverage
VI)	Contact-based delivery	Contactless delivery
VII)	Can deal with exceptional situation (example: giving way to ambulance).	Cannot deal with exceptional situation (example: giving way to ambulance)

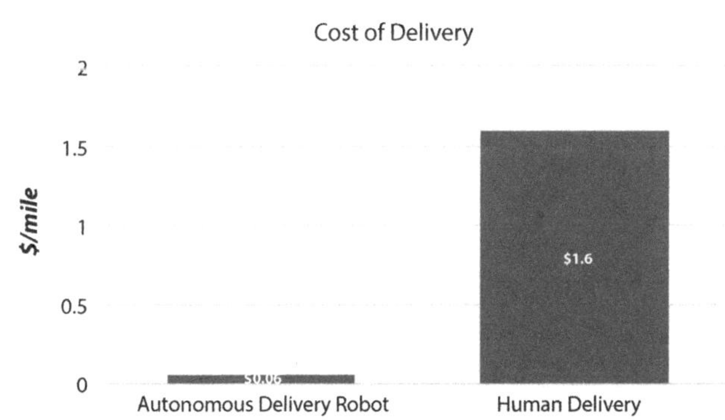

Figure 6.1 Cost of delivery for delivery robots and traditional robots.

In comparison to traditional delivery, delivery by robots eliminates the need for human intervention in the delivery process, reducing the risk of accidents and injuries. Moreover, robots can be available 24/7 and can deliver to a larger coverage area, providing more convenience and accessibility to customers. Delivery by robots also offers contactless delivery, which has become increasingly important in light of the COVID-19 pandemic. However, delivery robots may not be able to handle exceptional situations such as emergencies, requiring the need for human intervention. Overall, delivery robots offer several advantages over traditional delivery methods, making them a promising technology for the future of delivery services. The major contributions of the work are as follows:

- In this work, we have differentiated between traditional delivery system and delivery by robots. Also, a clear distinction is made between land-based delivery robots and aerial drones, highlighting their respective capabilities and limitations.
- Furthermore, we delve into the evolution of delivery robots, their working principles, and provide an overview of the delivery robot system (DRS).
- Additionally, we highlight the various benefits and applications of delivery robots, such as improved efficiency, reduced costs, and enhanced customer experience. This comprehensive overview of potential use cases highlights the broad impact that delivery robots can have on society.
- Moreover, we also explore the challenges faced by delivery robots, including technical limitations, legal and regulatory issues, and societal acceptance. The study also highlights the potential for future advancements in delivery robot technology.

6.2 Related Work

Delivery robots have received substantial attention in recent years for their potential to transform the transportation and delivery of goods. Researchers have conducted multiple studies and proposed diverse methods to enhance the performance of delivery robots in various settings. Figures 6.2 to 6.25 demonstrate various aspects of delivery robot deployment and applications, as referenced sequentially in the text. For example, Zeng *et al.* (2020) [2] presented a multi-robot task allocation method for the effective delivery of goods. This method incorporated a combination of genetic algorithms and a task partitioning algorithm to allocate tasks among multiple robots. In another study, Miao *et al.* (2021) [3] proposed a deep reinforcement learning–based approach for autonomous package delivery. This approach utilized a neural network to learn the optimal delivery policy, which was then employed to guide the robot's actions.

Additionally, Dong *et al.* (2020) [4] developed a DRS that integrated computer vision, natural language processing, and path planning algorithms to navigate indoor environments and deliver goods.

Sharma *et al.* (2020) [5] proposed a hybrid approach for path planning and obstacle avoidance in delivery robots. This method combined a genetic algorithm with a fuzzy logic controller to optimize the robot's path while avoiding obstacles. Furthermore, Huang *et al.* (2021) [6] presented a modular robotic system for last-mile delivery, which incorporated a combination of drones and ground-based robots to deliver packages in a cost-effective and efficient manner. These studies demonstrate the range of methods that researchers have explored to enhance the capabilities of delivery robots.

A multi-objective optimization method for scheduling delivery robots in a logistics network was proposed by Chen *et al.* (2020) to optimize delivery efficiency while minimizing delivery costs. Chen *et al.* (2019) proposed a swarm intelligence–based algorithm for task allocation in a large-scale delivery robot network. Wang *et al.* (2020) proposed a model predictive control–based approach for autonomous package delivery by aerial drones utilizing a predictive model to plan and execute delivery trajectories. Yuan *et al.* (2021) proposed a cooperative control strategy for a group of ground-based delivery robots utilizing a consensus-based algorithm to coordinate the movement of the robots and optimize delivery efficiency. Yang *et al.* (2020) proposed a path planning algorithm for autonomous delivery robots

Figure 6.2 The future of delivery robots [1].

that used a combination of Monte Carlo localization and occupancy grid mapping. Wu *et al.* (2021) proposed a swarm intelligence–based approach for autonomous parcel delivery in a large-scale logistics network utilizing a particle swarm optimization algorithm to optimize delivery routes. A study by A. Birolini provides a comparative review of delivery drones and robots [7], examining their applications, regulatory framework, and impact on society. The authors found that delivery drones and robots have the potential to reduce traffic congestion, carbon emissions, and delivery costs. However, the authors also highlight the need for clear regulations and guidelines to ensure safe and efficient use of the technology.

Overall, continued research and development are crucial to advance the field of delivery robots and address the challenges that arise with their integration into various environments. Such challenges include scalability, adaptability, robustness, and ethical concerns. The findings from these studies and further research can lead to the successful implementation of delivery robots in various industries and significantly impact the transportation and delivery of goods.

6.3 Evolution of Delivery Robot

Delivery robots were once considered a topic solely within the realm of science fiction. They have undergone several developmental stages, ranging from their early experimental prototypes to the advanced and efficient robots that we see today. The evolution of these robots can be briefly summarized as follows:

- Early Prototypes: The first delivery robots were developed in the early 2000s as basic machines that could transport small loads and navigate flat surfaces. However, these early prototypes were often unreliable, slow, and costly, requiring significant human intervention to function correctly.
- Segway-Based Robots: In the mid-2000s, several companies began developing delivery robots that were based on the Segway platform. These robots had improved capabilities to carry larger loads and navigate more complex environments. However, they remained relatively slow and had limited features.
- Advanced Autonomous Robots: In recent years, delivery robots have become increasingly advanced, thanks to improvements in autonomous technology, sensors, and

machine learning algorithms. These robots can now navigate complex environments, avoid obstacles, and interact with humans in various ways. They can also transport larger and heavier loads and can even climb stairs and open doors.

- Last-Mile Delivery Robots: One of the most notable developments in delivery robots has been the emergence of last-mile delivery robots. These robots are specifically designed to deliver packages directly to customers' homes, thereby reducing the need for human drivers and lowering delivery costs. Last-mile delivery robots are often lightweight and operate on sidewalks and bike lanes.

Overall, the evolution of delivery robots has been driven by technological advancements, a surge in demand for faster and more efficient delivery, and the necessity to reduce costs and enhance sustainability in the delivery industry. These factors have motivated researchers and developers to create delivery robots that can handle the complexities and demands of the modern world.

However, Starship, a company at the forefront of this technology, successfully deployed its first autonomous delivery robots commercially. Starship Technologies pioneered the utilization of delivery robots as its primary mode of delivery. Prior to this, the service underwent extensive testing in over 100 cities and 20 countries worldwide. Starship currently

Figure 6.3 An in-depth examination of a Starship delivery robot engaged in winter operation, with a visible array of cameras [8].

operates in various countries including the United States, the United Kingdom, Germany, Finland, and Estonia, with its primary focus on delivery services for college campuses since 2019 [2]. The company aims to expand its service to 100 university campuses in the United States, with a target of reaching one million students. During the COVID-19 pandemic, Starship expanded the use of its delivery robots to assist with grocery delivery in the UK and the US, as a response to the delivery driver shortage.

In March 2020, Starship made history as the first robot delivery service to operate in a British town center when it launched its service in Milton Keynes. By November 2020, Milton Keynes boasted the largest fleet of autonomous robots globally. As of March 2023, Starship was delivering in seven British cities.

In January 2019, Starship collaborated with Sodexo to launch robot food delivery services at George Mason University in Virginia, US. With a fleet of 25 robots at launch, this marked the most extensive implementation of autonomous robot food delivery services on a university campus at the time. In 2019, Starship expanded its services to other US universities, including Northern Arizona University, Purdue University, University of Pittsburgh, James Madison University, University of Wisconsin, University of Houston, and University of Texas at Dallas and, in 2020, to the University of Mississippi and Bowling Green State University. After the US universities reopened in 2020, Starship rehired many of its staff that it had previously made redundant.

As of October 2021, Starship had completed over 2 million deliveries worldwide, with over 100,000 road crossings daily. The company achieved 100,000 deliveries in August 2019 and 500,000 deliveries in June 2020. As of January 2022, Starship's autonomous delivery robots had completed over 2.5 million autonomous deliveries and traveled over 3 million miles globally, averaging around 10,000 deliveries per day.

Starship's delivery robots possess features that enhance their delivery capabilities. They operate through a combination of electric power, advanced sensor technology, artificial intelligence, and machine learning algorithms. Additionally, they employ computer vision–based navigation systems to meticulously map their surroundings, enabling them to identify the quickest and safest delivery routes. Consequently, these advanced capabilities significantly reduce both delivery times and the associated carbon footprint. The energy consumed by the average Starship delivery robot during an operation is equivalent to the amount required by a kettle to boil water for a single cup of tea.

Starship's delivery robots are electrically powered and designed for last-mile delivery. They can reach a maximum speed of 6 km/h (3.7 mph) on sidewalks, with remote control available in the event of autonomous operation failure. They are only suitable for local delivery over relatively short distances. These robots employ feature detection and mapping techniques to determine the navigability of terrain, with the ability to carry up to 20 pounds (9.1 kg) of deliveries and weigh 55 pounds (25 kg) unloaded. Their average battery life is 18 h, and a typical robot can travel around 40 km per day. These robots are equipped with various sensors, including cameras, GPS, inertial measurement, ultrasonic sensors, and radar, as well as loudspeakers for communication with humans. Users order Starship deliveries using the company's iOS and Android applications, and upon arrival for delivery, the robot's biometric authentication technology verifies the user's identity.

These delivery robots are powered by machine learning algorithms, constantly improving their efficiency and safety. While most work is carried out autonomously, human operators are available to intervene if required. The robots are equipped with sensors, including cameras with machine vision, radar, and ultrasonic sensors, to detect solid objects like curbs and walls.

The advent of delivery robots does not pose a threat to human employment but rather presents an opportunity for the creation of new job roles. Such roles may include those involved in maintaining the robots, providing services to merchants, and developing software applications for phones and tablets.

It is worth noting that land-based delivery robots have certain limitations in dealing with emergency situations, such as yielding to an ambulance. To address this issue, researchers are currently exploring the use of aerial drones for rapid delivery. This approach has the potential to overcome some of the challenges faced by ground-based robots while also creating additional employment opportunities in the field of drone technology.

6.4 Working Principal/Model of Delivery Robots

Delivery robots employ a range of distinct processes in order to function efficiently. In the following section, we present an overview of the key procedures that are integral to the operational model of these robots:

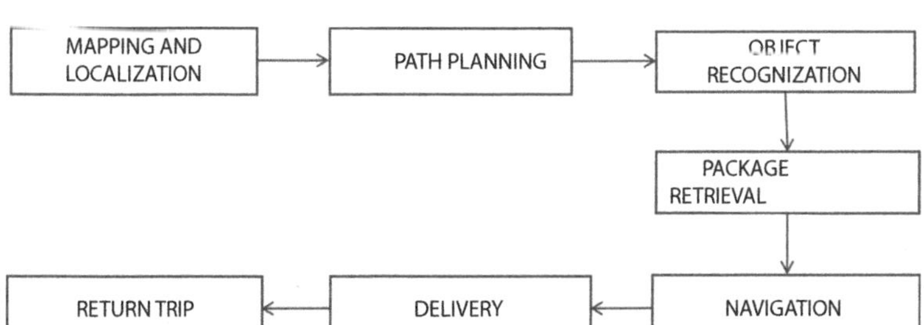

i. Mapping and Localization: Delivery robots employ a range of sensors and cameras to map their surrounding environment and to determine their location within this spatial context. By utilizing this information, delivery robots can effectively plan their route to avoid potential obstacles.
ii. Path Planning: Once the robot has generated a map of its environment, it uses an algorithm to optimize the most efficient path to its destination. This algorithm factors in variables such as distance, traffic, and potential obstructions.
iii. Object Recognition: Delivery robots are equipped with advanced sensors and cameras that enable them to identify and differentiate between various objects. This capability is crucial in enabling delivery robots to locate the specific package that they are tasked to deliver.
iv. Package Retrieval: Upon successfully identifying the package, the delivery robot employs a mechanical arm or other suitable mechanism to collect and securely store the package within its delivery compartment.
v. Navigation: The delivery robot utilizes the map and optimized path generated through the path planning algorithm in order to safely and efficiently navigate to its destination. The robot may employ a range of positioning systems such as GPS or inertial sensors to maintain accurate location information.
vi. Delivery: Once the robot has successfully reached the destination, it employs its mechanical arm or other suitable mechanism to deliver the package to the recipient.
vii. Return Trip: After successfully completing delivery, the robot may return to its starting point to collect another package, thereby initiating the delivery process once again.

In summary, delivery robots operate through a combination of advanced mapping, path planning, object recognition, navigation, and package delivery technologies, all of which function together to achieve safe and efficient transportation of packages from one location to another.

(The system includes delivery robots that transport objects from a warehouse to working stations located throughout a factory area. Each robot is battery-powered and autonomous, with specific features such as maximum speed, maximum weight, and the types of objects that it can transport. Robots can be of two types: fast or slow. They communicate with a

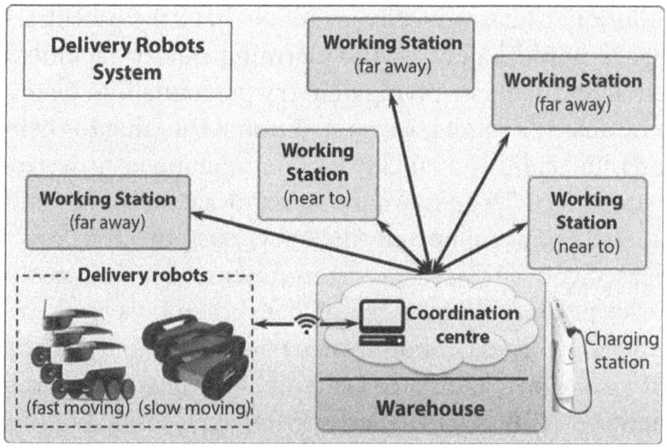

Figure 6.4 Delivery robots system overview [9].

coordination center to receive job requests and indicate their battery levels, availability, and speed. The coordination center is responsible for managing job requests from working stations and assigning them to available robots based on their characteristics and the features of the job requests. The performance requirements of the DRS include finding the system configuration that minimizes the average response time. The assignment policy of the coordination center has to consider the features of the robots and the types of job requests in order to select the most suitable robot for each task. Requests are queued and assigned to robots when they become available. The working stations generate requests of objects to the coordination center with either a certain frequency or a list of requests submitted simultaneously.)

6.5 Benefits of Delivery Robots

Over the recent years, there has been a noteworthy shift toward the adoption of online modalities, largely attributed to the onset of the COVID-19 pandemic. The pandemic has necessitated the minimization of physical contact, prompting the exploration of contactless means of exchanging goods with external markets. To address this need, delivery robots have surfaced as a viable solution. Although their utilization preceded the pandemic, their prevalence has experienced a marked increase during this time due to their myriad of advantages, which include but are not limited to contactless delivery, reduced reliance on human resources, and diminished levels of pollution. Moreover, delivery robots have the potential to significantly improve public safety, as the alarming rate of fatalities, resulting from vehicular accidents involving delivery personnel can be mitigated.

The use of delivery robots has gained popularity due to their ability to deliver goods efficiently and quickly while simultaneously decreasing costs and increasing safety. This essay aims to elaborate on the benefits of delivery robots, including enhanced efficiency, cost-effectiveness, improved safety, increased convenience, and environmental friendliness.

One of the primary advantages of delivery robots is their ability to improve efficiency. These robots can navigate through traffic and busy streets with ease, which allows for faster delivery of goods than traditional delivery methods. This is particularly crucial in densely populated urban areas, where traffic congestion and limited parking can make conventional delivery methods slow and inefficient. By employing delivery robots, businesses can enhance the speed and dependability of their deliveries, thereby gaining a competitive edge in the market.

Furthermore, delivery robots offer substantial cost savings, eliminating the need for human delivery personnel. The costs associated with hiring, training, and managing human personnel, coupled with benefits such as healthcare and retirement plans can be exorbitant. Conversely, delivery robots do not require such benefits and can work non-stop without getting tired or needing breaks. This translates into significant cost savings for businesses, particularly those that demand frequent or high-volume deliveries.

In addition to augmenting efficiency and reducing costs, delivery robots also increase safety. By eliminating the need for human delivery personnel, these robots reduce the risk of accidents and injuries associated with delivery. Human delivery personnel may be susceptible to accidents and injuries due to traffic accidents, falls, or other hazards, especially in busy urban areas. Delivery robots are designed to navigate these hazards safely and efficiently, mitigating the risk of accidents and injuries.

Delivery robots also offer increased convenience for customers. Traditional delivery methods are restricted by the availability of human delivery personnel, making it challenging to provide deliveries outside of regular business hours. By utilizing delivery robots, businesses can offer their customers 24/7 delivery services, enhancing convenience and customer satisfaction. Customers can receive deliveries at any time, which is particularly beneficial for those with unconventional work hours or busy schedules.

Lastly, delivery robots can be engineered to run on electricity or other clean energy sources, promoting a sustainable delivery system and reducing carbon emissions. Traditional delivery methods, such as delivery trucks and vans, can substantially contribute to air pollution and climate change. Delivery robots, on the other hand, can be designed to operate on clean energy sources, which can reduce emissions and promote sustainability, particularly in urban areas where air pollution can pose a severe health hazard. Table 6.2 shows the list of delivery robot types and their respective features.

In conclusion, the benefits of delivery robots are numerous and multifaceted. By improving efficiency, reducing costs, increasing safety, enhancing convenience, and promoting sustainability, delivery robots offer businesses and customers a range of advantages that conventional delivery methods cannot match. As technology advances, delivery robots are poised to become more sophisticated and versatile, further expanding their potential benefits. So, the main advantages that delivery robots offer are the following:

- mitigate environmental pollution and curtail emissions, thereby promoting sustainability;
- significantly enhance public safety and avert the loss of human lives;
- alleviate traffic congestion on roadways and promote more efficient transportation systems;
- augment last-mile delivery services, which are critical for ensuring the timely delivery of goods to end consumers;
- reduce the cost of transportation for businesses, which is instrumental in boosting economic competitiveness;
- diminish the expenses associated with maintenance and upkeep, further contributing to cost savings;
- enhance transport inter-connectivity and facilitate seamless connectivity across diverse transportation modes.

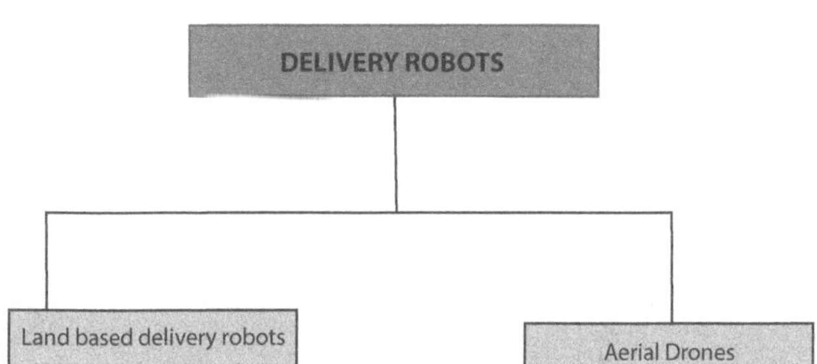

Table 6.2 Some difference between land-based delivery robots and aerial drones.

Basic information	The majority of ground-based delivery robots exhibit a box-shaped form factor, equipped with wheels for locomotion. These machines can be classified into three distinct categories: The first is confined to indoor environments, whereas the second category operates along pedestrian pathways and crosswalks, although not on public roads; the third category comprises autonomous vehicles designed for over-the-road transportation, enabled by advanced self-driving capabilities.	Aerial drones commonly are aircraft that lack a human pilot on board. Due to their high speed and agility, they are well-suited for rapid delivery of small packages over short distances. Moreover, they can be utilized to deliver goods to remote or geographically inaccessible locations, including rural areas and areas impacted by natural disasters.

(Continued)

Table 6.2 Some difference between land-based delivery robots and aerial drones. (*Continued*)

Advantage	• The implementation of a robot fleet can significantly expedite delivery times, eliminating the need to wait for the availability of delivery personnel. This can result in increased efficiency and customer satisfaction. • The utilization of robots in low-value tasks can free up human personnel to engage in higher-value activities, such as providing patient care or attending to customers in a restaurant. This can enhance the quality of service provided and potentially lead to improved outcomes. • Amidst labor shortages, the implementation of robots can reduce dependence on human personnel for low-value tasks. This can help mitigate the impact of labor shortages on businesses and organizations. • Robots are not subject to fatigue or downtime, resulting in more predictable delivery schedules. This can lead to increased efficiency and productivity. • The deployment of robots can lead to increased productivity, enabling organizations to accomplish more tasks with existing human resources. • The use of robots in transportation can be less costly than utilizing human personnel, potentially leading to significant cost savings for businesses and organizations. • In the context of a pandemic environment, contactless delivery is critical for ensuring the safety of customers and personnel. The implementation of robots can facilitate contactless delivery, enabling customers to retrieve their goods without the need for contact with another person.	• The implementation of aerial delivery robots may provide businesses with the opportunity to reduce their transportation expenses by eliminating the need for human drivers, fuel, and vehicle maintenance. • These robots can reduce the number of human-operated vehicles on the road, thereby reducing the risk of accidents and injuries that are often associated with traditional delivery methods. • The use of these robots can help decrease carbon emissions and other types of pollution that are linked to traditional delivery methods, such as delivery trucks and vans. • These can access remote or hard-to-reach areas, such as rural regions or regions affected by natural disasters that may be difficult or impossible to reach by conventional delivery methods. • In a pandemic environment, aerial delivery robots can offer contactless delivery, which enables customers to retrieve their items without the need for direct contact with another person.

(*Continued*)

Table 6.2 Some difference between land-based delivery robots and aerial drones. (*Continued*)

	 **Figure 6.5** Picture depicting the working station of autonomous delivery robots [10].	 **Figure 6.6** Aerial drones delivering the orders [11].
Limitations	• Autonomous systems may not have the capability to handle unexpected or exceptional situations, such as yielding to a blind person or an ambulance. This can be attributed to their limited ability to process and respond to unanticipated events or scenarios that fall outside of their programmed parameters. The inability of autonomous systems to address these exceptional situations may pose potential risks to the safety and well-being of individuals and may require human intervention to resolve.	• The adoption of delivery robot technology is hindered by safety considerations and regulatory approval. • The carrying capacity of these robots is restricted due to weight restrictions, prohibiting the delivery of larger and heavier packages. • Small unmanned aerial drones are vulnerable to harsh weather conditions and may be adversely impacted. Additionally, they may be damaged by bird strikes, which may compromise their overall safety and reliability.

6.6 Applications of Delivery Robots

Unmanned delivery robots possess a wide range of potential applications across various industries. The following are a few examples:

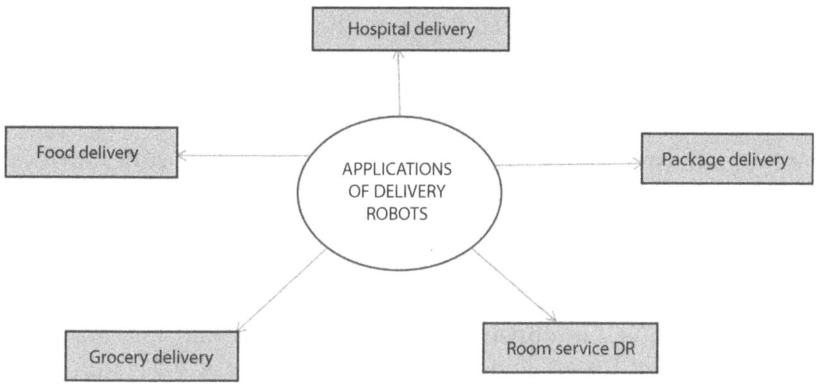

- Hospital Delivery

During the COVID-19 pandemic, delivery robots emerged as a safe means of conducting contactless delivery, prompting many companies to adopt them, particularly for food and medical door-to-door deliveries. In March 2021, the AIN pharmacy implemented autonomous delivery of medication

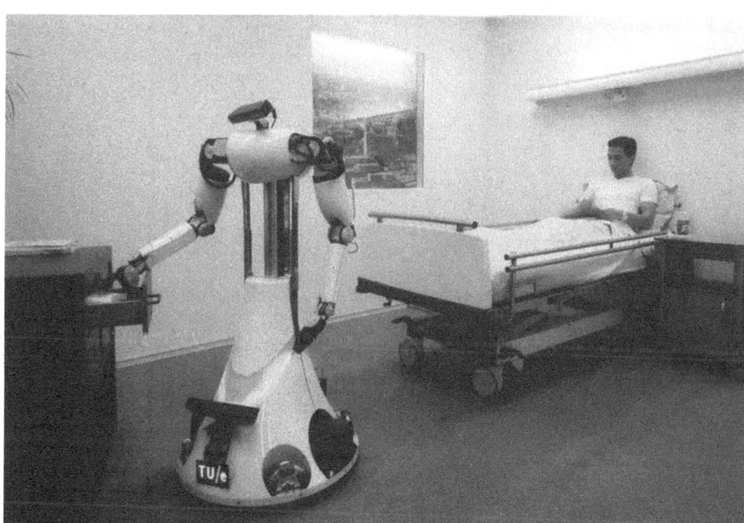

Figure 6.7 Robot taking care of the patient [12].

to patients' residences. Delivery robots have also been deployed in various hospitality and health care settings, such as guiding guests to their rooms, transporting items to customer rooms, providing food services, carrying luggage, and transporting waste to the disposal area. Moreover, delivery robots have been utilized for delivering test samples from patient rooms to laboratories, carrying soiled linens to the laundry, delivering food to patients' rooms, and delivering mail and packages to patients' rooms.

- Food Delivery

The food industry has been engaging in collaborative partnerships with delivery robot manufacturers in order to facilitate contactless and efficient food delivery. In addition to logistics and e-commerce sectors, food industries are incorporating delivery robots to deliver food directly to customers' doorsteps. An example of such a partnership is the collaboration between Domino's, a multinational pizza restaurant chain, and Nuro, Inc., a manufacturer of autonomous delivery robots. In April 2021, Nuro began providing driver-less deliveries of Domino's orders to customers through its autonomous delivery robot as part of the collaboration.

- Grocery Delivery

In the grocery industry, delivery robots are increasingly employed to offer customers convenient and efficient delivery services. These autonomous machines can navigate through city streets and sidewalks, bringing

Figure 6.8 DR are at work delivering food from Domino's Pizza [13].

Figure 6.9 Supermarket using robot's to deliver groceries [14].

groceries directly to the customers' doorstep, thereby eliminating the need for human delivery personnel. The utilization of delivery robots in grocery delivery offers various advantages such as faster delivery times, reduced delivery costs, and improved order accuracy. Large grocery retailers, including Walmart, Kroger, and Amazon, have already integrated delivery robot technology in select markets, and this trend is expected to expand in the future. Delivery robots have the potential to revolutionize the grocery delivery process and provide customers with a more convenient and seamless shopping experience.

- Package Delivery

The global delivery robot market is expected to witness significant growth due to advancements in the e-commerce industry and the increasing demand for contactless delivery services. The emergence of online shopping has resulted in a greater need for efficient and improved delivery services, leading to a rise in the adoption of last-mile options such as curbside pickup, parcel lockers, and automated delivery. This trend is further expected to augment the demand for delivery robots. Moreover, to cater to the surge in orders in the e-commerce industry, companies are collaborating with various delivery robot manufacturers to introduce robots for package delivery.

Figure 6.10 ANYmal robot delivering packages [15].

- Room Service Delivery Robot

Autonomous room service delivery robots have been developed to provide convenient and contactless delivery of food, beverages, and other amenities to guests residing in hotels or other hospitality establishments. These robots are capable of navigating through hallways and elevators and delivering the requested items directly to guests' rooms.

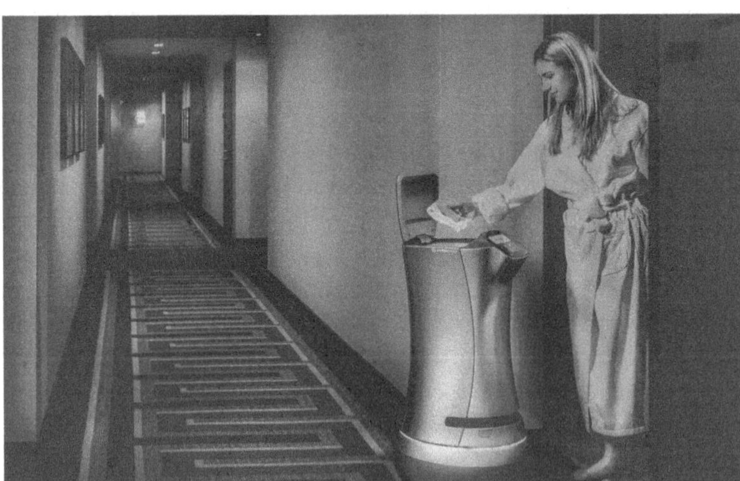

Figure 6.11 Robots giving room services to people [16].

Implementing room service delivery robots can result in a reduction of human staff needed for the delivery process, resulting in a saving of time and resources while ensuring accurate and prompt delivery to guests.

6.7 Development Projects

- Amazon Scout Robot

Amazon Scout [17] is a revolutionary delivery system that utilizes small, autonomous robots to deliver packages to customers. These robots are equipped with advanced sensors and algorithms [18] that allow them to navigate sidewalks and crosswalks to reach their destination. They are designed to operate in daylight hours and in good weather conditions, and they travel at a walking pace.

One of the primary advantages of using the Amazon Scout robots is that they are eco-friendly [19]. They use electric power and do not require any human intervention during delivery, which reduces the need for delivery vans and other delivery-related emissions. The Amazon Scout robots are currently being tested in select areas in the United States, including California, Georgia, Tennessee, and Washington. The testing phase will help Amazon fine-tune the robots' performance and address any issues before expanding the service to other locations. Overall, the Amazon Scout robots represent an innovative and sustainable solution for package

Figure 6.12 Six-wheeled Amazon scout robot.

delivery that can help reduce carbon emissions and improve the efficiency of the delivery process.

- Cleveron Delivery Robot

Cleveron [20] is a technology company that has developed an autonomous delivery robot designed to transport packages to customers. The robot, called Cleveron 701, is equipped with advanced sensors and algorithms that allow it to navigate sidewalks and other pedestrian areas safely.

The Cleveron 701 is designed to be efficient and eco-friendly, with the ability to deliver packages within a radius of 12 miles from its base station. It can carry up to 44 pounds of weight and has a delivery time of around 30 min, making it an ideal solution for last-mile delivery.

One of the key benefits of the Cleveron 701 robot is that it reduces the need for human delivery drivers, which can save time and money for businesses. Additionally, the robot's electric power source reduces carbon emissions associated with traditional delivery methods.

The Cleveron 701 is currently being tested in select locations in Europe and North America, and it has already shown promising results. As the technology continues to improve, it is expected that delivery robots like the Cleveron 701 will become increasingly popular for last-mile delivery.

Figure 6.13 The Cleveron 701.

Figure 6.14 Kiwibot delivery service.

- Kiwibot

Kiwibot is a delivery robot developed by Kiwibot Inc. that is designed to transport food, groceries, and other items to customers. The robot is equipped with advanced sensors and navigation systems that allow it to navigate sidewalks and pedestrian areas safely and efficiently.

The Kiwibot is designed to be small and agile, with a maximum speed of around 4 mph. It is powered by an electric battery, which makes it eco friendly and quiet. The robot can carry up to 40 pounds of weight and has a delivery range of around 3 miles.

One of the key benefits of the Kiwibot [21] is that it reduces the need for human delivery drivers, which can save time and money for businesses. Additionally, the robot's electric power source reduces carbon emissions associated with traditional delivery methods.

Kiwibot is currently being tested in select locations in the United States, and it has already shown promising results. As the technology continues to improve, it is expected that delivery robots like the Kiwibot will become increasingly popular for last-mile delivery, providing a safe, efficient, and eco-friendly solution for customers and businesses alike.

- Postmates Serve

Postmates Serve [22] is a delivery robot developed by Postmates, a popular delivery service company. The robot is designed to transport food, groceries, and other items to customers in urban areas.

Figure 6.15 Small and agile Postmates serve robot.

The Postmates Serve robot is equipped with advanced sensors and cameras that allow it to navigate sidewalks and pedestrian areas safely. It can carry up to 50 pounds of weight and has a delivery range of around 30 miles on a single charge.

One of the benefits of using the Postmates Serve robot is that it reduces the need for human delivery drivers, which can save time and money for businesses. Additionally, the robot's electric power source reduces carbon emissions associated with traditional delivery methods.

The Postmates Serve robot is currently being tested in select locations in the United States, and it has already shown promising results. As the technology continues to improve, it is expected that delivery robots like the Postmates Serve will become increasingly popular for last-mile delivery, providing a safe, efficient, and eco-friendly solution for customers and businesses alike.

- Refraction AI

Refraction AI is a delivery robot developed by a startup company based in Michigan, USA. The robot is called REV-1, and it is designed to deliver food and other items to customers in urban areas. The robot is equipped with advanced sensors and cameras that allow it to navigate sidewalks and other pedestrian areas safely.

The REV-1 robot is designed to be small and nimble, with a maximum speed of around 15 mph. It is powered by an electric battery, which makes

Figure 6.16 A cluster of refraction AI delivery robot providing services.

it eco-friendly and quiet. The robot can carry up to 20 pounds of weight and has a delivery range of around 4 miles. Refraction AI [23] is currently testing the REV-1 robot in select locations in the United States. One of the key benefits of the REV-1 robot is that it is designed to operate in inclement weather conditions, such as rain and snow. This makes it an ideal solution for delivery in areas where weather conditions can be unpredictable.

- Neolix

Neolix is a Chinese company that develops autonomous vehicles, including delivery robots. Its self-driving delivery robot, the Neolix NX1 [24], is designed to transport goods and parcels on sidewalks and roads. The robot is equipped with advanced sensors, cameras, and navigation systems that allow it to navigate complex environments safely.

The NX1 robot is designed to be small and efficient, with a maximum speed of around 20 km/h. It is powered by an electric battery, which makes it eco-friendly and quiet. The robot can carry up to 50 kg of weight and has a delivery range of around 100 km. Neolix is already testing its autonomous delivery robots in several locations around the world, including China and Europe.

One of the key benefits of the Neolix NX1 robot is that it reduces the need for human delivery drivers, which can save time and money for businesses. Additionally, the robot's electric power source reduces carbon emissions associated with traditional delivery methods.

Figure 6.17 Neolix autonomous delivery robot.

6.8 Challenging Issues with Delivery Robots

The use of delivery robots offers several advantages, yet there are also several challenges associated with their implementation. These challenges encompass various aspects, including but not limited to the following:

i) To get legal approval
The process of obtaining authorization for the use of autonomous vehicles in densely populated urban regions and open roads is a complex undertaking that requires a considerable amount of time and resources. Furthermore, cities remain wary of allowing robots to traverse sidewalks. Nonetheless, it is highly probable that droids capable of traveling at lower speeds within the last-mile radius may experience a shorter period to enter the market as compared to other alternatives that involve higher-speed transportation solutions.

ii) Exceptional Situations
The deployment of autonomous delivery robots may encounter occasional yet crucial exceptional circumstances that demand an appropriate response. One such scenario involves the ability of robots to react prudently when faced with emergency vehicles such as ambulances, police cars, and

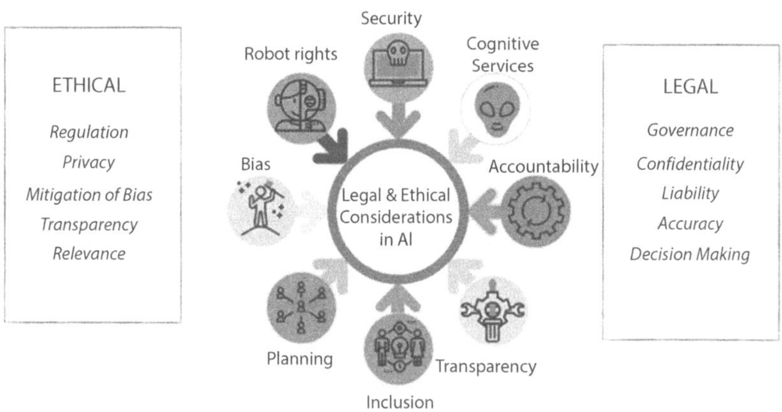

Figure 6.18 Some legal and ethical considerations of AI [25].

fire trucks. Additionally, delivery robots should consider the presence of disabled individuals requiring priority in traffic. Although such instances are infrequent, they can be more prevalent in densely populated urban regions. Hence, it is vital to develop and integrate effective algorithms and software that enable delivery robots to navigate through these challenging circumstances while ensuring the safety and well-being of all individuals involved.

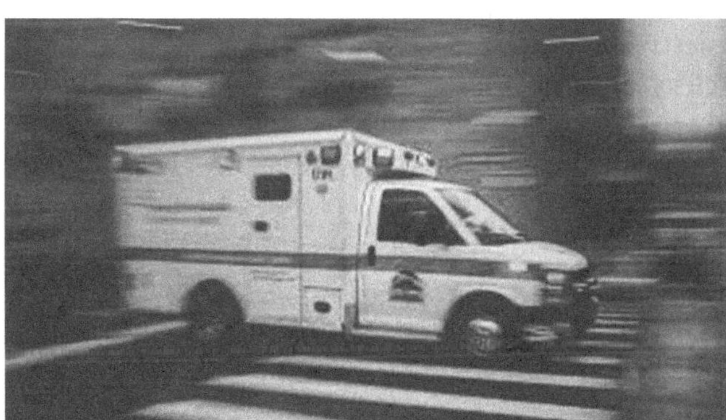

Figure 6.19 Exception situation (ambulance).

Figure 6.20 Exception situation (to give preference to specially-abled people).

iii) Dealing With Obstacles

Delivery robots interact with countless other participants in traffic, such as:

- other autonomous robots and vehicles
- human-driven vehicles
- pedestrians
- cyclists
- animals

The outcomes of these interactions are intricate and intricate to predict or control. Urban environments pose numerous challenges owing to their intricate nature.

Figure 6.21 Delivery robot interacting with real world environment [26].

iv) Social Acceptance

Social acceptance seems to be related to legislation: As long as the legislation is restrictive and prohibitive, social acceptance is likely to also remain low, and test pilots and deployments are rare, due to obvious reasons.

As we are making progress in regulating the autonomous delivery market; however, acceptance also improves: in France, for example, 63% of the population sees autonomous delivery positively.

We have a multitude of issues that are related to the social acceptance of autonomous delivery robots, such as:

- Safety concerns: A part of the population remains skeptical of new modes of transportation and does not trust the technology easily. With sufficient resources for development and testing; however, autonomous vehicles can become much safer than other means of transportation.
- Population density: Already busy cities are hesitant to allow autonomous delivery vehicles on their streets (like, for example, New York). However, autonomous delivery robots can in fact help alleviate traffic congestion by replacing delivery vans, which are typically much bigger, more polluting, noisier, and less efficient. Currently, we are working on a B2C autonomous delivery experiment in the heart of Helsinki, Finland, in which we are building a proof of concept of an

Figure 6.22 Safety concerns of robots [27].

alternative to both delivery vans and busy delivery points (such as kiosks).

- Job-related: Here, we could identify concerns about robots taking the jobs of human couriers, however, as we could see above, jobs are simply shifting, not disappearing. While fewer people might be delivering parcels themselves, operations will still need to be managed and staffed by humans.

As more and more people encounter autonomous vehicles in their daily lives, the vehicles become more readily accepted, and seen as a safe alternative to human-operated vehicles.

v) Operational challenges

Delivery robots face a range of operational challenges that need to be addressed for their successful implementation. One significant challenge is navigation. Delivery robots must be able to operate autonomously and navigate safely through a dynamic and often unpredictable environment. Safety is another critical challenge for delivery robots. They must be equipped with safety features, such as emergency stop buttons and collision avoidance systems, to prevent accidents and ensure the safety of both the robot and other road users.

Energy and battery life is a significant challenge as well. Delivery robots rely on batteries, and the distance they can travel is limited by battery life.

Figure 6.23 Robot's taking up human job [28].

Maintenance is another challenge. Delivery robots require regular maintenance to keep them operating at optimal levels. Security is also critical for delivery robots as they carry valuable goods. They must be secured against theft or tampering.

Finally, weather and environmental conditions are another challenge for delivery robots. They must be designed to operate in a wide range of weather and environmental conditions, such as rain, snow, and extreme temperatures. The robots must be robust enough to withstand these conditions and still be able to perform their tasks effectively.

vi) Ethical Values

Ethical considerations [25, 30] continue to be a prominent area of concern in the field of artificial intelligence and robotics. While robots are capable of performing sensitive tasks under human supervision, the advancement of autonomous systems has created the possibility of delegating such tasks entirely to robots. However, this presents several unforeseen challenges, such as a shortage of skilled personnel to maintain and manage these systems, and the potential for human employees to avoid accountability for their errors, which could have a ripple effect on the wider society. Delivery robots must be programmed to act ethically and transparently, and there must be mechanisms in place to hold them accountable for their actions. For example, if a delivery robot causes an accident or damages property, there must be a clear process in place for resolving the issue and compensating affected parties.

Figure 6.24 Robot is facing difficulty traversing in snow [29].

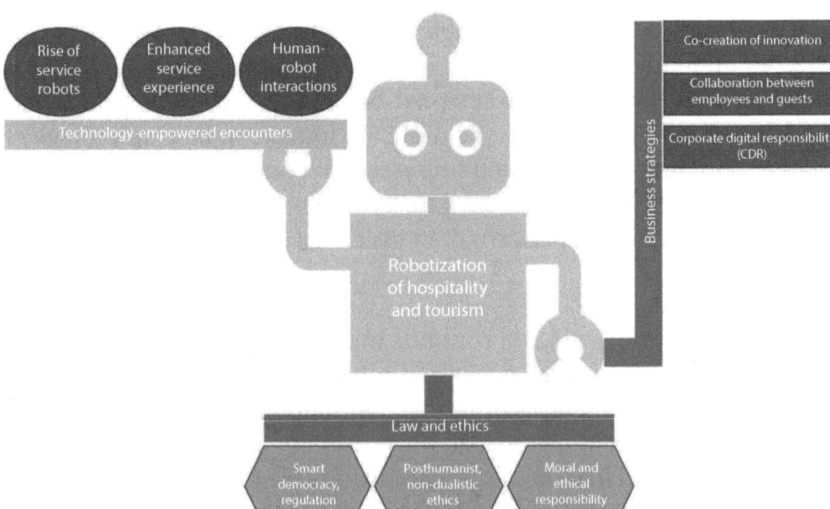

Figure 6.25 Just besides the manufacturing of robots are factor also plays a major role [30].

6.9 Conclusion and Future Work

In conclusion, delivery robots are likely to play an ever-increasing role in modern society, serving a wide range of organizations and applications. These robots can be used in various settings such as military bases, residential areas, university campuses, hospitals, and retail stores. The development of delivery robots with effective human-robot interaction, enhanced autonomy, and reduced delivery times is crucial to achieving success in this field.

One of the significant advantages of delivery robots is that they can improve efficiency and reduce costs. By using delivery robots, companies can reduce the time and cost associated with human labor, fuel, and vehicle maintenance. Furthermore, delivery robots can help businesses provide faster and more convenient delivery services to customers, thus improving customer satisfaction. However, there are still some barriers to overcome before delivery robots can be fully integrated into our daily lives. One of the significant challenges is developing algorithms that enable the robots to navigate through complex environments safely. In addition, there are concerns about the impact of delivery robots on employment opportunities and public safety.

Looking ahead, the future of delivery robots is promising. With continued investment and innovation, delivery robots have the potential to become even more sophisticated and capable. For example, researchers are exploring the use of drones and autonomous vehicles for last-mile delivery, which can improve the speed and efficiency of delivery services.

In the future, delivery robots may also be used for other applications such as home health care and disaster response. For example, robots equipped with medical supplies can be used to deliver medication and other essentials to patients at home. In disaster scenarios, delivery robots can be used to deliver food, water, and medical supplies to affected areas, reducing the risks to human responders.

In conclusion, the use of delivery robots is expected to become increasingly prevalent in modern society, and their potential benefits are vast. With continued investment and innovation, delivery robots have the potential to revolutionize the way we transport and deliver goods, making our lives more convenient and efficient. However, it is essential to address the challenges and concerns associated with delivery robots to ensure their safe and effective integration into our daily lives.

References

1. Marr, B., The Future of Delivery Robots, https://bernardmarr.com/the-future-of-delivery-robots/.
2. Zeng, Y., Huang, J., Xiong, R., Multi-Robot Task Allocation for Efficient Delivery of Goods. *IEEE Trans. Autom. Sci. Eng.*, 17, 2, 807–818, 2020.
3. Miao, Y., Chen, J., Chen, G., Deep Reinforcement Learning-Based Autonomous Package Delivery. *IEEE Trans. Ind. Inf.*, 17, 2, 1387–1397, 2021.
4. Dong, C., Zhao, Y., Wang, Y., A Delivery Robot System Based on Computer Vision, Natural Language Processing, and Path Planning Algorithms. *IEEE Trans. Ind. Inf.*, 16, 10, 6557–6566, 2020.
5. Sharma, A., Bhattacharjee, D., Bera, T.K., Obstacle Avoidance in Delivery Robots. *IEEE Trans. Ind. Inf.*, 16, 10, 6494–6503, 2020.
6. Huang, Y., Lin, S., Liu, Y., Modular Robotic System for Last-Mile Delivery. *IEEE Trans. Autom. Sci. Eng.*, 18, 2, 927–937, 2021.
7. Birolini, A., Delivery Drones and Robots: A Comparative Review of Applications. *Regulations Impact Soc.*, 14, 102–115, 2021.
8. https://en.wikipedia.org/wiki/Starship_Technologies.
9. Pagliari, L., Mirandola, R., Trubianil, C., Engineering Cyber-Physical Systems through Performance-based Modelling and Analysis: A Case Study Experience Report, July 2019. *J. Software: Evol. Process*, 32, 3, 45. DOI: 10.1002/smr.2179, Lab: EReS Research Lab.
10. Symonds, D., Starship deploys autonomous delivery robots in Greater Manchester, https://www.parcelandpostaltechnologyinternational.com/news/automation/starship-deploys-autonomous-delivery-robots-in-greater-manchester.html.
11. Pao, W., Robots and drones can offer these benefits amid covid-19, https://www.asmag.com/showpost/31432.aspx.
12. Medical Device Network, What are the main types of robots used in healthcare?, https://www.medicaldevice-network.com/.
13. Wessling, B., Teraki, DriveU.auto partner for teleoperated delivery robots.
14. Paden, J., Supermarket chain Lucky uses robots to deliver groceries, https://www.amadorvalleytoday.org/20267/news/lucky-uses-robots-to-deliver-groceries/.
15. Robotic Package Delivery with ANYmal, https://www.anybotics.com.
16. Millward, D., The rise of the robot butler – fad or the future of hotel room service?.
17. Meet Scout. About Amazon, 2019-01-23, Retrieved 2021-02-23. https://www.aboutamazon.com/news/transportation/meet-scout.
18. Vincent, J., Amazon has made its own autonomous six-wheeled delivery robot. *Verge*, 23, 200–210, 2019-01-23. Retrieved 2021-02-23.theverge.com/2019/1/23/18194566/amazon-scout-autonomous-six-wheeled-delivery-robot.

19. About Amazon Scout, www.amazon.com. Retrieved 2019-09-08. https://www.amazon.com/gp/help/customer/display.html?nodeId=GTGUQUQHMZ54B55F.
20. Cleveron delivery robot, 2022, May 21, Robotics Based Parcel Delivery Solution. Retrieved from https://cleveron.com.
21. Robots delivery service, 2022, May 28, Kiwibot. Retrieved from https://www.kiwibot.com.
22. Postmates Serve Self-Driving Vehicle (2022, May 28). Serve. Retrieved from https://www.forbes.com/sites/lanabandoim/2018/12/21/postmates-reveals-its-autonomous-delivery-rover-called-serve/.
23. Chick-fil-A taps Refraction AI for autonomous delivery pilot, Rebecca Bellan, https://techcrunch.com/2022/05/31/chick-fil-a-taps-refraction-ai-for-autonomous-delivery-pilot/.
24. Neolix delivery robot, 2022, May 28, Neolix. Retrieved from https://www.forbes.com/sites/davidsilver/2019/06/04/neolix-accelerates-the-autonomous-delivery-rush/.
25. Nithesh Naik, B.M., Hameed, Z., Shah, M., Legal and Ethical Consideration in Artificial Intelligence in Healthcare: Who Takes Responsibility? *Front. Surg.*, 8, 47–53, 14 March 2022. Sec. Genitourinary Surgery Volume 9 - 2022 | https://doi.org/10.3389/fsurg.2022.862322.
26. Wolfe, E., Pitt pauses testing of Starship robots due to safety concerns, October 21, 2019, News Editor.
27. McDonald, K., Robots, Safety, and the Future of Work, in: *Forbes*, 2020, November 18, https://www.forbes.com/sites/forbestechcouncil/2020/11/18/robots-safety-and-the-future-of-work/.
28. Coviello, J., Artificial Intelligence and Robots Will Cause Massive Unemployment, 6, 14, OCT 14, 2022. AM EDT.
29. Larson, S., Winter Is Coming: Robots Struggle to Navigate Snowy Terrain. *IEEE Spectr.*, 12, 120–130, 2019, December 20. https://spectrum.ieee.org/automaton/robotics/robotics-hardware/winter-is-coming-robots-struggle-to-navigate-snowy-terrain.
30. Fuste-Forne, F. and Jamal, T., Co-Creating New Directions for Service Robots in Hospitality and Tourism. *Tour. Hosp.*, 2, 1, 43–61, 2021.

7

Emergence of Cloud Computing in IoT Applications

Priyanshu Sonthalia* **and Doddi Puneet**

Kalinga Institute of Industrial Technology, Deemed to be University, Bhubaneswar, Odisha, India

Abstract

Cloud computing has enabled the accumulation, processing, and review of large volumes of Internet of Things (IoT) data in a more efficient manner. Cloud offerings such as Software as a Service, Infrastructure as a Service, and Platform as a Service are accessible across private, hybrid, public, and community cloud environments. This paper presents a detailed study of cloud computing on IoT with emphasis on privacy concerns for both technologies. The paper examines how cloud computing and IoT have common features and explores the benefits of their union. Furthermore, paper highlights the offering of cloud being used for computing purposes in IoT and how it has the potential to be used to improve its function. The cloud-based IoT architecture is composed of perception, network, middleware, and application layers that collect, process, and manage data gathered from IoT devices. This data is then used to add value to end-users. Message Queuing Telemetry Transport, Constrained Application Protocol, Advance Message Queueing Protocol, and Hypertext Transfer Protocol are some of the various cloud-based IoT standards and protocols. This research paper also explores the various potential use cases of this technology in health care, transportation, smart homes, and agriculture, as well as the challenges involved in integrating IoT with the cloud. The research paper presents two case studies that illustrate the application of cloud architecture that is IoT based on intelligent environment home automation and industrial IoT optimization. The paper concludes by outlining the potential of cloud computing applications in IoT and highlighting future scope in this emerging technology.

**Corresponding author*: 20051357@kiit.ac.in

Subhasis Dash, Manas Ranjan Lenka, S. Balamurugan, Ambika Prasad Tripathy and Amarendra Mohanty (eds.) Sustainable Resource Management in Next-Generation Computational Constrained Networks, (169–188) © 2025 Scrivener Publishing LLC

***Keywords*:** IoT, cloud storage, cloud infrastructure, virtualization, MQTT, CoAP, AMQP, HTTP

7.1 Introduction

Internet of Things (IoT) has transformed our interaction methods with our environment, allowing us to gather data from sensors and devices and use it to make more informed decisions. But as the number of IoT devices and size of the output that they generate continues to grow, traditional computing infrastructure is struggling to keep up. This is where cloud computing comes in—by leveraging the power of the cloud, we may store, process, and utilize vast amounts of IoT data more effectively than ever before.

This research paper will explore the benefits and challenges of integrating cloud computing with IoT, as well as the key concepts and architectures that underpin cloud-based IoT solutions. We will also examine two case studies—one in smart home automation and one in industrial process optimization—to illustrate the real-world applications of cloud-based IoT.

7.1.1 Characteristics of Cloud Computing

Computing done using cloud is an instrument for distributing resources such as compute, storage, database, and software, over a network [1]. It has several key characteristics:

1. Instantaneous provisioning: Users use resources, including servers and storage, if and when required without going through an individual intermediary.
2. Wide network availability: Resources are available across the internet from any device, including laptops, smartphones, and tablets.
3. Resource pooling: Multiple users can share the same physical resources, such as servers and storage, to increase efficiency and reduce costs.
4. Rapid flexibility: Resources could be adjusted quickly and efficiently for accommodating fluctuating demands.
5. Metered service: Resource use is tracked, allowing users to be charged for only the resources they consume.

Figure 7.1 shows the schematic diagram of cloud computing.

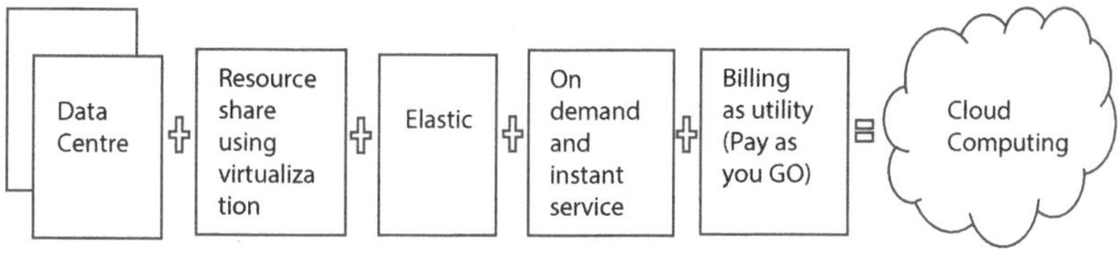

Figure 7.1 Schematic diagram of cloud computing.

7.1.2 Types of Cloud Deployment Models

Cloud computing can be applied in several different ways, depending on who takes the ownership of the infrastructure. The main deployment models are as follows:

1) In a public cloud, the available tools are owned and operated by a mediating cloud provider like Amazon or Microsoft.
2) In a private cloud, resources are owned as well as managed by a single organization, typically within its data center [2].
3) In a hybrid cloud, the resources are operated in a manner, which is an amalgamation of public and private clouds, wherein some services hosted in the public cloud and others hosted in the private cloud.
4) In a community cloud, resources are collectively utilized by a group of entities with similar needs, which may include government agencies or health care providers.

Table 7.1 shows the comparison of various deployment models in cloud.

Table 7.1 Relative study of various cloud deployment models.

Cloud type	Public	Private	Community	Hybrid
Used by	Common public and small businesses	Large businesses	Businesses having similar interests and objectives	Public businesses

(Continued)

Table 7.1 Relative study of various cloud deployment models. (*Continued*)

Cloud type	Public	Private	Community	Hybrid
Governed by	Cloud service providers	Businesses that own the cloud	Third-party organization or community using the cloud	Service providers and businesses
Security level	Extremely low	Extremely high	Higher than public clouds	Secure than public cloud
Scalability	Extremely high	Extremely low	Higher than private clouds	Higher than private clouds
Cost factor	Cheapest	Most expensive	Moderate cost	Cost effective
Best suited for	Small enterprises	Organizations dealing with sensitive information	Financial, health, and legal companies	Small- and medium-sized enterprises
Resources	Resources shared by a large group of users	Resources used by the organization owning the cloud	Resources used by community	Resources shared by businesses and general public

7.1.3 Categories of Cloud Computing Architectures

Cloud computing can be deployed using several different architectures, depending on the use case of the application. The main architectures are as follows:

1. Client-server: Resources are split between a client device, such as a laptop or smartphone, and a central server [3].
2. Peer-to-peer: Resources are distributed across multiple devices, which communicate with each other to perform a task.

3. Server-less: A cloud provider is responsible for handling all infrastructure management and scaling, and it also takes the responsibility of providing these resources as a service.

7.1.4 Types of Cloud Service Models

The most important types of cloud service models include the following:

1. Software as a Service: This service provides customers with the ability to utilize the provider's applications on a cloud infrastructure. These applications can be accessed from various client devices through either a lightweight interface like a web gateway (e.g., web-based email) or a software interface [4]. Customers do not oversee the underlying cloud infrastructure, including networks, servers, operating systems, and storage. The functionality of users to utilize these services may differ, with exceptions made for specific configurations tailored to individual consumer requirements.
2. Platform as a Service: The service offers features allowing clients to deploy their own or acquired applications on the cloud infrastructure using supported programming languages, libraries, services, and tools provided by the company. Although clients do not manage the underlying cloud infrastructure—comprising networks, servers, operating systems, and storage—they do maintain control over deployed applications and may adjust configuration settings within the application hosting environment.
3. Infrastructure as a Service: This provides customers with the capability to provision computing resources such as processing power, storage, and networks. Customers can install and run their own software, including operating systems and applications [5]. Although customers do not have direct control over the underlying cloud infrastructure, they retain control over operating systems, storage, and deployed applications. They may also have limited control over certain networking components like host firewalls.

Figure 7.2 shows the different cloud service models along with their vendors.

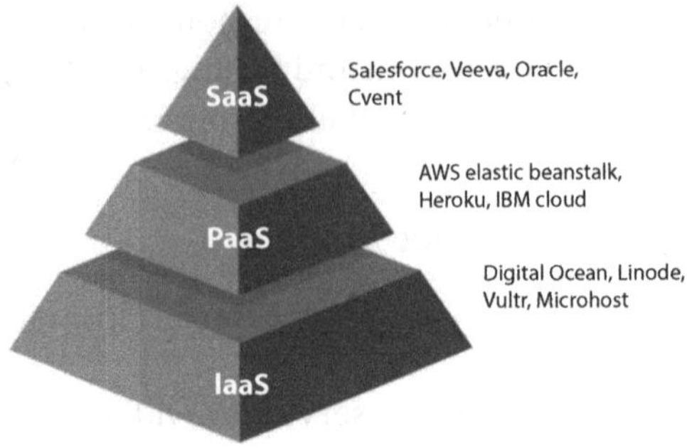

Figure 7.2 Different cloud service models and their service providers.

7.2 Benefits of IoT and Cloud Integration

The integration of IoT with cloud computing provides a variety of benefits, including scalability, reduced infrastructure costs, improved accessibility and availability, enhanced processing power, and increased innovation [3].

7.2.1 Scalability and Elasticity of Cloud Resources for Managing IoT Data

The most important advantage of cloud computing for IoT is the ability to adjust the capacity of resources being used from time to time. This is particularly important for managing large volumes of data generated by IoT devices. Cloud-based solutions can provide flexible and elastic store and process capabilities that is easily scaled to meet changing demands.

7.2.2 Reduced Infrastructure Costs with Cloud-Based Solutions

Cloud-based IoT solutions can significantly reduce infrastructure costs, as they eliminate the need for organizations to build and maintain their own data centers and servers. Instead, organizations can rely on cloud service providers to provide the necessary infrastructure, which can be accessed on a pay-as-you-go basis [6]. This helps significantly in reducing overall costs, largely for medium- and small-sized companies who do not have the bandwidth to expend extensively on infrastructure.

7.2.3 Improved Accessibility and Availability of IoT Services with Cloud Deployment

Cloud-based IoT solutions can also improve the accessibility and availability of IoT services. Cloud service providers typically offer global networks of data centers, which can provide high levels of availability and performance. This can be particularly important for organizations that operate in multiple locations or have customers in different parts of the world.

7.2.4 Enhanced Processing Power and Analytics Capabilities with Cloud Computing

Cloud computing can also provide enhanced processing power and analytics capabilities for IoT data. Cloud-based solutions can leverage sophisticated analytics tools to operate on large volumes of data in real time, enabling businesses to make real time decisions based on accurate data.

7.2.5 Reduced Time to Market and Increased Innovation with Cloud-Based IoT Development

Finally, cloud-based IoT development can reduce time to market and increase innovation. Cloud service providers offer a wide range of pre-built services and application programming interfaces (APIs) that can be leveraged to quickly develop and deploy IoT applications [7]. This can help organizations to make new product innovations and thus stay ahead of their competitors.

7.3 Cloud-Based IoT Architecture

Typically, this architecture comprises four layers: network, middleware, perception, and application layers.

7.3.1 Four Layers of Cloud-Based IoT Architecture

The IoT devices are responsible for collection of data. This data is then passed on to the perception layer. This layer uses device which operate using an Internet connection. The data is then transferred to the cloud using the network layer. This layer includes protocols as well as all types of wired and wireless mediums [8].

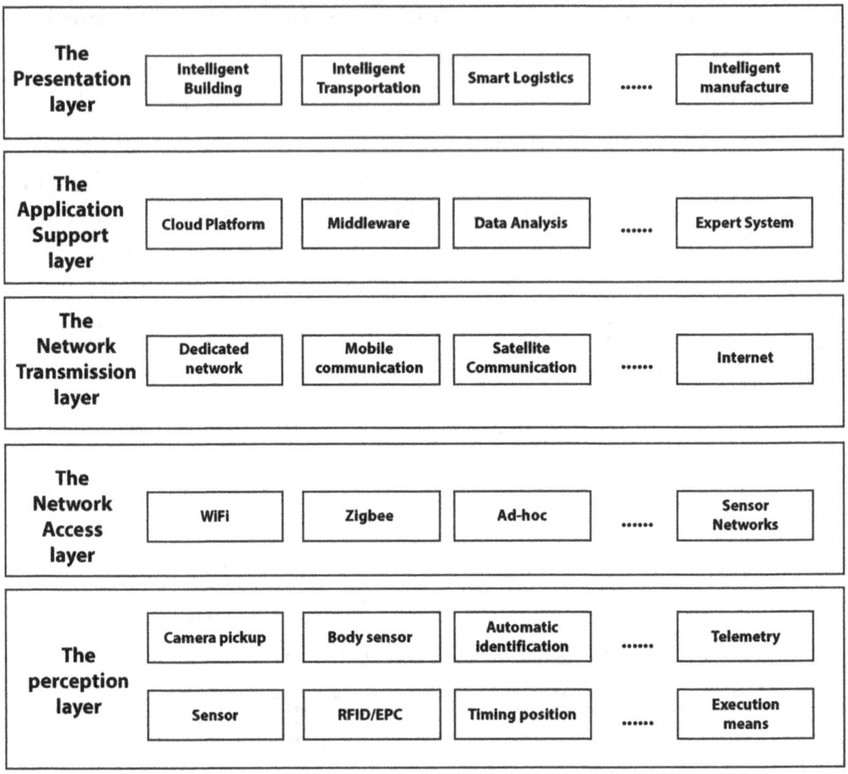

Figure 7.3 Five layers of IoT-based cloud architecture.

The middleware layer is responsible for processing and managing IoT data. This layer can include data storage, processing, and analytics services, as well as APIs that enable communication that connects IoT devices and cloud.

Finally, the application layer is responsible for delivering value to end-users. This layer can include IoT applications and services that provide real-time insights and actionable information. Figure 7.3 shows the five layers of cloud-based IoT architecture.

7.3.2 Role of Gateways in Linking IoT Devices to the Cloud

Gateways play an important role in bridging the gap between IoT devices and cloud. They form the intermediate layer that sits at the intersection of this cloud and the IoT devices; they collect data from IoT devices and send it to the cloud [9]. Gateways can also process data and filter it, which aids in minimizing the volume of data sent to the cloud.

7.3.3 Overview of Cloud-Based IoT Platforms and Services

Cloud-based IoT platforms and services can provide a range of capabilities, including data storage, processing, and analytics. Some examples of cloud-based IoT platforms and services include the following:

- AWS IoT
- Azure IoT
- Google Cloud IoT
- IBM Watson IoT
- Oracle IoT Cloud
- ThingWorx IoT

7.3.4 Cloud-Based IoT Standards and Protocols, such as MQTT, CoAP, AMQP, and HTTP

Standardization is essential for the interoperability and integration of IoT devices and cloud-based services [10]. Various standards and protocols have been coded to facilitate the communication and integration of IoT devices and cloud services. Some examples of cloud-based IoT standards and protocols include the following:

(a) MQTT (Message Queuing Telemetry Transport): This is a lightweight messaging protocol specifically designed for IoT applications, known for its efficiency and reliability, making it popular in cloud based IoT solutions.

Figure 7.4 shows the MQTT standard in IoT.

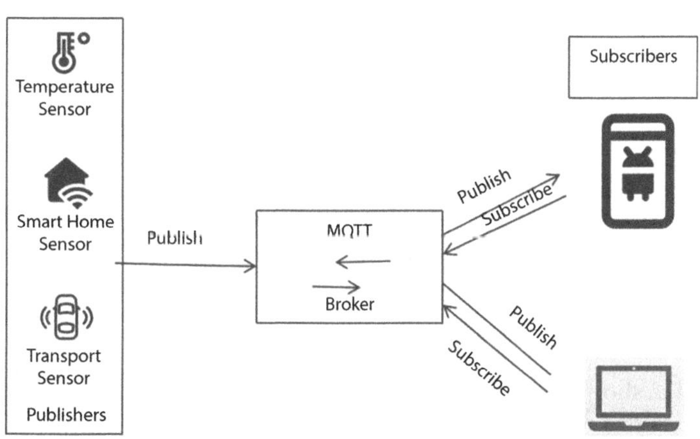

Figure 7.4 MQTT protocol in IoT.

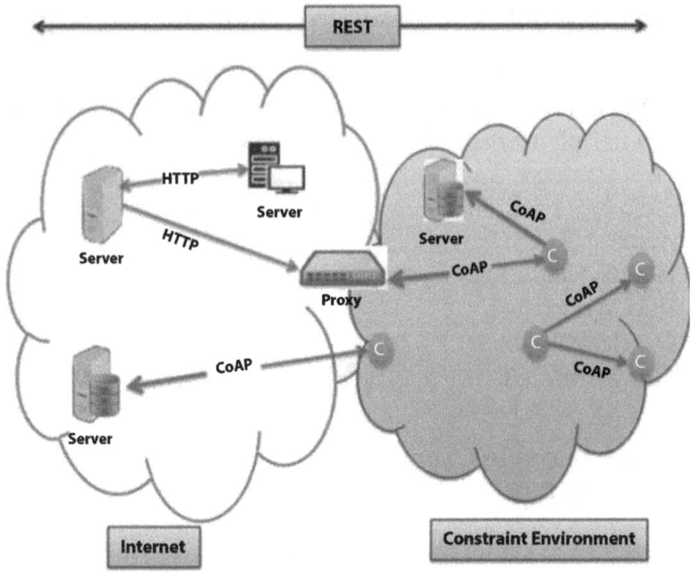

Figure 7.5 CoAP model in IoT.

(b) CoAP (Constrained Application Protocol): This is a standard designed for use in IoT devices such as sensors and actuators where the availability of resources is limited. It is commonly used in cloud-based IoT solutions due to its low overhead and simplicity. Figure 7.5 shows the CoAP model in IoT.

(c) AMQP (Advance Message Queueing Protocol): This is a messaging model developed for proprietary solutions to exchange large amounts of messages [11]. One of its important features is its high Interoperability and it is used for industrial and business management. It operates in the session layer. Figure 7.6 shows AMQP model in IoT.

(d) HTTP (Hypertext Transfer Protocol): This is a standard commonly deployed on net applications and is increasingly being used in cloud-based IoT solutions. It provides a standard method for transmitting data between IoT devices and cloud services.

Table 7.2 shows the comparison of various IoT standards and protocols.

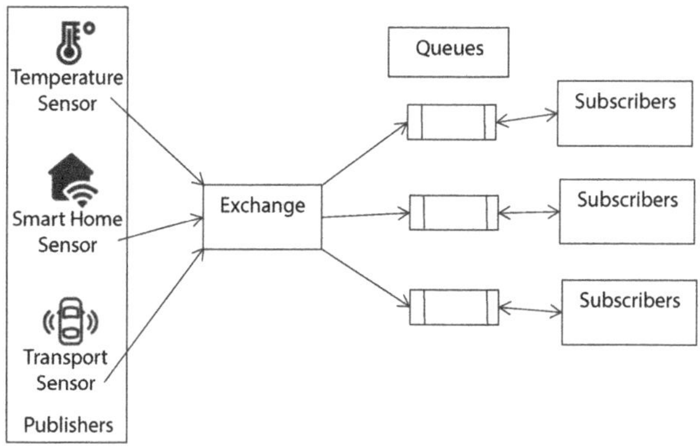

Figure 7.6 AMQP model in IoT.

Table 7.2 Relative comparison of various application layer messaging standards: MQTT, COAP, AMQP, and HTTP.

	MQTT	CoAP	AMQP	HTTP
Transport Layer Protocol	Support TCP	Support UDP, TCP	Support UDP, TCP	Support UDP, TCP
Safety	Lowest	Higher than MQTT	Highest	Higher than CoAP
Data size	Higher than CoAP	Lowest	Higher than MQTT	Highest
Message Pattern	Publishers send data to mediating, entity-broker, broker distributes data to consumers	Publishers send data to server, consumers request data from server	Publishers send data to mediating entity-broker, broker distributes data to consumers	Publishers send data to server, consumers request data from server
Message Overhead	Higher than CoAP	Lowest	Higher than MQTT	Highest
Header Size	2 byte	4 byte	8 byte	Undefined

(Continued)

Table 7.2 Relative comparison of various application layer messaging standards: MQTT, COAP, AMQP, and HTTP. (*Continued*)

	MQTT	CoAP	AMQP	HTTP
Binary Payload	Support	Support	Support	Does not support
Bandwidth	Higher than CoAP	Lowest	Higher than MQTT	Highest
Encoding	Binary	Binary	Binary	Text
Interoperability	Lowest	Higher than AMQP	Higher than MQTT	Highest
Performance	Highest	Higher than HTTOP	Lowest	Higher than AMQP
Security	Username and password, SSL/TLS	No security mode	SSL Certification, TLS Data Encryption	SSL/TLS

7.4 Cloud-Based IoT Applications

IoT can potentially transform various industries by providing data-driven insights and optimizing operations [12–14]. Cloud computing provides the architecture used to manage, store, and analyze the humungous amount of data generated by sensors, actuators, and other IoT devices. Here are some examples of IoT applications in different industries:

a. Health care: IoT devices such as wearable s and medical sensors can provide real-time health monitoring and disease management. Cloud-based IoT solutions can help store and process the data generated by these devices, providing insights into patient health and improving clinical decision-making. For example, the University of California, San Francisco (UCSF) Medical Center has implemented a cloud-based IoT platform to monitor patient health and improve patient outcomes.
b. Transportation: IoT devices have the potential to enhance transportation efficiency systems, improve traffic flow, and reduce carbon emissions. Cloud-based IoT solutions can provide real-time data on traffic conditions, weather, and other variables to help transportation systems adapt and

optimize their operations [15]. For example, the City of Barcelona has implemented a cloud-based IoT platform to manage its bus fleet and optimize its routes, reducing fuel consumption and improving air quality.

c. Agriculture: IoT devices can provide data on soil moisture, temperature, and other variables to help farmers optimize crop yields and reduce water usage. Cloud-based IoT solutions can process this data and provide insights into crop health and soil conditions. For example, Monsanto has implemented a cloud-based IoT platform to monitor soil conditions and optimize crop yields.
d. Smart Cities: The use of this can help optimize city services and improve the quality of life for citizens. IoT devices can provide real-time data on traffic, energy consumption, and other variables, which can be processed by cloud-based solutions to optimize city operations [16]. For example, the City of Copenhagen has implemented a cloud-based IoT platform to monitor and control streetlights, reducing energy consumption and improving public safety.

7.5 Challenges in IoT Cloud Integration

While the union of cloud computing and IoT has the ability to transform various industries, it also faces several issues that are yet to be solved, such as the following.

7.5.1 Security Risks and Challenges Associated with Cloud-Based IoT Solutions

Cloud-based IoT solutions may be susceptible to security risks like data breaches, hacking, and malware intrusions; it is crucial to enforce strong security protocols such to encrypt data, control the access, and authentication to safeguard both IoT devices and data [17].

7.5.2 Latency and Bandwidth Constraints of IoT Systems Hosted in the Cloud

The latency and bandwidth limitations of cloud-based IoT solutions can impact the performance of IoT applications, especially those that require real-time data processing. Edge computing, which involves processing data locally on the IoT device or gateway, can help overcome these limitations.

7.5.3 Interoperability Issues Between Different IoT Devices and Cloud Platforms

IoT devices may use different communication protocols and standards, which makes make it difficult to merge them with cloud-based solutions. The use of standardized protocols such as MQTT and CoAP can help address these interoperability issues.

7.5.4 Legal and Regulatory Challenges Associated with IoT Using Cloud Solutions

The use of cloud-based IoT solutions may raise legal and regulatory challenges such as data ownership and liability [18]. It is essential to comply with relevant laws and regulations and ensure that data privacy and ownership are clearly defined.

7.6 Open Issues and Research Directions

The integration of cloud computing and IoT presents several open issues and research directions, including the following.

7.6.1 Future Trends and Developments in Cloud-Based IoT Solutions

New advancements such as edge computing and server less processing are expected to have a significant impact on cloud-based IoT solutions. Future research should focus on optimizing these technologies for IoT applications.

7.6.2 Opportunities for Research in Cloud-Based IoT Solutions

There are several opportunities for research in cloud-based IoT solutions, such as optimizing data storage and processing, improving security and privacy, and enhancing the user experience.

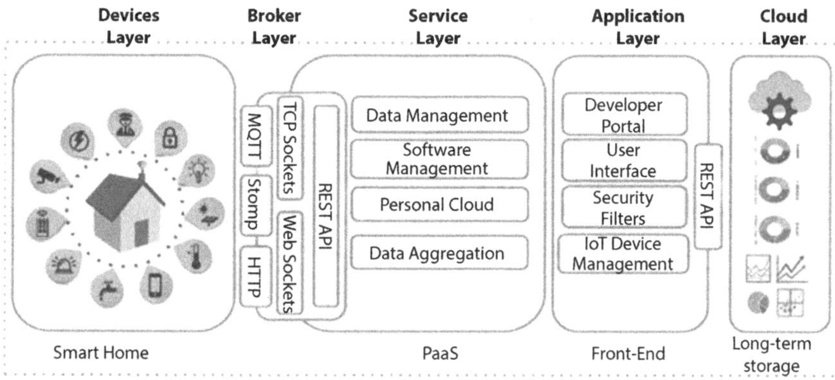

Figure 7.7 Five layers of smart home automation using cloud-based IoT.

7.6.3 Overview of Emerging Cloud-Based IoT Standards and Protocols

In addition, cloud-based IoT solutions also offer enhanced processing power and analytics capabilities, as cloud computing enables advanced data analysis techniques such as machine learning and artificial intelligence to be applied to IoT data. This can provide valuable insights and facilitate more informed decision-making in various industries.

7.7 Case Study 1: Smart Home Automation Using Cloud-Based IoT

One of the most promising applications of cloud-based IoT solutions is in the area of smart home automation. By connecting various devices and appliances in a home to the cloud, homeowners can control and monitor their home environment from anywhere in the world using their smartphone or another connected device [19].

A cloud-based IoT solution for smart home automation typically consists of several components, including sensors and actuators, a gateway device, cloud-based IoT platforms and services, and a user interface. The sensors and actuators collect and process data from the home environment and controlling various devices and appliances. The gateway device serves as the mediating link between the IoT devices, and the cloud and is responsible for transferring data to the cloud and receiving directions from the cloud. The cloud-based IoT platforms and services are responsible for storing and processing data, as well as providing analytics and other services. Finally, the user interface allows the homeowner to control and monitor the smart home system from their smartphone or another connected device.

One example of a cloud-based IoT solution for smart home automation is the Amazon Echo and Alexa. The Echo is a voice-activated smart speaker that allows users to interact with their home environment using natural language commands. Alexa, the intelligent personal assistant that powers the Echo, is built on Amazon's cloud-based IoT platform, AWS IoT. This allows the Echo to seamlessly connect with other IoT devices in the home and provide users with a variety of services, such as controlling home appliances, playing music, and ordering groceries. Figure 7.7 shows the five layers of smart home automation using cloud-based IoT architecture.

7.8 Case Study 2: Industrial IoT Optimization Using Cloud-Based IoT

In addition to smart home automation, cloud-based IoT solutions are also being used to optimize industrial processes. By connecting sensors and other devices in a manufacturing environment to the cloud, manufacturers can gain real-time insights into their operations and make data-driven decisions to improve efficiency and reduce costs.

A cloud-based IoT solution for industrial process optimization typically consists of several components, including sensors and actuators, a gateway device, cloud-based IoT platforms and services, and data analytics tools. The sensors and actuators collect and process data from the manufacturing environment and controlling various machines and processes. The gateway devices are the intermediate infrastructure connecting the IoT devices and the cloud. The devices also forward data to cloud and receive instructions from the cloud. The cloud-based IoT platforms and services are responsible for storing and processing data, as well as providing analytics and other services. Finally, data analytics tools are used to analyze the data collected from the manufacturing environment and provide insights into operational efficiency and other key metrics.

One example of a cloud-based IoT solution for industrial process optimization is general electric (GE's) Predix platform. Predix is a cloud-based platform that is specifically designed for industrial IoT applications. It allows manufacturers to connect their machines and sensors to the cloud,

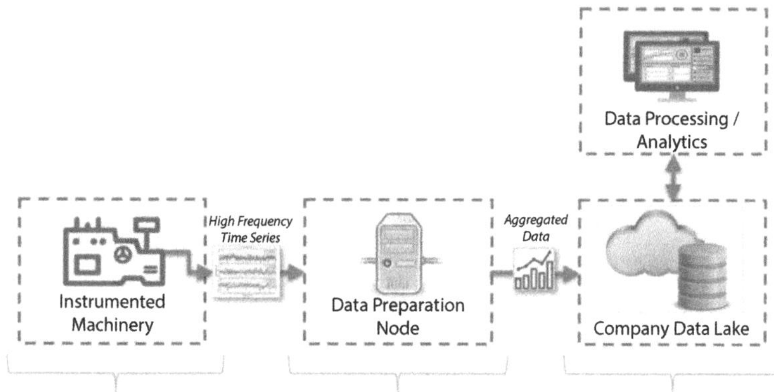

Figure 7.8 Architecture for industrial IoT scenario.

to store and process data, and to run analytics to gain insights into their operations. Predix also provides a suite of applications and tools that allow manufacturers to monitor and control their operations from anywhere in the world.

Figure 7.8 shows the architecture of industrial IoT scenario.

7.9 Conclusion

In conclusion, cloud computing has transformed the manner in which IoT data processing takes place, stored, and analyzed. The integration of IoT and cloud computing offers several benefits, such as scalability, reduced infrastructure costs, improved accessibility, enhanced processing power, and reduced time to market.

Cloud-based IoT typically this architecture comprises four layers: perception, network, middleware, and application layers, and gateways play a crucial role in connecting IoT devices to the cloud. Cloud-based IoT platforms and services offer several features, such as data storage, analytics, and visualization. Several cloud-based IoT standards and protocols, such as MQTT, CoAP, and HTTP, have emerged to address interoperability issues.

However, integrating IoT with cloud computing poses several challenges, such as security risks, latency, Interoperability issues, and legal and regulatory challenges. Future research and development in cloud-based IoT solutions should focus on optimizing data storage and processing, improving security and privacy, and enhancing the user experience. Emerging cloud-based IoT standards and protocols, such as 5G and LPWAN, also offer opportunities for research and development.

The two case studies presented in this research paper demonstrate the practical application of cloud-based IoT solutions. Smart home automation using cloud-based IoT offers several benefits, such as convenience, energy efficiency, and improved security. Industrial IoT optimization using cloud-based IoT offers several advantages like improved efficiency, minimized downtime, and enhanced safety.

Cloud computing for IoT has the potential to revolutionize several industries and sectors, such as agriculture, health care, and transportation. The union of IoT and cloud computing offers limitless possibilities for innovation and growth. It is up to researchers and developers to explore these possibilities and unlock the potential of cloud-based IoT solutions.

References

1. Atlam, H.F., Alenezi, A., Alharthi, A., Walters, R.J., Wills, G.B., Integration of Cloud Computing with Internet of Things: Challenges and Open Issues. *2017 IEEE International Conference on Internet of Things (iThings) and IEEE Green Computing and Communications (GreenCom) and IEEE Cyber, Physical and Social Computing (CPSCom) and IEEE Smart Data (SmartData)*, pp. 670–675, 2017.
2. Singh, N., Raza, M., Paranthaman, V.V., Awais, M.U., Khalid, M., Javed, E., Internet of Things and cloud computing. *Digital Health*, 151–162, 2021.
3. Dang, L.M., Piran, M.J., Han, D., Min, K., Moon, H., A Survey on Internet of Things and Cloud Computing for Healthcare. *Electronics*, 8, 1–49, 2019.
4. Rani, S., Bhambri, P., Nicolazzo, S., Big Data, Cloud Computing and Iot: Tools and Applications, pp. 442–448, Taylor & Francis group, New York, 2020.
5. James, A., Seth, A., Mukhopadhyay, S.C., Cloud Computing for IoT Systems, in: *Smart Sensors, Measurement and Instrumentation*, 2021.
6. Neumann, D., Stößer, J., Weinhardt, C., Nimis, J., A framework for commercial grids - economic and technical challenges. *J. Grid Comput.*, 6, 3, 325–347, 2008.
7. Mascolo, C., The Power of Mobile Computing in a Social Era. *IEEE Internet Comput.*, 14, 76–79, 2010.
8. Zhang, S., *et al.*, Cloud Computing Research and Development Trend, in: *Proceedings of International Conference on Future Networks*, 22–24, IEEE Jan., 2010.
9. Hossain, M.S. and Muhammad, G., Cloud-Assisted Industrial Internet of Things (IoT)-Enabled Framework for Health Monitoring. *Comput. Netw.*, 101, 192–202, 2016.

10. Guo, T. and Zhong, W., Design and implementation of the span greenhouse agriculture Internet of Things system. *Proc. of IEEE International Conf. on Fluid Power and Mechatronics (FPM)*, 2015.
11. Li, F., Voegler, M., Claessens, M., Dustdar, S., Efficient and Scalable IoT Service Delivery on Cloud. *Proceedings of the 2013 IEEE Sixth International Conference on Cloud Computing (CLOUD '13)*, IEEE, pp. 740–747, 2013.
12. Teixeira, C., Sousa, J., Ferreira, F., Oliveira, A., Teixeira, A., Pereira, C., Cloud Computing Enhanced Service Development Architecture for the Living Usability Lab. *Commun. Comput. Inf. Sci.*, 221, 289–296, 2011.
13. Moraes, T., Nogueira, B., Lira, V., Tavares, E., Performance comparison of iot communication protocols. *2019 IEEE International Conference on Systems Man and Cybernetics (SMC)*, pp. 3249–3254, 2019.
14. De Caro, N., Colitti, W., Steenhaut, K., Mangino, G., Reali, G., Comparison of two lightweight protocols for smartphone-based sensing. *Communications and Vehicular Technology in the Benelux (SCVT) 2013 IEEE 20th Symposium on*, pp. 1–6, 2013.
15. Guinard, D., Trifa, V., Karnouskos, S., Spiess, P., Savio, D., Interacting with the SOA-Based Internet of Things: Discovery, Query, Selection, and On-Demand Provisioning of Web Services. *IEEE Trans. Serv. Comput.*, 3, 3, 223–235, Jul. 2010.
16. Ali, Z.H., Ali, H.A., Badawy, M.M., A new proposed the internet of things (loT) virtualization framework based on sensor-as-a-service concept. *Wireless Pers. Commun.*, 97, 1, 1419–1443, 2017.
17. Fuentes, H. and Mauricio, D., Smart water consumption measurement system for houses using IoT and cloud computing. *Environ. Monit. Assess.*, 192, 1–16, 2020.
18. Yu, J. and Buyya, R., A budget constrained scheduling of workflow applications on utility grids using genetic algorithms, in: *IEEE Workshop on workflows in support of large-scale science*, pp. 1–10, 2006.
19. Mach, and Becvar, Z., Mobile edge computing: A survey on architecture and computation offloading. *IEEE Commun. Surveys Tuts.*, 19, 3, 1628–1656, 2017. 3rd Quart.

8

Conceptual Assessment of Sensory Networks and Its Functional Aspects

Barat Nikhita, Siddhant Prateek Mahanayak and Kunal Anand*

Kalinga Institute of Industrial Technology, Deemed to be University, Bhubaneswar, Odisha, India

Abstract
The Internet of Things (IoT) is a network of interconnected objects that interact over the internet. This technology has received a lot of attention in recent years, and its possible applications include healthcare, agriculture, industry, transportation, and other fields. This article presents an overview of the IoT, including its history, architecture, components, and main difficulties. The study also covers numerous IoT applications and their possible societal impact. It also discusses the present trends and future prospects of IoT. The goal of this article is to offer a thorough knowledge of IoT and its potential to transform the way we live and work.

***Keywords*:** Internet of things, smart city, smart agriculture, smart housing, smart traffic management, smart healthcare

8.1 Introduction

The "Internet of Things" (IoT) has grown in popularity significantly over the past several years and has already had a significant influence on how we perceive and interact with our environment. IoT has transformed our daily routines by allowing wearable technology and smart houses [1]. But, the real potential of IoT goes well beyond the present situation and holds tremendous promise for much more revolution in the ensuing 10 years. We should expect even more radical changes in our way of life and how we interact with the environment around us as a result of IoT in the future [2].

**Corresponding author*: kunal.anandfcs@kiit.ac.in

Subhasis Dash, Manas Ranjan Lenka, S. Balamurugan, Ambika Prasad Tripathy and Amarendra Mohanty (eds.) Sustainable Resource Management in Next-Generation Computational Constrained Networks, (189–220) © 2025 Scrivener Publishing LLC

The advent of the IoT is considered to be a highly transformative and disruptive technological innovation of the modern era. It has ushered in a new era of connectivity, facilitating the interaction of physical objects and devices with each other through a vast network of internet-connected devices [3]. This connectedness has allowed devices to be remotely monitored, controlled, and optimized, leading to unprecedented levels of efficiency and productivity in various industries [4]. IoT has transformed the way we interact with technology, as devices that were once isolated and disparate can now communicate and share data with each other. This ability to connect and communicate has created a world where information is accessible from almost any location [5], empowering data-driven decision-making and enabling real-time action-taking.

IoT technology has become an ever-present aspect of our lives, appearing in a variety of shapes and fulfilling various functions. These devices come in sizes ranging from minute sensors to colossal manufacturing machines or vehicles [6]. They are equipped with sensors, processors, and communication hardware that facilitate the collection of data from their environment and enable them to communicate with other devices via wired or wireless networks [7]. After the data is collected, it undergoes processing and analysis utilizing cloud computing, edge computing, or a combination of both. Cloud computing involves utilizing remote servers to store, manage, and process data, whereas edge computing entails processing data at the device's location before transmitting it to the cloud [8]. Edge computing is often more efficient and rapid, reducing the necessity for long-distance data transmission. The data insights obtained from analyzing IoT data have a broad range of applications in various industries [9]. Manufacturers can leverage IoT data to monitor their production processes and identify areas for improvement such as reducing downtime or optimizing energy consumption. In healthcare, IoT devices can monitor patients' vital signs and notify healthcare providers of any anomalies, enabling quick intervention that could potentially save lives. Furthermore, IoT data has the potential to enhance user experiences by providing personalized recommendations and improving product design. Retailers can utilize data from IoT-enabled beacons to track customers' movements in their stores and offer personalized promotions based on their preferences [10]. Similarly, car manufacturers can utilize data from IoT sensors to optimize the performance and safety of their vehicles. The incorporation of IoT in smart homes has revolutionized the way home-owners manage their household affairs. IoT devices enable homeowners to remotely control various home appliances using their smartphones, tablets, or laptops, thus providing them with unparalleled convenience and efficiency [11]. This technology allows them to manage their heating and cooling systems, lighting, and security systems even when they are away from home, giving them peace of mind. Smart thermostats, in particular, have gained immense popularity, owing to their ability to learn the homeowner's preferred temperature settings and adjust them automatically to save energy and minimize costs [12]. Additionally, IoT-based smart lighting systems are another prominent feature of smart homes. These systems utilize occupancy and time of day sensors to turn on and off lights, resulting in significant energy savings and greater convenience. For instance, a smart lighting system can be customized to activate the hallway lights when someone enters the house or switch off the living room lights when there is no movement for a specific period [13]. Consequently, the integration of IoT in smart homes is transforming the way homeowners experience comfort, security, and energy savings.

The impact of IoT on the healthcare industry cannot be overstated. Today, wearable devices like fitness trackers and smartwatches are ubiquitous and are revolutionizing healthcare. These wearable devices track and monitor vital signs such as heart rate, blood pressure, and oxygen levels, generating an abundance of valuable health-related data [14]. This data is analyzed by healthcare professionals to identify potential health issues and offer personalized recommendations, thus enhancing patient care [15]. Additionally, IoT-enabled medical devices like insulin pumps and pacemakers can transmit real-time data to healthcare providers, enabling remote monitoring and timely intervention in emergencies [16]. In the agricultural industry, IoT technology is also transforming the way farmers operate. Farmers face a plethora of challenges such as weather, pests, and plant diseases that can significantly impact crop yields and quality. By leveraging IoT technology, farmers can gain valuable insights into their operations and make data-driven decisions. For instance, smart sensors placed in fields can monitor soil moisture, temperature, and humidity levels, helping farmers optimize irrigation and reduce water waste [17]. Moreover, IoT-enabled drones can survey fields, identifying areas that require more attention and providing insights into crop health and potential disease outbreaks [18].

8.2 Evolution of IoT

The IoT has its roots in the early stages of internet development and the emergence of networking technology. The concept of connecting different devices and machines to the internet, thereby facilitating communication between them, dates back to the 1980s. However, it was not until 1999 that the term "Internet of Things" was coined by Kevin Ashton, a British technology pioneer and entrepreneur. At that time, Ashton was involved in a Procter and Gamble project that aimed to improve the efficiency of the company's supply chain using RFID (radio-frequency identification) technology. While working on the project, he realized that the technology could be utilized to connect a wide range of physical objects to the internet, allowing them to communicate with each other and creating a vast network of interconnected devices. As a result, the concept of the IoT was born, and it has since become a key driver of innovation and digital transformation in numerous industries.

In RFID Journal, "We require a way to link information from the physical world with information from the digital world. Similar to how the internet changed the world, the IoT has the potential to do the same. Maybe even more." IoT, according to Ashton, is a network of linked devices that can gather and share data, enabling higher levels of automation, efficiency, and insight. The idea has grown and changed throughout time to cover a wide range of sectors and applications, from wearables and smart homes to smart cities and industrial automation. The IoT sector is now expanding quickly, and, in the upcoming years, it is expected to provide economic value in the billions of dollars.

The evolution of IoT, which refers to the interconnectivity of physical devices over the internet, has progressed through distinct phases that are characterized by noteworthy technological breakthroughs and novel applications.

8.2.1 Phase 1: Early Adopters (Pre-2010)

The initial stage of IoT, which is also referred to as Phase 1, was a period characterized by experimentation, discovery, and progress. During this period, researchers and engineers were exploring the potential of wireless communication technologies to create interconnected networks of devices. Two of the most significant technologies that emerged during this stage were RFID and Bluetooth.

In the early days, RFID technology, which has been around since the 1940s, was an essential element of IoT. RFID employs radio waves to establish communication between a tag or label affixed to an object and a reader device. This technology allowed businesses to track assets and monitor inventory in real time, enhancing efficiency and minimizing errors [19]. In industrial and manufacturing settings, RFID was utilized to trace goods and materials as they traversed the supply chain, providing increased visibility and control [20]. Bluetooth, which was initially introduced in 1998, is a wireless technology that enables devices to communicate with each other over short distances. Although early versions of Bluetooth had restricted range and bandwidth, they were still useful in connecting devices like mobile phones and headsets. Bluetooth paved the way for the development of wireless sensors and other IoT devices [21].

In the initial phase of IoT, which is also known as Phase 1, the primary use of IoT was observed in the industrial and manufacturing sectors. The objective of businesses during this phase was to automate processes and increase efficiency, and IoT provided a viable solution to achieve this [22]. By connecting sensors and devices to the internet, companies were able to monitor equipment in real time and make necessary adjustments. For instance, businesses could utilize IoT to monitor the temperature and humidity levels in a warehouse or factory to ensure that products were stored under optimal conditions, which minimized spoilage or damage [23]. Asset tracking was another key application of IoT during Phase 1. Companies attached RFID tags to their equipment and goods to track their location and status in real time, which improved inventory management and reduced the risk of theft or loss [24].

8.2.2 Phase 2: Connectivity and Smart Devices (2010–2015)

The second phase of IoT was a pivotal moment for the technology, spanning from 2010 to 2015. During this phase, the emergence of powerful and cost-effective sensors, alongside wireless communication technologies like Wi-Fi and cellular networks, laid the foundation for the creation of smart devices like smartphones, tablets, and wearables [25]. These devices could gather and transmit data to the cloud, ushering in a new era of connectivity where devices could communicate and exchange information, opening up the potential for innovative use cases [26].

One of the significant factors driving this phase was the widespread adoption of smartphones and mobile devices. By 2010, smartphones had become ubiquitous, with more mobile devices in use than there were people on the planet. This demand for mobile applications spurred the development of new IoT applications and use cases, contributing to IoT's growth and expansion [27]. During this phase, the healthcare sector experienced substantial growth, with IoT-enabled medical devices such as wearables, blood glucose meters, and pulse oximeters becoming increasingly available. These devices enabled patients to monitor their health from home and share real-time data with healthcare providers, leading to better patient outcomes and cost savings [28].

During the second phase, the technology witnessed significant progress due to the availability of affordable and more advanced sensors, as well as wireless communication technologies such as Wi-Fi and cellular networks. This allowed for the creation of smart devices, including smartphones, tablets, and wearables, which could collect and transmit data to the cloud [29]. The rise of smartphones, in particular, led to an increase in demand for mobile applications, leading to the development of new IoT use cases. Besides, the second phase of IoT was not limited to industrial settings alone. Other industries, including healthcare, agriculture, and smart homes, also saw significant growth in their use of IoT [30]. Additionally, the popularity of smart homes surged during this phase, as consumers adopted IoT-enabled devices to enhance their daily living. Smart thermostats, lighting systems, and security systems became more widely available, allowing homeowners to control their homes remotely, save energy, and increase their convenience.

8.2.3 Phase 3: Big Data and Cloud Computing (2015 to Present)

The third phase of the IoT is marked by the widespread adoption of cloud computing and big data analytics, and it started in 2015 and continues until today. IoT devices have become increasingly advanced and produce massive amounts of data, which can be analyzed to gain insights for better decision-making and drive business outcomes [31]. This phase is characterized by the emergence of new IoT applications, which are designed to address real-world problems and have the potential to transform entire industries [32]. For example, smart cities use IoT technologies to optimize energy consumption, reduce traffic congestion, and improve public safety [33]. Connected cars are another area where IoT is making a big impact. Manufacturers can collect data on driver behavior, vehicle performance, and road conditions to improve the driving experience, reduce accidents, and develop new revenue streams [34].

Cloud computing has been a key enabler of this phase of IoT. By providing a flexible and scalable platform for storing and analyzing data, cloud computing has made it possible to process the massive amounts of data generated by IoT devices [35]. Cloud-based analytics tools have also made it easier for organizations to gain insights from this data without the need for expensive and complex on-premise infrastructure [36]. Another important trend in this phase of IoT is the move toward edge computing. Edge computing involves processing data at the edge of the network, closer to where it is generated. This approach can reduce latency and improve the performance of IoT applications. It also has the potential to reduce the amount of data that needs to be sent to the cloud, which can reduce bandwidth requirements and lower costs [37].

8.2.4 Phase 4: Artificial Intelligence and Edge Computing (Present and Future)

The fourth phase of the IoT is an emerging field, and it is anticipated that it will involve the integration of artificial intelligence (AI) and edge computing technologies. The emergence of this phase will take IoT to the next level.

Edge computing is a technique that involves processing data at the edge of the network or closer to the source, thereby reducing latency and improving efficiency [37]. This technique differs from traditional computing methods that transfer all data to a central server for processing. Edge computing has become an essential technology in the field of IoT as it allows for quick decision-making and efficient data processing [38]. On the other hand, AI has revolutionized the way we look at data. It can be used to analyze and make decisions based on the data collected by IoT devices, which enables autonomous decision-making and new levels of automation [39]. It can support equipment failure prediction and prevention, energy efficiency, customer experience enhancement, and business process automation. AI algorithms can also recognize patterns in data to help identify issues before they become critical [40]. Together, AI and edge computing can bring numerous benefits to the field of IoT. They can be used in numerous applications such as the development of autonomous vehicles, smart grids, and predictive maintenance in industrial settings. Autonomous vehicles are a prime example of how AI and edge computing can enhance the IoT experience. For navigation, they rely on data from a variety of devices, including cameras and sensors [41]. The vehicle can swiftly evaluate this data and decide when to change lanes or slow down, increasing safety thanks to edge computing [42]. AI and edge computing can assist utilities in managing energy supply and demand, enhancing distribution, and keeping track of the grid's health in smart grids [43]. Predictive maintenance in industrial settings is another illustration of how edge computing and AI may improve the IoT experience. By using machine learning (ML) algorithms to examine sensor data and forecast when equipment is likely to break, predictive maintenance enables businesses to plan repair before a problem happens [44].

8.3 Features of IoT

IoT features are numerous and varied, and they have the potential to change how we live and how we work. These are a few of the key characteristics of IoT:

1. **Security:** As the interconnectedness of devices offers potential threats, security is one of the fundamental aspects of IoT. Several procedures are put in place to offer protection against data breaches and unauthorized access because the security of IoT devices is of the utmost significance [45]. Strong encryption and authentication protocols are integrated into IoT devices to safeguard the privacy of user data. The use of firewalls, antivirus software, and intrusion detection systems is also common to identify and prevent potential security threats. Additionally, regular software updates and patches are necessary to mitigate any vulnerabilities that may arise. Ensuring the security of IoT devices is crucial, as any breach in data could lead to significant losses and compromise the privacy of individuals [46, 47]. Therefore, constant vigilance and adherence to best security practices are essential to keep IoT devices and their users safe.
2. **Connectivity:** IoT devices are intended to be connected to the internet, which permits them to share information and interact with other devices within the network. The ability to connect in this way allows for remote control and monitoring of IoT devices, making them ideal for a wide range of applications, including home and industrial automation [48]. With IoT connectivity, devices can communicate with each other and with central systems, enabling them to collect and analyze data in real time. This data can then be used to identify patterns, make predictions, and drive decision-making [49]. The seamless connectivity offered by IoT technology is transforming the way we interact with devices, and it has the potential to revolutionize a vast range of industries, from healthcare to transportation.

3. **Personalization:** The IoT has the potential to provide a customized experience for each user. With IoT devices, users can receive personalized recommendations based on their individual data [50]. For instance, a fitness tracker can collect and analyze data on a user's activity levels, heart rate, and sleep patterns to provide tailored advice on exercise and diet that suits their individual needs. This personalization can help users to make more informed decisions about their health and lifestyle, leading to better overall wellness [51]. With the integration of AI and edge computing technologies, this personalization can be further improved, allowing for even more advanced and accurate recommendation based on real-time data. As IoT continues to evolve, personalized experiences will become increasingly prevalent, enhancing the way we interact with technology and improving our quality of life [52].
4. **Sensor Technology:** IoT devices may collect data on a variety of environmental elements, including temperature, humidity, light, sound, and motion, thanks to sensor technology. Users might get useful insights from this data about patterns and trends that they would not have, otherwise, recognized [53]. In order to improve systems and processes and enable more informed decision-making, the collected data can be analyzed. IoT sensors may be included in a variety of gadgets, from basic home appliances to sophisticated industrial machines. In order to make better decisions and streamline operations, organizations may now gather and analyze data from a number of sources [54]. Moreover, sensor technology can aid in the detection of possible faults or equipment breakdowns, allowing maintenance staff to solve problems before they become significant. Overall, sensor technology is an essential part of the IoT, enabling both individuals and companies to leverage the power of data for better decision-making and increased productivity [55].
5. **Real-time Monitoring:** The ability of IoT devices to gather and transmit data in real time is a crucial advantage for both individuals and businesses. With this technology, people can easily track various metrics, such as traffic flow, energy usage, and machine performance, among others [55].

By monitoring data in real time, individuals and businesses can obtain valuable insights into their operations, identify areas for improvement, and enhance overall performance. For instance, companies can use real-time data monitoring to identify inefficiencies in their processes, reduce waste, and optimize performance, leading to increased productivity and profitability [56, 57]. Similarly, individuals can use real-time data to make informed decisions and adjust their behavior to achieve better outcomes. Real-time data monitoring, therefore, has the potential to transform the way we live and work, making our lives more efficient and productive.

6. **Predictive Analytics:** IoT devices can gather massive amounts of data, which can then be processed and analyzed using ML and AI algorithms. Predictive analytics, which involves identifying patterns and trends in the data to make predictions about future outcomes, can be achieved through these technologies [58]. By using predictive analytics, businesses can anticipate and identify potential equipment failures before they happen, allowing them to schedule maintenance and repairs proactively. This helps to reduce downtime and maintenance costs, ultimately improving business operations and productivity [59]. Predictive analytics can also be used in other applications, such as predicting consumer behavior or anticipating traffic congestion. Overall, the use of IoT devices and predictive analytics has the potential to revolutionize many industries, leading to greater efficiency, cost savings, and improved decision-making capabilities [60].
7. **Enhanced Safety:** The implementation of IoT devices holds promise for improving safety across various settings. One potential use case is through the installation of a smart home security system that can quickly alert homeowners of possible intrusions [61]. In addition, IoT devices can be integrated into smart city infrastructure to monitor traffic patterns and adjust signals in real time, which can help to reduce the likelihood of accidents on the road [62]. By leveraging IoT technology, it is possible to create a more

responsive and intelligent safety system that can detect and respond to potential dangers faster and more accurately. This can not only help to prevent accidents and minimize damage but also increase overall safety and security for individuals and communities alike [63]. As such, the integration of IoT devices into safety systems represents an important step toward building a safer and more connected world.

8.4 Architectural Framework of IoT

Data transfer across various devices, networks, and applications is made easier by the IoT architecture. The device layer, network layer, platform layer, and application layer are the four major layers that make up the IoT architecture, which is designed to accomplish this goal. Any IoT device, sensor, and actuator that gathers data and transmits it to the network layer is part of the device layer, which is the lowest layer. The network layer supports safe data transfer and provides dependable connectivity between IoT devices. IoT data management and processing, including data analysis, storage, and device management, are interfaced through the platform layer. With user-friendly interfaces and apps, the application layer distributes IoT data to end users. Figure 8.1 demonstrates the layers of IoT.

The IoT architecture can be broken down into several different levels, making it feasible to build a flexible and adaptable system that can scale to meet the changing demands of IoT applications.

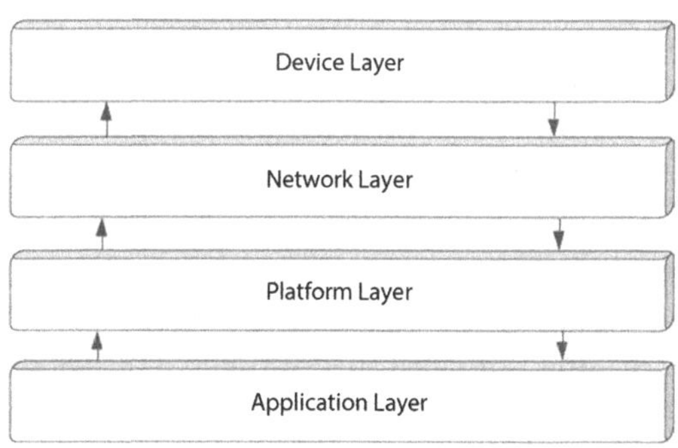

Figure 8.1 Layers of IoT.

8.4.1 Device Layer

The architecture of the IoT is built on the device layer (IoT). Physical objects or sensors make up this layer, which collects data from its environment and transmits it to the architecture's next level. In a sense, the device layer serves as the IoT's sensory organs, providing the basic information that is later examined and used to develop groundbreaking applications and insights.

A wide range of devices may be used in the IoT, from simple sensors that measure temperature, light, or humidity to more sophisticated ones that can track position, monitor a person's health, or operate machines. These gadgets may be incorporated into many different things, including people, appliances, buildings, cars, and even other people. Constrained and unrestrained devices make up the two main categories for IoT devices. Constrained gadgets are made to carry out easy activities and send minimal quantities of data and have restricted processing power, memory, and battery life.

Smart lightbulbs, temperature sensors, and motion sensors are a few examples of restricted devices. Unrestricted devices, on the other hand, have more processing power, memory, and networking possibilities, enabling them to carry out complicated tasks and send huge volumes of data. Smartphones, smart cars, and industrial robots are a few examples of unrestrained gadgets. The IoT's device layer may be distinguished by a number of characteristics, including sensor capacities, communication protocols, power supply, and form factor. The precise use cases and specifications for the IoT devices are determined by these qualities. A temperature sensor, for instance, would need to be able to precisely monitor a wide range of temperatures and communicate information through a low-power, long-range communication protocol. On the other hand, a smart car could require real-time data processing and high-speed networking.

IoT devices' sensing skills are essential to how well they work. They decide what information the gadgets may gather, and the sensing options can vary from proximity detection to temperature and pressure monitoring. Depending on the device and application, the sensing capabilities might vary in terms of accuracy, precision, and range. For instance, a proximity sensor must identify objects at different distances and angles, whereas a temperature sensor needs frequent calibration to guarantee reliable data. In order to send data to other IoT devices or networks, IoT devices rely on communication protocols. There are many frequencies and data formats that may be utilized with either wired or wireless communication methods.

The most popular networking technologies are cellular networks, Wi-Fi, Bluetooth, Zigbee, LoRaWAN, and others.

The choice of communication protocol is influenced by a number of variables, including range, bandwidth, power usage, and security.

In order for IoT devices to function without recharging or replacing the battery, power sources are also an important component. Many power sources, including batteries, solar panels, and energy harvesting, can power IoT devices. The choice of power source is influenced by a number of variables, including form factor, power consumption, and the availability of power sources. The physical properties of IoT devices, such as their size, shape, and design, are referred to as form factor. The gadgets' form factor influences how well they can be incorporated into other items or settings. IoT devices can be embedded systems, wearables, sensors, or actuators, among other things. The sensing capability, power supply, and communication protocol of the device all have an impact on the form factor selection. Device management, which gets increasingly difficult as the number of devices rises, is one of the major difficulties in the IoT device layer. Particularly in large-scale IoT installations, managing and maintaining devices is a difficult and time-consuming operation that comprises device registration, setup, monitoring, and firmware upgrades.

8.4.2 Network Layer

The IoT ecosystem's network layer is in charge of organizing and monitoring the device-to-device communication process. Establishing and maintaining a consistent, dependable connection and data transfer between the devices and the cloud is its fundamental goal. The primary hub for storing, processing, and analyzing the data produced by these devices is the cloud.

There are three main parts that make up the IoT network layer: gateways, network protocols, and cloud services. The numerous policies and practices that regulate data transmission throughout the network are outlined in a framework provided by network protocols. These protocols, which include Bluetooth, Wi-Fi, ZigBee, and message queuing telemetry transport (MQTT), offer recommendations for data format, data security, and data transfer. Gateways act as a connection point between devices and the cloud, translating data received from devices into a language that the cloud can understand. Gateways also offer security tools like encryption and authentication to guarantee safe data delivery. The last part of the network layer, cloud services, is in charge of processing, storing, and analyzing data produced by devices. They give programmers a solid foundation on which to build tools for the monitoring and management of devices. Moreover, cloud services include cutting-edge analytics capabilities that allow insightful analysis of the data produced by devices. The network layer is severely challenged by the IoT devices' constrained bandwidth and power. It can be difficult to transfer huge volumes of data over the network because IoT devices often have constrained processing and battery life. IoT devices frequently employ edge computing to solve this problem, which entails processing data locally, at the point of generation, before sending it to the cloud. By lowering the quantity of data that has to be transferred, this method helps to preserve bandwidth and electricity.

Due to their frequent vulnerability to assaults and the potential sensitivity of the data they generate, IoT device security is a significant problem at the network layer. As a result, to safeguard both the devices and the data they create, strong security measures like encryption, authentication, and access control are necessary. In controlling the connectivity between IoT devices and the cloud, the network layer is ultimately crucial. It can create and maintain an uninterrupted connection and data exchange by combining network protocols, gateways, and cloud services. Security is still a major problem at the network layer despite challenges such constrained power and bandwidth, necessitating the adoption of robust security methods like encryption, authentication, and access control.

8.4.3 Platform Layer

The entire structure, which consists of both hardware and software components, includes the platform layer of the IoT. Its primary objective is to streamline IoT device, application, and user interactions, data gathering, and processing. Moreover, it is essential for preserving the security, scalability, and dependability of IoT networks and assuring interoperability across various devices, protocols, and data formats. IoT gateways, serving as a bridge between edge devices and the cloud or data center, are at the heart of the platform layer. They enhance the latency, bandwidth, and availability of IoT applications by carrying out a variety of tasks such data aggregation, protocol translation, filtering, and preprocessing. IoT middleware, which offers software services and application programming interfaces (APIs) for developers to design, deploy, and manage IoT applications, is another crucial element. The platform layer includes a number of protocols and standards that enable smooth communication and interaction between IoT devices and apps. These protocols, which allow low-power, low-bandwidth, and sporadic communication conditions, include MQTT, constrained application protocol (CoAP), advanced message queuing protocol (AMQP), and hypertext transfer protocol (HTTP). The platform layer also includes governance and management structures with policies, laws, and standards in place that control the usage, sharing, and protection of IoT data and devices in order to assure compliance, privacy, and security of IoT systems.

The platform layer has a number of difficulties, including interoperability, scalability, security, and privacy, in spite of its significance. To solve this, it must give mechanisms for standardization and normalization, enable extensive deployments, and provide dependable security measures to safeguard IoT assets and data in a transparent and moral manner, in accordance with established norms and standards.

8.4.4 Application Layer

The IoT is a vast system of interconnected gadgets that can interact and share data with one another online (IoT). The IoT architecture's separation into several layers, each of which is in charge of a certain function, enables this. The application layer, which is the top layer, is responsible for managing the user interface (UI) and facilitating application interaction with IoT devices.

The application layer is crucial to the success of IoT because it provides services and apps that leverage the data provided by IoT devices to provide value to end-users. By creating a connection between users and IoT devices, the application layer enables users to manage, control, and monitor IoT devices. Moreover, it provides developers with a platform to create novel services and apps that can enhance the performance of IoT devices.

The application layer's key components include the UI, API, data management, security, application services, and application development. A key element is the UI, which provides users with a graphical or command-line interface to communicate with IoT devices and access the data they generate. Contrarily, the API provides a standard interface that can be utilized by several IoT platforms, enabling developers to create apps that can connect with IoT devices.

Because it enables the storing, processing, and analysis of data produced by IoT devices to produce important insights, data management is crucial to the application layer of an IoT architecture. The application layer provides databases, data analytics tools, and data visualization tools as part of its data management capabilities to help with this. Security at the application layer is equally important because it ensures that data generated by IoT devices is maintained securely and is protected from unauthorized access. Access control, authentication, and encryption are available as security capabilities at the application layer.

The application services, which give clients services using the data generated by IoT devices, are another crucial component of the application layer. Some of these services include location-based services, predictive maintenance, remote monitoring, and predictive analytics. The application layer also provides developers with platforms and tools to create new services and applications that can enhance the performance of IoT devices. Development tools include programming languages, integrated development environments, and software development kits.

8.5 Components of IoT

The IoT is a network of connected devices that enables data sharing and interoperability. These devices, which are typically referred to as "smart," can range from simple sensors to complex machinery and systems. Figure 8.2 exhibits the components of IoT. The following are the key components of IoT:

1. **Sensors and Actuators:** IoT requires sensors and actuators to function. Sensors are tools that can identify and quantify environmental changes in factors like temperature, humidity,

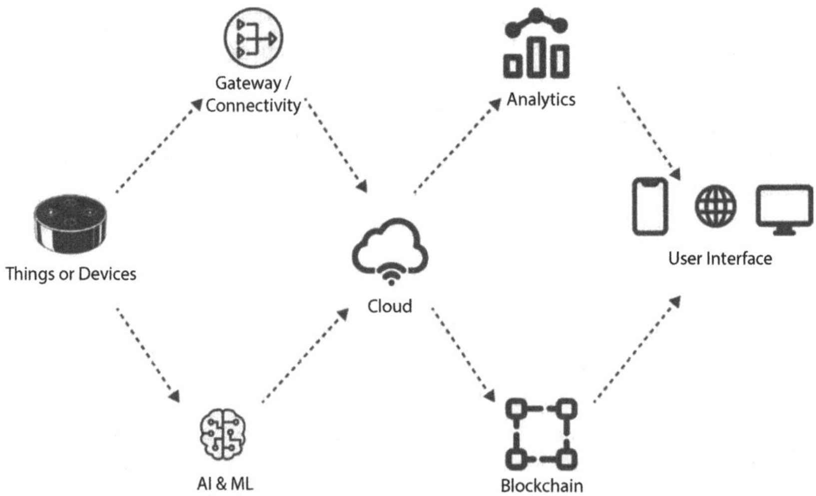

Figure 8.2 Components of IoT.

pressure, light, and sound. Actuators, which include things like motors, switches, and valves, are things that can control or alter the environment. For IoT systems to communicate with the real environment, these devices offer the input and output interfaces.

2. **Connectivity:** IoT connection is another essential component. Devices must be able to communicate with each other locally and over the internet in order for an IoT system to work. Networks like Wi-Fi, Bluetooth, Zig-Bee, RFID, and cellular ones may all be used to connect IoT devices and create communication. The individual requirements of the IoT application determine the communication method that is used.
3. **Cloud Computing:** IoT requires cloud computing as a critical component. Massive volumes of data generated by IoT must be handled, examined, and archived. The essential infrastructure to manage this data is provided by cloud computing. IoT data processing may be done using a variety of services provided by cloud platforms like Amazon Web Services and Microsoft Azure, including storage, analytics, and ML.
4. **Data Analytics:** Data analytics is yet another essential IoT component. IoT device data may offer insightful information about the environment and aid in decision-making for businesses. But, because of its size, speed, and diversity, this data can be difficult to analyze. IoT data may be processed and analyzed using data analytics technologies like Hadoop and Spark.
5. **User Interface (UI):** UI is an essential component of IoT. IoT technology needs to be straightforward to use and comprehend. Mobile apps, web programs, and voice assistants are just a few instances of many UIs. The Interface allows users to communicate with IoT equipment and obtain the data they generate.
6. **Artificial Intelligence (AI) and Machine Learning (ML):** AI and ML are being used more and more in IoT applications. Because to these technologies, IoT devices can now learn from data and make predictions based on that learning. An IoT system that monitors a machine's performance, for instance, may use ML algorithms to predict when the equipment is likely to malfunction, allowing repair to be scheduled before a malfunction occurs.

7. **Security:** IoT security is a key component. IoT devices are susceptible to cyberattacks, which can result in serious negative effects including data breaches, system failures, and bodily injury. To prevent unwanted access to IoT devices, security mechanisms including encryption, authentication, and access control must be put into place.
8. **Edge Computing:** Edge computing is starting to be integrated into IoT. Edge computing refers to the method of processing data locally as opposed to sending it to the cloud for processing. This tactic can help reduce latency, improve data privacy, and cut the cost of data transit.
9. **Blockchain:** Blockchain is an additional recently created IoT component. Blockchain, a distributed ledger technology, may be utilized to enable secure and transparent transactions between IoT devices. Blockchain, for example, may be used to create a tamper-proof record of the ownership and use of a certain item, like a car or a piece of equipment.

The IoT is a complex system made up of many different components, including sensors and actuators, connectivity, cloud computing, data analytics, AI, and ML, UI, security, edge computing, and blockchain. These components work together to create a network of interconnected devices that might help businesses and provide vital information about the environment.

8.6 Applications of IoT

An innovative and groundbreaking technology known as the IoT has significantly impacted both our personal and professional lives. By linking devices, sensors, and software, it enables the smooth interchange of data and communication between physical items and digital systems. This network of devices has completely changed several sectors thanks to its capacity to link various devices, and there is still a ton of room for expansion and improvement. IoT is a technology that is fast changing the way we live, and the breadth of potential applications is absolutely amazing.

1. **Agriculture:** The application of IoT technology in the agricultural sector holds immense promise for transforming traditional farming methods into a more efficient and profitable enterprise through the implementation of precision

farming. By leveraging an interconnected network of sensors and devices, farmers can collect and analyze critical data pertaining to soil moisture levels, temperature, and humidity in real time [64, 65]. The gathered data can be utilized to enhance the quality of crops and maximize yield by providing farmers with detailed insights on how to optimize crop growth [17]. Furthermore, IoT technology can help predict weather patterns and forecast disease outbreaks, allowing farmers to take timely action and implement preventative measures to protect their crops from potential damages.

In this way, IoT technology can enable farmers to make informed decisions and proactively address challenges, thereby enhancing the overall productivity and sustainability of the agricultural industry [66]. Figure 8.3 shows the application of IoT in agriculture field.

2. **Manufacturing:** The emergence of IoT has revolutionized the manufacturing industry by facilitating the creation of smart factories [67]. Figure 8.4 illustrates the application of IoT in manufacturing industry. These advanced factories rely on interconnected devices and sensors that can monitor

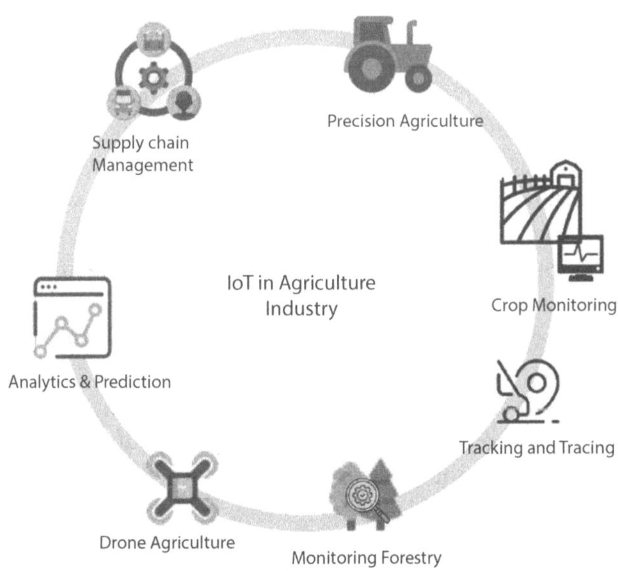

Figure 8.3 IoT in agriculture industry.

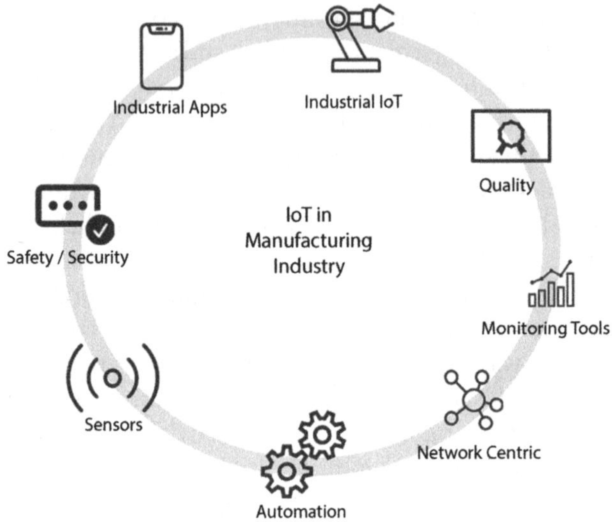

Figure 8.4 IoT in manufacturing industry.

the production process in real time, providing valuable insights into the performance of various equipment and processes [68]. Consequently, manufacturers can leverage this technology to optimize their operations and minimize downtime, resulting in increased productivity and profitability. Moreover, the utilization of IoT-enabled devices, such as predictive maintenance sensors, is a significant boon for the manufacturing industry [69]. These sensors are capable of detecting and predicting equipment failure, enabling manufacturers to take proactive measures to prevent costly downtime. This predictive maintenance approach can save businesses significant amounts of time and resources that would have been lost due to sudden equipment breakdowns. Therefore, the implementation of IoT technology in manufacturing can lead to substantial improvements in overall equipment effectiveness and operational efficiency.

3. **Medicine and Healthcare:** The healthcare industry is undergoing a significant transformation with the incorporation of IoT technology [15]. IoT is playing a pivotal role in revolutionizing healthcare by facilitating remote patient monitoring and providing personalized care. Figure 8.5 shows the application of IoT in healthcare system. By leveraging

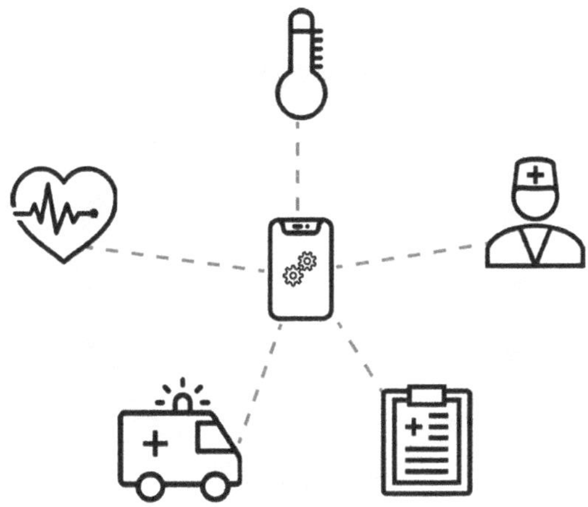

Figure 8.5 IoT in healthcare system.

the power of IoT-enabled devices, including wearables, sensors, and mobile applications, patient data can be tracked in real time and transmitted to healthcare providers for analysis [70]. This real-time data can be utilized to continuously monitor patient health, ensure medication adherence, and proactively detect any potential progression of disease. Additionally, IoT technology is empowering telemedicine, which allows patients to receive medical consultations and treatments from the convenience and safety of their homes, without compromising on the quality of healthcare services they receive [71]. These advancements in healthcare delivery through IoT are opening up new avenues for healthcare providers and patients to collaborate effectively and improving access to healthcare for patients in remote areas [72, 73].

4. **Transportation and Traffic Management:** The advent of IoT has led to a substantial revolution in the transportation industry through the introduction of connected cars and smart transportation systems [74, 75]. Figure 8.6 exhibits the application of IoT in transportation industry. The incorporation of IoT-enabled sensors and devices in connected cars enables them to establish seamless communication with other vehicles and infrastructure, thus promoting safer roads and reducing traffic congestion. Furthermore, smart transportation systems leverage the power of IoT

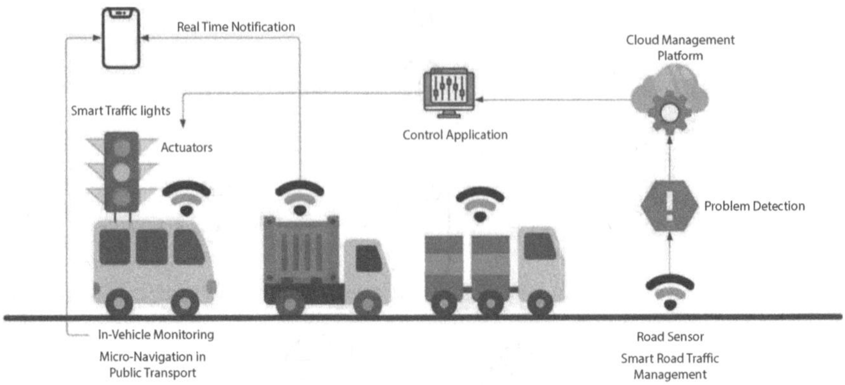

Figure 8.6 IoT in transportation industry.

to monitor traffic patterns and optimize routes, leading to reduced travel time and fuel consumption and, ultimately, resulting in lower emissions [76–78]. The application of IoT in the transportation sector has facilitated the deployment of advanced technologies that aim to streamline operations and elevate the overall user experience to unprecedented heights. In essence, the integration of IoT in the transportation industry has ushered in a new era of innovation, transforming the way we move from one place to another.

5. **Security Applications:** The application of IoT in the security industry is bringing about a major transformation, as it paves the way for the development of smart security systems. With the aid of connected devices such as cameras, sensors, and alarms, it is possible to keep homes and businesses under constant surveillance, providing real-time updates and notifications to security personnel in the event of an emergency [79]. Moreover, the integration of IoT-enabled security systems with other related technologies such as lighting and access control creates a comprehensive and cohesive security solution. This interconnectivity of IoT devices not only enhances security measures but also increases their efficiency and effectiveness.

   In addition, the integration of IoT in the security industry creates an opportunity for the deployment of predictive analytics and ML algorithms, which help to predict potential security breaches and improve response time in case of an emergency. As such, IoT-enabled security systems have become an indispensable tool in ensuring the safety and protection of individuals and businesses alike.

6. **Energy:** The application of IoT in the energy sector can bring about a significant improvement in energy efficiency and reduce waste [80]. By leveraging IoT devices, real-time monitoring of energy usage can be achieved, enabling both consumers and businesses to identify and curb energy wastage. Moreover, IoT devices can play a crucial role in optimizing the performance of renewable energy systems like solar panels and wind turbines, by tracking and analyzing weather conditions and making necessary adjustments to their output [81, 82]. Thus, IoT has the potential to revolutionize the energy sector by promoting sustainable practices and minimizing the environmental impact of energy generation and consumption.

8.7 Case Study

8.7.1 Overview of Barcelona Smart City Project

The Barcelona Smart City project is a significant example of the implementation of IoT technology in urban systems. The project's success depended on the involvement and support of different stakeholders, such as the city

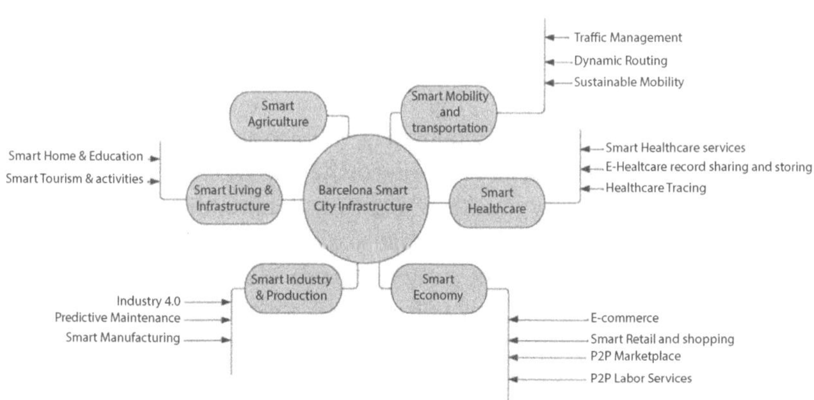

Figure 8.7 Overview of Barcelona smart city.

government, private companies, and citizens. A comprehensive methodology was followed, involving several key steps, such as defining the project's scope and objectives, identifying key stakeholders, developing a comprehensive plan, implementing the infrastructure, developing applications and services, testing and refining, and monitoring and maintaining. The project has become a model for other smart city initiatives globally, with a primary focus on improving the quality of life for citizens by integrating different urban systems into a unified platform. Figure 8.7 shows an overview of Barcelona city.

8.7.2 Methodology

The implementation of the Barcelona Smart City project followed a comprehensive methodology that involved several key steps. The first step in implementing the smart city solution was to define the project's scope and objectives. The project's primary objective was to improve the city's services and citizens' quality of life by leveraging the power of IoT technology. This involved identifying the various urban systems that needed to be integrated and the IoT technologies required for the project's implementation.

The success of the project depended on the involvement and support of different stakeholders, such as the city government, private companies, and citizens. Hence, the next step was to identify the key stakeholders and engage them in the project. The project team worked closely with stakeholders to ensure that their needs and expectations were met and that they were actively involved in the project's implementation.

A comprehensive plan was then developed to outline the project's implementation strategy. The plan involved identifying different urban systems that needed to be integrated, such as transportation, healthcare, energy, waste management, and public safety. The team also identified the IoT technologies required for the project's implementation, such as sensors, communication systems, and data management systems.

The project's implementation involved the deployment of IoT sensors and devices across the city to collect real-time data on different urban systems. The infrastructure included a network of sensors, communication systems, and data management systems to process and analyze the data. The project team worked closely with various stakeholders to ensure that the infrastructure was deployed in the most efficient and effective manner.

Based on the data collected by the IoT infrastructure, several applications and services were developed to improve the city's services and citizens' quality of life. For example, smart parking systems were developed to help drivers find available parking spots quickly, reducing traffic congestion and improving air quality.

Waste management systems were also implemented to help the city manage its waste more efficiently, reducing the amount of waste that ends up in landfills. Energy management systems were also developed to help the city reduce its energy consumption, lowering its carbon footprint and improving its environmental sustainability.

The applications and services developed were tested and refined based on feedback from citizens and other stakeholders. The project team worked closely with stakeholders to ensure that the applications and services developed were useful and effective in improving the city's services and citizens' quality of life. The success of the project depended on the usefulness and effectiveness of the applications and services developed.

The project's implementation involved the establishment of a monitoring and maintenance system to ensure that the infrastructure and applications developed functioned efficiently and effectively. The monitoring system allowed the project team to identify and address any issues that arose quickly. The maintenance system ensured that the infrastructure and applications were maintained regularly to ensure their long-term sustainability.

8.8 Conclusion

The IoT is a fast emerging technology with the potential to revolutionize the way we live and work. We have presented an introduction to IoT in this article, examining its history, architecture, components, applications, problems, and future prospects. We've seen how IoT has the ability to transform industries like healthcare, agriculture, manufacturing, and transportation by allowing real-time monitoring, automation, and data-driven decision-making. To guarantee that IoT is adopted responsibly and sustainably, governments, industry, and researchers must work together to address these difficulties.

In addition, we reviewed some of the present trends and future prospects of IoT. We have seen that the IoT is growing more common, with the number of linked devices anticipated to reach billions in the coming years. As a result, huge volumes of data will be created, necessitating the use of advanced analytics tools and methodologies to extract useful insights. Overall, IoT has enormous potential, and its effect on society will only rise in the future years. As a result, it is critical that we continue to investigate its potential and handle its obstacles in order to fully realize its advantages while reducing its hazards. We can create a more connected, intelligent, and sustainable world for future generations by doing so.

References

1. Ashton, K., *et al.*, That 'internet of things' thing. *RFID J.*, **22**, 7, 97–114, 2009.
2. Hassija, V., Chamola, V., Saxena, V., Jain, D., Goyal, P., Sikdar, B., A survey on IoT security: Application areas, security threats, and solution architectures. *IEEE Access*, **7**, 82721–82743, 2019, https://doi.org/10.1109/access.2019.2924045.
3. Ray, P.P., Dash, D., Salah, K., Kumar, N., Blockchain for iot-based healthcare: Background, consensus, platforms, and use cases. *IEEE Syst. J.*, **15**, 1–10, 2020, https://doi.org/10.1109/jsyst.2020.2963840.
4. Qin, W., Chen, S., Peng, M., Recent advances in industrial internet: Insights and challenges. *Digital Commun. Netw.*, **6**, 1–13, 2019, https://doi.org/10.1016/j.dcan.2019.07.001.
5. Kumar, S., Tiwari, P., Zymbler, M., Internet of things is a revolutionary approach for future technology enhancement: a review. *J. Big Data*, **6**, 1–21, 2019, https://doi.org/10.1186/s40537-019-0268-2.
6. Jadav, N.K., Kakkar, R., Mankodiya, H., Gupta, R., Tanwar, S., Agrawal, S., Sharma, R., Grade: Deep learning and garlic routing-based secure data sharing framework for iiot beyond 5g. *Digital Commun. Netw.*, **9**, 422–435, 2022, https://doi.org/10.1016/j.dcan.2022.11.004.
7. Garg, V.K., Wireless personal area networks: Low rate and high rate. *Wireless Commun. Networking*, 675–712, 2007, https://doi.org/ 10.1016/b978-012373580-5/50054-5.
8. Chellappan, S. and Dutta, N., Mobility in wireless sensor networks. *Adv. Comput.*, **90**, 185–222, 2013, https://doi.org/10.1016/ b978-0-12-408091-1.00003-8.
9. Ai, Y., Peng, M., Zhang, K., Edge computing technologies for internet of things: a primer. *Digital Commun. Netw.*, **4**, 77–86, 2018, https://doi.org/10.1016/j.dcan.2017.07.001.
10. Chen, P., Dairy Cow Health Monitoring System Based on NB-IoT Communication, 2019, https://doi.org/10.1109/EEI48997.2019.00091.
11. Reisinger, M.R., Prost, S., Schrammel, J., Fröhlich, P., User requirements for the design of smart homes: dimensions and goals. *J. Ambient Intell. Hum. Comput.*, 1–20, 2022, https://doi.org/10.1007/ s12652-021-03651-6.
12. Oturak, M. and Dursun, E., A cost-effective iot based smart home application. *2021 International Conference on INnovations in Intelligent SysTems and Applications (INISTA)*, 2021, https://doi.org/10.1109/inista52262.2021.9548468.

13. Fabi, V., Spigliantini, G., Corgnati, S.P., Insights on smart home concept and occupants' interaction with building controls. *Energy Procedia*, **111**, 759–769, 2017, https://doi.org/10.1016/j.egypro.2017.03.238.
14. Takiddeen, N. and Zualkernan, I., *Smartwatches as IoT Edge Devices: A Framework and Survey*, 2019, https://doi.org/10.1109/FMEC.2019.8795338.
15. Kelly, J.T., Campbell, K.L., Gong, E., Scuffham, P., The internet of things: impact and implications for healthcare delivery (preprint). *J. Med. Internet Res.*, **22**, 2020, https://doi.org/10.2196/20135.
16. Calvillo-Arbizu, J., Román-Martínez, I., Reina-Tosina, J., Internet of things in health: Requirements, issues, and gaps. *Comput. Methods Programs Biomed.*, **208**, 106231, 2021, https://doi.org/10.1016/j.cmpb.2021.106231.
17. Ayaz, M., Ammad-uddin, M., Sharif, Z., Mansour, A., Aggoune, e, H.M., Internet-of-things (IoT) based smart agriculture: Towards making the fields talk. *IEEE Access*, **7**, 1, 2019, https://doi.org/10.1109/access.2019. 2932609.
18. Israr, A., Abro, G.E.M., Sadiq Ali Khan, M., Farhan, M., Bin Mohd Zulkifli, SA., Internet of Things (IoT)-Enabled Unmanned Aerial Vehicles for the Inspection of Construction Sites: A Vision and Future Directions, 2021.
19. Majrouhi Sardroud, J., Influence of rfid technology on automated management of construction materials and components. *Sci. Iran.*, **19**, 381–392, 2012, https://doi.org/10.1016/j.scient.2012.02.023.
20. Wang, L.-C., Enhancing construction quality inspection and management using rfid technology. *Autom. Constr.*, **17**, 467–479, 2008, https://doi.org/10.1016/j.autcon.2007.08.005.
21. Bansal, N., Jayant, K.P., Singh, P., Pandey, S., Intelligent Extension with Smart Connections using Bluetooth with IoT, 2021, https://doi.org/10. 1109/ICOEI51242.2021.9452859.
22. Langley, D.J., van Doorn, J., Ng, I.C.L., Stieglitz, S., Lazovik, A., Boonstra, A., The internet of everything: Smart things and their impact on business models. *J. Bus. Res.*, **122**, 2020, https://doi.org/10.1016/j.jbusres.2019.12.035.
23. Zhang, S., Ang Jr., M.H., Xiao, W., Tham, Detection of activities by wireless sensors for daily life surveillance: eating and drinking. *Sensors*, **9**, 3, 1499–1517, 2009.
24. Khalid, R. and Ejaz, W., Internet of Things-based On-demand Rental Asset Tracking and Monitoring System, 2022, https://doi.org/10.1109/ICICT55905.2022.00023.
25. Pahlavan, K. and Krishnamurthy, P., Evolution and impact of wi-fi technology and applications: A historical perspective. *Int. J. Wireless Inf. Netw.*, **28**, 3–19, 2020, https://doi.org/10.1007/ s10776-020-00501-8.
26. Alam, T., Cloud-based iot applications and their roles in smart cities. *Smart Cities*, **4**, 1196–1219, 2021, https://doi.org/10.3390/ smartcities4030064.
27. Lee, U., Han, K., Cho, H., Chung, K.-M., Hong, H., Lee, S.-J., Noh, Park, Y.S., Carroll, J.M., Intelligent positive computing with mobile, wearable, and IoT devices: Literature review and research directions. *Ad Hoc Netw.*, **83**, 8–24, 2019, https://doi.org/10.1016/j.adhoc.2018.08.021.

28. Wan, J., Al-awlaqi, A.A.H., Li, M., O'Grady, M., Gu, X., Wang, J., Cao, N., Wearable iot enabled real-time health monitoring system. *EURASIP J. Wireless Commun. Networking*, 2018, 2018, https://doi.org/10.1186/s13638-018-1308-x.
29. Gardašević, G., Katzis, K., Bajić, D., Berbakov, L., Emerging wireless sensor networks and internet of things technologies—foundations of smart healthcare. *Sensors*, 20, 3619, 2020, https://doi.org/10.3390/s20133619.
30. Hussein, A.H., Internet of things (IoT): Research challenges and future applications. *Int. J. Adv. Comput. Sci. Appl.*, 10, 2019, https://doi.org/10.14569/ijacsa.2019.0100611.
31. Andersen, D.L., Ashbrook, C.S.A., Karlborg, N.B., Significance of big data analytics and the internet of things (IoT) aspects in industrial development, governance and sustainability. *Int. J. Intell. Netw.*, **1**, 107–111, 2020, https://doi.org/10.1016/j.ijin.2020.12.003.
32. Big IoT data analytics: Architecture, opportunities, and open research challenges. *IEEE Access*, **5**, 5247–5261, 2017, https://doi.org/10.1109/access.2017.2689040.
33. Syed, A.S., Sierra-Sosa, D., Kumar, A., Elmaghraby, A., IoT in smart cities: A survey of technologies, practices and challenges. *Smart Cities*, 4, 429–475, 2021, https://doi.org/10.3390/smartcities4020024.
34. Devi, Y.U. and Rukmini, M.S.S., IoT in connected vehicles: Challenges and issues — A review, 2016, https://doi.org/10.1109/SCOPES.2016.7955769.
35. Almurisi, N. and Tadisetty, S., Cloud-based virtualization environment for IoT-based wsn: solutions, approaches and challenges. *J. Ambient Intell. Hum. Comput.*, 13, 4681–4703, 2022, https://doi.org/10.1007/ s12652-021-03515-z.
36. Somani, G., Zhao, X., Srirama, S.N., Buyya, R., Integration of cloud, internet of things, and big data analytics. *Softw.: Pract. Exper.*, 49, 561–564, 2018, https://doi.org/10.1002/spe.2664.
37. Pérez, J., Díaz, J., Berrocal, J., López-Viana, R., González-Prieto, Edge computing. Computing, 2022, https://doi.org/10.1007/ s00607-022-01104-2.
38. Kadhum, M., Manaseer, S., Latif, A., Cloud-edge network data processing based on user requirements using modify mapreduce algorithm and machine learning techniques. *Int. J. Adv. Comput. Sci. Appl.*, **10**, 2019, https://doi.org/10.14569/ijacsa.2019.0101242.
39. Keshta, I., Ai-driven iot for smart health care: Security and privacy issues. *Inf. Med. Unlocked*, **30**, 100903, 2022, https://doi.org/10. 1016/j.imu.2022.100903.
40. Talmoudi, S., Kanada, T., Hirata, Y., An iot-based failure prediction solution using machine sound data. *2019 IEEE/SICE International Symposium on System Integration (SII)*, 2019, https://doi.org/10.1109/sii. 2019.8700357.
41. Hossai, M.R.T., Shahjalal, M.A., Nuri, N.F., Design of an iot based autonomous vehicle with the aid of computer vision. *2017 International Conference on Electrical, Computer and Communication Engineering (ECCE)*, 2017, https://doi.org/10.1109/ecace.2017.7913003.

42. Gong, J., Jiang, Y., Xiong, G., Guan, C., Tao, G., Chen, H., The recognition and tracking of traffic lights based on color segmentation and camshift for intelligent vehicles, in: *2010 IEEE Intelligent Vehicles Symposium, IEEE*, pp. 431–435, 2010.
43. Chen, Z., Amani, A.M., Yu, X., Jalili, M., Control and optimisation of power grids using smart meter data: A review. *Sensors*, **23**, 2118, 2023, https://doi.org/10.3390/s23042118.
44. Achouch, M., Dimitrova, M., Dhouib, R., Ibrahim, H., Adda, M., Sattarpanah Karganroudi, S., Ziane, K., Aminzadeh, A., Predictive maintenance and fault monitoring enabled by machine learning: Experimental analysis of a ta-48 multistage centrifugal plant compressor. *Appl. Sci.*, **13**, 1790, 2023, https://doi.org/10.3390/app13031790.
45. Mishra, N. and Pandya, S., Internet of things applications, security challenges, attacks, intrusion detection, and future visions: A systematic review. *IEEE Access*, 9, 59353–59377, 2021.
46. Mavrogiorgou, A., Kiourtis, A., Perakis, K., Pitsios, S., Kyriazis, D., IoT in healthcare: Achieving interoperability of high-quality data acquired by iot medical devices. *Sensors*, 19, 1978, 2019, https://doi.org/10.3390/s19091978.
47. Urla, P.A., Mohan, G., Tyagi, S., Pai, S.N., A novel approach for security of data in IoT environment. *Lect. Notes Netw. Syst.*, 251–259, 2019, https://doi.org/10.1007/978-981-13-7150-9 26.
48. Purnama, B., Sharipuddin, Kurniabudi, Budiarto, R., Stiawan, D., Hanapi, D., Monitoring connectivity of internet of things device on zig- bee protocol. *2018 International Conference on Electrical Engineering and Computer Science (ICECOS)*, 2018, https://doi.org/10.1109/icecos.2018.8605225.
49. Mukherjee, S. and Biswas, G.P., Networking for iot and applications using existing communication technology. *Egypt. Inf. J.*, 19, 107–127, 2018, https://doi.org/10.1016/j.eij.2017.11.002.
50. Lee, A.-R., Investigating the personalization–privacy paradox in internet of things (IoT) based on dual-factor theory: Moderating effects of type of IoT service and user value. *Sustainability*, **13**, 10679, 2021, https://doi.org/10.3390/su131910679.
51. Hong, S.G., Heo, T., Kim, N., Lee, K.B., ThumbUp : Dynamic updates of loT device applications for smart personalized services, 2016, https://doi.org/10.1109/ICTC.2016.7763535.
52. Mehrabani, M., Bangalore, S., Stern, B., Personalized speech recognition for internet of things. *2015 IEEE 2nd World Forum on Internet of Things (WF-IoT)*, 2015, https://doi.org/10.1109/wf-iot.2015.7389082.
53. Wason, V., Kumar, R., Johri, P., Smart Sensors Network using IoT technologies, 2021, https://doi.org/10.1109/ICACITE51222.2021.9404746.
54. Brous, P., Janssen, M., Herder, P., The dual effects of the internet of things (IoT): A systematic review of the benefits and risks of iot adoption by organizations. *Int. J. Inf. Manage.*, **51**, 2019, https://doi.org/10.1016/j.ijinfomgt.2019.05.008.

55. Tedeschi, S., Emmanouilidis, C., Mehnen, J., Roy, R., A design approach to iot endpoint security for production machinery monitoring. *Sensors*, **19**, 2355, 2019, https://doi.org/10.3390/s19102355.
56. Aboltins, U., Novickis, J., Romanovs, A., IoT Impact on Business Opportunities, 2020, https://doi.org/10.1109/ITMS51158.2020.9259315.
57. Dubey, Y., Patil, R., Sutaone, S., Kundu, S., Mhaski, A., Process Improvement of Finishing Machine by Real Time Monitoring using IoT, 2022, https://doi.org/10.1109/DELCON54057.2022.9753051.
58. Taneja, T., Jatain, A., Bajaj, S.B., Predictive analytics on IoT, 2017, https://doi.org/10.1109/CCAA.2017.8230000.
59. Elhami, E., Ansari, A., Farahani, B., Aliee, F.S., Towards IoT-Driven Predictive Business Process Analytics, 2020.
60. Mahmood, K. and Risch, T., Scalable Real-Time Analytics for IoT Applications, 2021, https://doi.org/10.1109/SMARTCOMP52413.2021.00084.
61. Wu, F., Wu, T., Yuce, M.R., Design and implementation of a wearable sensor network system for iot-connected safety and health applications. *IEEE Inst. Electr. Electron. Eng.*, 87–90, 2019, https://doi.org/10.1109/WF-IoT.2019.8767280.
62. Singh, S., Singh, B., Ramandeep, Singh, B., Das, A., Automatic Vehicle Counting for IoT based Smart Traffic Management System for Indian urban Settings, 2019, https://doi.org/10.1109/IoT-SIU.2019.8777722.
63. Cerbulescu, C.C., Marian, M., Ganea, E., *IoT* Big Data Management for Improved Response Time, 2021, https://doi.org/10.1109/ICCC51557.2021.9454644.
64. Dhanaraju, M., Chenniappan, P., Ramalingam, K., Pazhanivelan, S., Kaliaperumal, R., Smart farming: Internet of things (IoT)-based sustainable agriculture. *Agriculture*, 12, 1745, 2022, https://doi.org/10.3390/agriculture12101745.
65. Lakhwani, K., Gianey, H., Agarwal, N., Gupta, S., Development of IoT for Smart Agriculture a Review. *Proceedings of ICETEAS*, pp. 425–432, 2019, https://doi.org/10.1007/978-981-13-2285-3 50.
66. Xu, J., Gu, B., Tian, G., Review of agricultural iot technology. *Artif. Intell. Agric.*, 2022, https://doi.org/10.1016/j.aiia.2022.01. 001.
67. Kalsoom, T., Ahmed, S., Rafi-Ul-Shan, P.M., Azmat, M., Akhtar, P., Pervez, Z., Imran, M., Ur Rehman, M., Impact of iot on manufacturing industry 4.0: A new triangular systematic review. *Sustainability*, 13, 12506, 2021, https://doi.org/10.3390/su132212506.
68. Syafrudin, M., Alfian, G., Fitriyani, N., Rhee, J., Performance analysis of IoT-based sensor, big data processing, and machine learning model for real-time monitoring system in automotive manufacturing. *Sensors*, 18, 2946, 2018, https://doi.org/10.3390/s18092946.
69. Javaid, M., Haleem, A., Singh, R.P., Rab, S., Suman, R., Significance of sensors for industry 4.0: Roles, capabilities, and applications. *Sens. Int.*, 100110, 2021, https://doi.org/10.1016/j.sintl.2021.100110.

70. Gunturi, M., Kotha, H., Potluri, S., An iot based solution for health monitoring using a body-worn sensor enabled device. *J. Adv. Res. Dyn. Control Syst.*, 10, 646–651, 2018.
71. Abdellatif, M. and Mohamed, W., Telemedicine: An IoT based remote health- care system. *Int. J. Online Biomed. Eng. (iJOE)*, 16, 72, 2020, https://doi.org/10.3991/ijoe.v16i06.13651.
72. Baker, S.B., Xiang, W., Atkinson, I., Internet of things for smart healthcare: Technologies, challenges, and opportunities. *IEEE Access*, 5, 26521–26544, 2017, https://doi.org/10.1109/access.2017.2775180.
73. Verma, G. and Prakash, S., Internet of Things for Healthcare: Research Challenges and Future Prospects, pp. 1055–1067, 2020, https://doi.org/10.1007/978-981-15-5341-780.
74. Ushakov, D., Dudukalov, E., Kozlova, E., Shatila, K., The internet of things impact on smart public transportation. *Transp. Res. Procedia*, 63, 2392–2400, 2022, https://doi.org/10.1016/j.trpro.2022.06.275.
75. Manoj Kumar, N. and Dash, A., The internet of things: An opportunity for transportation and logistics, 2017.
76. Shashank, S., Kiran, P., Nischay, D., Vinay, M., Vatsala, B.R., Raj, D., Iot based traffic management system. *Int. J. Sci. Res. Comput. Sci. Eng. Inf. Technol.*, 184–187, 2021, https://doi.org/10.32628/CSEIT1217451.
77. Sarrab, M., Pulparambil, S., Awadalla, M., Development of an iot based real-time traffic monitoring system for city governance. *Global Transitions*, 2, 230–245, 2020, https://doi.org/10.1016/j.glt.2020.09.004.
78. Ms, S. and Newlin Rajkumar, M., IOT Based Smart System for Controlling Co 2 Emission, https://doi.org/10.13140/RG.2.2.26703.33444.
79. Ijaz, U., Ameer, U., Islam, D.-B., Ijaz, A., Aziz, W., Iot based home security and automation system. *NFC-IEFR J. Eng. Sci. Res.*, **4**, 58–63, 2016, https://doi.org/10.24081/nijesr.2016.1.0011.
80. Cristi, S., Birau, R., Ehsanifar, M.A., Dekamini, F., Khazaei, M., Bˇarbˇacioru, I., A sustainable pattern of waste management and energy efficiency in smart homes using the internet of things (iot). *Sustainability*, 15, 1–18, 2023, https://doi.org/10.3390/su15065081.
81. Chitra, L., Gowri, N.V., Maheswari, M., Uike, D., Medikondu, N.R., Al-Ammar, E.A., Metwally, A.S.M., Islam, A., Diriba, A., Iot-based solar energy measurement and monitoring model. *Int. J. Photoenergy*, 2022, 5767696, 2022, https://doi.org/10.1155/2022/5767696.
82. Andal, C.K. and Jayapal, R., Design and implementation of iot based intelligent energy management controller for pv/wind/battery system with cost minimization. *Renew. Energy Focus*, 43, 255–262, 2022, https://doi.org/10.1016/j.ref.2022.10.004.

9

System Security Using Artificial Intelligence and Reduction of Data Breach

M. Avrit[1], G. P. Siranjeevi[1], Shruti Mishra[2*], Sandeep Kumar Satapathy[2], Priyanka Mishra[1], Pradeep Kumar Mallick[3] and Gyoo Soo Chae[4]

[1]School of Computer Science and Engineering, Vellore Institute of Technology, Chennai, Tamil Nadu, India
[2]Centre for Advanced Data Science, Vellore Institute of Technology, Chennai, Tamil Nadu, India
[3]School of Computer Engineering, KIIT University, Odisha, India
[4]Division of ICT, Baekseok University, Cheonan, South Korea

Abstract

This presentation focuses on the integration of artificial intelligence (AI) with cloud security to address growing concerns about data breaches and strengthen security intelligence and audit processes. The problem statement highlights the difficulty of detecting malware files targeting sensitive data and cloud systems, as well as the significant impact of human error on data loss. The goal is to develop a defensive AI system that can adapt by self-learning using deep learning techniques for malware classification, intrusion detection, and mine intelligence detection. The motivation is the possibilities of AI technology to improve cybersecurity and minimize the vulnerabilities of cloud technology. The advantages include less data loss, improved security levels through deep learning and machine learning, malware detection and removal, and less human error. However, the downside is the need for advanced AI models, accurate data entry, third-party audits, AI security, and infrastructure requirements. The implementation plan includes two AI-powered servers, deep learning integration, and reverse tracking of corrupted data through censorship. The results of this presentation aim to strengthen cloud security, protect sensitive data, and prevent and mitigate data breaches.

**Corresponding author*: shrutim2129@gmail.com

Subhasis Dash, Manas Ranjan Lenka, S. Balamurugan, Ambika Prasad Tripathy and Amarendra Mohanty (eds.) Sustainable Resource Management in Next-Generation Computational Constrained Networks, (221–232) © 2025 Scrivener Publishing LLC

Keywords: Artificial intelligence, cloud security, data breach, deep learning, malware

9.1 Introduction

The use of cloud computing, which gives businesses scalable infrastructure and effective data management, has become pervasive in today's digital environment [1]. However, the growing reliance on cloud computing has brought about new difficulties, particularly in the area of security [1]. Organizations are constantly at risk of having their sensitive data and systems the target of cyberattacks, with malicious software continuously infiltrating systems and exploiting holes for a long time [2]. This makes it necessary for efficient security measures to identify and reduce such threats [3].

The difficulty in identifying and eliminating these malicious software files that target cloud-based systems is at the heart of the current problem statement [2]. Traditional security measures might not be able to completely protect users, which would result in an alarmingly high number of data breaches [3]. Furthermore, research has shown that a sizable portion of data loss—roughly 75%—is brought on by human error in connection with software, security, and malware [4, 15]. These elements emphasize the need for improved cloud security measures to counteract changing cyberthreats [5, 16].

Our goal is to create a defensive artificial intelligence (AI) system that is capable of self-adaptation and self-learning, with a focus on addressing security issues in cloud computing [6]. We want to build intelligent models that can classify malware, find intrusions, and provide threat intelligence by utilising AI technologies like deep learning [7]. We can effectively address the data imbalance brought on by malware and improve the security posture of cloud-based systems by implementing AI [8, 17]. The enormous development and potential of AI technology serves as the driving force behind the pursuit of this goal [8, 17]. AI has already made significant strides in coding and machine learning and applying it to security can completely transform the industry [9]. Organizations can significantly reduce human error–related vulnerabilities and eliminate the threat of data breaches by incorporating AI into cloud security practises [4].

It is possible to lessen the effects of data breaches, safeguard sensitive information, and restore the security of compromised systems by having the ability to reverse track breached data and offer censorship [6]. There are many benefits to using AI in cloud security [6]. It provides enhanced protection for sensitive information by first and foremost significantly reducing data loss brought on by breaches [7]. The development of strong antivirus security systems, capable of successfully tracking and removing malicious software, is made possible by AI's capacity for advanced levels of deep learning and machine learning [8, 10]. By automating security procedures and decreasing the likelihood of attacks on businesses using cloud computing, AI also lessens the effects of human error [5].

However, it is crucial to recognise the constraints and difficulties posed by AI in cloud security [8]. There is a need for more advanced and updated models in the future because the AI models in this field are only at a basic level right now [10]. To ensure the AI is effective, developers must provide accurate data for machine learning and deep learning [6, 11, 18]. To minimize the risks of AI being hacked or compromised, regular third-party checks and supervision are required throughout the self-learning and security development processes [6]. Additionally, putting in place an AI system requires a sizable amount of infrastructure and room [8]. Two AI-operated servers—one at a private level and another at a public level—are a part of the suggested implementation strategy for cloud security using AI [7]. Data in the public domain should only be subject to a minimal amount of control by AI at the public level, protecting data privacy [6]. The AI system will incorporate deep learning and machine learning techniques to mimic human-like neuron-level thinking [8]. The AI can develop advanced malware detection software with high accuracy by self-learning when given accurate information about security coding and breaches [9]. The risk of system attacks is greatly decreased by this proactive approach [6]. Reverse data tracking is used in the second procedure [8]. A breach tracker website will be used by the AI at the private user level to scan the system and confirm the data breach [1]. When a breach is discovered, the user level AI sends a client request to the public server level AI asking for action to be taken with regard to the compromised data [9]. The risks associated with data breaches are decreased when the public server AI receives the request, compares the records with breach data, and implements censorship measures to hide the breached data [11].

In essence, incorporating AI into cloud security holds enormous promise for lowering the risks of data breaches and improving information security analysis and audit procedures [6, 8]. Organizations can improve malware detection, fortify their defences against cyber threats, and restore the security of compromised systems by utilising AI's capabilities [7, 9]. Despite obstacles like the need for more sophisticated AI models and ensuring AI security, there are significant potential advantages [11–13]. A proactive step toward protecting sensitive data and ensuring the resilience of cloud-based systems in the face of evolving cyber threats is the implementation of AI-driven cloud security measures [8].

9.2 Related Work

There has been some research in this area. Below are the details:

Abeshu *et al.* [1] focused on the cybersecurity requirements for emerging IoT applications and the use of deep learning for distributed attack detection in fog-to-things computing. Similarly, Akhtar *et al.* [2] highlighted the vulnerability of deep neural networks to adversarial attacks, which can lead to incorrect predictions. They suggested the need for improvements in deep learning models to address this issue. Aul *et al.* [3] explored deep reinforcement learning algorithms that learn directly from camera inputs in the real world, enabling pixel-level detection and image sensing. Li *et al.* [6] discussed the integration of AI technologies, such as deep learning, into cybersecurity for tasks like malware classification and intrusion detection. It emphasizes the need for specific cybersecurity defense and protection technologies to combat adversarial machine learning.

Deng and Yu [7] presented an overview of deep learning methodology and its applications in signal and information processing tasks. It mentions areas like natural language processing, information retrieval, and multimodal information processing empowered by multi-task deep learning. Bost *et al.* [9] discussed the use of, particularly machine learning, in various applications such as medical predictions, spam detection, face recognition, and financial predictions. It emphasizes the importance of privacy-preserving protocols in these applications. Hatcher *et al.* [10] explored how deep learning is used in human-centred smart-world systems such as targeted advertisements and natural language assistants [14–16]. It discusses the platforms, applications, and emerging research trends deep learning.

Similarly, Golovko *et al.* [12] analyzed the main paradigms of learning in multilayer neural networks, including deep neural networks [17, 18]. It highlights the breakthrough achieved by deep learning in intelligent data processing.

9.3 Methodology

9.3.1 Implementation of Socket Programming Concept

This is the basic implementation of the entire process that is then implemented. We use socket programming to connect the server side and client side. In this code, we add conditions of "if client record similar to database in server," then the data is sent into censorship in the server-side database and a success statement is sent to the client.

9.3.2 Machine Learning

So, using the concept on our *C* code, we can convert it into JAVASCRIPT and combine it with a cascading style sheets (CSS) file and an html file to make it working at the internet level. The work of AI here is to improve itself on security using deep learning. It is also placed at client and server side as two separate functions. We implement our C socket logic here of censorship, where the AI implementation has its own levels of sending and receiving information and requests. It hence develops itself at client and security levels to increase its security. It also censors the data at server level according to our working program.

9.3.3 Deep Learning

This is used at the image level of data where grayscale images are scanned and then is detected. So, basically the client side private information can also be run into check by AI even with images to check for similar private data on the server to provide censorship.

9.3.4 Human Assistance

Because it is a developing program, it cannot be let at all on its own. Even at its highest level of understanding, an AI can be misled and can destroy the entire structure. Hence, an expert is also needed to maintain the system.

9.4 Proposed Model

Figure 9.1 represents our work flow model of AI security where the user accesses the network layer of the private AI server which has a self-updating security upon countering issues. It has machine learning and deep learning as its components that allow it to understand. It is a type of learning based on artificial neural networks in which multiple layers of processing are used to extract progressively higher level features from data. Deep learning, a pivotal aspect of the AI server's architecture, represents a powerful subset of machine learning. It revolves around artificial neural networks, where data undergoes processing through multiple layers to extract progressively higher-level features. This hierarchical approach to data analysis allows the AI to discern intricate patterns and relationships, thereby enhancing its comprehension and decision-making prowess.

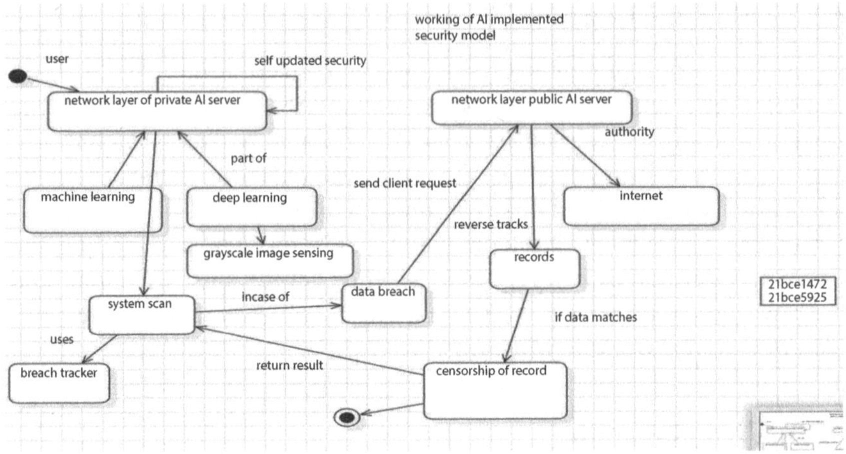

Figure 9.1 Workflow model of AI security model.

Notably, grayscale image sensing constitutes a critical feature within the AI server's capabilities. Leveraging this capability, the AI system becomes adept at processing and interpreting grayscale images, which is particularly advantageous for advanced malware detection. By converting data into grayscale images, the AI self-learns and progressively refines its malware detection software, consistently bolstering its accuracy and efficacy in safeguarding the private network from potential cyber threats. One of the main components of deep learning is grayscale image sensing. The AI self-learns and develops advanced malware detection software with accuracy as it is converted into greyscale images. The client side has a system scan that scans the data in the system and runs it in a data breach tracker system, upon detection, a request is sent alongside breached data to the public server level AI that refers similar records to the leaked file on the public database records of the internet. It then provides censorship to the leaked data so there is a minimal avoidance than a huge loss for breached data.

Moreover, the AI server's adaptability and resilience come into play after each data breach. Leveraging the power of both deep learning and machine learning techniques, the server evaluates the breach's circumstances and augments its defense mechanisms accordingly. By analyzing the breach's patterns, the AI system gains valuable insights, which are then integrated into its algorithms to fortify its resilience against future threats.

9.5 Experimental Result/Result Analysis

Client side

Pseudocode

1. *Declare socket file descriptor, buffer, and server address*
2. *Create socket file descriptor*
3. *If socket creation failed, print error message and exit*
4. *Fill server information with family, port, and address*
5. *Connect client socket to server socket*
6. *If connection failed, print error message and exit*
7. *Declare example data on client side*
8. *Send data to server for checking*
9. *For each record in client data:*
    a. *Send record to server*
    b. *Read response from server into buffer*
    c. *Print server response*
10. *Close socket file descriptor and return 0*

Algorithm of logic
Below is an algorithm covering the client-side pseudocode.

Algorithm 9.1 Client side algorithm

Declare connect, exit, socket descriptor
If sockfd = socket(socket descriptor)
        Do connect
        Else
        Do Exit(print "failure")
Declare data
Verify server ports
Do connect
Send record
Receive response

Algorithm 9.1 discusses the work of the client side. It verifies the ports and establishes connection to server side and receives response through buffer.

Server side

Pseudocode

1. *Create a socket file descriptor*
2. *If socket creation fails, print error message and exit*
3. *Initialize server address to zero*
4. *Assign IP and PORT to server address*
5. *Bind the socket to the given IP and verify*
6. *If binding fails, print error message and exit*
7. *Accept a data packet from the client and verify*
8. *If acceptance fails, print error message and exit*
9. *Initialize example data on the server side*
10. *While true:*
    a. *Read data from the client into a buffer*
    b. *Print the data sent by the client*
    c. *Initialize match_found to 1*
    d. *For each record in server data:*
        i. *If the buffer matches the record, set match_found to index of record and break loop*
    e. *If match_found is not 1, send "data is censored" response to client*
    f. *Delete matching record from server data by shifting all records after it one position to the left and setting last record to NULL*
    g. *Else, send "false" response to client*
11. *Close the socket file descriptor*

Algorithm of logic
Below is Algorithm 9.2 covering the server side pseudocode.

Algorithm 9.2 Server-side algorithm

Declare sock connections serveraddr, ports, buffer //declaring the port connections to
//verify a path,buffer has the server data

If socked connect=—-1
    Do write("socket creation failed")
    Exit
Set port, serveraddr, inaddr //Assign ip address
If socket bind==0

```
        Do write("socket bind failed")            //notifies socket bind has failed
int length
for length
        If match found //if similar record
                Do write("data is censored")
                Send client(message)
                Remove match
        Else
                Do Write(false')
end
```

Algorithm 9.2 discusses the server-side code that detects matching records and eliminates such records on port, sending the message to client side. The algorithm uses socket programming to connect the server and the client side. This is a basic knowledge only code as it is only for the logic of the working of the system.

Below is a table that states the difference between existing socket programming and implemented code and the output.

Table 9.1 discusses the changes done for a normal socket programming code and to the updated version.

Figure 9.2 shows the output 1 that takes two samples, record 1 and record 2, and displays data that is censored on matching records. At further updates some parts of socket programming will be shifted to AI. At the client side, it scans private data on client side as above and then sends it to the server. The code on finding similar records, deletes it in the server side.

Table 9.1 Comparison of existing socket programming and updated socket programming.

Sl. no.	Existing code	My code
1.	It is a normal socket programming code to make connections with ports.	Its updated so that it refers through the database on client and server sides.
2.	Information exchange process	Here, we send requests to delete data on the server side of the database.
3.	The code is just an experimental for the basics of socket linking.	We use this logic to pair it up with AI to scan records of database on two AI sides.

```
// Server side output:
Client sent: record1
Client sent: record2

// Client side output:
Server response: data is censored
Server response: false
```

Figure 9.2 Output 1 of the code.

This kind of method is not the most optimal as deletion requires a lot more authority on the network side and also on deletion on wrong records can have a huge effect. Hence, censorship is used to blind the view of data from the users and hence can be uncensored if anything goes out of hand. The above is the sample of similar execution but without an AI hence censorship execution is a little difficult. (*Note*: The entire project is to find similar data only for unreleased files which are private. It does not include verifying all data in database.)

Below is an image of how grayscale techniques can be used to find similarities in images.

Figure 9.3 shows that the project can be limited not only to text but also to image sensing. Hence, the censorship can also be carried out to image detection, although it is a very minimal level censorship to the data as many images can exist on similarities. Hence, as per results, the execution

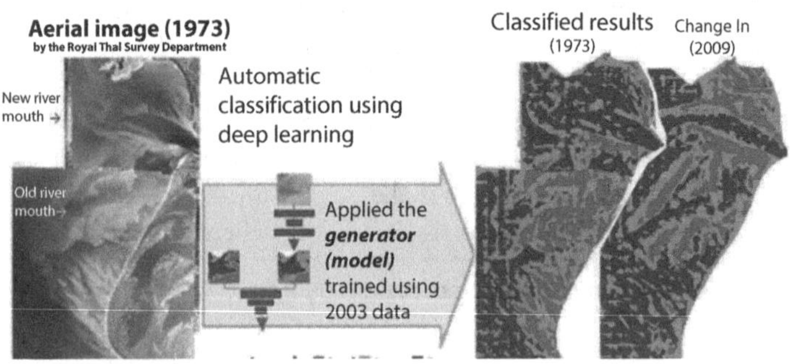

Figure 9.3 Using grayscale sensing to classify aerial images [18].

of the idea is possible according to the sources and, hence, can be put into work as an initial step for data breach censorship.

9.6 Conclusion and Future Work

Based on these evidences, we conclude that the idea of implementing such cybersecurity is possible if AI learning is more deeply defined in terms of research. Such an implementation has its advantages and disadvantages, but it also increases security by using self-learning AI, which greatly reduces data breaches on graphs. The integration of AI in cloud security promises to significantly reduce the risk of data breaches and improve information security analysis and review processes. By leveraging the capabilities of AI, organizations can strengthen their defenses against cyber threats, improve malware detection, and restore the security of compromised systems. Although there are challenges, such as the need for advanced AI models and ensuring the safety of AI, the potential benefits are significant. Implementing AI-based cloud security measures is a proactive step to secure sensitive data and ensure the resilience of cloud systems against evolving cyber threats.

In the future work area of the system, we want to increase the level of image processing from grayscale sensing to the updating image sensing processing techniques that provide even more detailed level of image detection by AI in records of database. We also want to improve the areas of security by feeding more data for deep learning techniques.

References

1. Abeshu, A. and Chilamki, N., Deep learning: the frontier for distributed attack detection in fog-to-things computing. *IEEE Commun. Mag.*, 56, 2, 169–175, 2018.
2. Akhtar, N. and Mian, A., Threat of adversarial attacks on deep learning in computer vision: a survey. *IEEE Access*, 6, 14410–14430, 2018.
3. Aulkumaran, K., Deisenroth, M.P., Brundage, M., *et al.*, Deep reinforcement learning: a brief survey. *IEEE Signal Process Mag.*, 34, 6, 26–383187–3196, 2017.
4. Cornejo, G.A., Human Errors in Data Breaches: An Exploratory Configurational Analysis, Nova Southeastern University, 2021, Doctoral dissertation.
5. Streeter, D.C., The effect of human error on modern security breaches. *Strategic Informer Stud. Publ. Strategic Intell. Soc.*, 1, 3, 2, 2013.

6. Li, J.H., Cyber security meets artificial intelligence: a survey. *Front. Inf. Technol. Electron. Eng.*, 19, 12, 2–1474, 2018.
7. Deng, L. and Yu, D., Deep learning: methods and applications. *Found Trend Sig. Process*, 7, 3–4, 197–387, 2014.
8. Prasad, R., Rohokale, V., Prasad, R., Rohokale, V., Artificial intelligence and machine learning in cyber security. *Cyber Security Lifeline Inf. Commun. Technol.*, 12, 1, 231–247, 2020.
9. Bost, R., Popa, R.A., Tu, S., *et al.*, Machine learning classification over encrypted data. *Network and Distributed System Security Symp.*, pp. 331–364.
10. Hatcher, W.G. and Yu, W., A survey of deep learning: Platforms, applications and emerging research trends. *IEEE Access*, 6, 24411–24432, 2018.
11. Saad, S., Briguglio, W., Elmiligi, H., *et al.*, The curious case of machine learning in malware detection, 2019, arXiv preprint arXiv:1905.07573.
12. Golovko, V.A., Deep learning: an overview and main paradigms. *Opt. Mem. Neur. Netw.*, 26, 1, 1–17, 2017.
13. Korczak, J. and Hemes, M., Deep learning for financial time series forecasting in a-trader system, in: *2017 Federated Conference on Computer Science and Information Systems (FedCSIS)*, IEEE, pp. 905–912, 2017, September.
14. Bahwaireth, K., Lo'ai, A.T., Benkhelifa, E., Jararweh, Y., Tawalbeh, M., Experimental comparison of simulation tools for efficient cloud and mobile cloud computing applications. *EURASIP J. Inf. Secur.*, 15, 1–14, 2016.
15. Booth, G., Soknacki, A., Somayaji, A., Cloud security: attacks and current defenses, in: *8th Annual symposium on information Assurance (ASIA'13)*, vol. 4, NYSCSC, New York, 2013, June.
16. Lo'ai, A.T. and Saldamli, G., Reconsidering big data security and privacy in cloud and mobile cloud systems. *J. King Saud Univ. Comput. Inf. Sci.*, 33, 7, 810–819, 2021.
17. Cui, Z., Xue, F., Cai, X., Cao, Y., Wang, G.G., Chen, J., Detection of malicious code variants based on deep learning. *IEEE Trans. Ind. Inf.*, 14, 7, 3187–3196, 2018.
18. Yamakita, T., Sodeyama, F., Whanpetch, N., *et al.*, A deep learning model determined seagrass extent using grayscale aerial, researchgate.com, https://www.researchgate.net/figure/A-deep-learning-model-determined-seagrass-extent-using-grayscale-aerial-photographs_fig1_333208017.

10

Mitigating DDoS Attacks: Empowering Network Infrastructure Resilience with AI and ML

Teja Pasonri[1], Saurav Singh[1], Vedant Shirapure[1], Sandeep Kumar Satapathy[2], Sung-Bae Cho[3], Shruti Mishra[2]* and Pradeep Kumar Mallick[4]

[1]School of Computer Science and Engineering, Vellore Institute of Technology, Chennai, Tamil Nadu, India
[2]Centre for Advanced Data Science, Vellore Institute of Technology, Chennai, Tamil Nadu, India
[3]Department of Computer Science, Yonsei University, 50 Yonsei-ro, Sudaemoon-gu, Seoul, South Korea
[4]School of Computer Engineering, KIIT University, Odisha, India

Abstract

DDoS attacks, short for distributed-denial-of-service attacks, have emerged as formidable tools in the hands of hackers on the internet. These malicious actors leverage the vast reach of the web to unleash chaos by inundating targeted websites with an overwhelming volume of requests. The sheer magnitude of these requests can overload servers and bring down websites, rendering them inaccessible to legitimate users. To understand and counter this growing threat, researchers dived into the world of DDoS attacks. By harnessing the power of artificial intelligence and machine learning, our model aims to enhance the resilience of network infrastructure to these attacks. By shedding light on the characteristics of each type of attack, our research provides a foundation for developing the required countermeasures. Armed with this deeper understanding, organizations can enhance their ability to detect and mitigate DDoS threats, bolstering their resilience against these potent attacks. By identifying connections that exhibit similar levels of security and compatibility, we strive to enhance the ability of organizations to thwart DDoS attacks effectively. In an era where cyber threats continue to evolve and proliferate, our

**Corresponding author*: shrutim2129@gmail.com

Subhasis Dash, Manas Ranjan Lenka, S. Balamurugan, Ambika Prasad Tripathy and Amarendra Mohanty (eds.) Sustainable Resource Management in Next-Generation Computational Constrained Networks, (233–250)

research endeavors to equip defenders with advanced tools and insights to safeguard web infrastructure from the disruptive forces of DDoS attacks.

Keywords**:** DDoS, ML, ping request, KNN, accuracy

10.1 Introduction

Distributed-denial-of-service (DDoS) attacks pose a significant risk to websites and network users by overwhelming them with a massive volume of traffic. Attackers exploit compromised systems to generate and direct this assault traffic, causing disruption and making services inaccessible. Understanding the subcategories and techniques of DDoS attacks is crucial for effective defense. These subcategories include SYN (synchronization) flood attacks [1], UDP (User Datagram Protocol) flood attacks [2], MSSQL (Microsoft SQL Server) attacks [3], LDAP (Lightweight Directory Access Protocol) attacks [4], Portmap attacks [5], and NetBIOS (Network Basic Input/Output System) attacks [6]. Machine learning (ML) and artificial intelligence (AI) play a vital role in combating DDoS attacks by training models to differentiate between normal network activity and attack traffic. Deep learning methodologies, such as convolutional neural networks (CNNs) and recurrent neural networks (RNNs), have shown success in categorizing specific attack types accurately. AI-based detection systems continuously learn and adapt to evolving attack techniques, facilitating real-time detection and mitigation. By integrating AI with network infrastructure, organizations can proactively respond to DDoS attacks and ensure service availability. The collaboration of AI, ML, and advanced detection systems equips organizations with the tools to enhance resilience against DDoS attacks and safeguard their digital assets.

Machine learning and deep learning have emerged as powerful tools within the field of AI, enabling us to solve complex problems across various domains with remarkable accuracy that rivals human performance. In this research endeavor, we have once again pushed the boundaries of AI by applying these methodologies to the realm of cybersecurity, specifically in detecting threats associated with DDoS attacks. The significance of this research lies in its application of AI in the cybersecurity domain, specifically in combating DDoS attacks [7]. By leveraging ML and deep learning techniques, we have demonstrated the potential for accurately detecting and classifying DDoS threats. This level of accuracy is crucial for organizations to effectively respond to and mitigate the impact of such attacks. Overall, our research has showcased the capabilities of AI in enhancing cybersecurity measures. By continuously advancing our understanding of DDoS attacks and developing robust detection mechanisms, we can empower organizations to safeguard their network infrastructure against the disruptive forces of cyber threats.

10.1.1 Categories of DDoS Attack

Categorizing and analyzing these attack types enables security professionals and researchers to develop robust defense mechanisms and strategies.

10.1.1.1 SYN Flood Attacks

One prominent subcategory of DDoS attacks is the SYN flood. In this type of assault, the attacker inundates the target server with an overwhelming number of SYN requests [1]. By exploiting the three-way handshake mechanism of the Transmission Control Protocol (TCP), attackers consume server resources, impeding the establishment of legitimate connections. This resource exhaustion leads to service disruption and renders the server inaccessible to genuine users.

10.1.1.2 UDP Flood Attacks

Another subcategory is UDP flood, where attackers flood the target network with a deluge of UDP packets. Unlike TCP, UDP does not require a handshake process, making it easier for attackers to generate a massive volume of traffic quickly [2]. This flood of UDP packets can exhaust network bandwidth, disrupt network operations, and impact the availability of online services.

10.1.1.3 MSSQL Attacks

MSSQL attacks target servers running Microsoft's popular relational database management system [3]. Attackers exploit vulnerabilities within the MSSQL server to initiate unauthorized and intensive operations. These operations cause significant resource consumption, ultimately resulting in service unavailability or degraded performance.

10.1.1.4 LDAP Attacks

LDAP attacks exploit vulnerabilities in LDAP servers, commonly used for centralized user authentication and directory services [4]. By overwhelming the LDAP server with a high volume of requests, attackers disrupt the authentication process and hinder user access to network resources.

10.1.1.5 Portmap Attacks

Portmap attacks specifically target the Portmapper service responsible for mapping Remote Procedure Call (RPC) services to network ports [5]. Attackers exploit weaknesses in the Portmapper service, flooding it with requests, causing resource exhaustion, and affecting the availability of network services reliant on RPC.

10.1.1.6 NetBIOS Attacks

NetBIOS attacks focus on systems utilizing the NetBIOS protocol, often found in older Windows operating systems [6]. Attackers flood the target network with NetBIOS requests, overwhelming network resources and disrupting communication between systems.

10.1.2 Harnessing Machine Learning for DDoS Threat Detection

One key aspect of AI in DDoS threat detection lies in ML techniques. By training models on extensive datasets containing network traffic patterns, IP addresses, and other relevant indicators, AI algorithms can learn to differentiate between normal network activity and DDoS attack traffic. This learning process empowers AI models to accurately identify and classify various types of DDoS threats.

10.1.3 AI Models for DDoS Threat Detection

Researchers have extensively analyzed log data generated during DDoS attacks to effectively detect and classify threats. By applying ML algorithms, to this data, researchers have trained AI models capable of distinguishing between normal network traffic and DDoS attack traffic with a high level of accuracy. Deep learning methodologies, including CNNs and RNNs, have displayed significant success in categorizing various DDoS threats [7]. These advanced models extract intricate patterns and features from the input data, enabling them to identify and categorize specific attack types with precision. Through the training of these deep learning models on extensive and diverse datasets, researchers have achieved classification accuracies that surpass previous methodologies.

10.1.4 Beyond Classification: AI for Real-Time Detection and Mitigation

The application of AI in DDoS threat detection extends beyond classification. AI models have the capability to continuously learn and adapt to evolving attack techniques, facilitating real-time detection and mitigation of DDoS threats. By merging AI-based detection systems with the network, organizations can respond to DDoS attacks, minimizing their impact and ensuring their availability in the market.

10.1.5 Collaboration and Knowledge Sharing

DDoS attacks continue to present a significant threat to websites and online services. Understanding the diverse subcategories and techniques employed by attackers is crucial for developing effective defense strategies. The utilization of AI, particularly ML and deep learning techniques, has shown great promise in detecting and classifying DDoS threats with high accuracy rates. By leveraging the power of AI and continuously evolving detection systems, organizations can enhance their resilience against DDoS attacks.

Additionally, this paper is organized as follows. Section 10.2 provides an insight on the works that have been done in this field. Section 10.3 talks about the approach that have been taken to get to a solution for the problem. Section 10.4 contains the proposed model for the methodology that has been followed. Section 10.5 displays the result obtained from the simulation/experiment done. Section 10.6 concludes the paper with some reference to the future works that can be done in this field.

10.2 Related Work

Liu *et al.* [8] have concluded that blockchain technologies have been proposed to support autonomous vehicles by improving security, providing shared storage, and optimizing vehicular functionalities. In the context of vehicular social networks. Li *et al.* [9] have discussed that a blockchain-based privacy-preserving scheme for multimedia data sharing has been proposed to secure sensitive user information, vehicle data, and reliable data sources. Similarly, in the work of Balasubramaniam *et al.* [10], a blockchain-based privacy-preserving vehicle-to-grid networks payment mechanism has been proposed to protect sensitive user information in the context of vehicle-to-grid networks. Blockchain can also be used to manage self-sovereign identity, allowing individuals to store and control their own identity data. Moreover, blockchain-based secure key management has been proposed to ensure communication security in autonomous vehicles.

In the work of Aljawarneh *et al.* [11], blockchain has been explored for storing road accidents, congestion, and delay-related data in an intelligent transportation system, enabling efficient tracking and management of transportation information. The approach based on blockchain aims to further develop security, data management, and privacy in autonomous vehicles. Shi *et al.* [12] have given the statement in their paper that, right now, DDoS attacks pose a serious threat to networks but with the help of ML, DDoS attacks can be detected, and it has recently gained significant attention. Zhang *et al.* [13] have talked about the main ML models that were proposed: gated repetitive units, multi-layer perceptron (MLP), auto-encoders, and bi-directional long-term and short-term memory have been introduced to classify the DDoS attacks based on network traffic patterns and characteristics. These models leverage supervised and unsupervised learning approaches to differentiate between normal and attack traffic. Stockburger *et al.* [14] talked about the supervised learning approaches that utilize labeled data to train ML models, whereas unsupervised learning approaches employ clustering and anomaly detection to identify abnormal traffic patterns associated with DDoS attacks. Kumar *et al.* [15] pointed out that hybrid approaches that combine supervised and unsupervised learning methods have also been explored to enhance detection accuracy. ML-based DDoS detection approaches provide valuable insights into network behavior and traffic characteristics, enabling efficient identification and mitigation of DDoS attacks.

Although, according to Alghamdi *et al.* [16], ML-based approaches show promise for DDoS attack detection, there are several limitations and challenges that need to be addressed. One challenge is the availability of large and diverse datasets for training ML models, as well as the need for continuous updating of these datasets to account for evolving attack techniques. Additionally, according to Cuzzocrea *et al.* [17], the dynamic nature of network traffic poses a challenge in terms of adapting ML models to changing traffic patterns. Evaluating the effectiveness and generalizability of proposed ML-based approaches using multiple datasets and real-world scenarios is crucial to assess their performance accurately. Future research directions in ML-based DDoS attack detection may include enhancing the scalability and efficiency of ML models to handle large-scale networks and real-time traffic analysis.

Exploring explainable AI techniques mentioned by Mebawondu *et al.* [18] can provide transparency and interpretability of ML models, enabling better understanding of their decision-making processes. Integration of ML-based detection mechanisms performed by Xinlong and Zhibin [19] with software-defined networking (SDN) and Internet of Things (IoT) environments can address emerging security challenges in these contexts. Additionally, investigating adversarial attacks against ML models for DDoS attack detection and developing robust defense mechanisms are important areas for future research.

However, as discussed by Nakayama *et al.* [20], addressing the limitations and challenges associated with ML-based approaches, such as dataset availability, dynamic traffic patterns, and evaluation in real-world scenarios, is crucial for their effective deployment. Further research is needed to improve the scalability, interpretability, and adaptability of ML models, as well as their integration with SDN and IoT environments, to effectively detect and mitigate DDoS attacks. Lastly, according to Nishani *et al.* [21], attack detection and prevention techniques offer significant potential for enhancing security, privacy, and data management in autonomous vehicles and intelligent transportation systems. It can support various applications such as secure multimedia data sharing, privacy-preserving transactions, self-sovereign identity management, and secure key management. Furthermore, as depicted by Revathi *et al.* [22], ML techniques have shown promise in detecting and mitigating DDoS attacks being utilized for classification based on network traffic patterns.

10.3 Methodology

The methodology employed in the provided approach involves two different code segments, each employing a different set of ML algorithms to tackle a classification problem. Pseudocode-1 utilizes a neural network model built using the Keras library, whereas Pseudocode-2 employs several classical ML algorithms from the scikit-learn library [23]. Both code segments start by loading the dataset, which is stored in the ARFF format (Attribute-Relation File Format). ARFF is a widely used data format for ML. The datasets are then processed to extract the feature values and corresponding labels. The data is pre-processed differently in each code segment.

10.3.1 Pseudocode-1: Jupyter Project Code

In this, the data is split into training and validation sets using a 90:10 ratio. The labels are converted into one-hot encoded categorical values using the to_categorical function. This ensures that the neural network can effectively handle the multi-class classification problem. It then defines a neural network model using the Keras Sequential API. The model architecture consists of multiple dense layers with ReLU activation functions, interspersed with dropout layers to prevent overfitting. The final layer uses a SoftMax activation function to produce the predicted class probabilities. The model is compiled with categorical cross-entropy loss and the Adam optimizer. During the training process, the model is fit to the training data using the fit function. The number of epochs is set to 2 in the provided code, but it can be increased to allow for more iterations and potentially improve the model's accuracy. The training progress is monitored using a TensorBoard callback.

Pseudocode 1:

1. *START*
2. *Import the required libraries and modules (Pandas, NumPy, scikit-learn, SciPy, etc.).*
3. *Load the dataset from an ARFF file into a DataFrame.*
4. *Preprocess the dataset by balancing the classes and splitting it into training and testing sets.*
5. *Standardize the feature values in the training and testing sets.*
6. *Train Support Vector Machine (SVM), K-Nearest Neighbors (KNN), and Gaussian Naive Bayes models on the training set.*
7. *Evaluate the accuracy of the models on the testing set.*
8. *Further split the training set into training and validation sets.*
9. *Train SVM, KNN, and Gaussian Naive Bayes models on the new training set.*
10. *Predict the labels for the validation set using the trained models.*
11. *Concatenate the validation set with the predicted labels for each model.*
12. *Prepare the testing set in the same format as the validation set.*
13. *Train a Random Forest model on the concatenated validation set.*
14. *Evaluate the accuracy of the Random Forest model on the testing set.*
15. *Save the trained Random Forest model to a file using pickle.*
16. *Load another ARFF file for prediction.*
17. *Preprocess the prediction data by encoding the labels and splitting it into training and validation sets.*
18. *Define a neural network model architecture using Keras.*

19. *Compile the model with appropriate loss function and optimizer.*
20. *Train the neural network on the training data and validate it on the validation data.*
21. *Evaluate the model's performance on the validation and training data.*
22. *Print the evaluation results.*
23. *END*

10.3.2 Pseudocode-2: Project KNN Model

In pseudocode-2, the dataset [24] is split into training and testing sets using an 80:20 ratio. The features are standardized using the StandardScaler to ensure that all features contribute equally to the training process. The labels are converted into numerical format. It then applies several classification algorithms to the pre-processed data. The code implements ML models such as the K-Nearest Neighbors (KNN), Naïve Bayes (NB), Support Vector Machine (SVM), and Random Forest (RF) Classifiers. In each of the classifiers, the training of the model is done on the training set with the use of the fit function. The trained models are then used to predict the labels for the testing set. The accuracy of each model is calculated using the accuracy_score function.

Pseudocode 2:

1. *START*
2. *Import the necessary libraries and modules.*
3. *Define a main() function to encapsulate the main functionality of the program.*
4. *Print the program description.*
5. *Get a list of network interfaces on the system.*
6. *Initialize variables for live iteration and allowed IP addresses.*
7. *Define a function to determine the IP layer name (IPv4 or IPv6) of a packet.*
8. *Define a function to display packet information.*
9. *Define a function to write packet information to a CSV file.*
10. *Define a function to retrieve network interface names from the Windows registry.*
11. *Define a function to perform label encoding on categorical data in a CSV file.*
12. *Define a function to load a saved machine learning model.*
13. *Define a function to choose a network interface for live packet capture.*
14. *Define a function to train or update a MLP model.*

15. *Define a function to perform live prediction using a trained MLP model.*
16. *Define a function to write packet information to a CSV file at regular intervals.*
17. *Define a function to perform label encoding on live data.*
18. *Define a function to display data in a CSV file.*
19. *Define a menu() function to display a menu and perform tasks based on user choice.*
20. *Call the main() function to start the program.*
21. *Call the menu() function to display the menu and perform tasks based on user choice.*
22. *END*

10.3.3 Hyperparameter Tuning and Evaluation

Additionally, Pseudocode-2 performs a stratified split of the training set into training and validation subsets. The validation subsets are used to tune hyperparameters and select the best-performing models. The predictions of each model on the validation set are concatenated with the corresponding feature values to create new input data. Finally, a RF classifier with 200 estimators is trained on the concatenated validation set input and the corresponding labels. The trained RF model is then evaluated on the concatenated testing set input to calculate the accuracy.

10.3.4 Enhancing Model Accuracy

To enhance the accuracy of the models, there are several ability adjustments that may be considered. These encompass growing the quantity of epochs, adjusting the model structure (e.g., wide variety of layers, units, and activation functions), exploring specific classification algorithms or ensemble techniques, tuning hyperparameters, performing characteristic choice or dimensionality reduction, and scaling or normalizing the input records. It is crucial to notice that the effectiveness of these adjustments can also vary relying on the unique dataset and problem at hand. It is usually recommended to test with distinct processes, compare their performance, and iterate on the methodology to locate the fine solution for the given category problem.

10.3.5 Ping Request and DDoS Attack

In addition to the above, it is important to take note of the IP addresses in the Linux machine (Target) as well as Kali Linux machine (Host). For us to understand, we are going to use SNORT detection system in Ubuntu to log all the ping requests that we are going to generate from Kali Linux, whereas, in Kali Linux, we are going to use hping3 command to flood the ping request as a mode of executing the DOS attack. Ping is a troubleshooting tool used by system administrators to manually test the connectivity between network devices, network delay, and transmission loss. The Ping command sends an ICMP echo request to the requested device (in our case from Kali -> Ubuntu) and the server (here: Ubuntu) immediately responds with an ICMP reply, to complete the request response cycle. According to network protocol standards [RFC (request for comments) standards], "every host must implement an ICMP echo server". Because this is mandatory, every server must send an ICMP reply to every ICMP request receival. This acts like a loophole and hackers or unauthorized group (or individuals) use this to orchestrate a DDoS attack. A genuine ping request is misclassified as "Attempted Information Leak". In the solution presented, we attempt to minimize misclassification with the help of neural networks, thus helping to boost the accuracy of the classification. 100% packet loss is obtained when a flood attack is generated.

10.4 Proposed Model

In our workflow model (as shown in Figure 10.1), we have categorized our approach into three main categories: supervised, unsupervised, and hybrid. Each category utilizes different methods to classify and analyze network traffic for detecting various types of DDoS attacks. In the supervised category, we make use of labeled data for classification. We deploy a lazy learning method called lazy meta-learning, specifically KNNs. KNN helps us identify similar data packets in order to analyze and detect video-based attacks. By comparing the characteristics of incoming packets with known patterns of attacks, we can classify them accordingly.

On the other hand, by considering factors such as the source and destination IP addresses, data size, and patterns associated with DDoS attacks, SVM helps us detect and classify potential malicious activities. Moving on to the unsupervised category, we focus on analyzing network traffic without relying on labeled data. One approach that we employ is partitioning using the K-means algorithm. K-means allows us to individually analyze each network node by splitting the incoming data packets. This helps us identify any abnormal patterns or potential DDoS attacks. By clustering data points based on similarities, we can uncover hidden trends and anomalies in the network traffic.

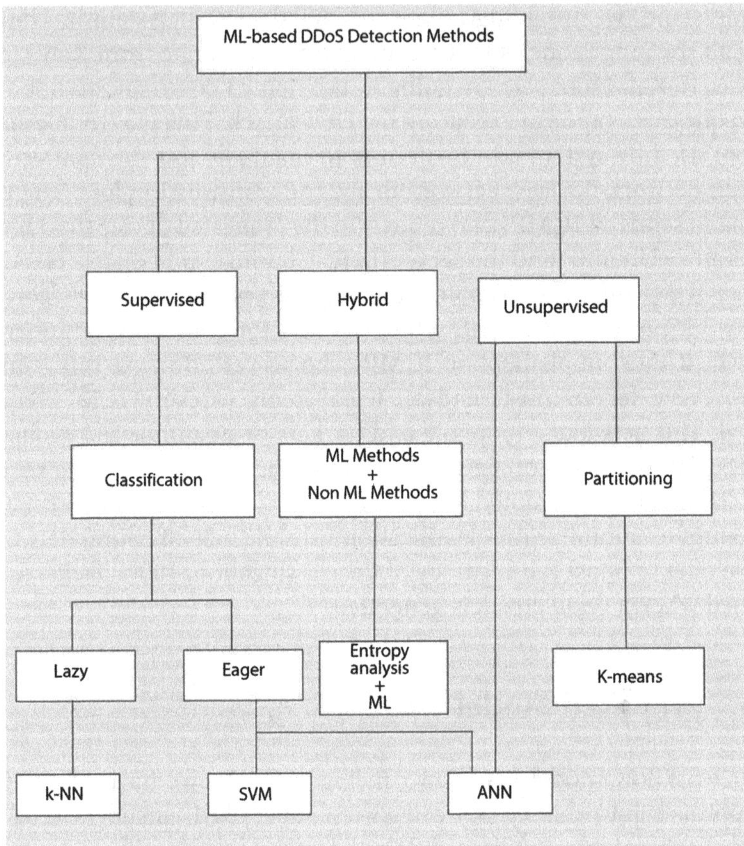

Figure 10.1 Proposed workflow model.

Another secondary method that is being used is the use of artificial neural networks (ANNs). ANN is a powerful tool for analyzing network data and detecting potential DDoS attacks. By leveraging the neural network's ability to learn and adapt, we can identify patterns and anomalies in the data traffic. ANN helps us protect against DDoS attacks by recognizing abnormal behaviors and taking appropriate action to mitigate the threats. Finally, in the hybrid category, we combine both ML methods and non-ML methods. One such non-ML method is entropy analysis. Entropy analysis will evaluate the randomness and unpredictability of the network data packets. By assessing the entropy of the packets, we can identify if any suspicious or malicious activities are present.

In summary, our workflow model encompasses supervised, unsupervised, and hybrid approaches for analyzing and classifying network traffic.

We utilize labeled data, lazy meta-learning with KNN, and eager learning with ANN to classify various types of attacks. In the unsupervised category, we employ K-means partitioning and ANNs to analyze network traffic without the need for labeled data. Lastly, the hybrid category combines both ML and non-ML methods, such as entropy analysis, to enhance the accuracy and effectiveness of our detection and classification system.

10.5 Experimental Result/Result Analysis

10.5.1 Demo of DDoS Attack

In an illustration of a DDoS attack from Kali to Ubuntu, Kali Linux is used as the attacker, and Ubuntu Linux serves as the victim. A DDoS attack objective is to weigh down a goal device's resources, rendering it inaccessible to legitimate users (as explained in Section 10.3.5). In this situation, the attacker, leveraging Kali Linux's tools and abilities, initiates a coordinated attack against the Ubuntu device. The attacker may hire techniques such as flooding the sufferer's network with too much traffic, exploiting vulnerabilities in network protocols, or deploying a botnet to amplify the attack (as shown in Figure 10.2).

As a result of the attack, the victim's Ubuntu gadget reviews an extensive increase in incoming site visitors, as its available assets are laborious, consisting of bandwidth, processing power, or reminiscence. This renders the Ubuntu system unresponsive to legitimate requests, efficaciously denying get entry to authorized customers. Such an indication highlights the disruptive nature and capability harm because of DDoS attacks. It emphasizes the importance of imposing strong safety features, consisting of network tracking, traffic filtering, and intrusion detection systems, to mitigate the impact of such assaults and make sure the supply and integrity of structures and offerings.

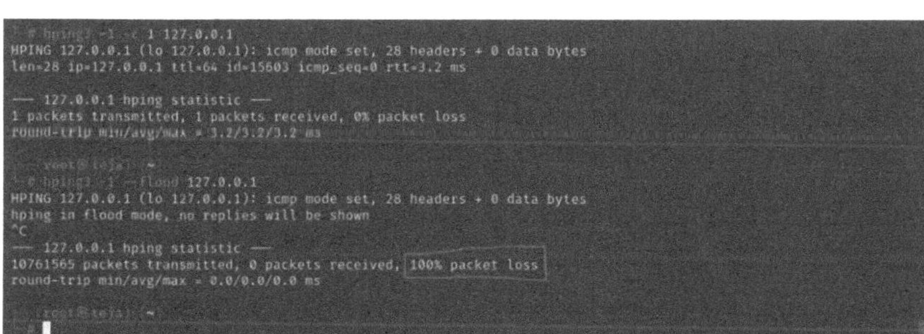

Figure 10.2 Successful flood attack.

Figure 10.3 DDoS model simulator.

10.5.2 Packet Sniffing and Detecting Traffic

The provided Python code below performs network packet analysis and ML tasks (as explained in Section 10.3.2). It captures packets, displays packet information, gathers packet data into a CSV file, pre-processes the data, trains a neural network model using the MLP algorithm, and performs real-time packet classification. The code allows users to interact through a menu-driven interface, where they can choose options for packet sniffing, data gathering, training neural networks, visualizing data, and live packet classification (as shown in Figure 10.3). It provides a comprehensive framework for network analysis and ML tasks.

10.5.3 Accuracy Graph

The graph shows that the accuracy of the model in detecting DDoS attacks increases as the number of sample datasets increases. This is because the model has more data to learn from, which allows it to better identify the patterns that distinguish DDoS attacks from normal traffic. The accuracy of the model plateaus at around 0.9989 (shown in Figure 10.4), which is a very high accuracy. This means that the model can correctly identify DDoS attacks with a very high degree of accuracy. The graph also shows that the average accuracy of the model decreases as the number of sample datasets decreases. This is because the model has less data to learn from, which makes it more difficult for the model to identify the patterns that distinguish DDoS attacks from normal traffic.

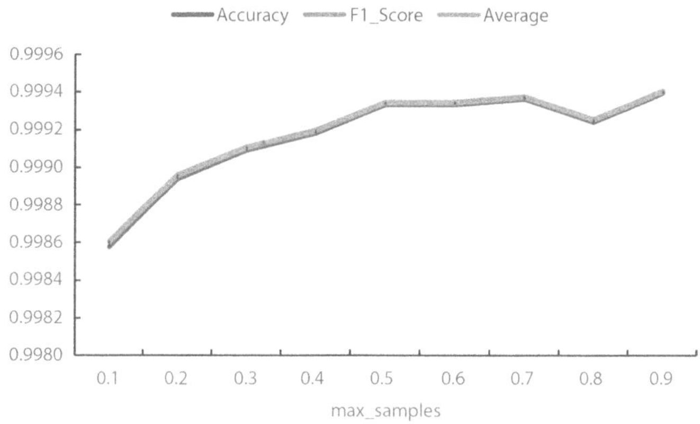

Figure 10.4 Accuracy graph [25].

Overall, the graph shows that the accuracy of the ML model in detecting DDoS attacks increases as the number of sample datasets increases. This is a positive finding, as it suggests that the model can learn from more data and improve its accuracy over time.

10.5.4 Precision Graph

The graph illustrates the precision percentages of different ML models in classifying traffic as either DDoS or normal. The KNN model demonstrate the highest precision for identifying normal attacks of various categories but falls short in identifying DDoS traffic at 89.4%. Importantly, the precision percentages are not flawless due to inherent data noise and imperfect differentiation between DDoS and normal traffic (as shown in Figure 10.5). Data quality and model parameters also impact the results.

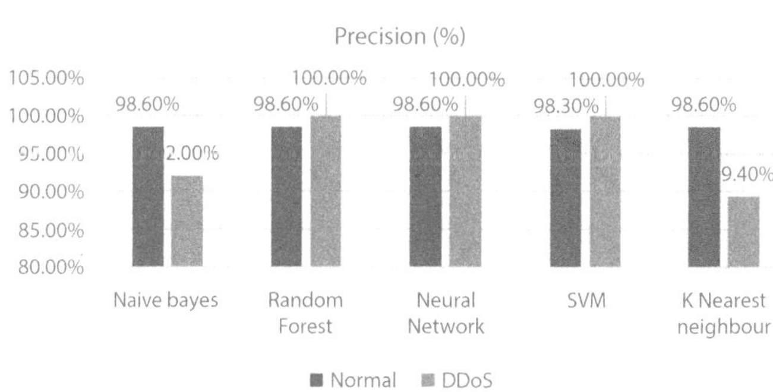

Figure 10.5 Precision graph [26].

In summary, the graph highlights the comparison of the method of KNN to various other ML models in DDoS detection, with NB and RF excelling in identifying DDoS traffic, whereas neural network and SVM perform well in recognizing normal traffic. Nonetheless, achieving perfect precision is challenging, considering data characteristics and model complexity.

10.6 Conclusion/Future Work

In conclusion, DDoS attacks pose a significant threat to the availability and performance of websites and network resources. The use of AI, specifically ML, has shown great promise in detecting and classifying DDoS threats with high accuracy rates. By training ML models on extensive datasets and analyzing network traffic patterns, IP addresses, and other relevant indicators, researchers have been able to differentiate between normal network activity and DDoS attack traffic. Deep learning methodologies, such as CNNs and RNNs, have been successful in categorizing various types of DDoS threats. These advanced models extract intricate patterns and features from the input data, enabling them to accurately identify and classify specific attack types.

Although ML-based DDoS attack detection has made significant progress, there are still important challenges and opportunities for future research. One key area is the availability of diverse and comprehensive datasets for training ML models. Another area is the development of techniques to enable ML models to adapt to dynamic traffic patterns in real time. Additionally, scalability and efficiency are crucial factors in handling large-scale networks and real-time traffic analysis. Lastly, exploring explainable AI techniques can provide transparency and interpretability of ML models, allowing security professionals and organizations to better understand the decision-making processes behind the detection and classification of DDoS attacks. By addressing these challenges and advancing research in these areas, we can bolster the resilience of network infrastructure against DDoS attacks, safeguarding the availability and functionality of web infrastructure in the face of evolving cyber threats.

References

1. Bogdanoski, M., Suminoski, T., Risteski, A., Analysis of the SYN Flood DoS Attack. *Int. J. Comput. Network Inf. Secur. (IJCNIS)*, 5, 8, 1–11, 2013.

2. Wei, H.C., Tung, Y.-H., Yu, C.-M., Countering UDP Flooding Attacks in SDN. *2016 IEEE NetSoft Conference and Workshops (NetSoft)*, 2016.
3. Kshirsagar, D. and Kumar, S., A feature reduction based reflected and exploited DDoS attacks detection system. *J. Ambient Intell. Hum. Comput.*, 13, 393–405, 2022.
4. Srinivasa, S., Pedersen, J.M., Vasilomanolakis, E., Deceptive directories and "vulnerable" logs: a honeypot study of the LDAP and log4j attack landscape. *IEEE Eur. Symp. Secur. Privacy Workshops*, 442–447, 2022.
5. Sadaf, K. and Sultana, J., Intrusion Detection Based on Autoencoder and Isolation Forest in Fog Computing. *IEEE Access*, 8, 167059–167068, 2020.
6. Chesney, S., Roy, K., Khorsandroo, S., Machine Learning Algorithms for Preventing IoT Cybersecurity Attacks. *Intell. Syst. Appl.*, 679–686, 2020.
7. Liu, Z., Qian, L., Tang, S., The prediction of DDoS attack by machine learning. *Third International Conference on Electronics and Communication; Network and Computer Technology*, 2021.
8. Liu, T., Sabrina, F., Jang-Jaccard, J., Xu, W., Wei, Y., Artificial Intelligence-Enabled DDoS Detection for Blockchain-Based Smart Transport Systems. *Sensors*, 22, 1, 1–11, 2021.
9. Li, J., Wu, J., Chen, L., Li, J., Lam, S.K., Blockchain-based Secure Key Management for Mobile Edge Computing. *IEEE Trans. Mob. Comput.*, 22, 1, 2021.
10. Balasubramaniam, A., Gul, M.J.J., Menon, V.G., Paul, A., Blockchain for intelligent transport system. *IETE Tech. Rev.*, 38, 438–449, 2021.
11. Aljawarneh, S., Aldwairi, M., Yassein, M.B., Anomaly-Based Intrusion Detection System through Feature Selection Analysis and Building Hybrid Efficient Model. *J. Comput. Sci.*, 25, 152–160, 2018.
12. Shi, K., Zhu, L., Zhang, C., Xu, L., Gao, F., Blockchain-based multimedia sharing in vehicular social networks with privacy protection. *Multimed. Tools Appl.*, 79, 8085–8105, 2020.
13. Zhang, Y., Zou, J., Guo, R., Efficient privacy-preserving authentication for V2G networks. *Peer-to-Peer Netw. Appl.*, 14, 1366–1378, 2021.
14. Stockburger, L., Kokosioulis, G., Mukkamala, A., Mukkamala, R.R., Avital, M., Blockchain-Enabled Decentralized Identify Management: The Case of Self-Sovereign Identity in Public Transportation. *Blockchain Res. Appl.*, 2, 100014, 2021.
15. Kumar, S. and Dutta, K., Intrusion Detection in Mobile Ad Hoc Networks: Techniques, Systems, and Future Challenges. *Secur. Commun. Netw.*, 9, 2484–2556, 2016.
16. Ndibwile, J.D., Govardhan, A., Okada, K., Kadobayashi, Y., Web Server Protection against Application Layer DDoS Attacks Using Machine Learning and Traffic Authentication. *Proceedings of the 2015 IEEE 39th Annual Computer Software and Applications Conference*, pp. 261–267, 2015.

17. Cuzzocrea, A., Fadda, E., Mumolo, E., Cyber-Attack Detection via Non-Linear Prediction of IP Addresses: An Innovative Big Data Analytics Approach. *Multimed. Tools Appl.*, 81, 171–189, 2022.
18. Alowolodu, O.D., Mebawondu, J.O., Adetunmbi, A.O., Network Intrusion Detection System Using Supervised Learning Paradigm. *Sci. Afr.*, 9, e00497, 2020.
19. Xinlong, L. and Zhibin, C., DDoS Attack Detection by Hybrid Deep Learning Methodologies. *Secur. Commun. Netw.*, 2022, e7866096, 2022.
20. Nakayama, H., Kurosawa, S., Jamalipour, A., Nemoto, Y., Kato, N., A Dynamic Anomaly Detection Scheme for AODV-Based Mobile Ad Hoc Networks. *IEEE Trans. Veh. Technol.*, 58, 2471–2481, 2009.
21. Nishani, L. and Biba, M., Machine Learning for Intrusion Detection in MANET: A State-of-the-Art Survey. *J. Intell. Inf. Syst.*, 46, 391–407, 2016.
22. Revathi, M., Ramalingam, V.V., Amutha, B., A machine learning based detection and mitigation of the DDOS attack by using SDN controller framework. *Wireless Pers. Commun.*, 127, 2417–2441, 2021.
23. Roy, K. and Khorsandroo, S., Machine Learning Algorithms for Preventing IoT Cybersecurity Attacks Steve Chesney. *IntelliSys*, 3, 679–686, 2020.
24. Steyn, J.V., DDOS Attack Network Logs Network traces from various types of DDOS attacks, https://www.kaggle.com/datasets/jacobvs/ddos-attack-network-logs.
25. Ma, R., Chen, X., Zhai, R., A DDoS Attack Detection Method Based on Natural Selection of Features and Models. *Electronics*, 12, 4, 1059–1069, 2023.
26. Maslan, A., Malik Bin Mohamad, K., Feresa Mohd Foozy, C., Feature selection for DDoS detection using classification machine learning techniques. *IAES Int. J. Artificial Intell.*, 9, 135–149, 2020.

11

CyberEDU: An Interactive Educational Tool for DDoS Attack Simulation and Prevention

Pulkit Srivastava[1], Vedant Shah[1], Priyanshu Singh[1], Sandeep Kumar Satapathy[2], Sung-Bae Cho[3], Shruti Mishra[2]* and Pradeep Kumar Mallick[4]

[1]*School of Computer Science and Engineering, Vellore Institute of Technology, Chennai, Tamil Nadu, India*
[2]*Centre for Advanced Data Science, Vellore Institute of Technology, Chennai, Tamil Nadu, India*
[3]*Department of Computer Science, Yonsei University, 50 Yonsei-ro, Sudaemoon-gu, Seoul, South Korea*
[4]*School of Computer Engineering, KIIT University, Odisha, India*

Abstract
This study focuses on the creation and assessment of a teaching tool for simulating and combating distributed-denial-of-service (DDoS) attacks on transmission control protocol/internet protocol (TCP/IP) servers. In the modern digital environment, DDoS attacks is a serious concern; thus, it is critical for professionals and students to have access to useful and engaging learning tools to comprehend the nuances of these attacks and learn how to defend against them. The study initially emphasizes the necessity for a teaching tool that can accurately model DDoS attacks on TCP/IP servers. Hands-on experiences and real-time simulations, which are crucial for understanding the intricacies of network security, are sometimes lacking in traditional training approaches. Students and professionals can learn about DDoS attack detection, mitigation, and prevention practically by using an educational application created expressly for this purpose. Overall, this study shows the effectiveness of a training tool for simulating and preventing DDoS attacks on TCP/IP servers. This application serves as a helpful resource for teachers, students, and network security professionals who want to advance their

**Corresponding author*: shrutim2129@gmail.com

Subhasis Dash, Manas Ranjan Lenka, S. Balamurugan, Ambika Prasad Tripathy and Amarendra Mohanty (eds.) Sustainable Resource Management in Next-Generation Computational Constrained Networks, (251–268) © 2025 Scrivener Publishing LLC

understanding and proficiency in fending off DDoS attacks by offering a practical and interactive learning environment.

Keywords: TCP/IP server, simulated attacks, intrusion detection system, AI-based IDS, DDoS attack, educational application

11.1 Introduction

In today's digital environment, networked system security is a crucial concern. The methods used by hostile actors to infiltrate networks and obtain unauthorized access to sensitive data evolve along with technology. Distributed-denial-of-service (DDoS) attacks have become a major threat for network users. Early DDoS attacks were games of underground communities. Attackers could get recognition via taking down popular web sites. As easy-to-use DDoS tools can be easily downloaded from the Internet, normal computer users can become DDoS attackers as well. DDoS attacks can also appear in illegal actions. Companies might use DDoS attacks to knock off their competitors in the market [1].

Network servers are particularly susceptible to attacks because they serve as the main nodes for data transfer and communication. It is essential to examine and comprehend the vulnerabilities that can be exploited in order to ensure their resilience against prospective attacks. During the first half of 2014 year, there were about 5,700 attacks with power more than 20 Gb/s. However, in 2013, less than 2,500 such DDoS attacks were detected. Therefore, network security from DDoS attacks is a very significant task [2]. TCP/IP servers, which enable data transmission between devices online, are essential for internet communication. They rely on IP addressing, which gives devices specific IDs for data transmission, and port numbers, which let various applications and services talk to one other through virtual endpoints. Whereas user datagram protocol (UDP) offers a connectionless and quicker option ideal for real-time applications, TCP assures dependable and orderly data transport through a connection-oriented strategy. TCP/IP servers are susceptible to DDoS attacks despite their importance. Attackers use methods including bandwidth and connection exhaustion, protocol exploitation, resource depletion, and application layer assaults to overwhelm servers and interrupt services by taking advantage of flaws in TCP/IP protocols as shown in Figure 11.1 [3]. Downtime, financial losses, and reputational harm might result from these assaults.

This research paper's goal is to look into how simulated attacks on a TCP/IP server are implemented and analyzed. We intend to evaluate the

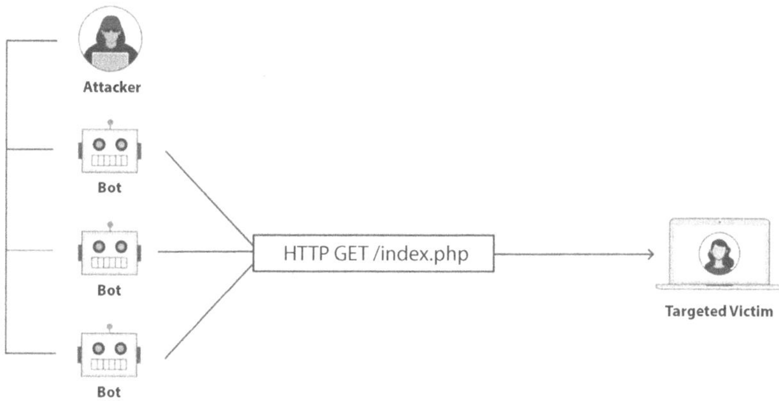

Figure 11.1 TCP/IP protocol and DDOS attack [3].

server's vulnerability by simulating several attack scenarios and investigate the capability of an artificial intelligence (AI)-based intrusion detection system (IDS) to identify and stop these attacks. The ser.py server code, the cli.py client code, the DDoS.py, and Password_Attacking.py attack codes, as well as other components used in the simulation, are all thoroughly examined. The basis of our investigation is the ser.py code. As a TCP/IP server, it accepts connections from clients and keeps a log of the packets that it receives in a packet.txt file. With this implementation, we are able to examine how the server responds to various attack scenarios. The packet.txt file can be improved to provide detailed insights into the packets' contents and enable more sophisticated analysis, even if it presently only represents a simple character count of the received strings. The ser.py code includes a password authentication method to ensure secure access to the server's services. The cli.py program operates as a straightforward client that communicates with the server by providing the right password. We may analyze the effects of password attacks and assess the server's defenses against threats based on authentication using this component.

The DDoS attack simulation portion of the DDoS.py module concentrates on the server. In a real-world scenario, such an assault effectively renders the server unusable by flooding it with a massive volume of data as shown in Figure 11.2 [4]. In our simulation, we want to examine how the server responds to heavy data traffic and create solutions to stop it from stalling or crashing. This study sheds light on the significance of proactive defense tactics against DDoS attacks. We combine all of the aforementioned elements into a thorough framework in the Both.py code. Users can engage with the simulation through this code and learn about the various

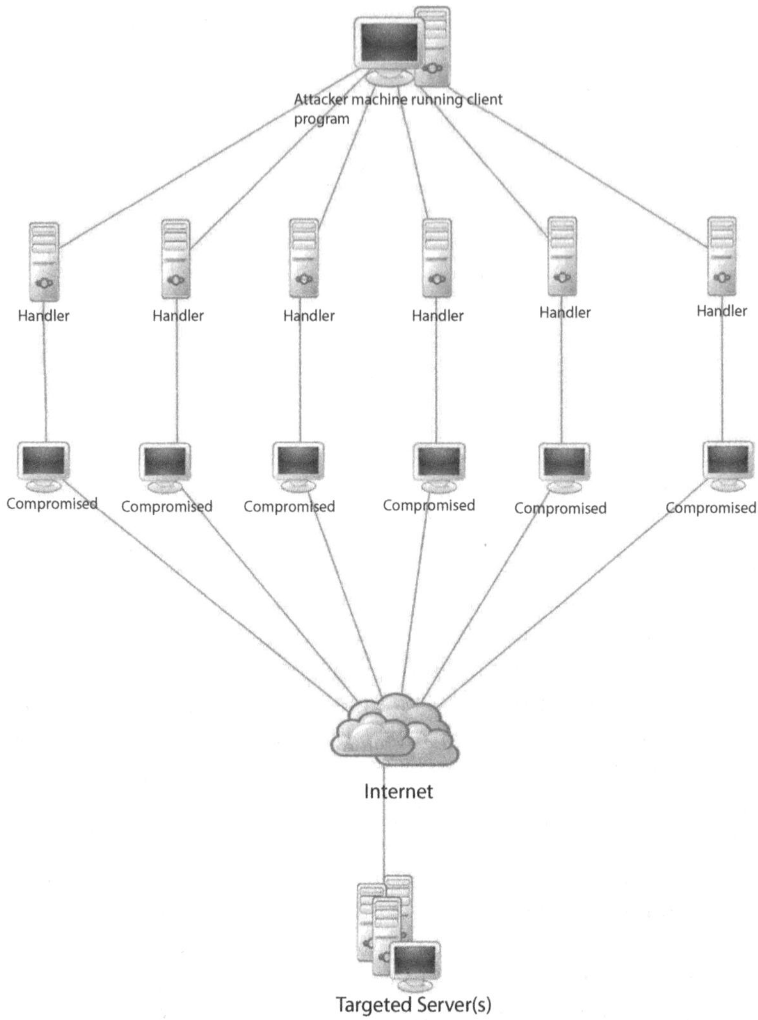

Figure 11.2 Flooding of DDOS attack [4].

attack types and the possible contribution of an AI-based IDS to threat mitigation. We emphasize the importance of education and awareness to equip users with the knowledge required to detect and respond to security breaches effectively.

Throughout this research paper, we will evaluate the server's performance under various attack scenarios, discuss potential defense mechanisms, and propose the utilization of AI-based IDS to enhance the server's security. By the end of this study, readers will gain a deeper understanding of the challenges faced in securing networked systems and the potential solutions offered by advanced intrusion detection technologies.

11.2 Related Work

Currently, an abundance of tools exists for generating DDoS attacks, with a variety of them being widely used and described in detail below.

DDoS simulator (DDOSIM) is a tool that can be used in a laboratory environment to simulate a DDOS attack against a target server. The test will show the capacity of the server to handle application specific DDOS attacks. DDOSIM simulates several zombie hosts (having random IP addresses) that create full TCP connections to the target server. After completing the connection, DDOSIM starts the conversation with the listening application (e.g., HTTP server) [5]. Trin00 [6] allows an attacker to control several hosts and makes them send a UDP flood to another host. Trin00 allows an attacker to control several hosts and makes them send a UDP flood to other hosts involved in the attack and also to configurate the transmitted packets parameters. The Trin00 master can make several requests to the Trin00 daemon: start flooding a host with UDP packets; stop flooding a host with UDP packets; and change the UDP flood configuration of the daemon. Trin00 is written in C and runs on Unix-like systems [1].

BoNeSi [7] generates internet control message protocol (ICMP), UDP, and TCP (HTTP) flooding attacks from a defined botnet size (different IP addresses). BoNeSi is highly configurable, and rates of data volume, source IP addresses, URLs, and other parameters can be configured. BoNeSi sniffs for TCP packets on the network interface and responds on all packets in order to establish TCP connections. For this feature, it is necessary, that all traffic from the victim web server is routed back to the host running BoNeSi. BoNeSi can be executed on Linux [1]. Tribe Flood Network [8] is a C++ program. It allows simulating such attacks as ICMP-flooding, SYN-flooding, UDP-flooding, and Smurf. Tribe Flood Network allows user to exploit the resources of a number of agents in order to coordinate an attack against one or more designated victims (host or network). Currently, UNIX, Solaris, and Windows NT platforms that are connected to the Internet, directly or indirectly, are susceptible to this attack [1].

CyberEDU and the paper on preventing DoS attacks in sensor networks are related in the sense that they both aim to prevent DoS attacks. However, they differ in terms of the context and the proposed solutions. CyberEDU is a platform that focuses on teaching students and professionals about

DDoS attacks and how to prevent them. It uses simulation and prevention techniques to provide a hands-on learning experience. The platform allows users to simulate various DDoS attack scenarios and learn how to prevent them using different mitigation techniques. It also provides real-time monitoring and alerts, which can help users identify and respond to DDoS attacks quickly. On the other hand, the paper proposes a game theoretic approach to prevent DoS attacks in wireless sensor networks (WSNs). WSNs are networks of small devices that are used to monitor and collect data from the physical environment. These devices are resource-constrained, which means that traditional security mechanisms are not effective in WSNs. The proposed approach models the sensor nodes as players in a non-cooperative game and the attacker as an adversary. The objective of the game is to minimize energy consumption while maximizing the network's lifetime. The authors show that this objective can be achieved by adopting a mixed strategy Nash equilibrium. Although both CyberEDU and the paper aim to prevent DoS attacks, they differ in terms of the context and the proposed solutions. CyberEDU focuses on teaching users about DDoS attacks and mitigation techniques, whereas the paper proposes a novel approach to prevent DoS attacks in resource-constrained WSNs. Both approaches are important in their respective contexts and can help improve the overall security of networks against DDoS attacks [9].

DDoS attacks are a common type of cyber-attack that can cause significant disruption to online services. They involve overwhelming a website or server with traffic from multiple sources, rendering it inaccessible to legitimate users. In recent years, DDoS attacks have become more frequent and sophisticated, making it increasingly important for organizations to have effective mitigation techniques in place. The article "DDoS Attack Mitigation Techniques: A Comprehensive Review" provides an overview of various techniques that can be used to defend against DDoS attacks. It covers both traditional and emerging techniques, including network-based and application-based approaches, as well as hybrid solutions that combine multiple techniques. The article highlights the importance of having a multi-layered defense strategy that includes both proactive and reactive measures. CyberEDU, an interactive educational tool for DDoS attack simulation and prevention, is a tool that uses simulation to educate users on how to prevent DDoS attacks. It provides a realistic simulation of a DDoS attack, allowing users to experience the impact of such an attack and learn how to prevent it. The tool also provides information on various mitigation techniques and best practices for defending against DDoS attacks.

Both the article and CyberEDU aim to increase awareness and understanding of DDoS attacks and how to protect against them. Whereas the article provides a comprehensive review of various mitigation techniques, CyberEDU provides a hands-on learning experience that can help users develop practical skills for preventing DDoS attacks. Together, they provide a valuable resource for organizations looking to defend against DDoS attacks and ensure the availability of their online services [10]. "DDoS Attack Detection and Prevention Techniques: A Review" is directly related to the topic of DDoS attacks as it provides a comprehensive review of various DDoS attack detection and prevention techniques. The paper discusses the strengths and weaknesses of each technique and provides insights into their effectiveness in mitigating DDoS attacks. The authors cover a wide range of techniques, including signature-based detection, anomaly-based detection, hybrid detection, and prevention mechanisms such as traffic filtering and rate limiting. The paper is relevant to those interested in understanding the various techniques available for detecting and preventing DDoS attacks. It provides a useful resource for researchers, network security professionals, and students who want to gain a deeper understanding of the different approaches to mitigating DDoS attacks. This paper can be used as a reference for those looking to evaluate the effectiveness of different DDoS mitigation techniques and choose the most appropriate one for their specific use case [11–14].

11.3 Methodology

1. Import essential libraries: The code gets started by importing subprocess, numpy, time, tkinter, threading, os, and sys.
2. Define global variables: A number of global variables are declared in order to manage the program's flow and save important data. They are c1, output, file_exists, threshold_factor, spike_counter, packets, running, server_process, client_process, and ddos_client_process.
3. Define the output redirection function: The standard output is directed to a Tkinter text widget using the redirect_output() function. In order to redirect the output to both the original sys.stdout and the text widget, it constructs a special class called OutputRedirector and overrides its write() method.
4. Implement server-side features: The start_server() and stop_server() functions are defined in the code, respectively, to start and stop the server. The subprocess is used by these operations. Using the Popen() technique, distinct server-related instructions can be executed.

5. Implement the numpy function: The numpy functionality is managed through the start_numpy_function(), stop_numpy_function(), and run_numpy_function() methods. Initializing the halted variable and invoking run_numpy_function() to launch the numpy process are both done by the start_numpy_function() function. The stopped variable is set to True by the stop_numpy_function() function, signaling that the numpy process has to be terminated. The mean and standard deviation of packet counts stored in the packets array are computed by the run_numpy_function() function. It looks for surges in packet counts and, if necessary, launches a DDoS assault. If stopped is False, then the method uses threading to call itself after a 0.5 s wait and changes the packet count label.
6. Implement DDoS functionality: The functions start_ddos() and stop_ddos() take care of DDoS functionality. The DDoS assault is launched via the start_ddos() method, which uses subprocess to run the DDoS.py script.Popen(), and the stop_ddos() method terminates the ddos_client_process, if one exists, to halt the DDoS attack.
7. Implement file manipulation functions: The code consists of routines for manipulating files, such as clear_text(), run_file(), stop_file(), clear_file(), and save_file(). These routines manage tasks like deleting the packet_count.txt file, executing the IDS.py script, pausing the running script, and saving the text box's contents to the IDS.py file.
8. Describe GUI components: The code produces a Tkinter window, selects a dark theme, and generates a number of GUI components, including buttons, text boxes, and labels. It also redirects the console output to the text box using the redirect_output() function.
9. Implement packet count update: The update_packet_count() function reads the packet_count.txt file and updates the label on the packet count with data like the total packet count, most recent packet count, mean packet count, spike counter, and standard deviation. The packet count display is updated once every second by continually invoking it using the root.after() method.
10. The clear_empty_lines() function reads the packet_count.txt file, removes any empty lines, and then rewrites the file

without the empty lines. Using the root.after() method, it is set to run once every 100 ms.

11. Set label position and window resizing: The update_label_position() function is defined in the code to put the packet count label in the middle of the window. It binds this function to the window resize event to ensure the label remains centered when the window size changes.
12. Start clearing empty lines and updating the packet count: The functions update_packet_count() and clear_empty_lines() are used to start updating the packet count display continuously and clearing out empty lines from the file, respectively.
13. Start the Tkinter event loop: The root.mainloop() function launches the Tkinter event loop, enabling the GUI to react to user input and carry out the specified functionality. Managing the first file's content Using a try-except block, the code tries to read the contents of the "IDS.py" file. If the file is present, then the initial_content variable is filled with its contents, and the file_exists flag is set to True. Initial_content is set to "#Write your code here" as a placeholder if the file cannot be located.
14. Update label position: The update_label_position() function is called to update the position of the packet count label within the window. It is bound to the window's resize event ("<Configure>") and calculates the new position based on the current window size, ensuring that the label remains centered.
15. GUI elements and layout: The code creates the necessary GUI elements using Tkinter's ttk module. These elements include buttons (get_basic_code_button, clear_button, save_button, stop_file_button, run_button, start_button, stop_button, clear_file_button,numpy_start_button,numpy_stop_button, ddos_start_button, and ddos_stop_button), text boxes (text_box and code1_output_text_box), and labels (packet_count_label and top_top_label). The elements are organized using frames (top_frame and button_frame) to control their placement and alignment within the window.
16. Functionality for basic code and file manipulation: The code includes functions such as write_the_basic_code() and save_file() to handle loading the basic code from a file and saving the content of the text box to the "IDS.py" file, respectively.

Additionally, there are functions for clearing the text box [clear_text()], running the "IDS.py" script [run_file()], and stopping the running script [stop_file()].

17. Packet count update: The update_packet_count() function reads the content of the "packet_count.txt" file and processes it using NumPy. It calculates the mean and standard deviation of the packet counts stored in the packets array and updates the packet_count_label with relevant information. The function is called repeatedly every second [root.after(1000, update_packet_count)] to ensure the packet count display stays up to date.
18. Clearing empty lines in the file: The clear_empty_lines() function reads the "packet_count.txt" file, removes any empty lines, and rewrites the file without the empty lines. It is scheduled to run every 100 ms [root.after(100, clear_empty_lines)] to maintain a clean and compact file.
19. Start updating packet count and clearing empty lines: The update_packet_count() and clear_empty_lines() functions are called initially to start the continuous update of the packet count display and the removal of empty lines in the file, respectively.
20. Run the Tkinter event loop: The root.mainloop() function is executed to start the Tkinter event loop. This loop continuously listens for user input, updates the GUI, and executes the defined functionality in response to events.

11.4 Proposed Model

With a graphical user interface (GUI) created with the Tkinter library (as shown in Figure 11.3), the provided code represents a DDoS simulator. It enables users to run IDS code, keep track of packet counts, and simulate DDoS attacks. Let us examine the code's detailed proposed model in more detail. The code starts by importing the required libraries, including tkinter, subprocess, numpy, and time. Additionally, it initializes a number of global variables that are used all through the code. These variables include stopped, which manages the simulator's main loop, and server_process, client_process, and ddos_client_process, which are each process objects that represent a different client process, such as a server, a regular client, or a DDoS client.

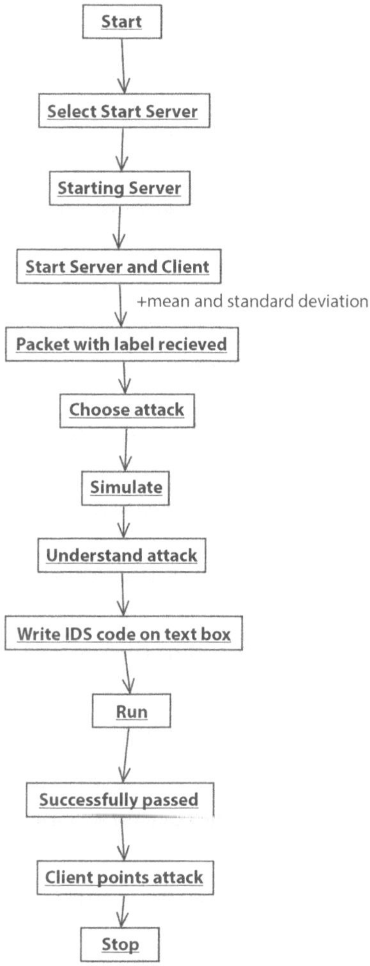

Figure 11.3 Flowchart of the proposed model.

Redirect console output to a text widget in the GUI by using the redirect_output function, which is defined. The output of the IDS code and other pertinent data are displayed within the GUI using this function. A DDoS attack, a numpy function, and other functions are also defined in the code. The server and client processes are started and stopped by the start_server and stop_server functions, respectively. The Numpy function that keeps track of packet counts, detects spikes, and handles DDoS attacks is started and stopped by the start_numpy_function and stop_numpy_function functions. By starting and stopping the DDoS client process, the start_ddos and stop_ddos functions, respectively, start and stop the DDoS attack.

The code includes functions for running, stopping, saving, and clearing the code in order to make editing and executing the IDS code easier. The run_file function runs the IDS.py file as a subprocess, directs the output to the GUI, and updates the text widget with the output as it is produced. The stop_file function halts the IDS code's execution. The IDS.py file is where the text widget's contents are saved using the save_file function. The "packet_count" is cleaned out by the clear_file function. Packet counts are kept in a ".txt" file.

Users can use the text widget as a starting point for their IDS code by using the write_the_basic_code function to write the basic code from the "basic_code.py" file. Additionally, the code has functions for clearing empty lines from the "packet_count" and updating the label for the packet count ".txt" file. The update_packet_count function reads the packet count data from the file, uses Numpy to compute statistics (like mean and standard deviation), and then modifies the GUI's label for the packet count. Any empty lines are removed from the "packet_count" by the clear_empty_lines function ".txt" file.

The code creates a Tkinter window called "DDoS simulator" to serve as the GUI. It uses the set_dark_theme function to set a dark theme for the GUI, which enhances user experience. The code redirects the console output to the newly created text widget, which will display the output of the IDS code. Additionally, it reads the first few lines of the IDS.py file to see if the file already exists. To provide control over the simulation, numerous buttons are made. These include switches for accessing the basic code, erasing the text widget, saving the code, halting execution, and running the IDS code. To carry out the corresponding functionalities, the aforementioned functions are bound to these buttons.

The code includes a packet count label that shows data on the packet count, most recent packet, mean packet count, spike counter, and standard deviation. By using the update_packet_count function, this label is updated on a regular basis. The code also manages the window resize event and modifies the packet count label's position appropriately. To start the simulation, the code enters the main Tkinter event loop by calling root.mainloop(), which keeps the GUI responsive and handles user interactions.

In conclusion, the proposed model provides a detailed understanding of the DDoS simulator code. It outlines the functions, global variables, and their roles within the simulation. The code's GUI components, such as the text widget, buttons, and packet count label, allow users to interact with the simulator effectively. With the provided functionalities for server and client management, Numpy-based packet monitoring, DDoS attack initiation, and IDS code execution, this simulator serves as a useful tool for studying DDoS attacks and developing intrusion detection mechanisms.

11.5 Experimental Result/Result Analysis

From the research paper, we can learn that DDoS attacks have become a significant threat in today's digital environment. The study highlights the need for a training tool that can faithfully simulate DDoS attacks on TCP/IP servers, because this will enable professionals and students to gain practical experience in DDoS attack detection, mitigation, and prevention. The suggested tool offers experts and students a hands-on, engaging learning environment to develop their knowledge and skills in thwarting DDoS attacks. The installation of server-side features, DDoS functionality, file manipulation capabilities, GUI components, and packet count update were all covered in detail along with the tool's methodology. The study showed the effectiveness of the training tool for simulating and preventing DDoS attacks on TCP/IP servers, which can serve as a helpful resource for teachers, students, and network security professionals.

Importing necessary libraries, creating global variables, putting server-side features in place, using the numpy function, putting in DDoS functionality, using file manipulation functions, describing GUI elements, and putting in packet count update are all part of the paper's methodology. The suggested solution (as shown from Figures 11.4 to 11.9) may mimic DDoS attacks on TCP/IP servers and offers practical training and real-time simulations that are essential for comprehending network security's intricate workings. Overall, this study offers insightful information on the development and assessment of a teaching tool for simulating and fending off DDoS attacks on TCP/IP servers. It is a useful tool for businesses trying to protect themselves from DDoS assaults and guarantee the availability of their online services.

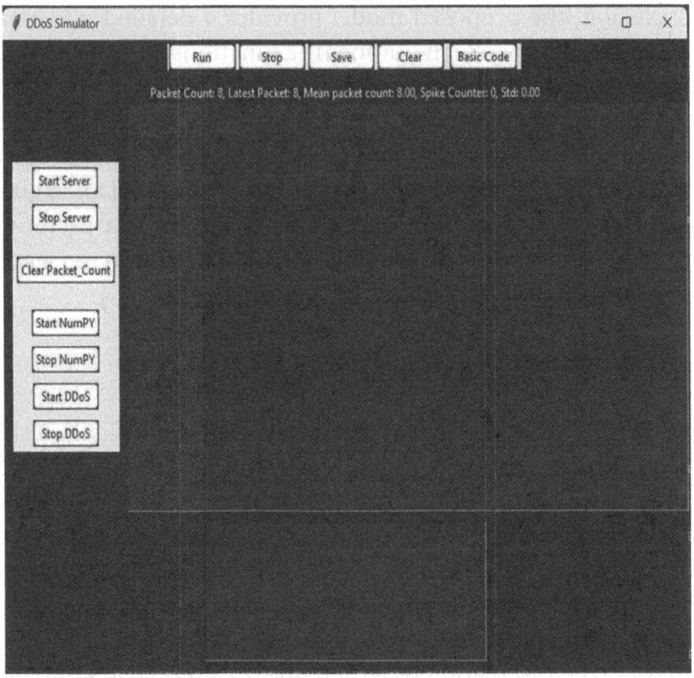

Figure 11.4 When we start the simulator.

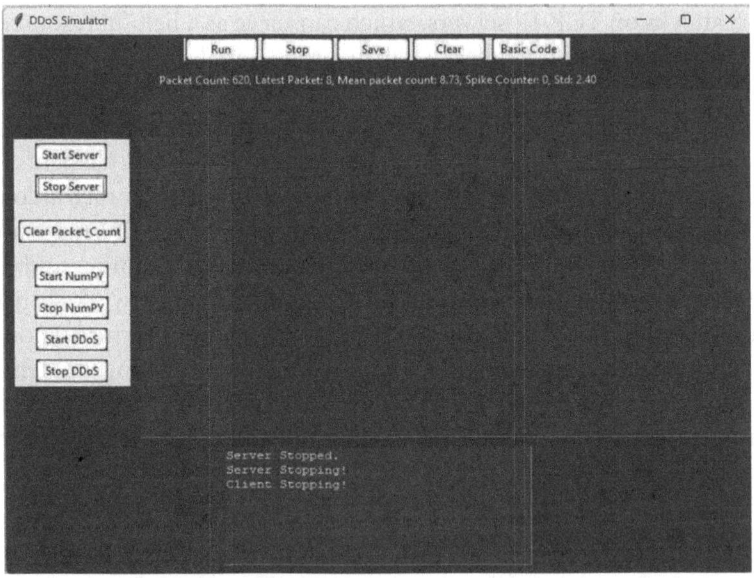

Figure 11.5 When we stop the server.

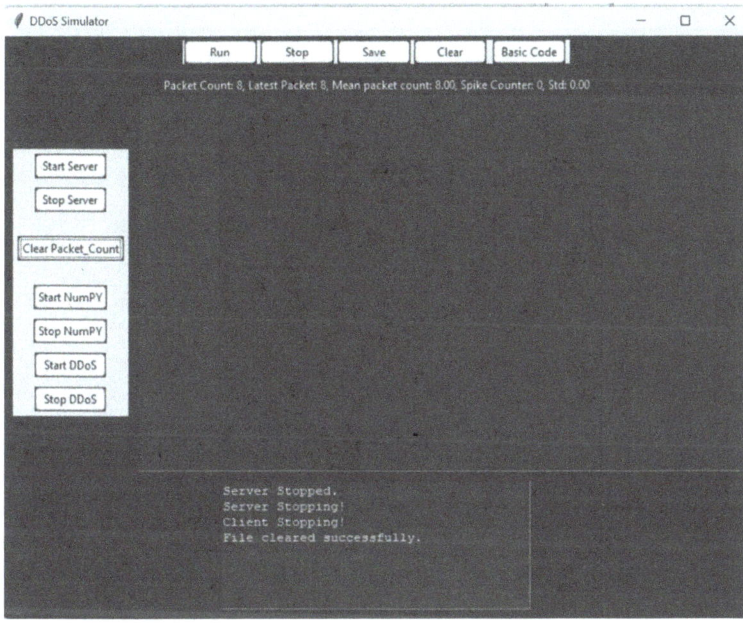

Figure 11.6 When we clear packet count.

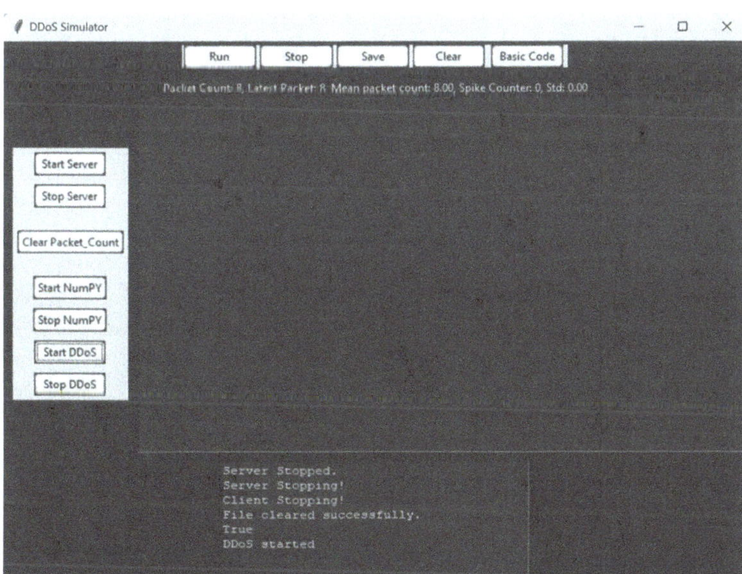

Figure 11.7 When DDoS started.

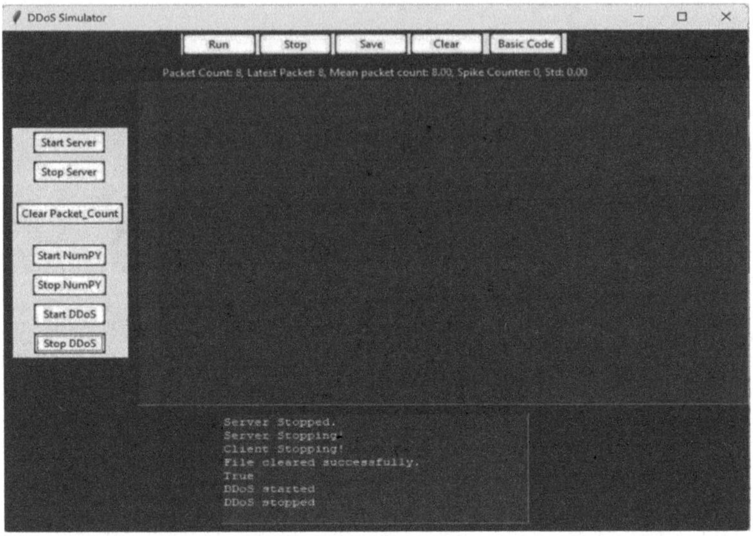

Figure 11.8 When DDoS stopped.

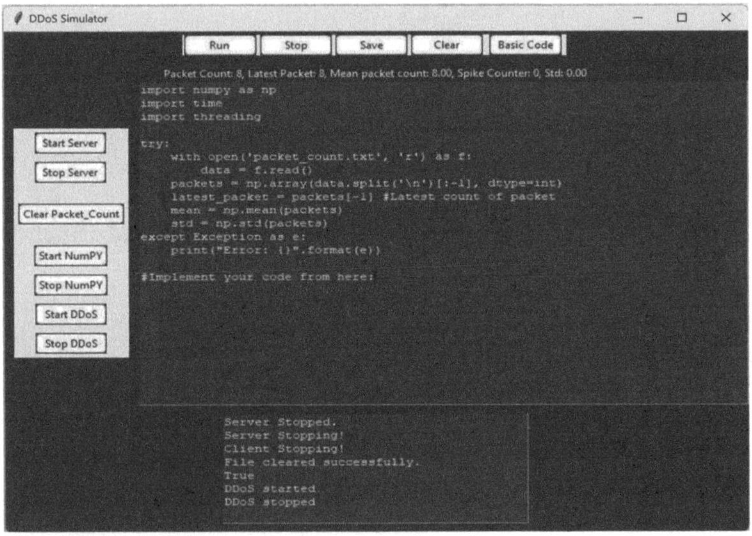

Figure 11.9 Basic functioning of packet count.

11.6 Conclusion and Future Work

In conclusion, the "CyberEDU" educational tool represents a vital step in bolstering cybersecurity education and preparedness against the rising threat of DDoS attacks. By providing users with realistic simulation environments and hands-on experience, this tool equips students and professionals with essential skills to learn to identify, mitigate, and prevent DDoS attacks effectively. Ultimately, the "CyberEDU" fosters a culture of awareness and preparedness, contributing to a more resilient and secure online ecosystem. By bridging the gap between theory and practical application, this educational tool plays a pivotal role in creating a skilled and vigilant workforce capable of countering the relentless threat of DDoS attacks and fortifying our digital infrastructure for a safer digital future.

The "CyberEDU" training program plans to include simulation and preventive modules for additional kinds of cyberthreats in the future, extending its application beyond DDoS assaults. This extension intends to combat a larger range of attack vectors, including malware, advanced persistent threats, phishing, and ransomware, in recognition of the changing nature of the cybersecurity field. The tool will give users full information and hands-on experience to protect against a wider range of cyber threats by including simulations for these various attack scenarios.

References

1. Bekeneva, Y., Shipilov, N., Borisenko, K., Shorov, A., Simulation of DDoS-attacks and protection mechanisms against them, in: *2015 IEEE NW Russia Young Researchers in Electrical and Electronic Engineering Conference (EIConRusNW)*, IEEE, pp. 49–55, 2015, February.
2. Gezelter, R., Security on the Internet, in: *Computer Security Handbook*, John Wiley & Sons, Inc., Hoboken, New Jersey, 1995.
3. https://cfassets.www.cloudflare.com/slt3lc6tev37/3jlyZeWRy9eBz3tyEk-9mxA/96eab064524495e8f6b2647f1f7b9d60/application_layer_ddos_example.png.
4. https://upload.wikimedia.org/wikipedia/commons/thumb/3/3f/Stachledraht_DDos_Attack.svg/1200px-Stachledraht_DDos_Attack.svg.png.
5. https://thehackernews.com/2011/01/ddosim-layer-7-ddos-simulator.html.
6. Trin00 analysis http://www.iss.net/security_center/reference/vuln/TrinOO_Daemon_Request.htm.
7. Aleksieva, Y. and Valchanov, H., Network Simulator for Botnet DoS Attacks.

8. Tribe Flood Network Analysis http:/packetstormsecurity.com/distributed/TFN2k_Analysis-I.3.txt.
9. Agah, A., Basu, K., Das, S.K., Preventing DoS attack in sensor networks: a game theoretic approach. *IEEE International Conference on Communications, 2005. ICC 2005*, vol. 5, IEEE, pp. 3218–3222, 2005, May 2005.
10. Singh, J. and Behal, S., Detection and mitigation of DDoS attacks in SDN: A comprehensive review, research challenges and future directions. *Comput. Sci. Rev.*, 37, 100279, 2020.
11. Kaur, A. and Kaur, S., DDoS attack detection and prevention techniques: A review. *J. Network Comput. Appl.*, 177, 102959, 2021.
12. Dharma, N.G., Muthohar, M.F., Prayuda, J.A., Priagung, K., Choi, D., Time-based DDoS detection and mitigation for SDN controller. *Network Oper. Manage. Symp. (APNOMS) 2015 17th Asia-Pac.*, 550–553, 2015.
13. Wei, L. and Fung, C., FlowRanger: A request prioritizing algorithm for controller DoS attacks in Software Defined Networks. *2015 IEEE Int. Conf. Commun. (ICC)*, 5254–5259, 2015.
14. Oshima, S., Nakashima, T., Sueyoshi, T., Early DoS/DDoS detection method using short-term statistics. *Complex Intell. Software Intensive Syst. (CISIS) 2010 Int. Conf.*, 168–173, 2010.

12

Resource Management and Performance Optimization in Constraint Network Systems

Amarendra Kumar Mohanty

Intel Corporation, Bangalore, India

Abstract
Efficient management of network resources is pivotal for optimizing packet processing performance within a network. This research delves into strategies aimed at enhancing network performance by wisely allocating and utilizing network resources. Various facets of resource management, including bandwidth, buffer space, computational assets, and prioritization techniques, are thoroughly examined. The exploration of optimization methodologies sheds light on achieving network efficiency, minimizing latency, and enhancing overall system performance. The study underscores the importance of resource allocation strategies in contemporary network architectures, ultimately fostering improved network performance and reliability. Emphasizing the critical role of resource management, the research highlights its contribution to enhancing system efficiency, alleviating bottlenecks, and meeting performance objectives within networks constrained by diverse limitations. These findings aid in the development of resource allocation and optimization strategies crucial for achieving superior performance in constrained network systems.

Keywords: Resource management, bandwidth, latency, throughput, jitter, queuing disciplines

Email: amarendra.kumar.mohanty@intel.com

Subhasis Dash, Manas Ranjan Lenka, S. Balamurugan, Ambika Prasad Tripathy and Amarendra Mohanty (eds.) Sustainable Resource Management in Next-Generation Computational Constrained Networks, (269–314) © 2025 Scrivener Publishing LLC

12.1 Introduction

In the contemporary landscape of network engineering, where technology and connectivity dominate, effective resource allocation and management have emerged as crucial factors influencing network performance. The inherent challenges posed by constraint networks, characterized by their inherent limitations on available resources, emphasize the urgent need for resource management techniques capable of mitigating these constraints.

This chapter initiates a comprehensive exploration of resource management intricacies within the context of constraint networks. It delves into the principles and methodologies governing resource allocation, network capacity, and performance optimization, all with the overarching objective of improving the efficiency, reliability, and overall performance of intricate constraint networks.

The changing terrain of networking technologies has introduced a wide range of constraints, spanning from bandwidth limitations to considerations of energy efficiency and scarcity of computational resources. Recognizing and tackling these constraints are essential for the effective design and operation of networks across diverse domains, such as telecommunications, cloud computing, and the Internet of Things (IoT). Skillful management of these limited resources poses a multidisciplinary challenge, drawing upon elements of computer science, engineering, and mathematics. As networks evolve and expand, resource management techniques must also evolve to usher in a new era of efficiency and performance optimization.

This chapter provides an in-depth perspective on the vital role of resource management in the design and operation of constraint networks. It explores a variety of resource management strategies and their practical application in real-world situations, empowering readers with the knowledge and tools needed to navigate the challenges of resource-constrained environments. Through a thorough examination of resource management within constraint networks, this chapter aims to enhance understanding of the intricacies of network optimization and provide valuable insights for both practitioners and researchers.

The structure of this chapter is designed to offer readers a systematic and thorough investigation into resource management techniques within constraint networks. By examining the principles, strategies, and applications of resource management [1–8] in constraint networks, this chapter aims to provide readers with a comprehensive understanding of the complex interplay between resource allocation and network performance. Whether you are a network practitioner, researcher, or a student embarking on network studies, this chapter offers valuable insights and knowledge to navigate the multifaceted world of constraint network resource management.

The rest of the chapter is organized as follows. Section 12.2 elucidates the key considerations and challenges inherent to efficiently allocating constrained resources. Section 12.3 delves into the concept of network capacity and its relationship with resource management. Section 12.4 explores strategies for performance optimization in constraint networks. To provide practical insights, Section 12.5 discusses the real-world applications of resource management techniques in various domains. Section 12.6 concludes the work with a glimpse into potential future directions and emerging trends in this dynamic field.

12.2 Resource Allocation Principles

In a computer networking environment, multiple data streams concurrently access and utilize shared network resources, including bandwidth, memory buffers, and processing capabilities of network routers. The phenomenon of congestion occurs when the demand from these competing data flows surpasses the available capacity of any given resource. An illustrative example of this is when the aggregate bandwidth requirement of all data streams converging on a specific output link surpasses the maximum bandwidth capacity of that link, necessitating the buffering or discarding of packets. This results in increased latency or packet loss, adversely affecting network performance. The strategic and fair allocation and management of resources under congestion conditions are critical for enhancing the efficiency and overall functionality of the system.

The flows of traffic traverse through a network and share with other flows a variety of resources like the following:

- Bandwidth Allocation: The fair distribution of bandwidth across network links has been the subject of thorough investigation within the scholarly community, particularly concerning edge segments of the Internet and wireless communication networks. Bandwidth stands out as a pivotal resource, necessitating an equitable allocation among all users vying for network access to ensure optimal network functionality and user satisfaction.
- Buffer Management: Network buffers play a crucial role in augmenting the throughput of data across output links.

In the absence of buffers, incoming packets to an overloaded link face immediate discard, leading to significant packet loss and diminished throughput. The incorporation of buffer resources, however, facilitates the temporary storage of packets during periods of congestion. This storage capability allows for the packets to be transmitted once the link has sufficient capacity, effectively mitigating packet loss and bolstering the overall throughput by enabling the queued traffic to be forwarded during idle periods of the link.

- Processor Utilization: In the realm of packet-switched networks, the processing units within switches and routers are tasked with executing a series of operations for each incoming packet. These operations encompass the extraction of relevant data from the packet's header, ascertaining the intended destination and the appropriate forwarding path, updating statistics related to traffic flow such as average arrival rates, and, in certain cases, altering the packet for purposes of network or traffic optimization. Each operation mandates the allocation of processing cycles from the central processing unit (CPU), highlighting its significance as an essential resource that is collectively utilized by all data flows. Despite the prevalent deployment of high-capacity optical links within the core segments of the Internet and the strategic overprovisioning in peripheral networks to mitigate congestion, the processing capacity of routers remains a bottleneck of paramount importance. Ensuring equitable access to processor resources among competing traffic flows is critical for maintaining optimal network performance and fairness. Each of these tasks requires the CPU to dedicate processing cycles, making it a vital shared resource for all traffic streams. Despite the widespread use of high-bandwidth long-haul optical links in the Internet backbone and occasional over-provisioning to alleviate congestion in edge networks, the router's processor remains a crucial resource. Ideally, all competing flows should receive fair access to this critical resource.

More than one of which resources could be congested at any given time; the allocation policy [9–13] with respect to any single resource can profoundly affect the overall performance and quality of service (QoS) experienced by flows within a network.

While fair scheduling of bandwidth allocation has been extensively studied, the ultimate objective is to achieve fairness in the combined allocation of all resources shared by traffic flows, rather than focusing solely on one resource such as link bandwidth.

The most popular resource allocation policies are max-min fairness, proportional fairness, and utility max-min fairness.

- Max-Min Fairness: The policy of max-min fair share, which allocates a shared resource among multiple flows with equal rights but varying demands, operates on the following principles:
    1. Allocation of the shared resource is prioritized based on increasing demand.
    2. No flow is granted a share of the resource exceeding its demand.
    3. Flows with unfulfilled demands are allocated equal shares of the resource.

- Utility-Based Max-Min Fairness Allocation: Within the framework of utility-based max-min fairness, each data flow is associated with a utility function as delineated in reference [16], where the equitable distribution of utility across flows is the primary objective. The utility function for a flow, given a specific resource allocation, quantifies the performance level attained by the flow as a consequence of this allocation. It is crucial to note that utility functions can differ among flows, mirroring their unique demands and priorities.
  For illustration, consider the utility functions for various traffic categories:
    1. Elastic Traffic: Applications such as E-mail, Telnet, and FTP are characterized by convex utility functions. The utility for these applications escalates rapidly with an increase in resource allocation, especially at lower levels of allocation. Nevertheless, there is a point of utility saturation, beyond which further resources do not substantially improve performance. This behavior indicates a diminishing return on utility as resource allocation continues to increase.
    2. Real-Time Traffic: Traffic for real-time applications, including video and audio streaming, necessitates a baseline level of resource allocation for utility to be considered

meaningful. The utility for this traffic type only becomes significant upon surpassing a minimum required threshold. Beyond this point, excessive provisioning of resources yields negligible improvements in utility. Consequently, the utility function for real-time traffic typically exhibits a threshold characteristic, correlating with its minimal resource requirements, above which additional allocation fails to substantially benefit performance.

12.3 Network Capacity and Utilization

Network capacity delineates the maximal quantity of data transferable between two nodes within a network over a defined temporal window. This metric is integral to the architecture and operational efficiency of network systems, influencing the speed and reliability of data exchange and, consequently, the quality of the end-user experience. Expressed in terms of bits per second (bps) and its derivatives, kilobits per second (Kbps), megabits per second (Mbps), or gigabits per second (Gbps), network capacity is a critical parameter for the assessment of network performance and the planning of data transmission strategies.

The practice of network capacity planning [14–16] involves a methodical examination and enhancement of network resources to guarantee optimal operation, continuous availability, and efficient data flow. This encompasses a thorough review of the existing infrastructure, an evaluation of bandwidth consumption, the identification of possible constraints, and the development of expansion strategies to accommodate future growth. This anticipatory strategy aims to ensure a fluid and effective networking experience for users while concurrently optimizing resource allocation, reducing operational costs, and enhancing the investment value in networking infrastructure.

One fundamental aspect of network planning involves determining the required bandwidth capacity for the network, considering both current usage and anticipated future growth. Accurate insights into bandwidth usage are essential for effective planning and provisioning. Network capacity planning also facilitates precise budgeting and resource allocation.

Furthermore, network capacity planning aims to identify conditions that could affect an organization's current and future network performance over a specified period. By predicting and addressing potential bottlenecks, performance lags, and availability issues within the network infrastructure, organizations can ensure optimal operation. In today's complex and diverse networks, which may include various network devices such as routers, switches, firewalls, servers, and storage hardware, network capacity planning plays a crucial role in maintaining optimal function and throughput. It helps network operators understand key metrics and identify potential flaws, misconfigurations, or other issues that could impact network availability within a specified timeframe. Overall, network capacity planning enables organizations to effectively manage and optimize their network resources to meet current and future demands. The network traffic is further classified as follows:

1. The capacity of existing network infrastructure
2. Network utilization in the network
3. Existing network traffic volumes for internal networks and external networks

By conducting this form of network assessment, analysts gain insights into the maximum potential of existing resources and the impact of integrating incremental new resources required to address future demands. Capacity planning not only aids in designing new network infrastructure but also assists in identifying the necessity for additional personnel or resources to manage and supervise the network effectively.

Network operations frequently establish a standard for network performance, with a pivotal inquiry in each operation being: What level of performance can be anticipated during routine operation? Network engineers forecast the optimal performance metrics, which can subsequently be utilized by network management tools. Essential metrics encompass the following:

- Bandwidth: The maximum rate of data transfer, usually measured in bits per second (bps).
- Throughput: The actual rate of data transfer.
- Latency: The time delay between data transmission and reception at the destination.
- Jitter: The variability in packet delay between the source and destination.
- Packet Loss: Expressed as the percentage of lost packets in relation to the total packets transmitted.
- Error Rate: The total number of corrupted bits in the transmitted data.

Network capacity planning is crucial to the following:

- Maintaining Network Performance and Dependability: Through the early detection and rectification of imminent congestion points, capacity planning plays a crucial role in upholding superior network efficiency and minimizing service interruptions. This preemptive approach contributes significantly to the continuity and reliability of network operations.
- Enhancing Resource Allocation Efficiency: Capacity planning empowers entities to execute strategic investments in network infrastructure based on a comprehensive understanding of current and projected resource demands. This facilitates the optimization of resource deployment, yielding cost savings and heightened operational efficiency.
- Projecting Future Network Requirements: Leveraging analysis of past network usage trends, organizations are equipped to foresee forthcoming demands on bandwidth. This foresight enables proactive adjustments to network capacity, ensuring readiness for evolving data transmission needs.
- Bolstering Network Security: A meticulously designed network framework allows for the seamless integration of security protocols, enhancing the ability to swiftly identify and neutralize potential cyber threats. This strategic alignment fortifies the network's defense mechanisms, safeguarding against breaches and vulnerabilities.
- Facilitating Organizational Expansion: By aligning network capacity with business growth trajectories, capacity planning aids organizations in scaling their network infrastructure. This alignment ensures that the network can support escalating demands, new technological deployments, and broader business objectives, thereby fostering expansion and innovation.

Efficient network capacity planning offers several key benefits to network operators, such as the following:

- Economic Efficiency: Through the strategic optimization of resource deployment and the exploration of potential for consolidation or shared resource utilization, organizations can significantly lower their expenditures related to network infrastructure.

- Enhancement of Network Performance: The anticipatory resolution of network congestion and capacity constraints is crucial for sustaining high network efficiency. Such proactive measures prevent network issues from adversely affecting user experience.
- Network Scalability: Capacity planning facilitates the systematic and effective growth of network infrastructure, ensuring that the network remains capable of accommodating surging demands without degradation in service quality.
- Informed Decision-Making: Capacity planning provides critical data and insights, enabling informed decisions regarding network investments and the allocation of resources. This strategic approach ensures that network planning is aligned with overarching business goals.
- Security Improvements: Strategic network planning underpins the implementation of strong security protocols, enhancing the network's ability to promptly identify and address potential security threats.

Key Metrics for Network Capacity Planning:

- Utilization Rate: This metric measures the ratio of current traffic volume to the total available bandwidth on a specific interface, offering insight into the degree of capacity utilization.
- Capacity Runout Prediction: By analyzing current utilization patterns, this metric forecasts the point at which traffic volume will surpass the available bandwidth of an interface. This projection aids in anticipating future capacity needs and preventing potential congestion scenarios.
- Latency: Measures the duration for a packet to travel from one point to another within the network, indicating network congestion or the need for additional capacity.
- Packet Loss: Occurs when data packets do not reach their intended destination, affecting network performance and suggesting a need for additional capacity or infrastructure enhancements.
- Error Rate: Quantifies the proportion of data packets that become corrupted or lost, indicating network infrastructure

problems or the need for additional capacity. Below are the best practices followed for network capacity planning:

1. Bandwidth Analysis and Metrics: Document the traffic generation from sources, destinations, devices, users, applications, protocols, and services. Utilize dashboard services that offer comprehensive visibility into bandwidth issues and provide metrics for both bandwidth utilization and device stress.
2. Reduce Expenses and Ensure Continuous Services: Utilize traffic metrics to assess performance and capacity benchmarks. By reviewing periodic reports, accurately projecting future bandwidth usage becomes achievable. Anticipating future bandwidth needs based on real data can prevent exceeding service provider limitations, particularly for growing or high-bandwidth–consuming sites.
3. Stay Mindful of Load Balancing Equipment: Another crucial aspect of network capacity planning involves managing CPU and memory resources. Excessive strain on a device's CPU can lead to performance throttling, potentially increasing latency or causing crashes. This could trigger a catastrophic chain reaction, burdening other devices further. Similarly, inadequate memory management might lead to failures in routing functions. Being vigilant about rising CPU and memory usage on devices can offer valuable insights into the network's health.
4. Guarantee Optimal Performance by Identifying Network Bottlenecks: Every link in a network may encounter congestion issues and sporadic spikes in traffic. Implementing network bottleneck policies is crucial to smoothing out traffic spikes and congestion peaks, while also allocating additional bandwidth to critical network traffic.

   Without appropriate policies in place, all traffic receives equal priority, potentially leading to insufficient bandwidth for essential business applications. For instance, without a comprehensive understanding of the traffic types traversing the network, it is challenging to determine if threshold parameters for services like VoIP are meeting target levels. Leveraging network analytics provides the insights necessary for effective network capacity planning and ensures optimal performance delivery.

5. Gain Insights Into Network Bandwidth Utilization: Monitoring network bandwidth is essential for understanding bandwidth requirements and network usage patterns. A bandwidth monitor tracks traffic, identifies trends, analyzes growth, and identifies bandwidth-consuming applications. Detailed reports provide real-time usage and historical trends. The bandwidth usage report summarizes utilization for specific devices/interfaces over defined periods. Data can be filtered by interfaces, hosts, traffic direction, and time frames. Additionally, features like top protocols and top applications display recorded and real-time usage. Classification-based reports monitor network bottleneck policies, comparing pre- and post-policy traffic to manage targets and identify critical issues like router saturation.
6. Acknowledge the Performance Capacity of Individual Components in Network Infrastructure: Bandwidth capacity planning involves proactive anticipation of future business needs and provisioning the necessary resources for the network to handle increased demand effectively. Additional strain on bandwidth can arise from advancements in technology usage (such as the adoption of a new VoIP communication system or media streaming service) and an increase in the number of end-users (such as expansion into new markets or mergers).
7. Managing Network Redundancy: Redundancy is a critical consideration, and when weighed against the cost of inevitable downtime, redundant connectivity proves its value multiple times over! When designing redundant connectivity, it is best practice to engage an alternate provider and utilize a link that is geographically separated from the primary connection. Verifying redundancy also entails auditing existing technology. Network flow monitoring tools can help identify patterns in traffic that necessitate redundancy checks.

Similar to how a design engineer employs computer-aided design to construct and evaluate the structural integrity of a tower, network engineers can utilize tools to strategize, design, and test an entire IT network even prior to its construction. Network capacity planning constitutes a vital component of robust network analytics. A resilient network possesses the scalability to accommodate future demands.

Network capacity planning offers resolutions to prospective "what if" scenarios, including alterations in bandwidth prompted by the implementation of new applications or technologies, shifts in traffic patterns, data center consolidation, and migrations within multi-vendor networks.

Network capacity planning encompasses numerous applications, tailored to the role within an organization and the unique requirements of the network. Several prevalent use cases comprise the following:

- Network Operations Expansion: With organizational growth comes the evolution of network requirements. Capacity planning is instrumental in determining the most opportune moments and locations for the integration of additional network devices, connections, or links to support this expansion effectively.
- Cost Optimization: By conducting ongoing assessments of network capacity and usage, entities can identify and strategically adjust or decommission underused resources. This process not only leads to financial savings but also ensures the efficient use of network resources.
- Performance Optimization: A key function of capacity planning is to maintain superior network performance, ensuring that the allocation of network resources is in alignment with both present and forecasted needs. This alignment is essential for delivering consistently high-quality user experiences.
- Enhancing Resilience for Disaster Recovery: Capacity planning is critical in the formulation and execution of disaster recovery and business continuity plans. An in-depth understanding of network capacity and its utilization patterns equips organizations to design more effective and resilient recovery strategies.
- Network Migration and Consolidation: As organizations evolve, there may arise a need to migrate or consolidate their networks. Capacity planning serves to assess the requirements of the new network, guaranteeing its ability to meet organizational needs while maintaining optimal performance.

12.4 Performance Optimization Strategies

A network resource is deemed congested when the influx of packets surpasses the resource's output capacity over a given timeframe. This congestion can lead to delays or even packet loss for arriving packets. Such congestion amplifies transit delays, variations in delay, packet loss, and undermines the predictability of network services. Clearly, congestion is an undesirable occurrence. Therefore, effectively mitigating congestion at a reasonable cost stands as a primary objective of Internet traffic engineering [17–20]. Efficient utilization of network resources by multiple traffic streams is a primary goal for packet-switched networks, particularly the Internet. A fundamental challenge in network operation is to enhance resource efficiency while minimizing the risk of congestion. Network resources such as link bandwidth, buffer space, and computational resources are essential targets for effective network resource management. Network survivability is another crucial aspect of network management, ensuring continuous service provision despite faults. While developing more reliable network elements enhances device-level survivability, it is imperative to implement failure and restoration capabilities across various network layers. Rerouting, traditionally employed at the IP layer, serves to restore service post-link and node outages. However, rerouting at the IP layer necessitates a period of routing convergence, which may range from seconds to minutes, potentially posing challenges in time-sensitive scenarios.

12.4.1 Resource Management in Physical Networks

Network resource optimization can be analogously understood through the concept of allocating dedicated pathways for distinct traffic types. This approach involves the strategic amalgamation of various network resources to create specialized pathways tailored for specific packet categories. Each pathway, or "network lane," can be provisioned with resources in a manner that reflects the unique demands of the traffic that it supports. For example, a lane handling higher volumes of traffic may be allocated additional resources to accommodate this demand. Through the intelligent configuration of these lanes, where resource distribution is meticulously aligned with the actual needs of the network traffic, the overall efficiency of packet processing within the system is significantly enhanced.

Key network resources instrumental in augmenting packet processing efficiency include:

- Bandwidth: This entails fine-tuning the data link's bandwidth to align precisely with the operational demands it is intended to support. Bandwidth represents the peak data transmission capacity of a network within a given timeframe. Networks characterized by higher bandwidth capacities are capable of handling larger data volumes in comparison to their lower-bandwidth counterparts. Nonetheless, the mere presence of high bandwidth does not inherently assure system performance optimization.

1. Gain insight into the current performance of your wired network: Prior to implementing optimization measures for wired performance, it is essential to comprehend the present state of both performance and bandwidth. The most effective approach to achieve this is by employing a network performance monitoring tool and bandwidth analyzer.
2. Enhance the efficiency of wire data flows: When aiming to enhance wire network performance, it is crucial to ensure that the movement of wire data between various points is optimized for streamlined operation. Implementing subnets for different segments of the wire network and adjusting topologies can facilitate the smooth flow of wire data and mitigate potential bottlenecks.
3. Enhance data efficiency: Enhancing bandwidth can be achieved effectively by optimizing wire data utilizing methods such as load balancing and traffic shaping. These optimization techniques aim to reduce overall bandwidth consumption or establish a prioritization system where critical wire data is given precedence, mimicking increased available bandwidth. Data optimization can be implemented at various points across the wire network.
4. Eliminate unnecessary data on the wire network: It is imperative to establish clear policies within the wire business, delineating which applications, websites, and services are permissible for access through the wire business network. Implementing blacklists and whitelists can assist in managing overly bandwidth-intensive services and websites effectively. Additionally, instituting an email attachment policy ensures wire employees understand how to transmit data more efficiently through the wire network.
5. Ensure optimal timing for backups and updates: While backups and updates are crucial for organizational operations, they can significantly impact bandwidth and may

even necessitate the shutdown of certain wire network functions. Failing to schedule these operations strategically can result in latency issues and compromise network performance. It is imperative to schedule all wire backups and updates outside of normal working hours to ensure that the network remains available for wire employees when needed.

6. Invest in a bandwidth-enhancing tool: To effectively boost wire bandwidth, investing in a network performance tool that provides comprehensive traffic and bandwidth monitoring and analysis is paramount. These tools equip you with the insights into your current wire network and bandwidth, enabling you to implement strategies to enhance performance. Additionally, they facilitate targeted actions to increase bandwidth without the need for investing in superfluous hardware.

- Latency: Latency, also known as delay, in a network refers to the total time taken for a complete message to travel from its source to its destination. It commences when the first bit of the message is sent from the source and concludes when the last bit arrives at the destination. Networks with minimal delays are termed "low-latency networks," whereas those with significant delays are categorized as "high-latency networks".

  High-latency presents challenges in network communication by creating bottlenecks, hindering data from fully utilizing the network capacity and consequently reducing the effective bandwidth. The impact of latency on bandwidth can vary depending on the root cause of the delays. Latency, typically measured in milliseconds (ms), is also commonly referred to as a ping rate.

  In simpler terms, latency can be understood as the time required for a packet to traverse a network. It can be measured in various ways, such as round trip or one-way latency. Latency can be influenced by any component involved in data transmission, including workstations, WAN links, routers, LAN, and servers. Moreover, for large networks, latency may be constrained by the speed of light.

$$Latency = PropagationTime + TransmissionTime + QueuingTime + ProcessingDelay \quad (12.1)$$

- Propagation Time: It refers to the duration necessary for a bit to journey from its point of origin to its destination. This timing can be computed by dividing the link length (distance) by the propagation speed across the communication medium. For instance, in the case of an electric signal, propagation time represents the duration required for the signal to traverse a wire.

$$Propagationtime = Distance/PropagationSpeed \quad (12.2)$$

Here are some alternative approaches to reduce latency and address various throughput concerns:

- Assess endpoint usage: Review the usage patterns of endpoints to identify and address potential latency caused by non-work–related applications.
- Opt for an Ethernet cable: Utilizing an Ethernet cable can mitigate latency and minimize packet loss, especially in comparison to wireless connections.
- Reboot the network: Restarting the network infrastructure can help eradicate software bugs and improve performance.
- Close unnecessary applications: Shutting down bandwidth-intensive programs can alleviate network congestion and reduce latency.
- Disable firewalls: In certain cases, firewalls may contribute to high traffic levels, disabling them temporarily can alleviate latency issues.
- Upgrade hardware: Consider upgrading routers and switches to newer models to enhance network performance and minimize latency.
- Consult your internet service provider: Collaborate with your internet service provider to identify and resolve potential issues affecting network performance.
- Measure network latency: Use latency measuring tools to assess the extent of latency issues. Typically, functional

network latency is less than 100 ms, with 20 ms to 40 ms being optimal for most applications.

- Opt for wired connections: If specific devices experience high latency, then consider using a wired connection to provide direct network access, which can help alleviate latency issues.
- Limit background operations: Reduce the number of simultaneous operations on your network-capable devices to prevent increased latency. Disconnecting unnecessary devices or background functions can help alleviate latency.
- Upgrade internet plan: If latency persists despite other attempts to resolve it, then consider discussing potential plan upgrades with your internet service provider to enhance network performance.
- Adjust device proximity to router: If using a wireless connection, then consider relocating closer to the router to strengthen the signal and reduce latency. Alternatively, invest in network boosting devices [21] to improve wireless connectivity over longer distances.

- Jitter: As illustrated in the referenced Figure 12.1, it is a crucial network performance metric that pertains to variations in packet delay, also known as "packet delay variance." This variability becomes particularly problematic in networks transmitting time-sensitive data, such as audio or video streams, where consistent timing is essential. Jitter is quantified in milliseconds (ms) and is a measure of the irregularities in the timing of data packet delivery.

  Fundamentally, jitter involves any fluctuation or displacement in the pulses of a high-frequency digital signal, which can affect aspects such as the amplitude, width, or phase timing of the signal. The primary sources of jitter include electromagnetic interference and signal crosstalk, both of which can significantly disrupt the integrity of signal transmission. The manifestations of jitter can range from flickering screens, degradation in processor performance on desktops or servers, introduction of unwanted artifacts in audio outputs, to loss of data across network devices.

  The impact of jitter on network performance is profound, as it can lead to congestion and packet loss, much like a traffic bottleneck where packets accumulate and slow down data

Figure 12.1 Jitter.

flow. Packet loss, a direct consequence of jitter, occurs when packets are delivered at inconsistent intervals, complicating the receiving system's ability to compile information accurately and resulting in gaps in data.

This irregularity can severely affect video streaming quality, leading to pixelation and frame skipping, which are indicative of jitter-induced losses. In the context of online gaming, such losses can disrupt the gameplay experience with sudden changes in player positions or interrupted scene transitions, thereby affecting the overall game fluidity.

In the depicted scenario, it is evident that the transmission time of packets does not align with their arrival time at the receiver's end. One packet experiences an unforeseen delay during transit and arrives later than anticipated, demonstrating jitter.

To alleviate the impact of jitter, the implementation of a jitter buffer is a common practice, applicable within networks, on routers or switches, or directly on endpoint devices. This approach involves the receiving system extracting network packets from the buffer rather than directly from the transmitting system. Packets are subsequently withdrawn from the buffer at a uniform pace. Additionally, in environments where traffic traverses multiple paths, a strategy to diminish jitter includes routing traffic via the most stable routes or consistently selecting routes that best match the intended packet delivery tempo.

- Priority plays a pivotal role in the processing of packets, facilitating the organization of packets based on their level of urgency. This prioritization mechanism significantly diminishes latency for high-priority packets by ensuring that they are processed prior to others. This concept is visualized through the implementation of a priority queue mechanism for managing both inbound and outbound traffic, as depicted in the referenced

Figure 12.2. Routers, critical to the network's operation, manage the flow of data by receiving packets on their input interfaces and forwarding them via their output interfaces. Nonetheless, routers are constrained by their finite memory capacity, potentially leading to situations where incoming packets exceed the router's ability to store them. This imbalance between packet arrival and departure rates may necessitate the discarding of new or existing packets to manage memory overload. To address these limitations, routers incorporate queuing strategies within their resource management protocols, determining the prioritization, buffering, or discarding of packets as required.

- Router queues frequently face congestion issues due to their limited buffer memory capacities. Congestion arises when incoming traffic volume exceeds the router's output interface's ability to efficiently forward it. Several factors can precipitate this condition, notably:
  1. Incoming traffic velocity outpacing the outgoing traffic rate.
  2. The cumulative traffic across all input interfaces exceeding the router's total output throughput.
  3. Challenges faced by the router's processor in managing the expansive forwarding table needed for routing path determination.
  4. Routers implement a variety of queuing disciplines [22–26] to manage packet allocation within their memory under congested conditions. The ensuing are prominent queuing disciplines adopted in router operations:
     (a) First-In, First-Out (FIFO) Queuing: This is the baseline queuing model for most routers, where packets are processed in the sequence they arrive. This approach requires minimal configuration on the

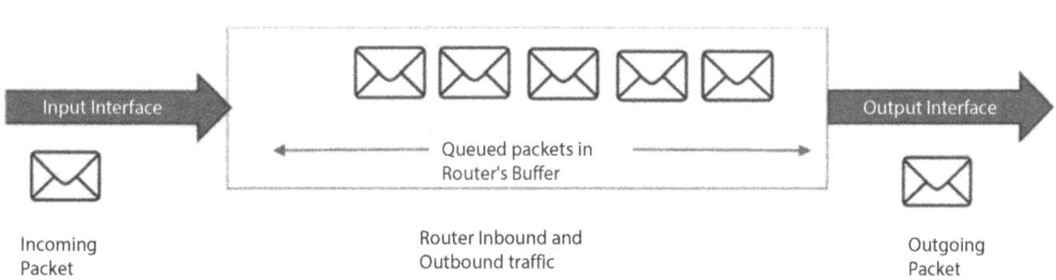

Figure 12.2 Router inbound and outbound traffic.

server side. Nevertheless, FIFO can lead to memory overflow scenarios.

(b) Priority Queuing (PQ): PQ involves dividing the router's memory into several queues, each classified by priority levels. Packets within each queue are processed in a FIFO manner, with the system cycling through the queues to process packets from each class. The queues are typically labeled as high, medium, or low priority, with processing precedence given to packets in the high-priority queue, followed by medium, and so on. This ensures that high-priority traffic is processed ahead of lower-priority traffic, which may only be addressed once higher-priority queues have been cleared. PQ is particularly beneficial for managing traffic with varying importance levels, as depicted in the associated figure illustrating the subdivision of queues within the PQ framework. One notable advantage of PQ is the prioritization of higher-priority traffic, ensuring it is always processed first. However, a significant drawback of the PQ scheme is the potential for low-priority queues to receive no service at all due to starvation. Continuous high-priority traffic can starve out the low-priority queues.

(c) Weighted Fair Queuing (WFQ) offers a solution to this issue. WFQ dynamically creates queues based on traffic flows and allocates bandwidth to these flows based on priority. The allocation of dynamically assigned bandwidths for sub-queues in WFQ is illustrated in

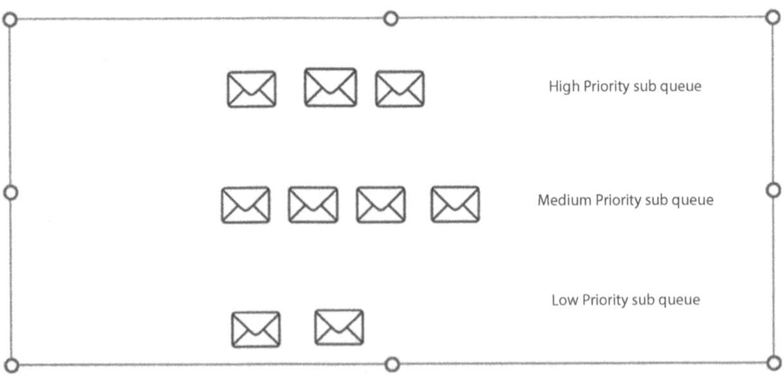

Figure 12.3 Multiple sub-queues used in priority queuing scheme.

> Figure 12.3. Each sub-queue is assigned bandwidth dynamically, ensuring fair distribution among active queues as illustrated in Figure 12.4. For instance, if three queues exist with bandwidth percentages of 20%, 30%, and 50% when all are active, and the 20% queue becomes idle, the freed-up bandwidth is redistributed among the remaining queues while maintaining the original bandwidth ratios. Consequently, the 30% queue is allocated (75/2)% bandwidth, and the 50% queue is allocated (125/2)% bandwidth.

Traffic flows are differentiated and categorized based on various header fields in the packets such as source and destination IP address, source and destination TCP (or UDP) port, IP protocol number, and type of service value (IP precedence or DSCP).

Packets are categorized and allocated to distinct queues based on their specific traffic characteristics, where packets belonging to the same traffic flow are grouped into a unique queue tailored for that flow. By default, routers are configured to support up to 256 distinct queues, with the potential to expand this capacity to 4,096 queues to accommodate diverse traffic needs.

Unlike PQ systems, WFQ mechanisms assign variable bandwidths to queues, reflecting their respective priorities. This ensures that higher-priority packets are processed before those of lower priority that arrive concurrently.

The influence of queuing disciplines on network performance is demonstrated through comprehensive analysis, as depicted in Figure 12.5. The choice of queuing discipline plays a pivotal role in shaping key performance indicators within the network, such as packet loss and latency. Through the utilization of simulation tools like Riverbed Modeler, the examination

Figure 12.4 Dynamically allocated bandwidths for sub-queues in WFQ.

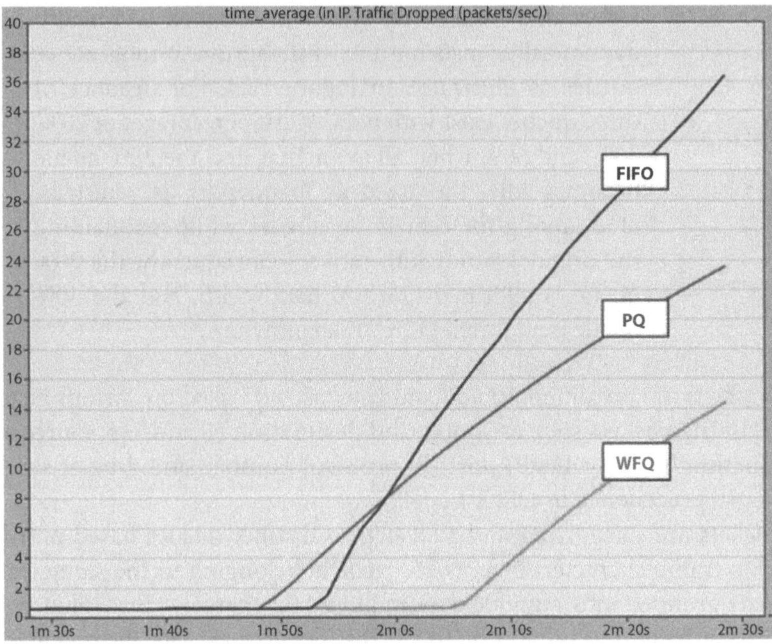

Figure 12.5 Effect of queuing disciplines on network.

of packet drop rates over time under various queuing schemes provides insightful observations into the differential impacts these methodologies have on network performance metrics.

Analysis of packet drop rates over time across different queuing disciplines, as simulated using Riverbed Modeler, reveals the following findings:

- Initially, no packet drops occur across all schemes. This initial period is due to the finite time required for router buffer memory to reach its capacity. Packet drops only occur once the buffer is full, leading to an absence of drops during this early phase.
- In the FIFO scheme, packet drops commence after PQ but before WFQ. Notably, FIFO experiences the highest number of dropped packets. This is because congested traffic from all applications is indiscriminately dropped once congestion occurs, without any discrimination.
- In the PQ scheme, packet drops begin earliest. PQ divides the queue based on priority levels, resulting in smaller individual queue sizes. Assuming a straightforward division

of memory into "important" and "less important" queues, the smaller queue size causes earlier filling and subsequent packet drops. These observations highlight the impact of queuing disciplines on packet drop rates and underscore the importance of selecting an appropriate scheme based on network requirements.

NIC rings refer to the transmit (Tx) and receive (Rx) rings, which are hardware resources utilized by network interface controllers (NICs) to send and receive network packets. Effectively managing and allocating these rings according to network traffic can enhance the efficiency of packet processing within the system.

Receive ring buffers are shared between the device driver and the NIC, serving as circular buffers where incoming packets are stored until they can be processed. These buffers are assigned by the NIC and are crucial for temporarily holding packets before they are passed to the kernel for further processing.

Upon receiving packets, the device driver drains the Rx ring using software interrupts, known as SoftIRQs. This process involves transferring incoming packets from the Rx ring buffer to a kernel data structure called an sk buffer or skb, from where they begin their journey through the kernel to the relevant application.

Similarly, the Tx ring buffer is utilized to hold outgoing packets destined for transmission over the network. These buffers play a critical role in the packet transmission process and are located at the bottom of the network stack. However, it is essential to note that packet drops can occur at the Tx ring buffer, potentially leading to adverse effects on network performance.

Configuring NICs, especially adjusting the size of Rx and Tx ring buffers, is a crucial aspect of network performance tuning, particularly when dealing with large data volumes. The ring buffers contain descriptors or pointers to kernel buffers holding packet data.

To determine the current configuration of NICs and adjust settings accordingly, the ethtool command can be utilized. For instance, running the command "ethtool -g" allows users to view the current configuration and adjust parameters such as the Rx and Tx ring buffer size to optimize network performance.

ethtool -g eth0: The following sections show a sample output:

Ring parameters for eth0: Pre-set maximums: RX: 2,040; RX Mini: 0; RX Jumbo: 8160; TX: 255.
Current hardware settings: RX: 255; RX Mini: 0; RX Jumbo: 0; TX: 255.

The section labeled "pre-set maximums" displays the highest allowable values that can be configured for each parameter, providing users with an understanding of the upper limits for adjustment. Conversely, the "current hardware settings" section presents the current configuration details, offering insight into the existing setup.

Opting for a smaller buffer size results in reduced latency, which is advantageous in scenarios where minimizing delay is crucial. However, this reduction in latency may come at the expense of throughput, as smaller buffers may not be able to handle large volumes of data efficiently. To achieve higher throughputs, it is recommended to configure larger buffer ring sizes for both RX and TX.

Informatica advises utilizing the ethtool command to assess the current hardware settings and determine the maximum supported values for each parameter. Subsequently, users can adjust the settings based on these maximum values, taking into account compatibility with the operating system in use. For instance, if the maximum supported value for RX is 2,040, the ethtool command can be employed to set the RX value to this maximum, ensuring optimal configuration.

ethtool -G eth0: RX 2040. Setting a low ring buffer size for data transfer can increase the likelihood of packet drops. To ascertain whether packets are being dropped, you can utilize commands such as netstat and ifconfig.

Figure 12.6 shows a sample output of the netstat command.

The RX-DRP column displays the count of packets that were dropped. Adjust the RX value to ensure that no packets are dropped, resulting in the RX-DRP column showing 0. You may need to experiment with different values to achieve optimal performance. Figure 12.7 illustrates a sample output of the ifconfig command.

The status messages provide information about the number of packets that were dropped.

Figure 12.6 Out of netstat command.

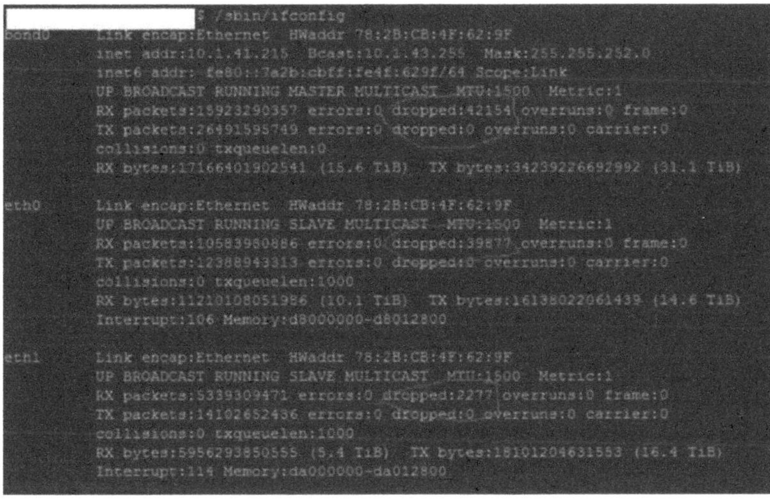

Figure 12.7 Output of ifconfig command.

- CPU pool: It allows for the creation of CPU pools that are associated with specific zones. These pools can then be allocated to datalinks to manage the network processes within their respective zones.

In systems with multiple CPUs, it is possible to designate a certain number of CPUs for specific network processing tasks. By utilizing the pool link property, network resource management can be more closely integrated with CPU allocation and administration within zones. This property enables the assignment of a CPU pool to networking processes associated with a particular zone. When a link is designated as the network interface for a zone and the pool property is set for that link, it becomes bound to the CPU pool of the zone. If the zone is configured to be exclusive, the CPU resources allocated to its pool are restricted for use by other links not assigned to the zone.

Figure 12.8 shows how pools work when the pool property is assigned to a datalink. In the illustration, the system comprises eight CPUs. By default, when no pools are configured, all CPUs are part of the default pool and serve the global zone. However, in this scenario, a custom pool named pool99 has been established, encompassing CPU 3 and CPU 4.

This pool is linked to zone1, an exclusive zone. If pool99 is attributed as a property of vnic1, then it becomes dedicated to managing vnic1's networking operations. Upon assigning vnic1 as the network interface for zone1, the CPUs within pool99 are earmarked for managing both networking and non-networking tasks within zone1.

The pool property exhibits dynamic characteristics. Zone pools can be configured with a specified range of CPUs, and the kernel autonomously determines which CPUs are included in the pool's CPU set. Any alterations to the pool are automatically applied to the associated datalink, streamlining pool management for that link. In contrast, utilizing the cpu property to assign specific CPUs to the link necessitates explicit specification of the CPUs to be assigned. This property must be set each time changes to the CPU components of the pool are desired.

For instance, if CPU 4 is taken offline as depicted in Figure 12.8, the dynamic nature of the pool property ensures seamless adjustment. The software automatically incorporates an additional CPU into the pool, thereby maintaining the pool's original configuration of two CPUs.

From the perspective of vnic1, this change is transparent. The adjusted configuration is shown in Figure 12.9.

• Managing Network Resources With Datalink Properties: Utilizing datalink properties enhances the system's capacity to process packets efficiently. These properties can be configured during the creation of the link, allowing for precise control over the allocation of network resources. Whether dealing with virtual or physical networks, the procedures for resource allocation remain consistent. Network resources can be allocated to datalinks to

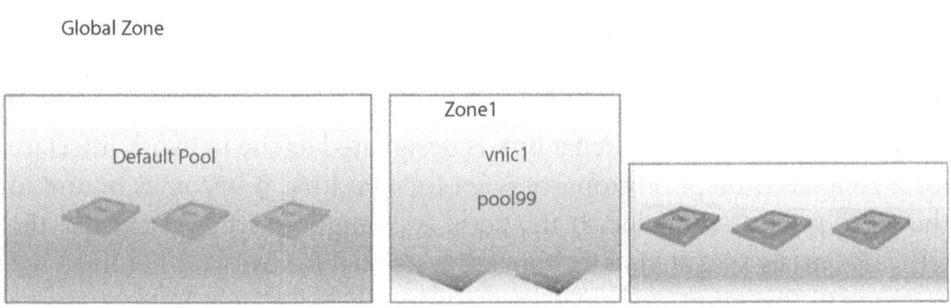

Figure 12.8 Pools work when the pool property is assigned to a datalink.

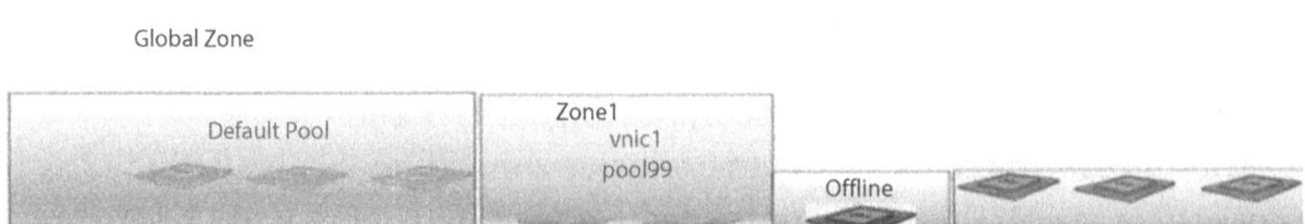

Figure 12.9 Automatic addition of CPU to maintain two CPU configuration.

optimize packet processing efficiency, either during the creation of a new datalink or by applying properties to an existing one. The following datalink properties can be configured to allocate network resources: maxbw specifies the maximum bandwidth allocation for a datalink. rxrings and txrings determine the number of receive and transmit rings of a NIC assigned to a specific datalink. Pool identifies the CPU pool containing sets of CPUs allocated to manage network processes efficiently. cpus specifies the CPUs assigned to a datalink. The following use case exemplifies the enhancement of system efficiency through the configuration of both datalink and flow properties, as depicted in the following configuration scenario shown in Figure 12.10.

The illustration portrays two physical hosts interconnected, with Host1 configured as follows:
One non-global zone serving as a server and router, with two interfaces assigned: net0 connects to the Internet, and net1 connects to the internal network, including Host2. Flows configured over net1 for traffic isolation and resource control over the respective packets.

• Managing Network Resources Using Flows: A flow categorizes network packets based on attributes derived from packet headers. After setting datalink properties for network resource management, flows further regulate resource utilization for processing network packets. Flows can be created based on single or combined attributes, such as:

Local or Remote IP address Transport protocol name (UDP, TCP, and SCTP) Differentiated Services Field (DS Field) attribute (for IPv6 packets) Combination of transport protocol name with local or remote application port number. Customizing flow resource usage involves setting properties such as bandwidth and priority.

Host2's Configuration:

Three non-global zones with respective VNICs configured over net0, supporting ring allocation.

1. Optimization of NIC Ring Utilization: The NIC (Network Interface Card) utilizes hardware-based receive (Rx) and transmit (Tx) rings for the efficient handling of incoming and outgoing packets, respectively. The strategic allocation of these rings based on the volume and nature of network traffic significantly boosts packet processing capabilities. For example, enhancing the allocation of Rx rings for a link with a high influx of packets

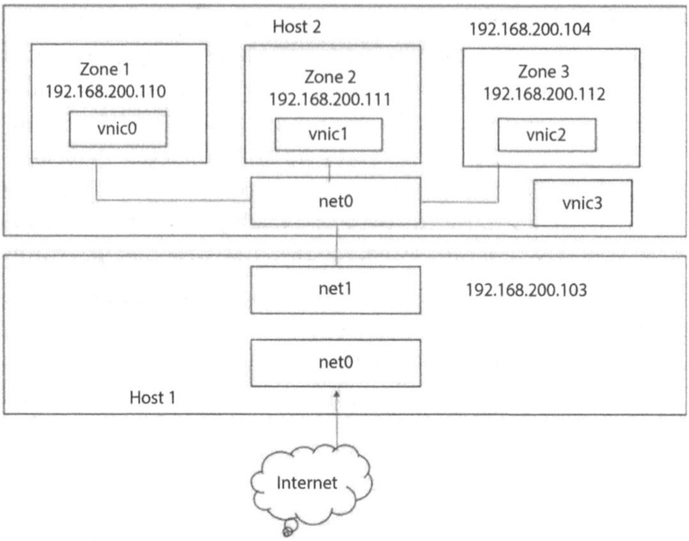

Figure 12.10 Network resource management by using datalink properties.

markedly improves throughput. The workload on network resources varies across different zones. Consider a setup where zone1 operates as an HTTP client, and zones 2 and 3 serve as SSH clients connecting to Host1. Zone1 experiences voluminous, albeit less time-critical, traffic, whereas zones 2 and 3 encounter lower volumes of time-sensitive traffic. Prioritizing the network traffic for zones 2 and 3 by capping the bandwidth for zone1 ensures timely processing, preventing bandwidth monopolization by zone1 to the detriment of zones 2 and 3. In this context, each zone is equipped with a Virtual Network Interface Controller (VNIC), functioning as a software-driven client, tailored to its specific traffic handling requirements.

2. Distribution of Rings to MAC Clients: MAC (Media Access Control) clients, encompassing both physical datalinks and Virtual Network Interfaces (VNICs), are pivotal in facilitating network interactions. These clients are categorized based on their operational basis:
   - Hardware-Based Clients: These entities exclusively control one or more NIC rings, with ring assignments

contingent upon the NIC's support for specific ring allocations.

- Software-Based Clients: Unlike their hardware counterparts, these clients share NIC rings with other software-based clients or default to the primary client, dependent on the prioritization of hardware-based clients in ring allocation.

Key tasks include the following:

- Creating and configuring flow control: Flows are established over net1 to exert separate resource control over packets received by net1 on Host1.
- Configuring network resource properties for VNICs on Host2: Each zone's VNIC is configured with a dedicated set of rings based on processing load. Additionally, a separate VNIC is configured without dedicated rings as an example of a software-based client.

3. rxrings and txrings: These parameters specify the number of receive rings and transmit rings of a NIC assignable to a specific datalink.

12.4.2 Resource Management in Virtual Networks

This is crucial for optimizing performance, scalability, and efficiency in modern computing environments. Virtualization technology [27–31] allows for running multiple workloads on the same physical server, thereby reducing costs and improving resource utilization. However, it also introduces new challenges such as increased traffic, congestion, latency, and security risks. To ensure optimal performance, network configuration and bandwidth need to be optimized according to specific needs and goals.

Optimizing Virtual Network Performance: Virtual networks play a vital role in enabling cloud computing, remote access, and scalability. However, they pose challenges in terms of latency, bandwidth, security, and configuration. To enhance virtual network performance, several best practices can be followed. These include the following:

- Configuring Virtual Network Adapters (VNAs): VNAs connect virtual machines (VMs) to the physical network and emulate the functionality of physical network cards. Optimizing VNA settings to match the characteristics of the physical network and VMs is essential. This involves enabling features like jumbo frames, link aggregation, port mirroring, VLAN tagging, TCP segmentation offload, and VM queues to reduce overhead and enhance throughput.

- Monitoring Virtual Network Traffic: Monitoring virtual network traffic helps identify bottlenecks, errors, and anomalies. Tools that capture and decode virtual network packets can provide valuable insights into traffic patterns, protocols, and performance metrics. Additionally, tools for generating and simulating virtual network traffic aid in testing capacity, latency, and resilience.
- Updating and Optimizing Virtual Network Components: Regular updates and optimization of virtual network components such as the virtualization platform, VNAs, virtual switches, VMs, and applications are essential. This involves keeping components up-to-date with patches, drivers, and firmware, as well as tuning parameters and removing unused features to enhance efficiency and resource utilization.
- Evaluating and Improving Virtual Network Performance: Benchmarking and comparing virtual network performance with industry standards and physical network performance helps assess optimization efforts. Tools that provide feedback and suggestions for further improvement aid in identifying gaps, inefficiencies, and conflicts. Regular review and adaptation of optimization strategies ensure alignment with changing needs and goals.
- Assessing Network Requirements: Before optimizing the network, understanding current and future network requirements is essential. Factors such as the number and type of VMs, supported applications and services, expected traffic volume and patterns, QoS requirements, and security and compliance standards should be considered. Network analyzers, performance monitors, and capacity planners assist in collecting and analyzing relevant data for identifying gaps and prioritizing areas for improvement.

- Choosing the Right Network Architecture: The network architecture chosen for the virtualization environment significantly impacts performance and scalability. Different architectures such as traditional, converged, or hyperconverged networks offer varying levels of flexibility, management complexity, and scalability. Selecting the architecture that best aligns with budget, resources, and goals is crucial for optimizing virtualization performance.
- Optimizing Network Devices and Protocols: Optimizing network devices such as routers, switches, firewalls, and load balancers, along with network protocols like TCP/IP, UDP, HTTP, and HTTPS, improves overall network performance. Enabling features such as jumbo frames, link aggregation, port mirroring, VLAN tagging, TCP offloading, and SSL acceleration enhances bandwidth, reduces overhead, and improves security and efficiency.
- Implementing Network Virtualization: Network virtualization abstracts the physical network infrastructure, creating logical network entities such as virtual switches, routers, firewalls, and networks. This enhances flexibility, scalability, efficiency, and security by allowing dynamic creation and modification of virtual network entities without changes to the physical network. Granular security policies and controls improve compliance and visibility while segmenting and isolating network traffic prevents unauthorized access and interference.
- Monitoring and Troubleshooting Network Performance: Regular monitoring and troubleshooting of network performance are essential for maintaining optimal virtualization performance. Tools for capturing metrics and logs, visualizing network performance, and diagnosing network problems help identify issues and anomalies. Techniques such as ping, traceroute, iperf, and Wireshark aid in diagnosing and resolving network problems or bottlenecks, ensuring optimal virtualization performance and scalability.
- Virtual Network Functions (VNFs) Enhance Performance: VNFs are software implementations of network functions deployed on virtual resources such as VMs. They enable agile, secure, and cost-effective service

architectures while supporting modern business models. VNFs provide flexibility, scalability, and agility by virtualizing network services, separating each function from underlying hardware, and enabling on-demand deployment and scaling. VNFs improve service lifecycle management, resource utilization, high availability, and scalability while reducing hardware costs and resource usage.

12.4.3 Resource Management in Software-Defined Networking (SDN)

SDN decouples control and data planes using a centralized controller component, simplifying network administration and management. SDN controllers create and manage a unified view of the network and abstract network resources for SDN applications. Centralized and distributed SDN controller architectures offer different advantages and challenges in terms of scalability, reliability, and performance. Dynamic resource allocation based on traffic load improves SDN controller performance and prevents bottlenecks. VM migration in SDN environments requires reimplementation of network policies and routing configurations, presenting challenges in ensuring seamless migration and performance optimization. Optimizing network resources in virtual networks is essential for achieving optimal performance, scalability, and efficiency. By following best practices, assessing network requirements, choosing appropriate architectures, and leveraging technologies like VNFs and SDN, organizations can enhance virtualization performance, improve resource utilization, and adapt to changing business needs and goals. Regular monitoring, troubleshooting, and optimization ensure continuous improvement and alignment with evolving requirements and industry standards as shown in Figure 12.11.

It should be noted that, in this scenario, a minimum memory of 512 MB must be reserved for the DOM0. This is crucial because if DOM0 crashes or fails to execute, the hypervisor would be unable to operate and allocate memory. Dynamic memory management in the XenServer hypervisor is facilitated by a specialized memory management unit known as DMC.

It is worth mentioning that this feature is available in the XenServer hypervisor version 5.6 and later. Similarly, the allocation of CPUs to a VM can be dynamically managed. Upon installation of the XenServer

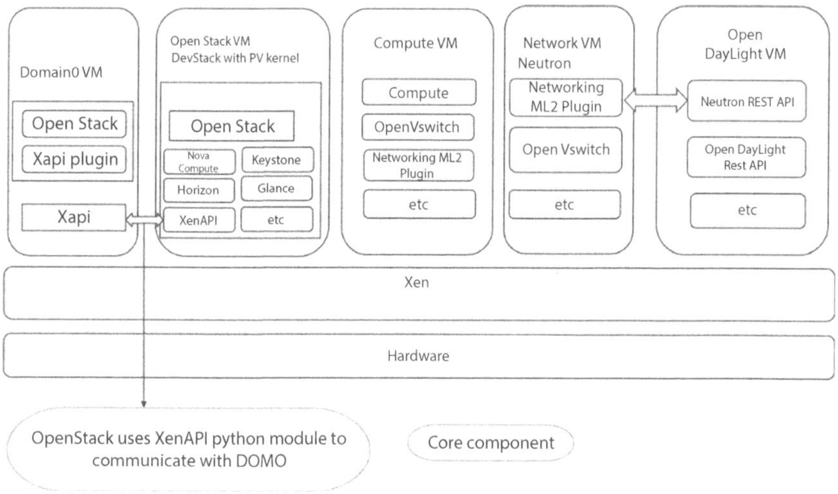

Figure 12.11 XenServer hypervisor.

hypervisor, each physical CPU (CPU core) is abstracted as a virtual CPU (VCPU), dividing CPU cycles for each core, allowing multiple VMs to access a physical core through time sharing. Consequently, an increase in the number of VMs utilizing a single shared VCPU results in fewer CPU cycles available to each virtual machine. All VCPUs are managed by a local queue on a physical CPU, which prioritizes VCPUs based on their assigned priority values. Each VCPU receives a fair share of CPU resources, with the manager administrating priorities by adjusting the values of CAP and Weight parameters. The weight parameter determines the number of cycles a domain or VM can receive relative to others, where a higher weight value grants more cycles. For instance, a VCPU with a weight of 128 can receive twice as many cycles as one with a weight of 64. On the other hand, the CAP parameter dictates the maximum usage rate of CPU cycles by a domain and is expressed as an absolute value. For example, a CAP value of 100 for a VCPU implies that it can utilize 100% of the CPU cycles of a physical host. Leveraging these concepts, XenServer implements adaptive resource allocation.

Network resource management enables the isolation, prioritization, tracking, and control of data traffic on an individual system without the need for complex QoS rule definitions. It proves useful for various tasks including provisioning the network, establishing service-level agreements, billing clients, and diagnosing security problems.

12.5 Real-World Applications

In real-world scenarios, resource optimization and performance improvement in physical IP networking can be achieved through various technologies. Among the most common are fast path processing and the Data Plane Development Kit (DPDK) library. Virtual Machine Device Queues (VMDQ) also stands out as a technology in virtual networking. Fast path processing in IP networking refers to the rapid handling of network packets through a streamlined and optimized path within networking equipment like routers or switches. Key aspects of fast path processing include:

- Packet Forwarding: Fast path processing primarily focuses on promptly forwarding incoming packets by leveraging destination addresses and routing information. This entails making swift and straightforward decisions regarding the routing of packets to their subsequent destination.
- Routing Lookups: Efficient methods for conducting routing table lookups are crucial. This frequently entails employing specialized data structures such as tries or hash tables to rapidly identify the next hop for a provided destination IP address.
- Caching and Acceleration: Fast path processing might include caching commonly accessed data, like route entries, to hasten subsequent lookups. Additionally, hardware acceleration, including the utilization of specialized ASICs (application-specific integrated circuits), can be leveraged to offload and expedite specific processing tasks.
- Access Control Lists (ACLs) and Firewall Rules: Fast path processing involves swiftly assessing ACLs and firewall rules to ascertain whether a packet adheres to specified security policies, thereby determining whether it should be permitted or denied.
- Quality of Service (QoS): Fast path processing may entail rapid packet classification based on QoS markings, enabling the prioritization or differentiation of traffic flows in accordance with service-level agreements.

- Packet Header Manipulation: Removing redundant headers and altering packet headers, such as decrementing the Time-to-Live field, are typical functions executed in the fast path to enhance packet processing efficiency.
- Checksum Verification and Correction: Swiftly verifying and rectifying checksums, when needed, constitutes a component of fast path processing aimed at preserving the integrity of incoming packets.
- Handling Common Protocols: Fast path processing frequently encompasses specialized treatment of prevalent protocols like TCP and UDP, enabling expedited decision-making based on the unique attributes of these protocols.
- Multicast and Broadcast Handling: The fast path incorporates efficient mechanisms for managing multicast and broadcast traffic, ensuring their appropriate distribution across the network.
- Error Handling and Logging: Although the primary goal of fast path processing is to minimize overhead, certain error handling and logging mechanisms might still be integrated to capture critical issues.

Optimizing these facets of fast path processing enables networking devices to achieve high-performance packet forwarding, a critical requirement for delivering low-latency and high-throughput networking services. This optimization is particularly vital in environments with stringent networking demands, including data centers, telecommunications networks, and service provider networks.

Efficient resource utilization in fast path processing is pivotal for enhancing system efficiency and performance, especially in contexts where low latency and high throughput are imperative. Fast path processing typically pertains to the primary execution path or the critical path of a system responsible for handling time-sensitive tasks. Here are several strategies for optimizing resources in fast path processing:

1. Parallelization: Leverage parallel processing techniques to execute multiple tasks concurrently. This can be accomplished through methods such as multi-threading or parallel programming, enabling the system to handle various aspects of the fast path simultaneously. Nonetheless,

it is crucial to effectively manage synchronization and prevent conflicts over shared resources.

2. Batch Processing: Grouping similar tasks together and processing them in batches reduces the overhead of task switching and resource allocation, thereby improving overall efficiency.
3. Data Locality: Enhance cache locality by optimizing data access patterns. This entails organizing data structures and algorithms to minimize cache misses, thereby significantly improving processing speed.
4. Memory Management: Efficient memory management is vital for fast path processing. Reduce unnecessary memory operations and overhead by minimizing memory allocations and deallocations. Consider using memory pools or object reuse to optimize memory usage.
5. Optimized Algorithms: Select algorithms tailored for fast path processing, prioritizing efficiency over complexity. Evaluate trade-offs between algorithmic intricacy and resource utilization to identify the most optimal solution for the given scenario.
6. Hardware Acceleration: Utilize hardware accelerators such as graphics processing units (GPUs) and field programmable gate arrays (FPGAs) for tasks requiring intensive computation. These dedicated processors can notably enhance the speed of specific computations, thereby offloading the CPU and enabling it to handle other tasks efficiently.
7. Asynchronous Processing: Implement asynchronous programming models to overlap computation with I/O operations, effectively reducing idle time and ensuring continuous system activity, thereby enhancing overall throughput.

In a production environment, it is crucial to minimize logging and debugging activities to avoid unnecessary overhead. Selective use of logging and debugging is recommended, with consideration given to conditional logging based on the severity of issues.

- Resource Reservation: Allocate resources specifically required for fast path processing, guaranteeing that essential tasks receive priority access to the necessary resources. This might entail establishing processor affinity, memory reservations, or employing other resource allocation techniques.

- Dynamic Resource Scaling: Develop a system that dynamically adjusts its resource allocation in response to fluctuations in workload. This may include modifying thread counts, reallocating memory, or scaling resources in real-time to effectively manage system load.
- Profile and Monitor: Consistently conduct system profiling and monitoring to pinpoint bottlenecks and areas ripe for enhancement. Employ performance analysis tools to identify resource-heavy tasks and optimize them for improved efficiency.
- Energy Efficiency: Factor in energy efficiency when optimizing resources, particularly in situations where power usage is crucial. Employ low-power modes when applicable and tailor algorithms to minimize energy consumption.

By integrating a blend of these tactics, the resource optimization for fast path processing within a system can experience notable enhancement, resulting in heightened performance and responsiveness.

Fast path processing is instrumental across diverse real-world contexts where rapid and effective data or task management is imperative. Here are several concrete instances spanning various domains:

- Routing and Forwarding: In networking equipment, fastpath processing is crucial for quickly determining the next hop and forwarding network packets based on routing information.
- This is essential for achieving low-latency and high-throughput communication [32] in IP networks.

Firewalls and Security Appliances:

- Access Control Lists (ACLs): Fastpath processing is used to rapidly evaluate access control lists and make decisions on whether to allow or deny packets based on specified security policies. This helps maintain network security without introducing unnecessary delays.

- Load Balancers: Load balancers use fastpath processing to quickly distribute incoming traffic across multiple servers or resources based on predefined algorithms. This ensures efficient resource utilization and high availability.

Wireless Access Points:

- Packet Forwarding and QoS: In wireless networks, fastpath processing is employed to quickly forward packets, implement QoS policies, and manage traffic efficiently to provide a seamless and responsive user experience.
- Flow Control: SDN controllers use fastpath processing to manage and control the flow of network traffic dynamically. This allows for real-time adjustments to network conditions, optimizing performance and resource utilization.

High-Frequency Trading (HFT) Systems:

- Algorithmic Trading: In financial systems, especially in HFT, fastpath processing is critical for executing trading algorithms with minimal latency. Quick decision-making and order execution are essential for capitalizing on market opportunities.
- Call Routing: Telecommunications switches utilize fastpath processing to quickly route voice and data calls, ensuring efficient call setup and connection establishment.
- Content Delivery Networks (CDNs): CDNs leverage fastpath processing to quickly cache and deliver content to end-users, reducing latency and improving the overall performance of web applications.
- Edge Computing: In edge computing environments, fastpath processing is used to quickly analyze and respond to data at the edge of the network. This is particularly important for applications that require real-time or low-latency processing, such as IoT devices.

12.5.1 Data Plane Development Kit Libraries

The DPDK [33] is a set of libraries and drivers designed to accelerate packet processing workloads in user space. DPDK can significantly enhance resource management and performance optimization in networking applications. Here are ways in which DPDK achieves these goals:

- User Space Packet Processing: DPDK operates in user space rather than the traditional kernel space, allowing applications to have direct control over packet processing without the overhead of kernel context switching. This reduces latency and improves performance.
- High-Speed Packet I/O: DPDK provides high-performance packet I/O mechanisms that enable applications to efficiently handle network packets at line-rate speeds, contributing to low-latency communication and increased throughput.
- Poll-Mode Drivers (PMDs): DPDK includes poll-mode drivers that enable applications to directly poll and handle incoming packets. This eliminates the need for interrupts, reducing overhead and improving the efficiency of packet reception.
- Batch Processing: DPDK supports batch processing, allowing applications to process multiple packets in a single operation. This reduces the overhead associated with processing individual packets and improves overall throughput.
- Optimized Memory Management: DPDK provides a memory management system that allows applications to allocate and manage memory in a way that minimizes fragmentation and improves memory access patterns. This is particularly beneficial for packet buffers and descriptors.
- Lockless Data Structures: DPDK includes lockless data structures, such as ring buffers, which enable multiple threads to efficiently exchange data without the need for locks. This helps in achieving better parallelism and scalability.
- Hardware Offload: DPDK leverages hardware offload capabilities, such as checksum offload and large receive offload (LRO), to offload certain packet processing tasks to NICs. This reduces the workload on the CPU and improves overall system performance.
- Multi-Queue Support: DPDK supports multiple queues for packet processing, allowing applications to scale across multiple CPU cores. This enables better parallelism and utilization of available processing resources.

- Optimized Polling Mechanisms: DPDK provides efficient polling mechanisms, such as busy-wait loops, that enable applications to continuously poll for incoming packets without the overhead of traditional interrupt-based packet handling.
- Unified API: DPDK provides a unified and consistent API for various networking functionalities. This abstraction simplifies the development of high-performance networking applications and makes it easier to achieve optimization goals.
- Fastpath Processing: DPDK is commonly used in fast-path processing scenarios, such as in network function virtualization (NFV) and software-defined networking (SDN), where low-latency and high-throughput packet processing is crucial.

By incorporating these features and optimizations, DPDK empowers developers to build high-performance networking applications that can efficiently manage resources and achieve optimal performance in a variety of scenarios, including data centers, telecommunications networks, and network appliances. The DPDK is widely used in various real-world applications where high-performance packet processing is crucial. Here are some examples of how DPDK is employed in different domains:

- Network Function Virtualization (NFV): DPDK is extensively used in NFV deployments to accelerate the packet processing performance of virtualized network functions (VNFs), such as firewalls, load balancers, and virtual routers.
- Software-Defined Networking (SDN): DPDK can be integrated into SDN controllers to achieve high-speed packet processing in SDN environments. This enables efficient handling of control plane and data plane separation.
- Network Security: DPDK is employed in Intrusion Detection and Prevention Systems (IDPS) applications to enhance the performance of deep packet inspection and threat detection, allowing for rapid analysis and response to security events.
- Cloud Computing: DPDK is used in virtual switches to accelerate packet forwarding within virtualized

environments, ensuring that communication between VMs is performed with minimal latency.

- Telecommunications: DPDK is utilized in packet core networks to optimize the performance of functions such as packet gateway and serving gateway in LTE and 5G networks, where low latency is critical.
- Edge Computing: DPDK can be applied in edge computing devices to accelerate packet processing at the edge of the network, supporting real-time applications and services with reduced latency.
- Load Balancers: DPDK is employed in load balancers and application delivery controllers (ADCs) to efficiently distribute incoming network traffic across multiple servers, ensuring optimal resource utilization and high availability.
- Storage Networking: DPDK is used to accelerate packet processing in storage networking applications, particularly in iSCSI-based storage solutions and storage controllers.
- 5G Networking: In 5G networks, DPDK is often applied in the User Plane Function to handle high-throughput data plane traffic, supporting services like enhanced mobile broadband (eMBB) and ultra-reliable low-latency communications (URLLC).
- Packet Brokers: DPDK is utilized in network packet brokers to efficiently capture, filter, and forward network traffic for monitoring and analysis purposes.
- High-Frequency Trading (HFT): DPDK is employed in HFT systems to achieve low-latency packet processing and rapid execution of trading algorithms, enabling financial institutions to react quickly to market changes.
- Internet Service Providers (ISPs): DPDK is used in edge routers and aggregation devices to handle high-speed packet forwarding in ISP networks, ensuring efficient data transfer.

12.5.2 Virtual Machine Device Queues (VMDQ)

It is a technology used in NICs to enhance the efficiency of network communication in virtualized environments. VMDQ enables improved network performance and resource utilization in scenarios where multiple VMs share a physical network interface. Here are key aspects of VMDQ:

1. Virtualization Context: VMDQ is specifically designed for virtualized environments, where multiple VMs run on a hypervisor sharing the same physical network interface.
    - Problem Addressed: In traditional setups, VMs on a host might contend for network resources, leading to suboptimal performance and inefficient use of available bandwidth. VMDQ addresses this issue by providing a mechanism for efficient and isolated packet processing for each VM.
    - Isolation of Queues: VMDQ isolates network traffic into multiple queues, each dedicated to a specific VM. This prevents contention and ensures that the network traffic for one VM is processed independently of others.
    - Queue Assignment: NICs supporting VMDQ are capable of dynamically assigning queues to VMs based on criteria such as VLAN tags. This allows for flexible and dynamic allocation of resources.
    - Performance Improvements: By isolating and dedicating queues to specific VMs, VMDQ helps in achieving improved network performance. Each VM can access the NIC resources independently, leading to better throughput and reduced latency.
    - Multicast and Broadcast Filtering: VMDQ-enabled NICs can efficiently filter multicast and broadcast traffic, preventing unnecessary processing and distribution of such packets to VMs that do not require them.
2. VLAN Tagging Support: VMDQ supports VLAN tagging, allowing for the differentiation of traffic based on VLAN identifiers. This is useful in environments where VLAN segmentation is employed.
3. Coexistence with SR-IOV: VMDQ can coexist with single root input output (I/O) virtualization (SR-IOV), another virtualization technology for NICs. Both technologies can be used together to enhance network performance in virtualized environments.

4. Enhanced Security and Isolation: VMDQ enhances security by isolating network traffic for different VMs. This isolation helps in preventing unauthorized access to network data between VMs.
5. Scalability: VMDQ provides a scalable solution for virtualized environments, allowing for the efficient sharing of network resources among multiple VMs without compromising performance.
6. Vendor-Specific Implementations: Different network equipment vendors may implement VMDQ in their own ways. VMDQ is often supported by Intel NICs, and other vendors may have similar technologies with different names.

VMDQ plays a significant role in optimizing network communication in virtualized environments, contributing to improved performance, resource utilization, and isolation between VMs on a host.

12.6 Conclusion and Future Directions

This research has rigorously explored the crucial role of efficient resource management in enhancing network performance. Through detailed examination of various aspects such as bandwidth allocation, buffer space utilization, and computational resource management, the study has highlighted effective strategies for optimizing packet processing within networks. The findings underscore the significance of intelligent resource allocation and its direct impact on minimizing latency, alleviating bottlenecks, and boosting overall system performance.

The research demonstrates that strategic resource management is not only fundamental in achieving high efficiency in current network architectures but is also vital for maintaining reliability and meeting stringent performance goals in environments constrained by diverse limitations. The insights gleaned from this study contribute significantly to the development of advanced resource allocation and optimization strategies, which are indispensable for superior performance in constrained network systems.

By addressing these areas, future research can build upon the foundations laid by this study, driving innovation and improvements in network resource management that will be critical for the next generation of network technologies.

References

1. Wu, W., Li, M., Qu, K., Zhou, C., Shen, X., Zhuang, W., Li, X., Shi, W., Split learning over wireless networks: Parallel design and resource management. *IEEE J. Sel. Areas Commun.*, 41, 1051, 2023, https://doi.org/10.1109/JSAC.2023.3242704.
2. Wang, Y., Yin, B., Chen, Z., Xia, B., Aggregation design and resource allocation for decentralized learning over wireless networks, 2023, https://doi.org/10.1109/ ICCC57788.2023.10233435.
3. Balakrishnan, R., Akdeniz, M., Dhakal, S., Himayat, N., Resource management and fairness for federated learning over wireless edge networks, vol. 2020-May, 2020, https://doi.org/10.1109/SPAWC48557.2020.9154285.
4. Khan, L.U., Guizani, M., Hong, C.S., Resource optimized hierarchical split federated learning for wireless networks, 2023, https://doi.org/10.1145/3576914. 3590148.
5. Kim, M., Derieux, A., Saad, W., A bargaining game for personalized, energy efficient split learning over wireless networks, vol. 2023-March, 2023, https://doi.org/10.1109/WCNC55385.2023.10118601.
6. Chen, M., Saad, W., Yin, C., Virtual reality over wireless networks: Quality-of-service model and learning-based resource management. *IEEE Trans. Commun.*, 66, 5621, 2018, https://doi.org/10.1109/TCOMM.2018.2850303.
7. Zhou, X., Deng, Y., Xia, H., Wu, S., Bennis, M., Resource allocation for time-triggered federated learning over wireless networks, vol. 2022-May, 2022, https://doi.org/10.1109/ICC45855.2022.9838329.
8. Chen, H., Huang, S., Zhang, D., Xiao, M., Skoglund, M., Poor, H.V., Federated learning over wireless iot networks with optimized communication and resources. *IEEE Internet Things J.*, 9, 16592, 2022, https://doi.org/10.1109/JIOT.2022. 3151193.
9. Mai, Y.T. and Hu, C.C., Design of dynamic resource allocation scheme for real-time traffic in the lte network. *EURASIP J. Wireless Commun. Networking*, 2022, 2022, https://doi.org/10.1186/s13638-022-02095-6.
10. Maule, M., Vardakas, J.S., Verikoukis, C., Multi-service network slicing 5g nr orchestration via tailored harq scheme design and hierarchical resource scheduling. *IEEE Trans. Veh. Technol.*, 72, 5021, 2023, https://doi.org/10.1109/TVT.2022.3223252.
11. AlQahtani, S.A., Cooperative-aware radio resource allocation scheme for 5g net- work slicing in cloud radio access networks. *Sensors*, 23, 2023, https://doi.org/ 10.3390/s23115111.
12. Tchendji, V.K., Yankam, Y.F., Sihomnou, I.C.K., Game theory-based dynamic resource allocations scheme in virtual networks. *J. Inf. Telecommun.*, 7, 1, 2023, https://doi.org/10.1080/24751839.2022.2117125.
13. Kim, S., Hierarchical multi-service resource allocation scheme for future wireless network virtualization. *IEEE Access*, 11, 87859, 2023, https://doi.org/10.1109/ ACCESS.2023.3304632.

4. Mortier, R., Multi-timescale internet traffic engineering. *IEEE Commun. Mag.*, **40**, 125–131, 2002.
15. He, J., Bresler, M., Chiang, M., Rexford, J., Towards robust multi-layer traffic engineering: Optimization of congestion control and routing. *IEEE J. Sel. Areas Commun.*, 25, 868, 2007, https://doi.org/10.1109/JSAC. 2007.070602.
16. Heidari, S. and Fotuhi-Firuzabad, M., Integrated planning for distribution automation and network capacity expansion. *IEEE Trans. Smart Grid*, 10, 4279, 2019, https://doi.org/10.1109/TSG.2018.2855218.
17. Gong, Y., He, B., Li, D., Network performance aware optimizations on iaas clouds. *IEEE Trans. Comput.*, 66, 672, 2017, https://doi.org/10.1109/TC.2016. 2609387.
18. Wang, Y., Zhang, S., Chow, D., Kuckelkorn, J.M., Evaluation and optimization of district energy network performance. *Present Future*, 2021, https:// doi. org/10.1016/j.rser.2020.110577.
19. Natkaniec, M. and Kras, M., An optimization of network performance in ieee 802.11ax dense networks. *Int. J. Electron. Telecommun.*, 69, 2023, https:// doi.org/10.24425/ijet.2023.144347.
20. Alghamdi, R., Alhadrami, R., Alhothali, D., Almorad, H., Faisal, A., Helal, S., Shalabi, R., Asfour, R., Hammad, N., Shams, A., Saeed, N., Dahrouj, H., Al-Naffouri, T.Y., Alouini, M.S., Intelligent surfaces for 6g wireless networks: A survey of optimization and performance analysis techniques. *IEEE Access*, 8, 202795, 2020, https://doi.org/10.1109/ACCESS.2020.3031959.
21. Vaishnav, A., Swain, A.R., Lenka, M.R., Device discovery approaches in d2d communication: A survey, in: *2022 OITS International Conference on Information Technology (OCIT)*, pp. 391–396, 2022, https://doi.org/10.1109/ OCIT56763.2022.00080.
22. N. Sugirtham, R.S.J., Impact of queuing disciplines on the performance of multi- class traffic in a network. *INF. TECHNOL. IND.*, 9, 2021, https://doi. org/10.17762/itii.v9i1.188.
23. Hussein, S.A.I., Zaki, F.W., Ashour, M.M., Mathematical model for forwarding packets in communication network. *IET Networks*, 11, 2022, https://doi. org/10. 1049/ntw2.12035.
24. Mone, P., Athalye, H., Borse, C., Kshirsagar, D.D., Patil, S.D., Testbed based analysis of Linux queue disciplines over Internet traffic mix, 2022, https:// doi. org/10.1016/j.simpat.2022.102601.
25. Velmurugan, T., Chandra, H., Balaji, S., Comparison of queuing disciplines for differentiated services using opnet, 2009, https://doi.org/10.1109/ ARTCom.2009.128.
26. Lee, C.H. and Kim, Y.T., Qos-aware hierarchical token bucket (qhtb) queuing disciplines for qos-guaranteed diffserv provisioning with optimized bandwidth utilization and priority-based preemption, 2013, https://doi. org/10.1109/ICOIN. 2013.6496403.

27. Tam, P., Math, S., Kim, S., Adaptive partial task offloading and virtual resource placement in sdn/nfv-based network softwarization. *Comput. Syst. Sci. Eng.*, 45, 2141, 2023, https://doi.org/10.32604/csse.2023.030984.
28. Lin, B.-S.P., Lin, Y.-B., Tung, L.-P., Lin, F.J., Exploring network softwarization and virtualization by applying sdn/nfv to 5g and iot. *Trans. Netw. Commun.*, 6, 2018, https://doi.org/10.14738/tnc.64.4825.
29. Kiran, N., Liu, X., Wang, S., Yin, C., Vnf placement and resource allocation in sdn/nfv-enabled mec networks, 2020, https://doi.org/10.1109/WCNCW48565. 2020.9124910.
30. Polverini, M., Galan-Jimenez, J., Lavacca, F.G., Cianfrani, A., Eramo, V., A scalable and offloading-based traffic classification solution in nfv/sdn network architectures. *IEEE Trans. Netw. Serv. Manage.*, 18, 1445, 2021. https://doi.org/10.1109/TNSM.2020.3047468.
31. Barakabitze, A. and Hines, A., *Network Softwarization and* Virtualization in Future Networks: The promise of SDN, NFV, MEC, and Fog/Cloud Computing, 2022, https://doi.org/10.1002/9781119800828.ch6.
32. Vaishnav, A., Swain, A.R., Lenka, M.R., Improved affinity propagation clustering for d2d communication in 5g, in: *2022 OITS International Conference on Information Technology (OCIT)*, pp. 403–408, 2022, https://doi.org/10.1109/OCIT56763.2022.00082.
33. Data Plane Development Kit (DPDK), 2020, https://doi.org/10.1201/9780429353512.

13

Resource-Constrained Network Management Using Software-Defined Networks

Sayan Bhattacharyya, Manas Ranjan Lenka* and Subhasis Dash

School of Computer Engineering, KIIT Deemed to be University, Bhubaneswar, India

Abstract

Over the past few decades, there has been a concerted effort to create a sophisticated network architecture that is programmable, centrally controlled, and able to address the shortcomings of traditional network systems. This cutting-edge network technology is called software-defined networking or SDN for short. As a newcomer to the topic, this article gives a detail overview of SDN, including its meaning, ways it overcomes the limitations of conventional networks, its underlying architecture and components, workflow considerations, as well as the challenges and use cases associated with this innovative technology. In addition, this paper will explore upcoming research on SDN as it has the power to significantly improve network management and address issues that arise in resource-constrained networks.

***Keywords*:** Software-defined network, resource management, SDN controller, southbound API, northbound API

13.1 Introduction

In this digital age, networks have become a critical component of our daily lives, connecting individuals, organizations, and devices worldwide. As more and more devices get connected and the volume of data traffic,

**Corresponding author*: manasy2k3@gmail.com

Subhasis Dash, Manas Ranjan Lenka, S. Balamurugan, Ambika Prasad Tripathy and Amarendra Mohanty (eds.) Sustainable Resource Management in Next-Generation Computational Constrained Networks, (315–336) © 2025 Scrivener Publishing LLC

network management has become increasingly complex, challenging, and resource-intensive. Managing network resources efficiently and effectively is crucial to ensure the delivery of reliable and high-quality services to end-users. SDN [1] has come up as a promising solution to tackle these challenges by enabling centralized network control, automation, and programmability.

Unlike hardware-controlled systems, SDN [2] is software-based and managed through software-controlled APIs, enabling remote use and upgrades, as well as better network monitoring and visualization. SDN is composed of three main parts: application, control, and data plane, which are connected by two protocols: the northbound protocol allows communication between the application and control planes, and the southbound protocol allows communication between the control and data planes. The control plane is considered the most intelligent component of SDN [3], as it stores all the logic and routing rules, whereas the data plane handles packet forwarding. The Ternary Content Addressable Memory (TCAM) in the data plane is a critical [4] component for flow table management, as it stores all the flows and determines which flow to install or discard based on match and control plane policies.

However, SDN itself also requires adequate resources to operate effectively, which may pose a significant challenge in resource-constrained environments with limited network infrastructure and limited budgets. In such scenarios, network operators face a trade-off between providing high-quality services and keeping the operational costs low, while also ensuring optimal resource utilization and network security.

Therefore, this paper explores the challenges and opportunities of resource-constrained network management using software-defined networks [5]. Specifically, we will investigate the state-of-the-art techniques and tools for efficient network resource management in SDN environments, including traffic engineering, load balancing, fault detection and recovery, network slicing, and security [6]. We will also discuss the benefits and limitations of SDN in resource-constrained scenarios and highlight the potential research directions for future advancements in this area.

The rest of the paper is structured as follows. Section 13.2 gives an overview of software-defined network architecture and its key components. Section 13.3 discusses the challenges and opportunities of SDN in resource-constrained scenarios. Section 13.4 presents the state-of-the-art techniques and tools for efficient network resource management in SDN environments. Section 13.5 evaluates existing techniques and tools performance using a case study. Finally, Section 13.6 concludes the paper and discusses the potential future research directions.

13.2 Software-Defined Network Architecture and Its Key Components

SDN provides a new way of managing networks [7] that makes things simpler by separating the control plane from the data plane depicted in Figure 13.1, as opposed to the traditional network management depicted in Figure 13.2.

By segregating control plane from data plane, SDN enables network administrators to manage network resources and traffic more efficiently and effectively. SDN also enables the development of new network applications that can leverage the control from a central place and programmability of the network to provide new services and improve network

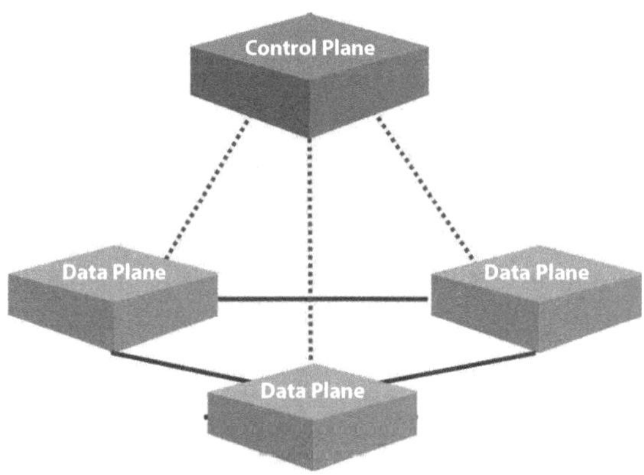

Figure 13.1 Decoupled control and data plane in SDN.

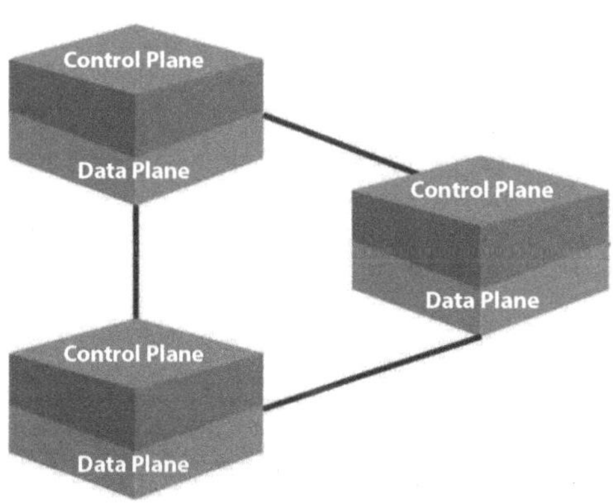

Figure 13.2 Coupled traditional network management.

performance. However, the adoption of SDN also poses some challenges, such as security and scalability, that need to be solved to fully unlock its potential.

The SDN architecture given in Figure 13.3 consists of three major components: the control, data, and application plane.

The control plane [8] decides how traffic moves through the network. In SDN architecture, the control plane is like a central server that talks to network devices like switches and routers using the OpenFlow protocol. The controller maintains a global view of the network topology and uses this information to make forwarding decisions based on the policies defined by the network administrator.

The data plane [9] handles sending network traffic as per the decisions made by the control plane [10]. In an SDN architecture, the data plane is implemented in network devices, referred to as OpenFlow switches and routers that uses the OpenFlow protocol. Each OpenFlow switch maintains a flow table that stores the forwarding rules. Once a packet receives at the switch, it checks the flow table to decide what to do next, like sending the packet to a particular place or ignoring it.

In the SDN infrastructure [11], various network applications run in the application plane. These applications can leverage the control from a central place and programmability of the network to provide new services, such as network slicing, load balancing [12], and security. Examples of

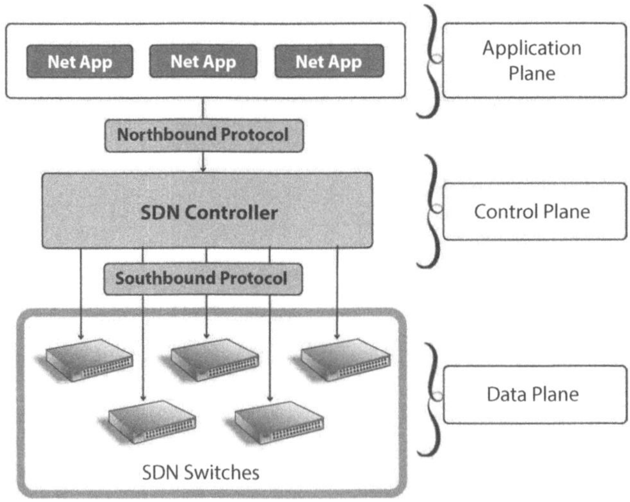

Figure 13.3 Overview of SDN architecture.

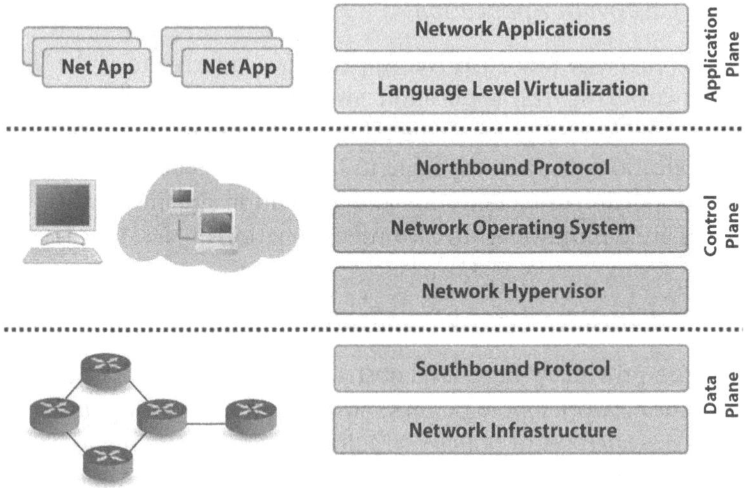

Figure 13.4 Layered architecture of SDN.

SDN applications include traffic engineering, network monitoring, and network security.

The SDN architecture can be represented using a layered architecture model, as shown in Figure 13.4. The lower layers [13], including the data and the control plane, are meant for forwarding and controlling network traffic [14].

The higher layers, including the application plane and the orchestration layer, are responsible for managing network resources and services.

The orchestration layer provides [15] a higher level of abstraction that helps administrators to define and manage network services and resources. It includes components such as the network service orchestrator, which manages the lifecycle of network services, and the resource orchestrator, which manages the allocation of network resources [16].

The followings three important layers that make up SDN architecture are discussed here.

13.2.1 Application Plane

Network applications [17] (Net Apps) run on the application plane, a layer that gives users the freedom to develop their own network logic. It consists of the following components.

13.2.1.1 Network Application

These are otherwise known as Net Apps and are referred to as the "brains" of the network [18]. This application contains the logic that would be presented on the control plane. Depending on the requirements of the user, these applications contain the logic to behave as a load-balancer, switch, router, firewall, intrusion detection and prevention systems, etc. High-level languages are typically used in the implementation of Net Apps [19].

13.2.1.2 Language-Level Virtualization

This feature provides a high-level abstraction of the network objects that make up the network topology. These abstraction network topology objects and the associated set of policies simultaneously conceal the information and provide the programmers with the necessary services. Another type of language is virtualization [20], which uses static sliding to split the network according to the description of the application layer.

13.2.2 Control Plane

This layer can execute the control logic that will be used to facilitate the following elements. As previously discussed, we separated the data plane and control plane [21] from the traditional network system. Hence, the control plane now has overall control, and the system will be centralized. This layer has been split into two parts with the idea of virtualization.

13.2.2.1 Network Operating System (NOS)

The NOS [22] is the location where the control logic of the SDN network runs. NOS can provide abstraction, essential service, and common API [23]. NOS supports features that generate network configuration based on the network operators policy.

13.2.2.2 Network Hypervisor

Infrastructure as a service [24], which includes virtualization and the provision of virtual machines, helps in a variety of ways where physical infrastructure is lacking. These cloud virtual machines can be easily created, migrated from various physical infrastructures [25], and deleted. The cloud virtualization concept of today allows us to make the best use of physical infrastructure. SDN controllers will run on a NOS in the case of SDN architecture. This operating system will run on virtual machines managed by a specialized hypervisor known as a Network hypervisor [26]. The network topology and address space vary arbitrarily across different locations in a large network area [27]. These concepts allow us to allocate sufficient resources based on network topology so that an efficient and powerful physical infrastructure can be shared by all SDN controllers [28].

13.2.3 Data Plane

The data plane is decoupled from the traditional network component and is used to have embedded software of its own to treat autonomous decisions, but, currently, it simply has forwarding components.

13.2.3.1 Network Infrastructure

This layer contains networking equipment. The traditional network component [29] has embedded control to make autonomous decisions in this layer only. In the case of SDN, however, this has been removed.

It only contains forwarding components such as switches, routers, and middlebox appliances. After the autonomous decision-making component is removed, the decision must be made by the central management component, which is the SDN controller [30], interacting via southbound protocols.

13.2.4 SDN Protocols

SDN architecture includes several protocols [31] for remote interaction as follows.

13.2.4.1 Northbound Protocol

The northbound protocol [32] shown in Figure 13.5 is a software ecosystem, not a piece of hardware [33]. It is made up of a number of APIs that communicate with each other between the control and application plane. Because the use cases for this interface are still being developed, it does not have a standard implementation, in contrast to the southbound protocol [34]. In the development of networking protocols [35], the representational state transfer (REST) architectural style is gaining popularity and is increasingly chosen for the top-level interface of SDN [36]. It enables

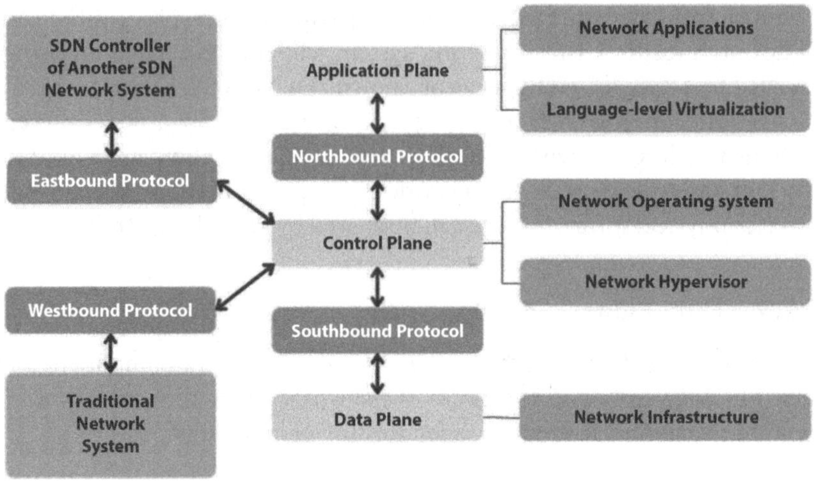

Figure 13.5 Hierarchy of SDN components and protocols.

communication between a lower-level and a higher-level or more central network component. Some examples are simple network management protocol (SNMP) transaction language 1 (TL1), systems management architecture for server hardware (SMASH), and simple object access protocol (SOAP).

13.2.4.2 Southbound Protocol

A number of APIs make up the southbound protocol [37], which is the actual interface between the control and data plane. OpenFlow is the name of its standard implementation. It makes it possible for a network component at a higher level to communicate with a component at a lower level [38]. The forwarding components of the physical or virtual network infrastructure remain closely tethered to these APIs, nevertheless.

13.2.4.3 Eastbound Protocol

This protocol helps in interaction between two SDN controllers that are located in different places as shown in Figure 13.6. Examples like SDN, HyperFLow, and Onix are eastbound protocols [39, 40].

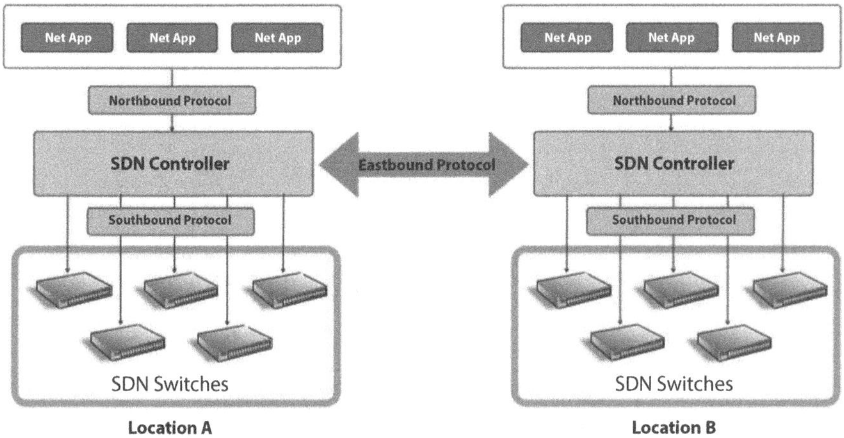

Figure 13.6 Communication using eastbound protocol.

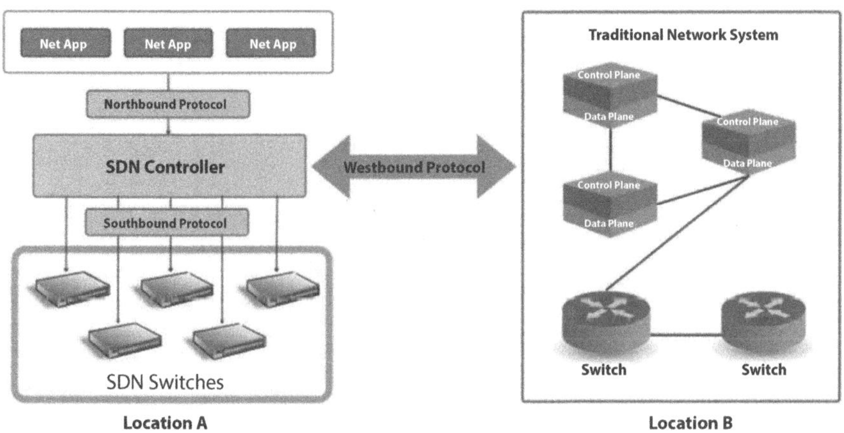

Figure 13.7 Communication using westbound protocol.

13.2.4.4 Westbound Protocol

This protocol facilitates communication between traditional network components and SDN controllers. Only upcoming modifications of network design with SDN are also compatible with the conventional network architecture due to this protocol [41], as shown in Figure 13.7. RouteFlow, SDN-IP, and BTSDN are well-known examples of this protocol.

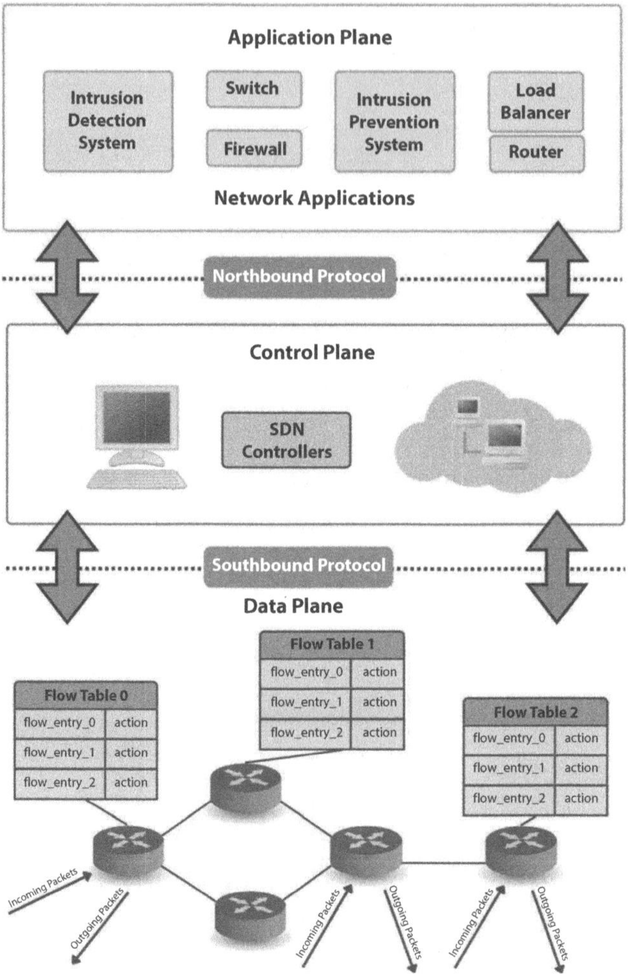

Figure 13.8 Overview of SDN workflows.

13.2.5 SDN Workflows

SDN manages and controls network infrastructure using software applications [42, 43]. Figure 13.8 illustrates how the SDN Architecture functions, utilizing the application, control, and data planes [44]. Here is a detailed workflow of SDN:

- Application Plane: Applications used in networks may perform specific functions such as acting as load balancers, switches, or routers etc. All of these programs need to be installed exclusively in the application layer.

SDN-enabled applications can be developed to provide additional functionality, such as network monitoring, optimization, and automation [45]. These applications integrate with the SDN controller through northbound APIs.

• Control Plane: Here, the NOS will run over the network hypervisor and the network applications installed in the application plane will run over this NOS. The control plane talks to the application plane via the Northbound protocol. The layer must provide the infrastructure for those applications to run over distributed computing [46].

The SDN controller is the central component of the SDN architecture. It initializes and starts running on a server or cluster of servers within the network. Common SDN controllers include OpenDaylight, ONOS, and Ryu.

The SDN controller uses the southbound APIs to discover the network topology. It learns about the connected switches, routers, links, and the relationships between them. Topology information is crucial for making intelligent decisions about network traffic.

Network administrators define high-level network policies and rules through northbound APIs provided by the SDN controller. These policies express the desired behavior of the network, such as quality of service (QoS), security policies, and traffic routing preferences.

The SDN controller translates the high-level network policies into specific configurations that can be understood and implemented by the network devices. This translation process involves mapping policies to specific rules and actions that should be taken by the switches and routers.

The SDN controller makes centralized decisions based on the network policies and the present state of the network. It computes optimal paths, determines how traffic should be sent, and updates the flow tables of the switches accordingly.

SDN controllers continuously monitor the network through southbound APIs. They collect real-time data on traffic patterns, network performance, and link states. Analytics tools can be used to gain insights into the network's behavior and performance.

SDN controllers enforce security policies by controlling access to the network. They can dynamically adjust access control lists and firewall rules based on network policies and real-time threat intelligence.

SDN allows for dynamic adaptation to changing network conditions. The controller can respond to events such as link failures, congestion, or changes in traffic patterns by dynamically updating network policies and flow tables [47].

• Data Plane: SDN-enabled switches and routers register with the SDN controller.
This registration process includes exchanging information about the capabilities of the devices and establishing a communication channel between the controller and the devices.

Most importantly, data plane contains flow table that contains all the rules that define how switches should manage packets based on factors like where they came from, where they are going, what type of data they carry, and which ports they are using. At first, the flow tables follow a set of rules. The control plane gradually updates the flow table after the flow of network packets. When a network packet arrives at the forwarding components, the flow table must provide the associate rule using wild card or exact match. In the absence of a flow entry, the controller receives a request to create a flow entry for that particular packet and update the corresponding flow table. The TCAM [48] is used to create flow tables.

The SDN workflow is iterative, allowing for continuous improvement and adaptation. Network administrators can update policies, add new services, and respond to changing requirements without making extensive changes to the underlying hardware. By following this workflow, SDN enables centralized control, programmability, and automation in network management, offering flexibility and efficiency in adapting to the evolving needs of modern networks.

13.3 Challenges and Opportunities of SDN in Resource-Constrained Scenarios

SDN offers a number of opportunities for improving network management and resource utilization in various scenarios. However, there are also several challenges associated with deploying SDN in resource-constrained environments [49]. Here, we discuss some key challenges and opportunities of SDN in resource-constrained scenarios, including use cases.

One of the main challenges of deploying SDN in resource-constrained scenarios is limited hardware resources, such as memory and processing power. In such scenarios, SDN controllers may struggle to handle large-scale networks or complex policies. To address this challenge, researchers have proposed solutions such as distributed SDN controllers or hybrid SDN architectures that combine centralized and distributed control [50].

Another challenge is the lack of standardized APIs and protocols for SDN, which can make it difficult to integrate different components of the network. To address this challenge, the SDN community has developed a number of standardization efforts, including the Open Networking Foundation and the OpenDaylight Project [50].

Despite these challenges, SDN also presents a number of opportunities for resource-constrained scenarios. One such opportunity is improved resource utilization, which can help to minimize the costs and improve the network performance. For example, SDN can enable network administrators to allocate network resources dynamically based on changing demands, such as traffic load or user behavior [51].

Another opportunity is the ability to provide network services and applications that were previously difficult to implement. For example, SDN can enable the deployment of network virtualization and network slicing, which can help optimize network resources and provide customized services for different applications and users.

A use case for SDN in a resource-constrained scenario is wireless sensor networks (WSNs). WSNs are typically deployed in remote and harsh environments, where resources such as battery life and bandwidth are limited. SDN can help optimize the energy consumption of WSNs by dynamically adjusting the network topology and traffic flow based on changing demands [52]. For example, SDN can enable the deployment of routing algorithms that take into account energy consumption and data aggregation.

Another use case for SDN in a resource-constrained scenario is in cloud computing environments. SDN can help optimize resource allocation in cloud data centers by enabling dynamic network reconfiguration based on changing demands. For example, SDN can enable the deployment of load-balancing algorithms that can dynamically allocate network resources to different virtual machines based on their workload [53].

13.4 State-of-the-Art Techniques and Tools for Efficient Network Resource Management in SDN Environments

Efficient network resource management is a critical requirement for modern networks, and SDN environments have opened up new possibilities for managing network resources. This section discusses some of the state-of-the-art techniques and tools for efficient network resource management in SDN environments.

One of the key techniques for efficient network resource management in SDN environments is network slicing. It lets multiple virtual networks share the same physical infrastructure, each with its own network resources, policies, and performance requirements. This allows network resources to be used efficiently by different applications and users and can help improve overall network performance. Tools such as the Network Service Header and the Segment Routing architecture have been proposed for implementing network slicing in SDN environments [54].

Another technique for efficient network resource management in SDN environments is network function virtualization (NFV). NFV allows network functions like load balancers, firewalls, and intrusion detection systems as software, rather than in hardware. This provides greater flexibility in resource allocation and enables more efficient use of network resources. Tools such as Open vSwitch (OVS) and OpenFlow have been proposed for implementing NFV in SDN environments.

In addition to network slicing and NFV, machine learning (ML) techniques are also useful for efficient network resource management in SDN environments. ML algorithms can help predict network traffic patterns and adjust network resource allocation in real time, based on changing demands [55]. ML tools such as TensorFlow and scikit-learn are used for implementing ML-based network resource management in SDN environments.

Another key technique for efficient network resource management in SDN environments is traffic engineering. Traffic engineering enables network administrators to optimize network performance by controlling the flow of network traffic. SDN enables more fine-grained traffic engineering by allowing administrators to control network traffic at the flow level, rather than at the packet level. Tools such as the Open Network Operating System (ONOS) and the Floodlight controller have been proposed for implementing traffic engineering in SDN environments [56].

Finally, software-defined WAN (SD-WAN) is another technique for efficient network resource management in SDN environments. SD-WAN enables organizations to use multiple WAN connections, such as broadband and LTE, to create a virtual WAN with more reliable and efficient network performance. SD-WAN can be implemented using SDN controllers and tools such as Viptela and VeloCloud [57].

13.5 Performance of the Existing Techniques and Tools with Use Case

This section discusses the performance of some of the existing techniques and tools for efficient network resource management in SDN environments, using case studies.

- Network slicing: One of the important benefit of network slicing is that it enables multiple virtual networks to be present on the same physical infrastructure, each with its own network resources, policies, and performance requirements. This enables the allocation of network resources efficiently to different applications and users and can help improve overall network performance [58]. A case study of the performance of network slicing was conducted in a 5G network environment, where network slicing was used to support different types of applications with different QoS requirements. The study found that network slicing enabled better resource allocation and utilization and helped improve the overall network performance, especially for applications with stringent QoS requirements such as remote surgery and augmented reality.
- NFV: This provides greater flexibility in resource allocation and enables more efficient use of network resources. A case study of the performance of NFV was conducted in a data center environment, where NFV was used to implement virtual network functions such as firewalls and load balancers. The study found that NFV enabled more efficient use of network resources, reduced operational costs, and improved scalability and agility.
- Machine learning (ML): ML algorithms are used to predict network traffic patterns and adjust network resource allocation in real time, based on changing demands. ML tools such as TensorFlow and scikit-learn are used for implementing ML-based network resource management in SDN environments [59]. A case study of the performance of ML-based network resource management was conducted in a cloud data center environment, where ML algorithms were used to predict network traffic and adjust resource allocation

accordingly. The study found that ML-based resource management enabled more efficient use of network resources, reduced congestion and latency, and improved overall network performance.

- Traffic engineering: Traffic engineering enables network administrators to optimize network performance by controlling the flow of network traffic [60]. SDN enables more fine-grained traffic engineering by allowing administrators to control network traffic at the flow level, rather than at the packet level. A case study of the performance of traffic engineering was conducted in a campus network environment, where traffic engineering was used to optimize network performance for different applications and users. The study found that traffic engineering enabled better resource utilization, reduced congestion and packet loss, and improved overall network performance.
- Software-defined WAN (SD-WAN): SD-WAN enables organizations to use multiple WAN connections, such as broadband and LTE, to create a virtual WAN with more reliable and efficient network performance. SD-WAN are implemented using SDN controllers and tools such as Viptela and VeloCloud. A case study of the performance of SD-WAN was conducted in a multi-site enterprise network environment, where SD-WAN was used to optimize network performance and reduce costs. The study found that SD-WAN enabled better utilization of available WAN resources, reduced WAN costs, and improved overall network performance, especially for applications such as video conferencing and file transfers [61].

13.6 Conclusion and Future Scope

In conclusion, the use of SDN in resource-constrained scenarios has great potential to address challenges related to efficient network resource management. Various techniques and tools, such as network slicing, NFV, ML, traffic engineering, and software-defined WANs, have been developed and evaluated for their effectiveness in resource-constrained scenarios.

The existing techniques and tools have been shown to provide significant benefits, such as improved network performance, reduced energy consumption, and better scalability. However, still there is a room for improvement, and future research could focus on addressing some of the remaining challenges, such as ensuring the security and privacy of the network, developing more effective algorithms for resource allocation and scheduling, and investigating the integration of SDN with other emerging technologies, such as blockchain and edge computing.

References

1. Waseem, Q., Din, W.I.S.W., Aminuddin, A., Mohammed, M.H., Aziza, R.F.A., Software-defined networking (sdn): A review, 2022, https://doi.org/10.1109/ICOIACT55506.2022.9972067.
2. Farooq, M.S., Riaz, S., Alvi, A., Security and Privacy Issues in Software-Defined Networking (SDN). *A Syst. Lit. Rev.*, 12, 3077, 2023, https://doi.org/10. 3390/electronics12143077.
3. Letswamotse, B.B., Malekian, R., Chen, C.Y., Modieginyane, K.M., Software defined wireless sensor networks (SDWSN): A review on efficient resources, applications and technologies, 2018, https://doi.org/10.3966/160792642018091905003.
4. Afridi, S.K., Iqbal, S., Qureshi, K.N., Majeed, S., Jeon, G., Integration of interdomain flow-rule in software-defined networks for embedded internet of things devices. *Electron. (Switzerland)*, 12, 1172, 2023, https://doi.org/10.3390/ electronics12051172.
5. Lu, J., Xiong, H., He, F., Zheng, Z., Li, H., A mixed-critical consistent update algorithm in software defined time-triggered ethernet using time window. *IEEE Access*, 8, 65554, 2020, https://doi.org/10.1109/ACCESS.2020.2984749.
6. Rehman, A.U., Aguiar, R.L., Barraca, J.P., Fault-tolerance in the scope of software-defined networking (sdn). *IEEE Access*, 7, 124474, 2019, https://doi.org/10. 1109/ACCESS.2019.2939115.
7. Narwaria, A. and Mazumdar, A.P., Software-Defined Wireless Sensor Network: A Comprehensive Survey, 2023, https://doi.org/10.1016/j.jnca.2023.103636.
8. Romanov, O., Nesterenko, M., Mankivskyi, V., Zhuk, O., Principles of building modular control plane in software-defined network, vol. 548, 2023, https://doi. org/10.1007/978-3-031-16368-5 17.
9. Hauser, F., H¨aberle, M., Merling, D., Lindner, S., Gurevich, V., Zeiger, F., Frank, R., Menth, M., A survey on data plane programming with P4. *Fundamentals Adv. Appl. Res.*, 212, 103561, 2023, https://doi.org/10.1016/j.jnca.2022.103561.
10. Ren, Q., Guo, Z., Wu, J., Hu, T., Jie, L., Hu, Y., He, L., Sdn-esrc: A secure and resilient control plane for software-defined networks. *IEEE Trans. Netw. Serv. Manage.*, 19, 2366, 2022, https://doi.org/10.1109/TNSM.2022. 3163198.

11. Mehra, M., Maurya, S., Tiwari, N.K., Network load balancing in software defined network: A survey. *Int. J. Appl. Eng. Res.*, 14, 245, 2019.
12. Wang, Z., Li, Y., Guan, S., A robust-link controller placement model for large-scale software defined networks. *Trans. Emerging Telecommun. Technol.*, 34, 2023, https://doi.org/10.1002/ett.4765.
13. Samadi, P., Fiorani, M., Shen, Y., Wosinska, L., Bergman, K., Flexible architecture and autonomous control plane for metro-scale geographically distributed data centers. *J. Lightwave Technol.*, 35, 1188, 2017, https://doi.org/10.1109/JLT.2017.2652480.
14. Meena, R.C., Bhatia, S., Jhaveri, R.H., Shukla, P.K., Kumar, A., Varshney, N., Malibari, A.A., Enhancing software-defined networks with intelligent controllers to improve first packet processing period. *Electron. (Switzerland)*, 12, 600, 2023, https://doi.org/10.3390/electronics12030600.
15. Núñez-Gómez, C., Carrión, C., Caminero, B., Delicado, F.M., S-hidra: A blockchain and sdn domain-based architecture to orchestrate fog computing environments. *Comput. Netw.*, 221, 109512, 2023, https://doi.org/10.1016/j.comnet.2022.109512.
16. Sim, D.H., Shin, J., Kim, M.H., Software-defined networking orchestration for interoperable key management of quantum key distribution networks. *Entropy*, 25, 943, 2023, https://doi.org/10.3390/e25060943.
17. Tapiero, R., Security in sdn networks and their applications. *Ingenier´ıa Solidaria*, 17, 2021, https://doi.org/10.16925/2357-6014.2021.02.09.
18. Zhao, Y., Li, Y., Zhang, X., Geng, G., Zhang, W., Sun, Y., A survey of networking applications applying the software defined networking concept based on machine learning. *IEEE Access*, 7, 95397, 2019, https://doi.org/10.1109/ACCESS.2019.2928564.
19. Zhang, C., Wang, X., Li, F., He, Q., Huang, M., Deep learning–based network application classification for sdn. *Trans. Emerging Telecommun. Technol.*, 29, 2018, https://doi.org/10.1002/ett.3302.
20. Paolucci, F., Cugini, F., Castoldi, P., Osinski, T., Enhancing 5g sdn/nfv edge with p4 data plane programmability. *IEEE Netw.*, 35, 154, 2021, https://doi.org/ 10.1109/MNET.021.1900599.
21. Jingjing, Z., Di, C., Weiming, W., Rong, J., Xiaochun, W., The deployment of routing protocols in distributed control plane of sdn. *Sci. World J.*, 2014, 2014, https://doi.org/10.1155/2014/918536.
22. Gong, J. and Rezaeipanah, A., A fuzzy delay-bandwidth guaranteed routing algorithm for video conferencing services over sdn networks. *Multimed. Tools Appl.*, 82, 1, 2023, https://doi.org/10.1007/s11042-023-14349-6.
23. Jacobs, A.S., Pfitscher, R.J., Ferreira, R.A., Granville, L.Z., Refining network intents for self-driving networks, 2018, https://doi.org/10.1145/3229584.3229590.
24. Liao, L.X., Wang, J., Chao, H.C., Qin, B., Distributed and efficient network hypervisor for sdn virtualization. *J. Internet Technol.*, 22, 2021, https://doi.org/10.3966/160792642021052203012.

25. Blenk, A., Basta, A., Reisslein, M., Kellerer, W., Survey on network virtualization hypervisors for software defined networking, 2016, https://doi.org/10.1109/COMST.2015.2489183.
26. Hassan, M.K., Ariffin, S.H.S., Syed-Yusof, S.K., Ghazali, N.E.B., Kanona, M.E.A., Mohamed, K.S., Khairi, M.H.H., Hamdan, M., Dlvisor: Dynamic learning hypervisor for software defined network. *IEEE Access*, 11, 84144, 2023, https://doi.org/10.1109/ACCESS.2023.3302266.
27. Yoo, Y., Yang, G., Shin, C., Lee, J., Yoo, C., Control channel isolation in sdn virtualization: A machine learning approach, 2023, https://doi.org/10.1109/CCGrid57682.2023.00034.
28. Mahdi, S.S. and Abdullah, A.A., Implementation of network slicing for multi-controller environment based on flowvisor, vol. 1764 CCIS, 2023, https://doi.org/10.1007/978-3-031-35442-710.
29. Krishnan, P., Jain, K., Aldweesh, A., Prabu, P., Buyya, R., Openstackdp: a scalable network security framework for sdn-based openstack cloud infrastructure. *J. Cloud Comput.*, 12, 1, 2023, https://doi.org/10.1186/s13677-023-00406-w.
30. Ahmad, S. and Mir, A.H., Scalability, consistency, reliability and security in sdn controllers: A survey of diverse sdn controllers. *J. Netw. Syst. Manage.*, 29, 2021, https://doi.org/10.1007/s10922-020-09575-4.
31. Bannour, F., Souihi, S., Mellouk, A., Distributed sdn control: Survey, taxonomy, and challenges. *IEEE Commun. Surv. Tutorials*, 20, 333–354, 2018, https://doi.org/10.1109/COMST.2017.2782482.
32. Wang, C., Ni, H., Liu, L., An enhanced message distribution mechanism for northbound interfaces in the sdn environment. *Appl. Sci. (Switzerland)*, 11, 4346, 2021, https://doi.org/10.3390/app11104346.
33. Faisal, M., Siddiqua, H., Islam, M.J., Rahman, A., An SDN-based secure model for iot network in smart building, 2022, https://doi.org/10.1109/STI56238.2022.10103295.
34. Mahrach, S., Makkaoui, K.E., Esbai, R., SDN Southbound Protocols: A Comparative Study, vol. 147, 2023, https://doi.org/10.1007/978-3-031-15191-0 39.
35. Lam, J., Lee, S.G., Lee, H.J., Oktian, Y.E., Securing SDN southbound and data plane communication with ibc. *Mobile Inf. Syst.*, 2016, 2016, https://doi.org/10.1155/2016/1708970.
36. Braun, W. and Menth, M., Software-defined networking using openflow: Protocols, applications and architectural design choices. *Future Internet*, 6, 302, 2014, https://doi.org/10.3390/fi6020302.
37. Latif, Z., Sharif, K., Li, F., Karim, M.M., Biswas, S., Wang, Y., A comprehensive survey of interface protocols for software defined networks, 2020, https://doi.org/10.1016/j.jnca.2020.102563.
38. Islam, M.D.S., Al-Mukhtar, M., Khan, M.D.R.K., Hossain, M., A survey on sdn and sdcn traffic measurement: Existing approaches and research challenges. *Eng.*, 4, 124474, 2023, https://doi.org/10.3390/eng4020063.

39. Nikolova, K., Atanasov, I., Pencheva, E., Software defined networks and openflow: A survey, vol. 18, 2018, https://doi.org/10.5593/sgem2018/6.3/S27.090.
40. Nadeem, M.W., Goh, H.G., Aun, Y., Ponnusamy, V., Detecting and mitigating botnet attacks in software-defined networks using deep learning techniques. *IEEE Access*, 11, 49153, 2023, https://doi.org/10.1109/ACCESS.2023.3277397.
41. Lam, J.H., Lee, S.G., Lee, H.J., Oktian, Y.E., Securing distributed sdn with ibc, vol. 2015, August, 2015, https://doi.org/10.1109/ICUFN.2015.7182680.
42. Javanmardi, S., Shojafar, M., Mohammadi, R., Persico, V., Pescapè, A., S-fos: A secure workflow scheduling approach for performance optimization in sdn-based iot-fog networks. *J. Inf. Secur. Appl.*, 72, 103404, 2023, https://doi.org/10.1016/j.jisa.2022.103404.
43. Aktas, M.F., Haldeman, G., Parashar, M., Scheduling and flexible control of bandwidth and in-transit services for end-to-end application workflows. *Future Gener. Comput. Syst.*, 56, 284, 2016, https://doi.org/10.1016/j.future.2015.09.011.
44. Xu, X., Cao, H., Geng, Q., Liu, X., Dai, F., Wang, C., Dynamic resource provisioning for workflow scheduling under uncertainty in edge computing environment, vol. 34, 2022, https://doi.org/10.1002/cpe.5674.
45. Aditya, T., Donald, A.D., Thippanna, G., Kousar, M.M., Madilety, C., SDN application plane where intelligence meets networking. *Int. J. Adv. Res. Sci. Commun. Technol.*, 3, 512, 2023, https://doi.org/10.48175/ijarsct-8529.
46. Yan, Q., Yu, F.R., Gong, Q., Li, J., Software-defined networking (SDN) and distributed denial of service (DDOS) attacks in cloud computing environments: A survey, some research issues, and challenges, 2016, https://doi.org/10.1109/COMST.2015.2487361.
47. Maleh, Y., Qasmaoui, Y., Gholami, K.E., Sadqi, Y., Mounir, S., A comprehensive survey on SDN security: threats, mitigations, and future directions, 2023, https://doi.org/10.1007/s40860-022-00171-8.
48. Zhao, Z., Yang, W., Wu, B., Flow aggregation through dynamic routing overlaps in software defined networks. *Comput. Netw.*, 176, 107293, 2020, https://doi.org/10.1016/j.comnet.2020.107293.
49. Pathak, G., Gutierrez, J., Rehman, S.U., Security in low powered wide area networks: Opportunities for software defined network-supported solutions. *Electron. (Switzerland)*, 9, 2020, https://doi.org/10.3390/electronics9081195.
50. Segura, G.A.N., Chorti, A., Margi, C.B., Centralized and distributed intrusion detection for resource-constrained wireless sdn networks. *IEEE Internet Things J.*, 9, 7746, 2022, https://doi.org/10.1109/JIOT.2021.3114270.
51. González, C.C., Pupo, E.F., Atzori, L., Murroni, M., Dynamic radio access selection and slice allocation for differentiated traffic management on future mobile networks. *IEEE Trans. Netw. Serv. Manage.*, 19, 2022, https://doi.org/10.1109/TNSM.2022.3150978.

52. Zhu, B., Jiang, H., Wu, L., Yi, S., Wang, H., A dynamic bandwidth allocation solution based on user behavior and software defined eps. *China Commun.*, 13, 80, 2016, https://doi.org/10.1109/CC.2016.7582300.
53. Karnani, S. and Shakya, H.K., Leveraging sdn for load balancing on campus network (cn), 167, 2021, https://doi.org/10.1109/CICN51697.2021.9574640.
54. Tayyaba, S.K. and Shah, M.A., Resource allocation in sdn based 5g cellular networks. *Peer-to-Peer Networking Appl.*, 12, 514, 2019, https://doi.org/10.1007/s12083-018-0651-3.
55. Guo, Y., Wang, W., Zhang, H., Guo, W., Wang, Z., Tian, Y., Yin, X., Wu, J., Traffic engineering in hybrid software defined network via reinforcement learning. *J. Netw. Comput. Appl.*, 189, 103116, 2021, https://doi.org/10.1016/j.jnca.2021.103116.
56. Oginni, O., Bull, P., Wang, Y., Constraint-aware software-defined network for routing real-time multimedia. *ACM SIGBED Rev.*, 15, 2018, https://doi.org/10.1145/3267419.3267425.
57. Wood, M., Top requirements on the sd-wan security checklist. *Network Secur.*, 2017, 9, 2017, https://doi.org/10.1016/S1353-4858(17)30070-3.
58. Barakabitze, A.A., Ahmad, A., Mijumbi, R., Hines, A., 5g network slicing using sdn and nfv: A survey of taxonomy, architectures and future challenges. *Comput. Netw.*, 167, 2020, https://doi.org/10.1016/j.comnet.2019.106984.
59. Haseeb, K., Ahmad, I., Awan, I.I., Lloret, J., Bosch, I., A machine learning SDN-enabled big data model for iomt systems. *Electron. (Switzerland)*, 10, 2228, 2021, https://doi.org/10.3390/electronics10182228.
60. Dinh, K.T., Kukliński, S., Osiński, T., Wytrebowicz, J., Heuristic traffic engineering for sdn. *J. Inf. Telecommun.*, 4, 251, 2020, https://doi.org/10.1080/24751839.2020.1755528.
61. Wei, Y., Zhang, X., Xie, L., Leng, S., Energy-aware traffic engineering in hybrid sdn/ip backbone networks. *J. Commun. Netw.*, 18, 2016, https://doi.org/10.1109/JCN.2016.000079.

14

Vehicles Smoke Monitoring Using Internet of Things and Machine Learning

Dhavakumar P.[1]* and Selvakumar Samuel[2]

[1]*School of Computer Science and Engineering (SCOPE), Vellore Institute of Technology, Chennai, India*
[2]*Asia Pacific University of Technology & Innovation, Kuala Lumpur, Malaysia*

Abstract
Global warming is the most important problem of our time. CO_2 emissions through various means are the main reason for this problem. One of the major contributors among the means of CO_2 emissions is vehicle smoke. In this chapter, this issue has been discussed. A system has been proposed using the Internet of Things and a convolutional neural network–support vector machine hybrid machine learning model. This system can help monitor the level of vehicle emissions and alert the Road Transport Department if CO_2 emissions exceed the permitted level. This system can help the government alleviate the CO_2 emission problems of vehicles to some extent. This is a small initiative to support the green environment.

Keywords: IoT, machine learning, global warming, CO_2 emissions, vehicle emission monitoring, road transport department (RTD)

14.1 Introduction

Carbon dioxide (CO_2) is a chemical compound comprising one carbon atom and two oxygen atoms. It occurs naturally as a greenhouse gas in small amounts in the Earth's atmosphere and transforms into dry ice when in its solid state. The primary origins of CO_2 releases entail the combustion of carbon-based fuels and the decomposition of vegetation. Colorless and

**Corresponding author*: dhavakumar.p@vit.ac.in

Subhasis Dash, Manas Ranjan Lenka, S. Balamurugan, Ambika Prasad Tripathy and Amarendra Mohanty (eds.) Sustainable Resource Management in Next-Generation Computational Constrained Networks, (337–358) © 2025 Scrivener Publishing LLC

odorless CO_2 is essential in regulating the Earth's climate by capturing solar heat and stopping it from dissipating into space. While many gases also became an cause for the global warming, CO_2 accounts for around 75% of the total warming influence.

Due to the human activities, such as burning fossil fuels, have greatly contributed to the abudent rise in atmospheric CO_2 levels. CO_2 emissions have surged, with an annual per capita increase of 1.1% in the 1990s and over 3% from 2000 to 2004. Whereas industrialized countries, notably the United States, mainly drive CO_2 emissions, developing nations like China have also experienced a noticeable increase. In 2004, industrialized nations, including the United States, accounted for 71% of CO_2 emissions.

Since 1750, advanced countries have been responsible for approximately 77% of the 315 billion tonnes (286 billion metric tons) of CO_2 emissions. Conversely, less wealthy nations have encountered a rapid increase in their emissions recently. The majority (73%) of the surge in CO_2 emissions in 2004 occurred in swiftly growing emerging nations such as China, where likely to surpassed the United States in the emissions, whereas emissions from developing world were much lower. In 2004, the average American produced 20.4 tons of CO_2, whereas the typical Chinese citizen emitted 3.8 tons. The next part will discuss CO_2 emissions from automobiles.

14.2 Vehicle CO_2 Emissions

Under the previous arrangement, cars within a single lane produced CO_2, and there is no evident remedy for this issue. Driving in the equal lane can result in the discharges of the carbon dioxide and other detrimental greenhouse gases. These discharges originate from the combustion of fossil fuels and contribute to the progression of global warming by confining heat in the atmosphere. Carbon emissions elevate global temperatures by confining solar energy in the atmosphere.

Vehicle usage has a harmful impact on the environment, leading to air pollution and subsequent health issues. Investing in public transportation and railways can help decrease CO_2 emissions and air pollution in the long run by reducing the dependency on more polluting transportation methods. The next section will outline the primary effects of vehicle emissions.

The following two information graphics show vehicle CO_2 emission details in Japan (Figure 14.1) and Europe (Figure 14.2).

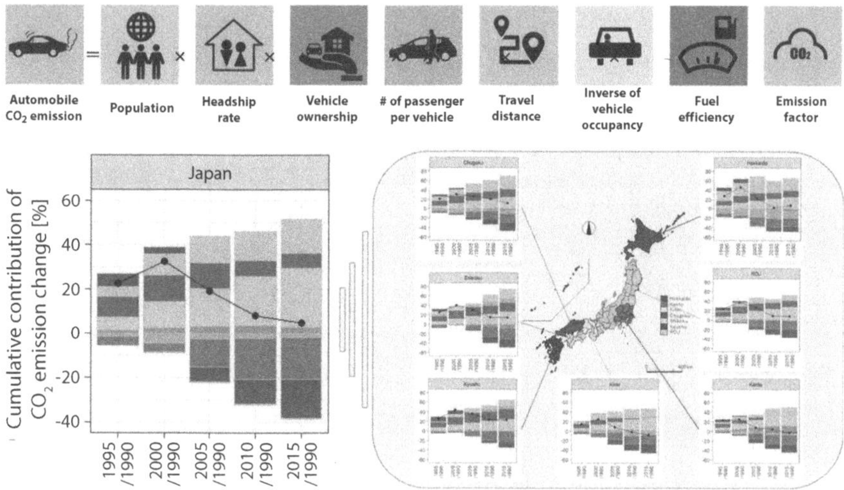

Figure 14.1 Graphical abstract of automobile CO_2 emissions in Japan [1].

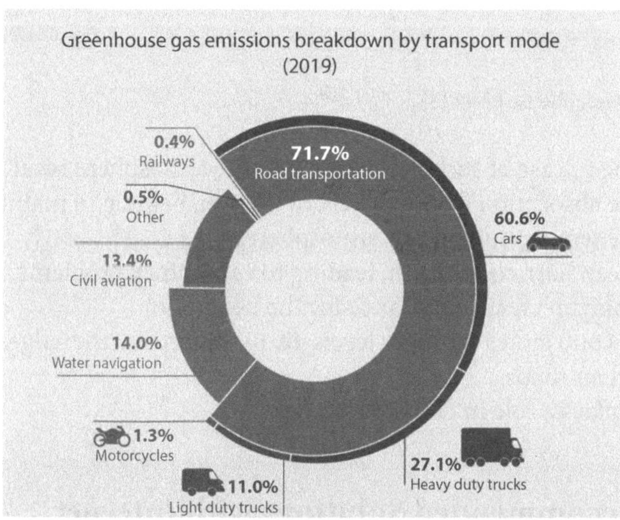

Figure 14.2 Transport emissions in the EU [2].

14.2.1 Impacts of CO_2 Emissions

Figure 14.3 illustrates the greenhouse effect in detail. Here are some of the significant impacts of CO_2 emissions given:

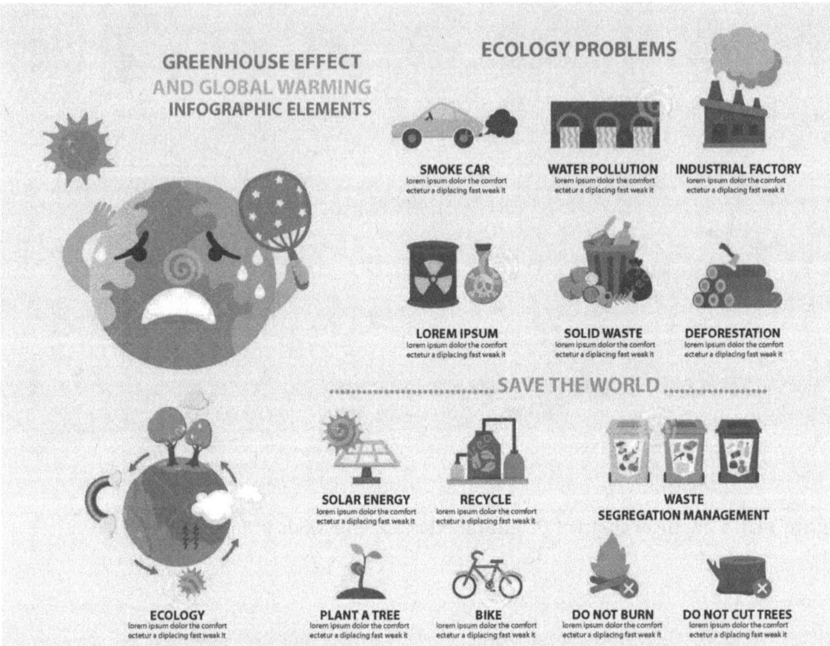

Figure 14.3 Greenhouse effect [3].

- The release of carbon dioxide into the atmosphere results in the absorption from the heat of the sun, helping to maintain the temperature in our atmosphere.
- It can harm our health, leading to respiratory problems.
- This can create a nuisance for the neighbor.
- It contributes to high levels of pollution on the edges of urban roads.
- It plays a role in climate change.

14.3 Recommended Solutions with Internet of Things

14.3.1 IoT System and CO_2 Sensors

Internet of Things (IoT) is a system consists of the data collection sensors and related technologies for data transfer, storage, processing/analysis, and display of outcomes. The main application of IoT is automated data collection. Depending on the data that we want to collect, the respective sensors can be used. CO_2 sensors are also available to detect CO_2 emissions. Below, a couple of CO_2 sensors are given in Figure 14.4.

The proposed system utilizes CO_2 sensors to evaluate the vehicle emitting the highest level of the pollution. This article delves into the low carbon initiatives of manufacturing execution systems (MESs) by studying the carbon emission flow in transmission and distribution stages. More specifically, the analysis focuses on detecting any further pollution emissions during vehicle transmission analysis. If such emissions are identified, then a warning is transmitted to the Road Transport Department (RTD).

When the vehicle's speed crosses a specific limit at the distribution level, an alert is sent to the RTD. The vehicle will stop once it gets the signal, as a result of emitting excessive carbon. Case studies involving MESs at different scales demonstrate that the suggested carbon emission flow reduces carbon emissions more effectively than existing solutions.

The IPCC emphasizes the necessity of halving global annual carbon emissions by 2050 to address global warming. This paper investigates the government's selection of carbon emissions trading systems and emission thresholds to encourage companies to adopt and implement low-carbon technologies.

Analog Electrochemical Carbon Dioxide Sensor (0-10000 ppm) [4]

Wireless CO_2 Sensor [5]

Figure 14.4 CO_2 sensors.

However, as the utilization of low-carbon technologies increases, carbon emission prices are expected to decrease. Conversely, regulations on emission pricing notably curtail economic activities in energy-intensive sectors. Additionally, the escalating price of CO_2 carries significant distributional consequences.

14.3.2 Benefits of the IoT System

There are many ways to create values from IoT system for various applications. Here, we have listed some of the important benefits that we can create from the IOT system related to environmental factors.

Some of the benefits are as follows:

- It reduces regional pollution and reduction of CO_2
- It protects the environment to mitigate climate change and safeguards the health of individuals, neighborhood livability is improved, and safety is enhanced.
- The concentration of carbon in the atmosphere will decrease gradually.
- It enhances air quality while decreasing emissions of greenhouse gases.

In addition to the above benefits, here, we have included information graphics (Figure 14.5) to clarify the significance of the built environment

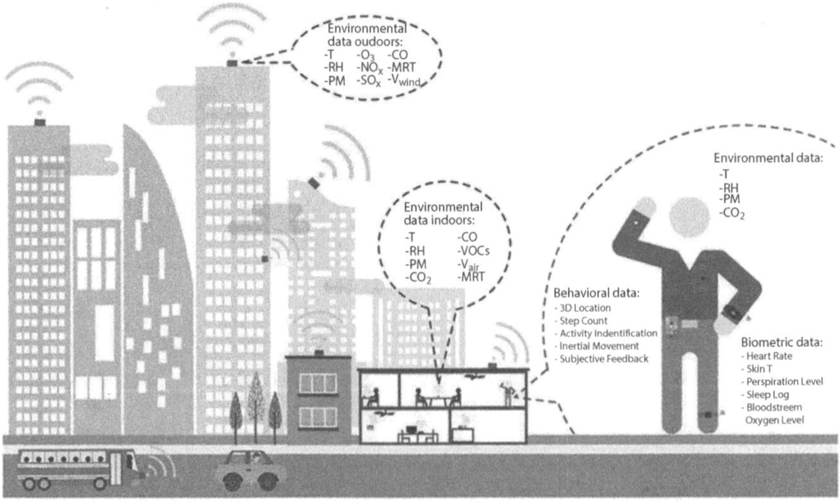

Figure 14.5 Three scales of environmental parameters [6].

in assessing air quality and thermal comfort, evaluations are carried out across building, urban, and human dimensions. These dimensions encompass changes in environmental variables, with the human dimension additionally considering biometric and behavioral data.

14.3.3 Air Quality Monitoring System (AQMS)

In 2020, Kashif Hussain and colleagues [7] showcased a real-time air quality monitoring system which use of IoT and cloud computing. The system is self-sufficient and uses solar panel and battery for power. It is linked to a cloud application through an AVR microcontroller (Atmega32) and a GSM modem (Sim900). This method is economical and adaptable, enabling the installation of approximately 50 devices in different spots like roundabouts, market squares, residential areas, and industrial zones.

The air quality monitoring system gauges the levels of CO_2, CO, O_2, SO, NO/NO_2 (NO_x), hydrocarbons, humidity, temperature, and noise with the help of a small vacuum pump (operating at 5-volt DC). This pump regulates and ensures a steady airflow through a manifold equipped with electromechanical sensors. By default, air sampling is conducted once every hour, but this frequency can be altered depending on fluctuations in air quality, making the system adaptable and energy-efficient, consequently prolonging the sensor's lifespan.

Data analytics and artificial intelligence methods will be used to analyze information gathered from the cloud application, with the aim of conducting data mining to uncover insights about locations producing substantial and detrimental environmental emissions.

The analysis is intended to help prevent accidents, focusing on Karachi, a large city in Pakistan, as it transitions to a smart city. The author proposes a design for an air quality monitoring system using IoT technology, with a focus on energy efficiency. For power, the design includes a combination of a solar panel and a battery to ensure self-sufficiency and independence.

Imran Ali Tasadduq *et al.* (2020) [8] highlight the annual pilgrimage (HAJJ) to the holy city of Mecca, where millions of Muslims use pedestrian and vehicular tunnels. To maintain acceptable air quality levels in these tunnels, open-loop air circulation systems are often employed. Nevertheless, overcrowding and congestion result in prolonged periods spent by pilgrims in the tunnels, which leads them to the harmful gases that lead to the vehicle pollutants such as volatile organic compounds such as the carbon oxides, fine particulate matter, and elevated humidity levels. Additionally, peoples and individuals in open vehicles or on motorcycles also encounter substantial exposure to harmful gases in case of accidents or ventilation system failures.

This study introduces a tailored surveillance and management setup created for municipal the authorities. It leverages the IoT to supervise air quality and pollution levels in vast underground passages. The setup incorporates forecasting techniques and reporting approaches grounded in data scrutiny. It features specialized sensors placed at specific points throughout the tunnel, alongside base station nodes. These sensors send gathered data to the cloud for storage and processing to produce reports, recommendations, queries, and alarm notifications.

The system regulates the ventilation and aeriation systems of the tunnel based on various contaminant set points. When air pollution levels become hazardous, it alerts tunnel passengers through electronic display panels.

Ghalib A. Shah *et al.* (2020) [9] discuss the challenges in designing and analyzing network security systems, particularly focusing on network traffic generation. Traditional tools for network traffic generation struggle to replicate IoT-specific protocol traffic poses a challenge because of the varied nature of IoT networks, encompassing devices, applications, and protocols. This complexity renders them ineffective for testing IoT-specific security solutions.

The article highlights two key challenges in developing an IoT-based traffic generation system: modeling IoT devices and generating normal and attack IoT traffic simultaneously. To tackle these challenges, the authors present an open-source framework to generate IoT traffic, which supports message queuing telemetry transport (MQTT) and constrained application protocol (CoAP), two widely utilized IoT application layer protocols.

With this framework, users can generate IoT use cases, alter IoT devices, and generate both legitimate and malicious IoT traffic within an actual network. The authors further illustrate the framework's practicality by simulating a real-time IoT smart home scenario, highlighting its effectiveness in devising security solutions for IoT smart homes.

Martin Nordal-Petersen and colleagues (2020) [10] investigate the present initiatives focused on enhancing the dependability of IoT gadgets, particularly those used in critical missions. The aim is to increase device resilience and fault tolerance, ensuring that, if the primary communications technology fails, then backup technology can provide a secondary channel to maintain minimal functionality without interruption. This approach can lead to quicker recovery times while preserving connectivity for end users. The primary goal is to achieve optimal performance reliability while minimizing any adverse effects on the device's battery life.

Considering the varied array of tracking applications and their unique demands, this study concentrates on employing IoT devices for asset tracking as a primary example. Specifically, the research seeks to bolster the robustness of radio connectivity and location acquisition in IoT devices dedicated to asset tracking. The study entails the creation of an IoT device integrating diverse radio communication technologies and evaluating the precision of a location service based on triangulation.

Solomon Raju Kota and colleagues (2020) [11] examine the crucial importance of the sensor in the IoT. The primary goal of IoT is to deliver continuous services to any entity, irrespective of time or place. Following the internet and information and communication technology (ICT), IoT technologies are considered as crucial elements in various fields, marking the fourth wave of transformative technologies. The research and development community anticipates that IoT will have a more profound impact on society than the Internet and ICT, ultimately enhancing the well-being of both society and industries.

The objective of this study is to inspire researchers and students to develop present model, energy-saving and more secure IoT applications by showcasing the recent progress in IoT functional components and their emerging applications. The paper delineates the structure of the IoT and offers insights into contemporary IoT designs.

To design more robust real-time IoT applications, this study emphasizes the system-level challenges and strengths of IoT. With hundreds of millions of devices exchanging data through various communication protocols,

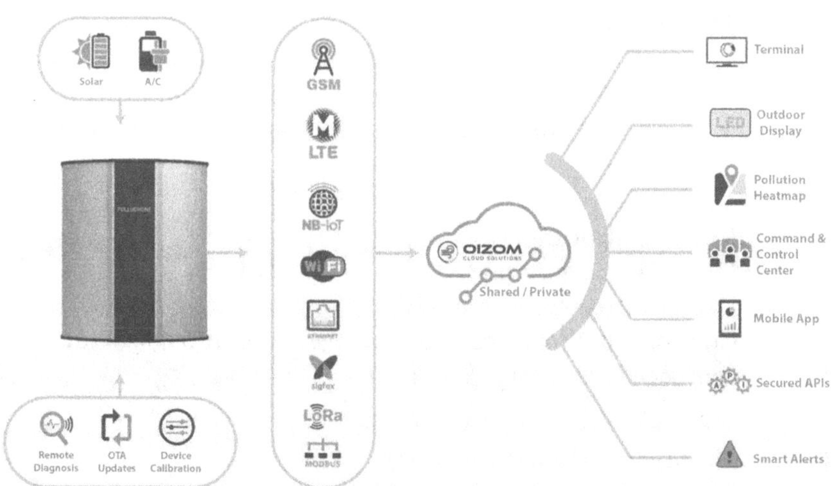

Figure 14.6 A sample of air quality monitoring system architecture [13].

Figure 14.7 Air quality monitoring system in realtime [13].

interoperability becomes a significant concern [12]. The research offers an exhaustive examination of the existing communication requirements and application layer protocols employed within the IoT. Furthermore, IoT leverages computing paradigms like Cloud, Cloudlet, Edge Computing, and Fog, which offer services such as data offloading and asset and device management.

Figure 14.6 shows an example of an air quality monitoring system architecture, and Figure 14.7 shows how this system was implemented in a real-world environment. This is a product of OIZOM [13].

14.4 ML Algorithms

Machine learning (ML) algorithms could be used to automate the proposed system. In this section, four relevant ML algorithms were evaluated. These are the following:

- K-means algorithm (KM)
- Naive Bayes algorithm (NB)
- Decision Tree Algorithm (DT)
- Control of unlimited carbon flow operations through an ML approach (CULTML)

14.4.1 K-Means Algorithm (KM)

K-means is the most commonly used method for clustering. It involves allocating data points to K clusters based on their distances from the cluster centers. This method has various applications the data mining like image segmentation, market segmentation, and anomaly detection. However, it has some restrictions like sensitivity to initial centroid placement, a predefined number of clusters, and difficulties in dealing with noise and outliers.

14.4.2 Decision Tree Algorithm (DT)

One way to conduct unsupervised learning is by using decision tree analysis. This method is suitable for regression and classification tasks and allows the creation of a predictive model with training data. Decision trees can handle both numerical and categorical data and are easy to understand and interpret but can overfit and become complex with complex datasets. When we are using the decision trees for record classification, the process starts by evaluating the root attribute's value and comparing it with the record's attribute value and then moves along the associated branch to the next node in the tree based on the outcome [14].

14.4.3 Naive Bayes Algorithm (NB)

Naive Bayes is frequently employed in various classification tasks due to its foundation in Bayes' theorem. The Naive Bayes classifier aids in constructing swift and precise ML models owing to its simplicity and effectiveness. Consequently, the categorization of characteristics is not dependent on a single approach. These methods are part of a bigger group of methods. However, practical situations usually include several X factors. When these attributes are separate, Bayes' rule can be expanded to form what is called naive Bayes. In this situation, the X factors are considered to be unrelated to each other, thus the term "naive." Naive Bayes is commonly used in natural language processing and text categorization tasks. It is straightforward, effective, and capable of handling extensive datasets. However, Naive Bayes assumes independence among features, a condition that may not always apply in practical real-world scenarios, presenting both advantages and limitations [15].

14.4.4 Controlling Carbon Unlimited Flow Operation with Machine Learning Approach (CULTML)

The e-learning methodology has been improved with some extra and new information for repeated use. The reinvention method can effectively use live data from recurring Wi-Fi devices, but staying updated on current issues can be difficult. The research aims to identify the appropriate ML approach for quickly and accurately identifying wireless devices based on topic categories and subtopics. This enables umastering queries to be automatically resent as needed. Recent studies show that CULTML has made significant progress in decreasing carbon emissions compared to other methods. By using data analytics, CULTML can improve the accuracy and efficiency of optimizing the pollution of the carbon emissions in vehicles [16].

14.5 Proposed System Architectures and Designs

The proposed system in Figure 14.8 has four major units; these are as follows:

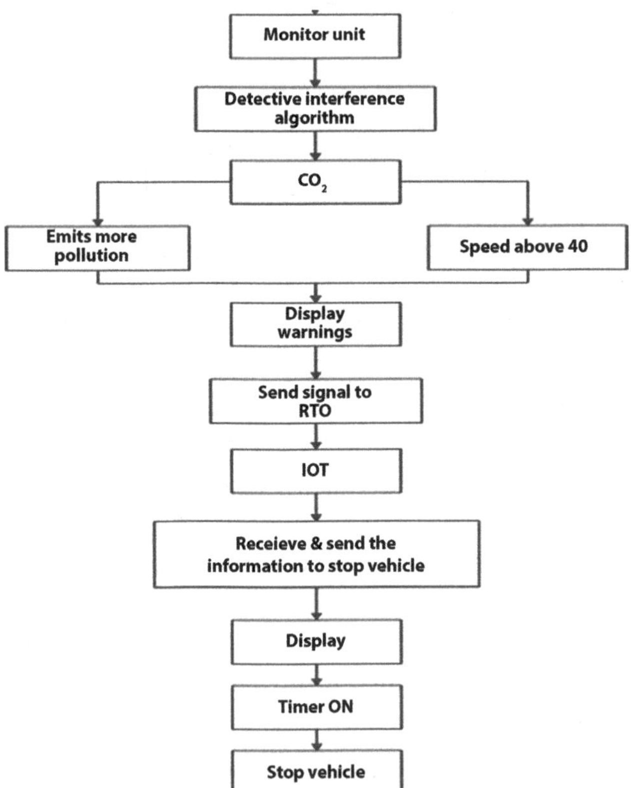

Figure 14.8 Architecture diagram.

(i) Monitoring units using detective interference algorithm
(ii) Analysis flow of CO_2
(iii) Send warning to RTO
(iv) Send signal to stop vehicle

14.5.1 Vehicular Unit

In Figure 14.9 describes the vehicular unit. A switching power supply (SMPS) is made up of a rectifier, capacitor, DK 112, and step-down transformer. These components are powered by a 230-V AC input voltage. The rectifier changes AC to pulsating 230-V DC. The switch's analog input is connected to the rectifier toward its positive and negative edges that are connected toward the capacitor. The DK112 IC converts 230-V DC to 30-V AC, whereas the step-down transformer lowers 30-V AC to 12-V AC. Whereas the rectifier turns the 12-V AC into 12-V DC, a 1000-uf ceramic capacitor is used to eliminate harmonics in the power line.

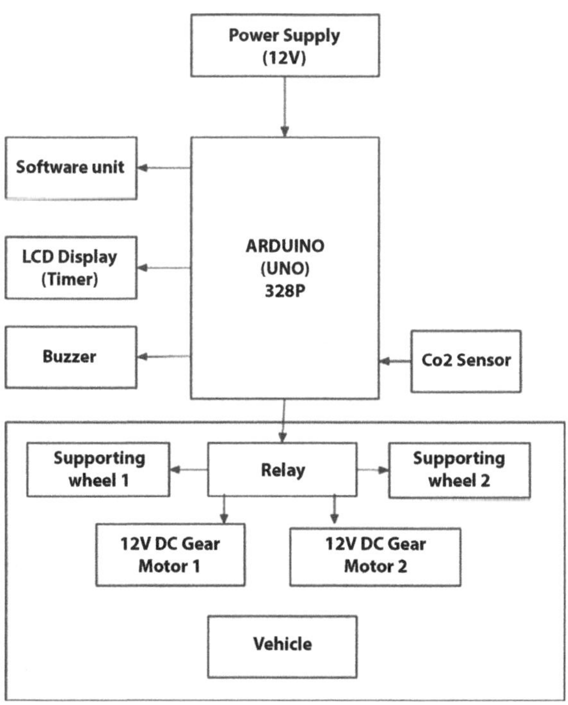

Figure 14.9 Vehicular unit.

The primary function of the Arduino Uno microcontroller is to oversee the entire system. Our main goal is to reduce CO_2 emissions and combat environmental pollution. The vehicle has a total of four wheels, with two serving as support and the other two as DC gear motor wheels. The Arduino microcontroller is connected to a relay and is used to control the car's movement. We also integrated IoT technologies into the project. A CO_2 sensor is connected to the microcontroller to monitor CO_2 levels. If high carbon emissions are detected, then warnings will be shown on the LCD screen.

14.5.2 Software Unit

In this Figure 14.10 explained the various software unit. By utilizing USB communication, the Arduino microcontroller's input output port is linked to a computer or laptop. The HyperTerminal software processes each signal, and Visual Studio (.Net) takes input from HyperTerminal and sends a signal to the NodeMCU, referred to as the IoT device, to the server.

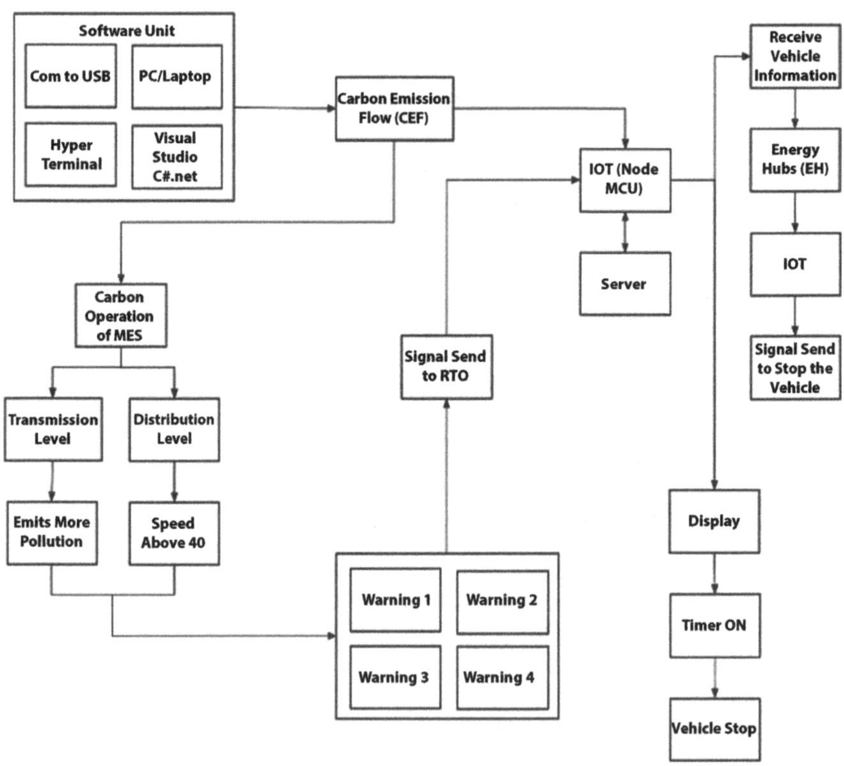

Figure 14.10 Software unit.

At the same time, the MES monitors carbon emissions during operation and has two levels of transmission and distribution. The transmission level is activated when pollution reaches a certain threshold, and the distribution level is activated when the speed exceeds 40 units. We have analyzed the carbon emission stream and issued warnings labeled as warning 1, 2, 3, 4, and 5, which are then transmitted to the RTD via the NodeMCU (microcontroller), which we refer to as the IoT device.

14.5.3 Road Transport Office (RTO) Unit

In this Figure 14.11 illustrates the road transport office unit. When the level of carbon emissions exceeds a specified threshold, a Node MCU is used to send a message to an RTO office and validate the ASP code. Once the signal is received, an RTO officer will use IoT to press a button that stops the vehicle. A relay is installed between the support wheels and connected to a 12-V DC motor. When a signal is received from the RTO unit, the controller will bring the vehicle to a halt. A buzzer and an LCD display are used to convey warnings. This paper discusses reducing CO_2 emissions in the environment.

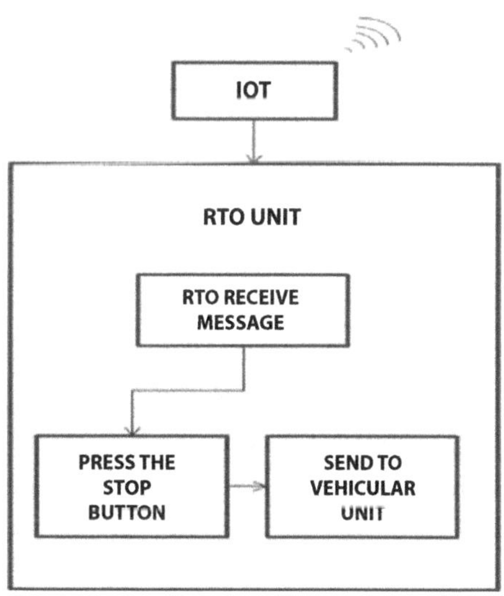

Figure 14.11 Road transport office unit.

14.6 Logical Design of the Proposed System

14.6.1 Summation Detector Using Artificial Intelligence

1. First step is to establish an objective function called f(X) I'm that X represents a group of variables that are utilized in forming an beginning population of n host nests (Xi, i = 1, 2, ..., n).
2. Proceed through a desired number of iterations or until it gets satisfied. During each iteration, use a levy flight process to randomly select a cuckoo and assess its fitness level (Fi).
3. Randomly pick one of the n nests (j) to compare with the newly chosen cuckoo.
4. If the newly selected cuckoo demonstrates better quality than the chosen nest, substitute the chosen nest with the new solution.
5. Repeat steps 2-4 until the maximum number of iterations or the stopping condition is met.
6. Discard a fraction (Pa) of the nests with the poorest quality solutions and generate new ones to replace them.
7. Observe and maintain records of the nests with high-quality solutions.
8. Assess and recognize the best solution at the present stage.
9. Continue iterating through step 2-8 until the maximum number of iterations or the stopping condition is met.
10. Carry out post-processing and visualization on the final outcomes.
11. Conclude the procedure.

14.6.2 Digit Recognition

The innovative hybrid ML method that we are using combines convolutional neural networks (CNN) and support vector machines (SVMs) to detect the carbon meter numbers in cars. The process of this hybrid model is as follows:

1. Initially, a fundamental CNN undergoes training on a handwritten numbers dataset to extract vital data from input images as features.
2. Afterward, the ultimate layer of the CNN is utilized to acquire concise image representations, known as features.

3. Subsequently, a classifier, namely, SVM, is educated using these extracted features to anticipate the category for each image.
4. Through integrating the CNN and SVM models, this fusion algorithm exploits the advantages of both. The CNN grasps crucial image data, whereas the SVM adeptly utilizes this data for predictions.

In Figure 14.12 it explains the proposed architecture of the hybrid CNN-SVM model. The CNN is a type of neural network with several fully connected layers and operates through supervised learning. It mimics the functioning of the human brain and has the ability to learn distinct local

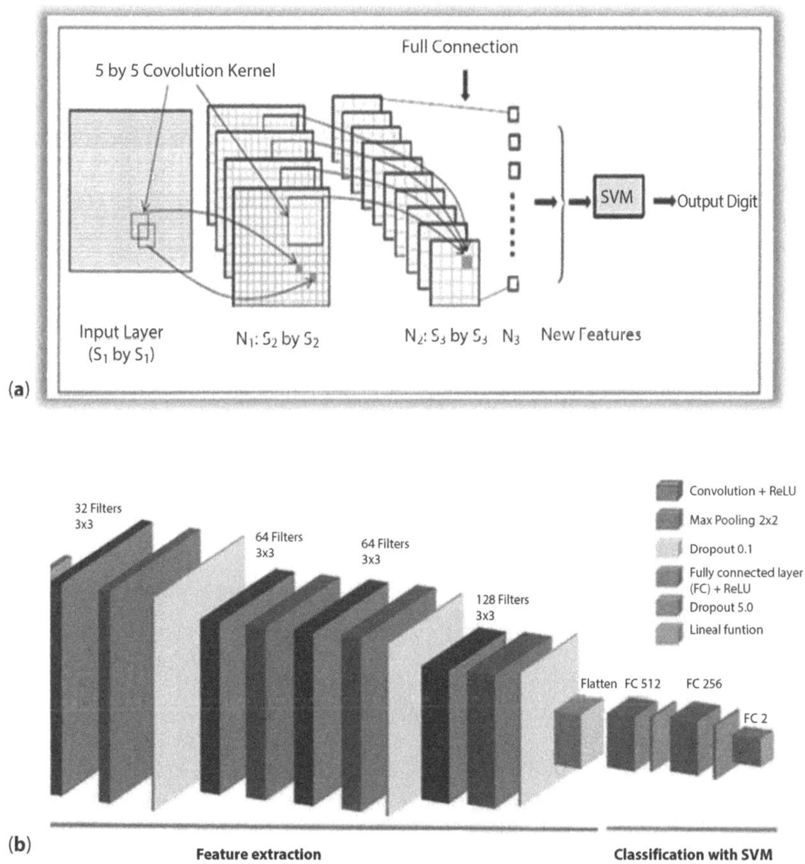

Figure 14.12 (a, b) Architecture of the proposed hybrid CNN-SVM model.

features from raw digital images. It uses a 5 × 5 filter to identify important features within the raw images.

On the other hand, the SVM is designed to separate multi-dimensional data points of distinctive classes using a hyperplane in a high-dimensional space. The SVM classifier reduces generalization errors on unseen data and is effective in binary classification. However, its shallow architecture makes it challenging for SVM to learn complex, deep functionalities.

The hybrid CNN-SVM model utilizes an SVM as a binary classifier, replacing the CNN's softmax layer. In this approach, the CNN serves as a feature extractor, with the SVM using these features for making predictions. By combining the CNN's feature extraction with the SVM's prediction accuracy, this model proves effective for handwritten digit classification.

14.7 Experimental Results

Figure 14.13 shows the throughput of the experimental results. Figure 14.14 shows the cost of the model. Figure 14.15 shows, high performance

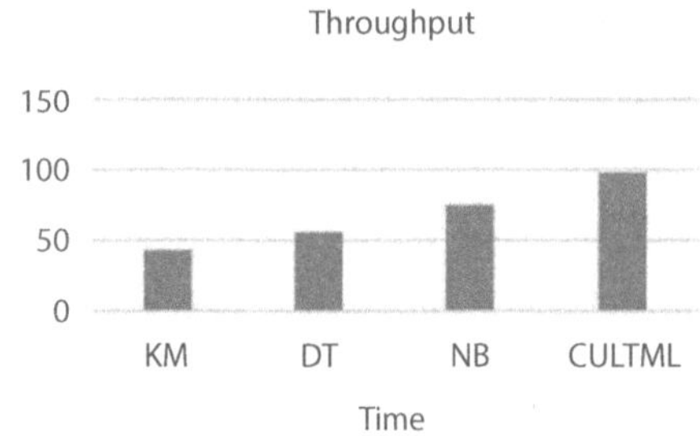

Figure 14.13 Throughput.

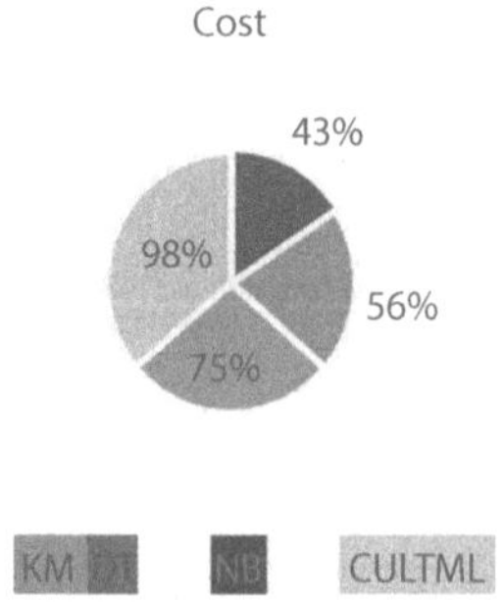

Figure 14.14 Cost.

of this method. Table 14.1(a) shows the evaluation metrics for the hybrid CNN-SVM vs. SVM model & Table 14.1(b) shows the evaluation metrics for the hybrid CNN-SVM vs SVM model.

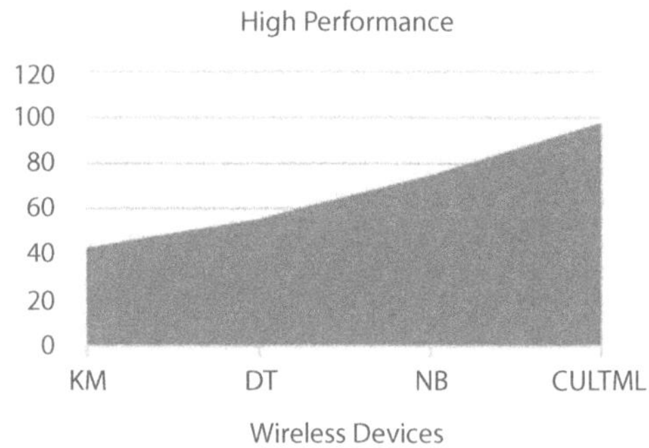

Figure 14.15 High performance.

Table 14.1(b) Evaluation metrics for the hybrid CNN-SVM vs SVM model.

	Accuracy	Recall	F1-score	Precision
Classic	95.67%	95.66%	95.66%	95.66%
Hybrid	96.20%	96.20%	96.20%	96.20%

Table 14.1(a) Evaluation metrics for the hybrid CNN-SVM vs. SVM model.

	Parameters			Percentage accuracy (SVM)		Percentage accuracy	
S. no.	Gamma	Degree	Decision function	Training	Testing	Training	Testing
1	1	3	One Vs One	97.80	97.52	98.80	98.82
2	1	3	One Vs One	97.38	97.74	98.48	98.74
3	1	5	One Vs One	96.18	96.37	97.38	97.39
4	0.1	3	One Vs One	97.95	97.85	98.95	98.95
5	0.1	3	One Vs One	98.93	97.84	98.93	98.84
6	0.1	5	One Vs One	98.35	97.68	99.28	98.88

14.8 Physical Design of the Proposed System

The physical design of the given system is shown above in Figure 14.16 (a) and Figure 14.16 (b) with all interactions of hardware connections.

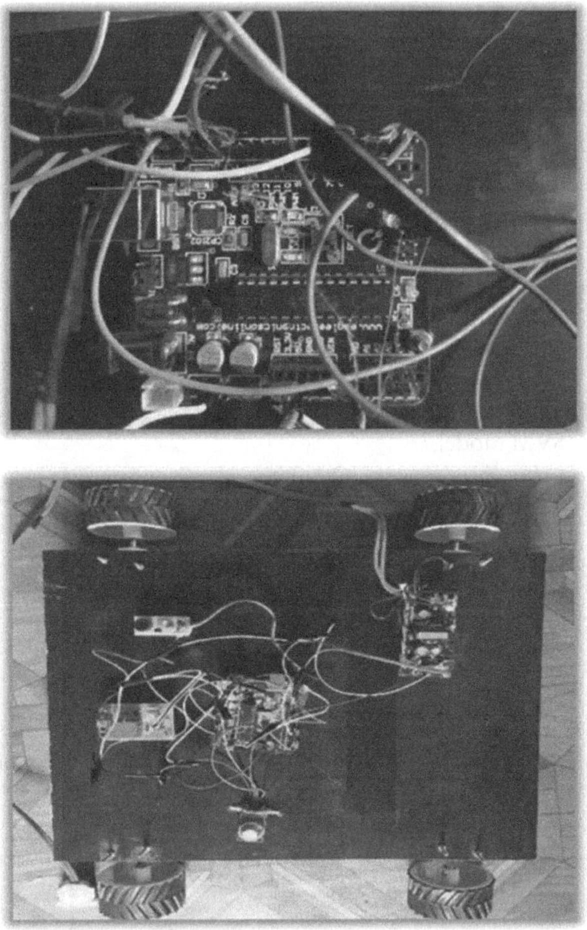

(a) (b)

Figure 14.16 (a, b) Physical design view.

14.9 Conclusion

In this chapter, CO_2 emissions from vehicles have been discussed. An IoT-based system was designed and developed. Thus, the said objectives of supporting the environment and the government to monitor CO_2 emissions have been achieved.

The CO_2 sensor identifies the car with the highest pollution emissions. This section evaluates the low-carbon performance of the MES by examining carbon emission flows in transportation and distribution (CEF). It checks the car for any additional emissions and notifies the Direction des Transports Routiers (RTD) if any are found. An alert is sent to the RTD if the vehicle exceeds the speed limit during distribution, and the vehicle is halted to prevent unnecessary emissions.

Case studies illustrate how the suggested carbon emission flow effectively reduces emissions in comparison to current solutions. The carbon emission flow is incorporated to minimize emissions. The CEF model evaluates carbon emissions from different energy systems and resolves conjunction oscillation with a bisection-based method.

Based on case studies involving two systems, the proposed strategy can effectively support the low-carbon operation of MES. By implementing carbon reduction targets, greater use of low-carbon energy sources can help decrease overall carbon emissions.

In the future, there will be a reduction in manpower, as well as a decrease in the frequency of communications sent to RTD agents and car owners. This will help individuals reduce pollutants in the air. For calculating CO_2 emissions from vehicles, a model for estimating CO_2 emissions is employed. The simulation findings show that the suggested method can efficiently decrease vehicle CO_2 emissions in contrast to other control techniques. There are intentions to include the gas compression gas usage in a broader simulation of the natural gas network. However, implementing the three-variable non-separable gas consumption equation for compressors using tetrahedral triangulations would necessitate additional binary variables and could potentially render the resulting problem unsolvable.

References

1. Shiraki, H., Matsumoto, K., Shigetomi, Y., Ehara, T., Ochi, Y., Ogawa, Y., Factors affecting CO_2 emissions from private automobiles in Japan. *Impact Vehicle Occupancy Appl. Energy*, 259, 114196, 2020. ISSN 0306-2619, https://doi.org/10.1016/j.apenergy.2019.114196.

2. Claros, G.E. and Pape, M., Transport CO_2 emissions in focus, EPRS. *Eur. Parliament*, 2020, Journal 2015.
3. Greenhouse Effect And Global Warming Infographics, Vector Stock Vector - Illustration of industrial, environment: 69784987. (n.d.), Www.dreamstime.com. https://www.dreamstime.com/stock-illustration-greenhouse-effect-global-warming-infographics-vector-illustration-image69784987.
4. Gravity: Analog CO_2 Gas Sensor for Arduino (MG-811 Sensor) - DFRobot.com. (n.d.), https://www.dfrobot.com/product-1023.html.
5. Wireless CO_2 Sensor PS-3208. (n.d.). PASCO Scientific, https://www.pasco.com/products/sensors/wireless/ps-3208.
6. Pantelic, J., Nazarian, N., *et al.*, Transformational IoT sensing for air pollution and thermal exposures, doi.org/10.3389.
7. Hussain, AI.M., Aleem, S., Karim, A., Hai, M., Hussain, K., *et al.*, Design of Low Cost, Energy Efficient, IoT Enabled, Air Quality Monitoring System with Cloud Based Data Logging, Analytics, 2020.
8. Murad, M., Yousuf Irfan Zia, M., Tasadduq, I.A., *et al.*, Monitoring Pollution and Air Quality of Pedestrian and Automotive Tunnels in the City of Makkah, 2020.
9. Ghazanfar, S., Hussain, F., Ur Rehman, A., Fayyaz, U.U., Shahzad, F., Shah, G.A., *et al.*, IoT-Flock: An Open-source Framework for IoT Traffic Generation, 2020.
10. Ballal, K.D., Dittmann, L., Ruepp, S., Nordal Petersen, M., *et al.*, IoT Devices Reliability Study: Multi-RAT Communication, 2020.
11. Swamy, S.N., Raju Kota, S., *et al.*, An Empirical Study on System Level Aspects of Internet of Things (IoT), 2020.
12. Thibault, L., Pognant-Gros, P., *et al.*, Real-Time Air Pollution Exposure and Vehicle Emissions Estimation Using IoT,GNSS Measurements and Web-Based Simulation Models, 2018.
13. https://oizom.com/product/polludrone-air-pollution-monitoring.
14. IEA, Fuel Consumption of Cars and Vans, 2020, June, Retrieved from https://www.iea.org/reports/fuel-consumption-of-cars-and-vans.
15. Erbach, G., CO_2 emission from cars facts, European Parliamentary Research Service, 2023.
16. Amin, A.B., Patel, H.P., *et al.*, IOT Based Vehicle Anti-Collision And Pollution Control System, 2019.

15

Enhancing Home Security through IoT Innovation: Recommendations for Biometric Door Lock System to Deter Break-Ins

Muhammad Ehsan Rana[1*], Kamalanathan Shanmugam[1], Lim Enya[1] and Hrudaya Kumar Tripathy[2]

[1]Asia Pacific University of Technology and Innovation, Technology Park Malaysia, Bukit Jalil, Kuala Lumpur, Malaysia
[2]School of Computer Engineering, Kalinga Institute of Industrial Technology, Deemed to be University, Bhubaneswar, Odisha, India

Abstract
Home security has consistently occupied a vital role in Malaysia due to the recurring instances of residential break-ins. The prevalence of these incidents has led to a heightened awareness among Malaysians regarding the vulnerability of their homes, prompting the adoption of diverse strategies to reinforce security measures. Among the conventional methods embraced are the installation of alarm systems and the deployment of closed-circuit television surveillance. However, a particularly noteworthy advancement in this domain is the introduction of biometrically operated door locks, which offer the potential to enhance residential security and mitigate the risks of break-ins substantially. In this chapter, extensive research has been conducted to comprehensively investigate the gravity of the issue and underscore the exigency of implementing such a progressive security solution. Furthermore, a meticulous review of existing systems has been undertaken to foster a deeper understanding of the current landscape. The research culminates in incisive deliberations on avenues for refining and augmenting the biometric door lock system, representing a significant step forward in fortifying residential security paradigms.

**Corresponding author*: muhd_ehsanrana@apu.edu.my

Subhasis Dash, Manas Ranjan Lenka, S. Balamurugan, Ambika Prasad Tripathy and Amarendra Mohanty (eds.) Sustainable Resource Management in Next-Generation Computational Constrained Networks, (359–392) © 2025 Scrivener Publishing LLC

***Keywords*:** Smart home security, biometric door locks, residential break-ins, biometric technology, machine learning

15.1 Introduction

The term "ubiquitous computing" was coined by Mark Weiser back in 1991. This concept revolves around the idea of connecting small devices wirelessly, enabling them to gather data from their surroundings and provide valuable information as output [1]. This notion closely aligns with concepts like pervasive computing, ambient intelligence, and the Internet of Things (IoT) [1]. Even though many might not realize it, ubiquitous computing is all around us. Instances of its application include retail, industrial settings, logistics, personal identification, and healthcare [1]. In the contemporary context, home security has emerged as a pressing concern in Malaysia. According to data from the Department of Statistics Malaysia, there were a staggering 16,497 reported cases of house break-ins in 2019 alone [2]. This figure is alarmingly high, underscoring the need for Malaysians to remain vigilant and take effective measures to safeguard their residences.

The emergence of biometric technology has ushered in a paradigm shift with far-reaching implications, particularly within the realm of security. In its essence, biometrics revolves around the identification of individuals through their distinctive physical traits, encompassing elements like fingerprints, facial features, and ocular attributes [3]. Through the strategic integration of biometric authentication within a home security system, harmonized with the scope of ubiquitous computing, a compelling and comprehensive solution materializes. This integrated approach possesses the inherent potential to strengthen the safeguarding of residential spaces. By leveraging biometric characteristics, this technology adds an extra layer of defense. Furthermore, its incorporation within the framework of ubiquitous computing, where interconnected devices synergize to facilitate seamless data exchange, amplifies its efficacy. The blend of these concepts provides a dynamic safeguarding mechanism to mitigate the vulnerability of homes to unlawful break-ins. This research proposes a design of a smart home door lock system using biometrics technology to enhance home security and reduce house break-ins by providing convenient and secure access control through the integration of fingerprint and facial recognition. This will improve the quality of life for users by making it easier and safer to access their homes.

The study of biometric door locks resonates with sustainable resource management in IoT by potentially curbing physical resource demands, such as keys, and facilitating automation for energy conservation. The following points outline the pivotal considerations for this research concerning sustainable resource management:

- Biometric door locks constitute integral components of smart home systems, operating within the IoT framework. They interface with networks, gather data (such as fingerprint scans), and interact with other devices through avenues like smartphone applications. Consequently, the focus lies on optimizing these devices' network operations to minimize their energy footprint.
- Investigating the utilization of low-power communication protocols and energy-efficient components represents a promising avenue in door lock research.
- Biometric door locks obviate the necessity for physical keys, which are prone to loss or misplacement, necessitating replacements and additional resource consumption for manufacturing and distribution.
- Exploring integration with smart home systems capable of automating actions based on user presence represents another avenue of inquiry. This integration could encompass actions such as dimming lights or deactivating appliances during periods of vacancy, thereby fostering reduced energy consumption.

The research presented in this chapter tackles the critical need for improved home security. It delves into the seriousness of break-ins and explores biometric door locks as a potential solution. The researchers conducted a comprehensive analysis of the problem, existing lock systems, and potential areas for improvement. This research aims to provide valuable insights for developing and implementing secure biometric door locks, ultimately strengthening home security measures in Malaysia.

15.2 Literature Review

Malaysia is witnessing increasing concerns about property crime, particularly home break-ins, which are common for landed homes lacking proper security measures. Gated and guarded communities (GGCs) have gained popularity in response to these challenges, offering more privacy, security, and favorable locations. Homeowners are adopting security measures like security cameras and alarms, but advanced technologies like biometrics offer a more comprehensive solution. Biometrics involves recognizing and validating individual identity based on physical and behavioral traits. Continuous advancements refine biometric accuracy and applicability, making it a valuable tool for security and authentication. Biometrics integration in smart homes offers secure entryways, using physiological traits like fingerprints and behavioral traits like gait recognition. This enhances security and overall quality of life. This section provides a detailed account of these topics and compares two existing smart door lock systems in terms of their features and effectiveness.

15.2.1 Home Security Concerns in Malaysia

In Malaysia, the increasing concern about property crime creates a sense of worry for the population. The distressing issue of home break-ins has unfortunately become a common occurrence for Malaysians. This worry is especially strong for landed homes, which often lack proper security measures, making them vulnerable to break-ins. The vulnerability of such homes to unauthorized entries creates a feeling of heightened unease. In the current landscape, an interesting trend has appeared in the construction of residential areas across Malaysia—the rise of "gated" communities. These housing developments involve homes being enclosed within protected areas, guarded by security personnel. The introduction of this "gated and guarded community" (GGC) concept is a direct response to the challenge of break-ins [4]. A survey on this topic highlights Malaysians' preference for GGC living, driven by the promise of more privacy, better security, and favorable locations [4]. The importance placed on these aspects shows how security concerns greatly influence housing decisions.

In parallel with the growing popularity of GGCs, homeowners are actively seeking ways to secure their homes. Steps like installing security cameras (closed-circuit television) and alarm systems are among the strategies chosen. However, it is interesting to note that, despite their common use, these methods are not the most favored options for achieving strong home security [5]. This contradiction underscores the delicate balance homeowners seek between convenience and effectiveness. Amidst these considerations, the integration of advanced technologies such as biometrics within the framework of ubiquitous computing becomes crucial. The potential to combine the advantages of GGCs, traditional security practices, and modern authentication methods offers a comprehensive approach to addressing the various aspects of the home security challenge in Malaysia. Through this combination, a stronger, multifaceted, and effective strategy emerges to tackle the complex dimensions of the home security issue.

15.2.2 Introduction to Biometric Solutions

The notion of biometrics can be distilled as a technique to recognize and validate an individual's identity based on their physical and behavioral attributes. Physical traits encompass characteristics like fingerprints, facial features, iris patterns, electrocardiogram readings, and finger veins. Conversely, behavioral traits encompass aspects such as voice patterns, signatures, typing styles, and walking mannerisms. However, inquisitiveness has arisen surrounding the operational mechanisms of biometrics and the reliability of the authentication process. This authentication journey is split into two core phases: enrollment and verification. During the enrollment phase, a person's biometric data is gathered and temporarily stored within a database. Subsequently, in the verification phase, this data is cross-referenced with pre-existing records in the database. The system then identifies parallels between the two datasets to confirm the person's identity [3]. Figure 15.1 details the diverse behavioral and physiological characteristics employed in biometric systems.

Errors within the verification phase can be classified as either a false match (false positive) or a false rejection (false negative). A false match arises when the system inaccurately verifies an individual. Conversely, a

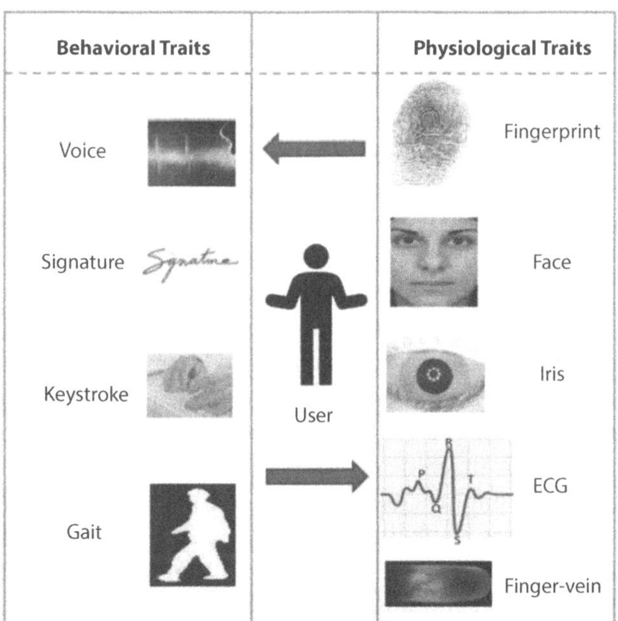

Figure 15.1 Example of behavioral and physiological traits [3].

false rejection transpires when the system fails to correctly recognize the authentic person [6]. These potential errors underline the intricate nature of biometric systems. While the technology is incredibly advanced, it is not devoid of challenges. Factors such as variations in physiological traits due to factors like lighting conditions or age can occasionally lead to false positives or negatives. Similarly, the system's performance may vary with the type of biometric being used. For instance, fingerprint recognition might experience differing accuracy levels compared to voice recognition.

Addressing these challenges necessitates continuous refinement of biometric algorithms and the integration of sophisticated techniques. Researchers and engineers work tirelessly to enhance the accuracy of these systems, making them more reliable and less susceptible to errors. Over time, the potential for errors decreases as technology advances and adapts to various real-world scenarios. In essence, while biometrics represent a remarkable leap forward in identity authentication, they are not devoid of limitations. Nevertheless, ongoing advancements continue to refine their accuracy and applicability, ensuring that biometrics remain a valuable tool in security and authentication systems across a myriad of contexts.

15.2.3 Enhancing Biometrics with Machine Learning

Biometrics frequently incorporates the power of machine learning to refine accuracy and bolster security. This collaboration gives rise to four main approaches: supervised, unsupervised, semi-supervised, and reinforcement learning. Notably, the supervised learning method stands out as the most dependable and favored algorithm [7].

Supervised learning involves teaching the machine using labeled data. It learns from this data, making predictions or decisions based on the patterns it identifies. This method's reliability is attributed to the fact that it learns from known examples, continuously refining its accuracy over time. It is like a teacher guiding the machine through a set of examples to recognize various traits accurately. Unsupervised learning, on the other hand, involves machine learning from unlabeled data. It attempts to uncover patterns and relationships in the data without explicit guidance. This method is akin to the machine exploring the data on its own, seeking hidden structures or groupings. Semi-supervised learning is a blend of both these methods. It uses a small amount of labeled data along with a more extensive pool of unlabeled data. This hybrid approach leverages the benefits of both supervised and unsupervised learning to achieve more robust outcomes. Lastly, reinforcement learning involves machine learning from the feedback it receives based on its actions. It makes decisions through trial and error, to maximize rewards and minimize penalties. This method is similar to a student learning by receiving feedback from a teacher after attempting different approaches to solve a problem.

In the realm of biometrics, these machine learning approaches elevate the technology's accuracy and efficiency. Supervised learning, with its structured guidance, tends to produce consistent and reliable results. By leveraging these advanced algorithms, biometrics not only enhances security measures but also evolves to handle the intricacies of identifying and authenticating individuals in increasingly sophisticated ways. This fusion of biometrics and machine learning exemplifies how technology continues to advance, positively impacting aspects of security and identification.

15.2.4 Biometrics in the Realm of Smart Home Security

Within the vast realm of smart homes, a symphony of technologies, including ubiquitous computing, artificial intelligence (AI), and the IoT, intertwines to orchestrate seamless living experiences [8]. Encompassing automation, security enhancements, energy efficiency, and the facilitation of convenience, smart homes epitomize the fusion of modern innovation with daily living. One instrumental facet of this orchestration involves the integration of biometric technologies, which significantly elevate the security landscape within smart homes [8].

A. Secure Entryway: Imagine a smart home that not only welcomes its occupants with open arms but also validates their identity through cutting-edge biometric systems. At the forefront of this application lies the installation of a biometric system at the home's entrance, creating a formidable barrier against unauthorized access. This technology is akin to a digital bouncer, ensuring only authorized individuals gain entry.
B. The Power of Physiological Traits: Incorporating the physiological traits of residents, such as fingerprints, facial features, or even eye patterns, this biometric system effectively differentiates between residents and potential intruders. When a resident approaches the front door, the biometric system scans their chosen physiological trait. This trait acts as a unique key, unlocking access to the home for legitimate residents. The process not only boosts security but also encapsulates convenience, eliminating the need for traditional keys.
C. Behavior as an Identifier: Delving further into the tapestry of biometric possibilities, smart homes can also harness

behavioral traits as identifiers. Gait recognition, a sophisticated technique that identifies individuals based on their distinctive walking patterns, adds layer of security. This application becomes especially valuable in recognizing unfamiliar or irregular movements around the home. Like a digital guardian, the smart home alerts residents when an anomalous gait is detected, potentially indicating the presence of an intruder.

D. Elevating Home Security: The integration of biometrics within smart homes resonates beyond mere security enhancement; it catalyzes an overall elevation of the quality of life for residents [9]. This symbiotic relationship between technology and lifestyle revolves around the empowerment of users through advanced control mechanisms [9]. By interfacing with the smart home's systems, residents can seamlessly manage door locks and alarm systems, thereby taking active charge of their home's security [9].
E. A Shield Against Intrusion: In the unfortunate event of a break-in, smart homes equipped with biometric security systems promptly relay notifications to residents. This instant awareness arms homeowners with the knowledge they need to respond effectively, whether by alerting authorities or taking appropriate measures themselves. This direct and immediate interaction between residents and their home's security systems exemplifies the marriage of technology with a proactive defense.
F. Technological Confluence: The foundation for these advancements lies in extensive research and experimentation within the domain of smart homes. Engineers and innovators harness various technologies such as wireless mesh networks, Arduino microcontrollers, Bluetooth communication, and microchips to create these integrated living environments [9]. The synergistic interplay of these components not only fortifies security but also shapes the very fabric of modern living, fostering an environment that accommodates both safety and convenience.

In conclusion, the integration of biometrics within the fabric of smart homes exemplifies the harmonious blend of technology and everyday living. This integration marks a pivotal stride forward in security by melding physiological and behavioral traits to craft impenetrable shields against unauthorized access. Moreover, it heralds a new era of interactivity, where homeowners wield the reins of security and engagement with their abodes. As these technologies continue to evolve, the smart home landscape morphs into a realm that seamlessly incorporates the innovative marvels of the digital age into the sanctity of domestic life.

15.2.5 Review of Existing Commercial Systems

This section critically examines and contrasts two similar commercial systems, aiming to provide a comprehensive overview of their functionalities, advantages, limitations, and other relevant attributes.

15.2.5.1 Samsung Smart Door Lock

The DR 708 (Figure 15.2) represents an innovative smart door lock leveraging cutting-edge biometric technology, featuring a fingerprint sensor

Figure 15.2 Samsung DR 708 [10].

crafted by Samsung [10]. Samsung, a prominent digital technology provider hailing from South Korea, has a storied history dating back to its establishment in 1969. Over the years, the company has been at the forefront of delivering a diverse array of digital products catering to consumer needs, including smartphones, televisions, home appliances, and beyond [11]. Notably, Samsung extends its expertise to encompass a dedicated product line of smart door locks, exemplified by the DR 708. In addition to its biometric capabilities, this intelligent lock offers multifaceted access options, including smartphone app integration, NFC, password entry, and traditional physical keys [12].

The smartphone application, readily available for download from the Google Play Store, serves as a centralized control hub. From within the app, users gain real-time insights into the door's status, whether locked or unlocked, and access a comprehensive log detailing the comings and goings of household occupants. Furthermore, the application empowers users with proactive notifications, such as alerts when a family member arrives home. Additionally, users have the convenience of generating one-time passwords for visitor access, streamlining entry for guests while maintaining security [12]. Figure 15.3 illustrates Samsung SmartThings App on Google Play Store, a mobile application for controlling and monitoring Samsung smart door locks.

Figure 15.3 Samsung smart door lock app on Google Play Store [13].

Besides that, Samsung prioritizes security, implementing a robust suite of protective measures. Recognizing the susceptibility of smart systems to potential attacks and addressing privacy concerns, Samsung introduces a feature to wipe all data in the event of a lost smartphone. Furthermore, the company employs a trifecta of advanced technologies to safeguard user data, encompassing white-box cryptography, secure encapsulation for the application layer, and app hardening. Enhancing safety within the home, the system incorporates a high-temperature alarm capable of detecting abnormal temperatures and promptly notifying users while automatically unlocking the door for swift egress, particularly crucial in emergency scenarios such as fires. Additionally, a built-in intrusion detection alarm serves as a deterrent against forced entry attempts, alerting users to potential security breaches such as burglary [12].

15.2.5.2 Philips EasyKey

Philips, founded in The Netherlands by the visionary duo of Frederik and Gerard in 1891 [14], embarked on its illustrious journey as a light bulb manufacturer. Over the decades, the company has metamorphosed into a renowned provider of cutting-edge digital and electrical home appliances, boasting a diverse portfolio spanning sound and vision products, personal care essentials, household items, health solutions, automotive accessories, and beyond [14]. Notably, Philips has made significant strides in the realm of smart security, exemplified by its line of innovative products.

At the forefront of Philips' smart security offerings stands the Philips DDL702-8HWS (Figure 15.4), a groundbreaking facial recognition smart lock that epitomizes the integration of biometric technology [15]. In addition to its facial recognition prowess, this intelligent lock incorporates a fingerprint sensor, offering consumers versatile alternatives for unlocking their doors. Utilizing a dual camera system, the Philips smart door lock employs advanced 3D data collection technology to accurately discern faces, even in scenarios where users may wear makeup [15]. Equipped with ultrasonic sensors, the lock intelligently detects user proximity, automatically activating the facial recognition sensor from its dormant state for swift and seamless authentication [15].

Philips complements its hardware with a user-friendly mobile application, easily accessible for download from the Google Play Store (Figure 15.5) [16]. This intuitive application serves as a gateway for users to connect with the smart lock via Wi-Fi, providing functionalities such as access logging and PIN code management. Users can effortlessly generate temporary PINs for visitors, streamlining entry procedures with convenience [15].

Figure 15.4 Philips DDL702-8HWS [15].

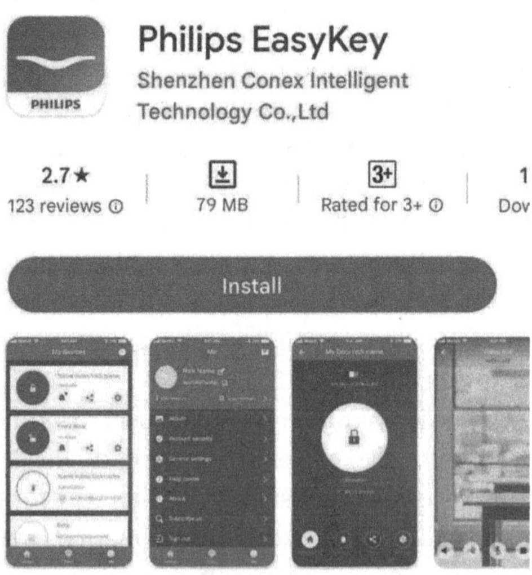

Figure 15.5 Philips EasyKey app on Google Play Store [16].

Furthermore, Philips prioritizes security with a suite of robust features integrated into its smart door lock. Users have the option for dual verification, necessitating the use of two authentication methods for door access—a combination of facial recognition, fingerprint sensing, and PIN code entry [15]. Moreover, the system is fortified with an alarm system that promptly alerts users to any detected anomalies, ensuring proactive security measures. Additionally, Philips employs a unique pin tumbler design for the physical lock, augmenting resistance against sophisticated lock-picking techniques employed by potential intruders [15].

15.2.5.3 Comparison of Systems

Table 15.1 summarizes the key features of the Samsung DR-708 and Philips DDL702-SHWS smart door locks in terms of the features they offer.

Table 15.1 Comparison between Samsung smart door lock and Philips EasyKey.

Features	Samsung smart door lock	Philips EasyKey
Authentication mechanisms	Five mechanisms available: Fingerprint, mobile app, password, NFC, and physical key	Four mechanisms available: Fingerprint, facial recognition, PIN, and physical key
Biometric options	Fingerprint	Fingerprint, Facial Recognition
Convenience for busy hands	No (requires fingerprint scan)	Yes (facial recognition)
Mobile application	Available	Available
Temporary password setting	Available	Available
Dual verification	Not available	Available
Alarm	Available	Available
Security features	Improved user data security and alarm for high-temperature	Unique pin tumbler design

Both the Samsung DR 708 and Philips DDL702-8HWS smart door locks offer multiple authentication methods catering to users' diverse needs. Samsung provides five authentication options including a mobile app, fingerprint, NFC, password, and physical key, whereas Philips offers four methods comprising facial recognition, fingerprint, PIN code, and physical key. While both locks boast mobile applications downloadable from the respective app stores, allowing users to manage access logs, and user data, and create temporary passwords, Philips' door lock distinguishes itself with dual verification capability. This dual authentication process heightens security by requiring users to pass through two authentication steps, such as PIN entry followed by fingerprint scanning. In contrast, Samsung's offering lacks this additional layer of security.

Furthermore, both locks feature an alarm system to detect abnormal activities and notify users accordingly. However, Samsung's lock goes the extra mile with enhanced user data security measures and a high-temperature alarm function, automatically unlocking the door in case of a fire emergency. Conversely, Philips' lock stands out with its unique pin tumbler design, fortifying the physical keyhole against forced entry attempts, thus enhancing overall security.

Both offer fingerprint scanning and traditional key access, but Samsung adds NFC for a total of five methods. Philips counters with facial recognition for a convenient hands-free approach, especially useful when carrying groceries. If you prioritize versatility, then Samsung might be the better choice. However, for those who value ease of use, Philips' facial recognition might be more suitable. While the Philips DDL702-SHWS might lack some authentication options compared to Samsung, it compensates with a robust physical security feature. Its keyhole boasts a specially designed pin tumbler mechanism that hinders forceful break-ins. This unique design adds an extra layer of defense against unauthorized entry, potentially deterring burglars and giving you peace of mind. Consider factors like price, smart home compatibility, and design aesthetics to make the best decision for your smart home.

15.3 Recommendations for the Implementation of the Proposed Biometric Door Lock System

The proposed implementation of a smart home door lock system leveraging biometric technology presents a robust solution to augment home security standards in contrast to conventional methodologies. The core aspiration of this proposed system is to target the challenges identified within the literature review section effectively. Additionally, the system offers an avenue for enhanced user convenience, thereby elevating the overall quality of their residential experience. By harnessing the recommended tools, the researchers portray an innovative and robust security solution that not only improves prevailing concerns but also increases user convenience, ultimately improving their residential security.

15.3.1 Software Requirements

The selection of appropriate software components plays a pivotal role in the successful realization of the proposed system. Table 15.2 provides a recommended list of software tools to facilitate the construction of the system. The Interactive Development Environment (IDE) that emerges as the developer's choice is the Arduino IDE. This selection is rooted in the IDE's compatibility and seamless integration with the microcontroller utilized in the system. Notably, the Arduino IDE furnishes the requisite support to build, compile, and debug the program, with the added advantage of easy program transfer to the microcontroller through a standard USB cable connection.

The development process centers on the strategic integration of libraries, required to ensure the appropriate functioning of distinct components. In this context, two key libraries are recommended. The Adafruit_fingerprint library assumes high importance as it extends support to the fingerprint scanner module, enabling its optimal operation within the system framework. Similarly, the HUSKYLENS library is endorsed as it underpins the camera module's functionality for facial recognition processes. In tandem with the software elements, the operating system that underpins the development environment requires careful consideration. Windows 11, in its 64-bit iteration, emerges as the recommended operating system for the computer that orchestrates the system development. The selection is rooted in the compatibility of this operating system with the tools and libraries harnessed for the system's construction, thereby fostering a seamless and efficient developmental workflow.

Table 15.2 Software requirements for the proposed system.

Interactive development environment (IDE)	**Arduino IDE**
Libraries	Adafruit_fingerprint.h, HUSKYLENS.h
Operating system	Windows 11 (64-bit)

15.3.2 Key Hardware Requirements

To build the proposed smart door lock system, the following hardware components are selected.

15.3.2.1 Arduino Nano

This work leverages the Arduino Nano (as seen in Figure 15.6) as a microcontroller due to its ideal size for discreet door integration. Unlike bulkier boards, the Nano's compact form minimizes space constraints when mounted on the door. Beyond its size advantage, the Nano offers familiarity for hobbyists as it shares functionalities with the popular Arduino Uno, making it a versatile choice for various projects [17]. Additionally,

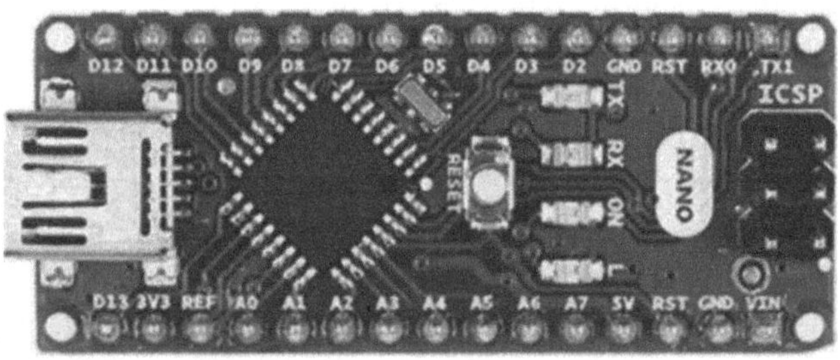

Figure 15.6 Arduino Nano [17].

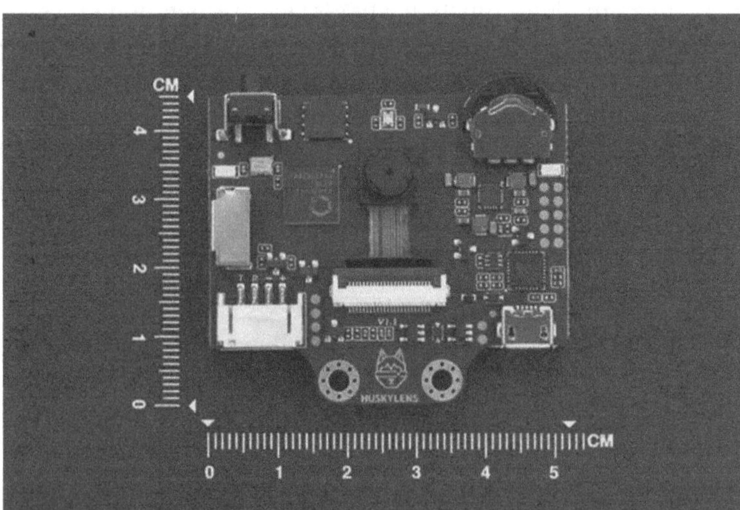

Figure 15.7 DFRobot HuskeyLens [18].

its compact design translates to a cost-effective option compared to other microcontrollers on the market.

15.3.2.2 DFRobot HuskyLens

The DFRobot HuskyLens (Figure 15.7) stands out as a perfect choice for the face scanner in this smart door lock system due to its versatility and user-friendly features. This AI vision camera boasts an impressive array of built-in functions straight out of the box, including face recognition, object recognition, line tracking, color recognition, and even QR code recognition [18]. This eliminates the need for complex programming or custom algorithms. Additionally, the HuskyLens seamlessly integrates with the Arduino Nano used in the system, ensuring compatibility. But that is not all! The HuskyLens's machine learning capabilities [18] allow it to continuously learn and improve its accuracy over time, making it an ideal long-term solution for the smart door lock system.

15.3.2.3 DFRobot UART Fingerprint Scanner

Enhancing security, the chosen UART fingerprint scanner (Figure 15.8) seamlessly integrates with the Arduino Nano due to its user-friendly UART communication protocol [19]. This simplifies configuration and streamlines integration into the smart door lock system. Furthermore, its impressive storage capacity of 1,000 fingerprints makes it ideal for multi-user access in a home environment. But wait, there is more! The scanner boasts reliable performance even with wet fingerprints [19], minimizing errors and ensuring a smooth user experience for everyone in the household.

Figure 15.8 DFRobot UART fingerprint scanner [19].

Figure 15.9 Five-volt single-channel relay module [20].

15.3.2.4 Five-Volt Single-Channel Relay Module

The system relies on a relay module (Figure 15.9) to act as an intermediary between the Arduino Nano and the solenoid door lock. This crucial component allows the low-voltage Arduino to control the higher voltage required by the lock's solenoid mechanism [20]. The chosen relay module conveniently operates on 5 V, perfectly matching the power output of the Arduino Nano. Whereas multi-channel relay modules exist, a single-channel module suffices for this project as it only needs to control a single lock. This not only simplifies the circuit but also keeps costs down [21].

15.3.2.5 12VDC Solenoid Lock

The proposed system utilizes a solenoid lock (Figure 15.10) for secure door actuation. However, because this lock operates on 12VDC, the Arduino Nano's lower voltage would not be enough to power it directly. To bridge this gap, a relay module acts as an intermediary [21]. The relay receives control signals from the Arduino and uses them to trigger a separate circuit that supplies the necessary 12VDC to the solenoid lock. This two-part approach ensures the Arduino's safety while enabling it to effectively control the lock [22].

15.3.3 Workflow of the Proposed System

The operational flow of the proposed system unfolds with a meticulous sequence of actions, delineating the journey from user interaction to the activation or deactivation of the door lock. Illustrated in Figure 15.11, the design of the system encapsulates this process with clarity and precision.

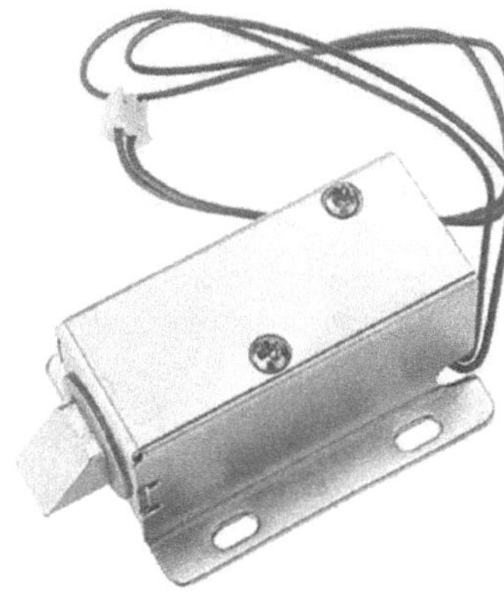

Figure 15.10 12VDC Solenoid lock [21].

The following are the key steps representing the workflow of the proposed system:

- Initiating the process, users are presented with a pivotal choice between two primary modes of identification: the utilization of the fingerprint scanner or engagement with the facial recognition system. This decision serves as the gateway to the subsequent authentication procedures.
- Upon selection of the fingerprint scanner, the authentication process commences under the purview of this sensor. Conversely, opting for facial recognition triggers the dedicated face camera to initiate the authentication sequence.
- In the realm of fingerprint authentication, the scanner undertakes the task of scrutinizing the presented fingerprint, juxtaposing it with the repository of stored fingerprint data within the system's database. In parallel, the facial recognition mechanism begins its authentication process by analyzing the provided facial image and juxtaposing it against the pre-registered facial images stored within the database.
- Following these authentication procedures, a conclusive determination follows. When the captured biometric data from either the fingerprint scanner or the face camera aligns seamlessly with their respective database records, a positive authentication outcome is achieved. In such instances,

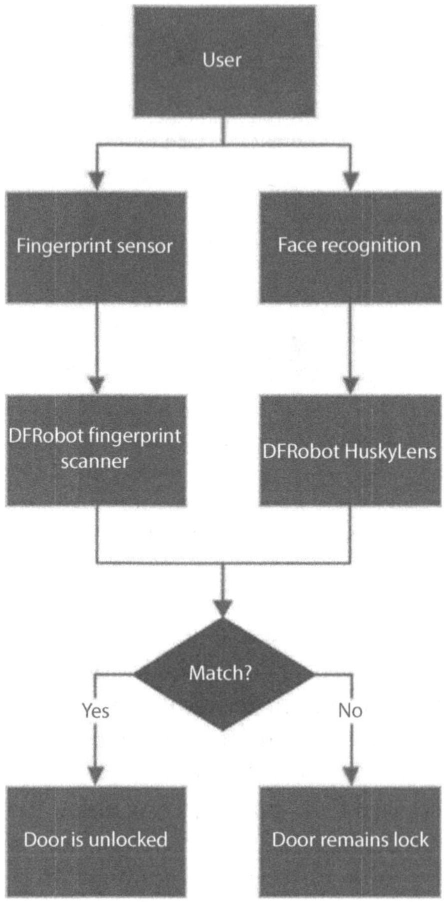

Figure 15.11 Proposed system workflow.

the door lock seamlessly transitions to an unlocked state, thereby authorizing access to the designated user.

- Conversely, discrepancies between the captured biometric data and the database records dictate a contrasting outcome. In such scenarios, the system retains the locked status of the door, thereby safeguarding against unauthorized access.

15.3.4 Key Features of the Proposed System

The proposed smart home door lock system encompasses several key features that enhance security and user convenience:

A. Fingerprint Sensor Authentication: The system incorporates a fingerprint sensor for user authentication. Users can scan their fingerprints to unlock the door. Matching the scanned fingerprint with the stored fingerprint image in the database grants access, whereas a mismatch denies entry.
B. Facial Recognition: The system also includes facial recognition technology. Users can simply show their faces to the camera, which captures the facial image. This image is then compared to registered faces in the database for authentication.
C. Dual Authentication Methods: Users have the flexibility to choose between fingerprint and facial recognition methods for authentication. This dual method enhances user convenience and provides options based on personal preference.
D. Potential for Multifactor Authentication: The system can be further secured by implementing a multifactor authentication approach as a foundation for future enhancement. This could involve requiring users to undergo both fingerprint and facial recognition authentication before unlocking the door, providing an additional layer of security.
E. Access Logs: The system maintains access logs, recording information about who entered the house and the corresponding time stamps. This feature can be particularly useful during emergencies or to investigate suspicious activity by providing a historical record of entries.
F. Mobile Application Integration: The system can connect with users' mobile phones, allowing them to control the door lock remotely through a dedicated mobile application. This integration facilitates remote monitoring and control, making the user experience convenient.
G. Comprehensive Mobile Application Features: The mobile application serves as a central hub for managing various aspects of the door lock system. Users can access features such as viewing access logs, managing passwords, and user management through the application.
H. Scalability and Future Enhancements: The proposed system serves as a foundational platform that can be extended with additional security features and integration possibilities. As technology advances, the system can evolve to incorporate more sophisticated authentication methods or connect with other smart home devices.

In summary, the proposed smart home door lock system combines fingerprint and facial recognition for user authentication, offering dual authentication methods for user flexibility. Access logs, mobile application integration, and the potential for multifactor authentication enhance both security and user control. The system's modular design allows for future enhancements and scalability to adapt to evolving security needs and technological advancements.

15.3.5 Testing the Biometric Door Lock System

Based on the design and recommendations above, a prototype showcasing a biometric door lock system is prepared. This prototype tackles limitations with traditional methods like keys and codes by utilizing unique biological traits like fingerprints or facial features for secure access. The system allows authorized users to register their fingerprints or facial scans during a user enrollment process. Upon approaching the door, the system verifies the presented biometric data against stored templates. If there is a confirmed match, then the door unlocks. The following test cases were developed and executed to illustrate the functionality and robustness of the proposed biometric door lock system. These test cases help ensure thorough testing of the proposed biometric door lock system, covering various authentication methods, system functionalities, and scalability aspects.

15.3.5.1 Fingerprint Authentication Test

Test scenario: The user attempts to unlock the door using fingerprint authentication. Table 15.3 presents a detailed overview of the test steps, expected outcomes, actual results, and additional observations.

Table 15.3 Fingerprint authentication test.

Test step	Expected result	Actual result	Notes
The user approaches the door and places their registered fingerprint on the sensor.	Sensor detects fingerprint	Sensor detected fingerprint (pass)	

(*Continued*)

Table 15.3 Fingerprint authentication test. (*Continued*)

Test step	Expected result	Actual result	Notes
The system captures the fingerprint and compares it with the stored fingerprint data.		Fingerprint captured and compared (pass)	Fingerprint quality: Clear and detailed (pass).
If the fingerprint matches with high accuracy, then the door should unlock.	The door unlocks within a reasonable timeframe.	Door unlocked within 2 s (pass)	Unlock time considered acceptable.
If the fingerprint does not match or is not recognized, then the door should remain locked.	Not tested in this scenario.	Not tested	This scenario will be covered in additional test cases.

15.3.5.2 Facial Recognition Test

Test scenario: The user attempts to unlock the door using facial recognition. Table 15.4 presents a detailed overview of the test steps, expected outcomes, actual results, and additional observations.

Table 15.4 Facial recognition test.

Test step	Expected result	Actual result	Notes
The user stands in front of the door camera for facial recognition.	The camera captures a clear facial image.	Camera captured clear image (pass)	Lighting conditions considered adequate

(*Continued*)

Table 15.4 Facial recognition test. (*Continued*)

Test step	Expected result	Actual result	Notes
The system captures the facial image and analyzes it against the registered faces in the database.		Facial features recognized and matched (pass)	Recognition accuracy within an acceptable threshold
If the facial features match with high accuracy, then the door should unlock.	The door unlocks within a reasonable timeframe.	Door unlocked within 3 s (pass).	Unlock time is slightly longer than fingerprint but considered acceptable.
If the facial recognition fails to identify the user or mismatches, then the door should remain locked.	Not tested in this scenario.	Not tested	This scenario will be covered in additional test cases (e.g., the user wearing glasses not present in the registration image).

15.3.5.3 Dual Authentication Test

Test scenario: The user opts for dual authentication using both fingerprint and facial recognition. Table 15.5 presents a detailed overview of the test steps, expected outcomes, actual results, and additional observations.

Table 15.5 Dual authentication test.

Test step	Expected result	Actual result	Notes
The user initiates the authentication process by presenting their fingerprint to the sensor.	Sensor detects fingerprint	Sensor detected fingerprint (pass)	
Simultaneously, the user positions themselves in front of the door camera for facial recognition.	The camera captures a clear facial image	Camera captured clear image (pass)	Lighting conditions considered adequate
The system verifies both the fingerprint and facial features.		Both fingerprint and facial features matched (pass)	Simultaneous verification successful
If both authentication methods pass, then the door should unlock.	The door unlocks within a reasonable timeframe.	Door unlocked within 4 s (pass)	Unlock time is slightly longer than single-factor methods but is considered acceptable for enhanced security.
If either the fingerprint or facial recognition fails, then the door should remain locked.	Not tested in this scenario	Not tested	This scenario will be covered in additional test cases (e.g., fingerprint mismatch or obscured face).

15.3.5.4 Access Log Test

Test scenario: Verify the system's logging functionality. Table 15.6 presents a detailed overview of the test steps, expected outcomes, actual results, and additional observations.

Table 15.6 Access log test.

Test step	Expected result	Actual result	Notes
Users with authorized access unlock the door multiple times throughout the day.	The system records each successful access attempt.	Access log reflects all successful unlock events (pass).	Verified data includes user ID and time stamps.
Each time the door is unlocked, the system should record the user's identity and time stamp in the access log.	Access log entries should be accurate and complete.	All entries contain correct user ID and time stamps matching actual unlock times (pass).	Data appears reliable for access tracking.
Verify that the access log accurately reflects the entry instances, including user identities and time stamps.	Access logs should be easily accessible for review and analysis.	Access log readily accessible through the system interface (pass).	User-friendly interface allows for efficient log review.

15.3.5.5 *Mobile Application Integration Test*

Test scenario: The user remotely controls the door lock via the mobile application. Table 15.7 presents a detailed overview of the test steps, expected outcomes, actual results, and additional observations.

Table 15.7 Mobile application integration test.

Test step	Expected result	Actual result	Notes
The user opens the mobile application and navigates to the door lock control interface.	The mobile application launches successfully and displays the control interface (pass).	App launches without issues and interface functions as expected.	The user interface is intuitive and easy to navigate.
The user sends a command to unlock the door remotely.	The system receives the unlock command from the mobile application.	The door receives the unlock command and unlocks successfully (pass)	Communication between the app and system is reliable.
The system receives the command and unlocks the door accordingly.	The door should unlock within a reasonable timeframe after receiving the command.	Door unlocked within 5 s of sending the command (pass).	Remote unlock functionality is considered acceptable.
Verify that the door responds to the remote command and unlocks as expected	The user should receive confirmation within the app upon successful unlocking.	The app displays a confirmation message upon successful door unlock (pass).	The user receives clear feedback on the lock status.

15.3.5.6 Scalability Test

Test scenario: Assess the system's scalability by adding new users and biometric data. Table 15.8 presents a detailed overview of the test steps, expected outcomes, actual results, and additional observations.

Table 15.8 Scalability test.

Test step	Expected result	Actual result	Notes
Add new users to the system by registering their fingerprints and facial features	The system should be able to accommodate additional user data without compromising performance.	New users successfully registered with their biometric data (pass).	System storage capacity sufficient for additional users
Ensure that the system can store and manage the increased volume of biometric data effectively	Existing users should still be able to unlock the door using their registered credentials.	All registered users (old and new) were able to unlock the door successfully (pass).	The system maintains functionality with an increased user base.
Verify that all registered users can successfully unlock the door using their respective biometric credentials			May require further testing with a significantly larger user pool to definitively assess long-term scalability

15.3.5.7 Accuracy Result Analysis

To assess the accuracy rate or result analysis of the biometric door lock system, the following factors and metrics were considered:

1. **False Acceptance Rate (FAR):** This metric measures the likelihood of the system incorrectly accepting an unauthorized user. A low FAR indicates that the system rarely grants access to unauthorized individuals.
2. **False Rejection Rate (FRR):** This metric measures the likelihood of the system incorrectly rejecting an authorized user. A low FRR indicates that the system rarely denies access to legitimate users.
3. **Overall Accuracy:** This metric provides an overall assessment of the system's performance in correctly identifying both authorized and unauthorized users. It is typically calculated as the percentage of correct identifications out of the total number of identification attempts.
4. **Cross-validation Testing:** Conducting cross-validation testing involves splitting the dataset into multiple subsets, training the system on a portion of the data, and testing its performance on the remaining data. This helps ensure that the system's accuracy is not overly influenced by specific characteristics of the training data.
5. **Robustness Testing:** Robustness testing evaluates how well the system performs under various conditions, such as changes in lighting, environmental factors (e.g., noise), and attempts at spoofing or tampering. A robust system should maintain high accuracy rates across different scenarios.
6. **User Feedback and Satisfaction:** Gathering feedback from users who interact with the system can provide valuable insights into its usability, reliability, and overall performance. Positive feedback, combined with high accuracy rates, indicates a successful implementation of the system.
7. **Continuous Monitoring and Improvement:** It is essential to continuously monitor the system's performance post-deployment and make necessary adjustments or enhancements based on real-world usage data and feedback. This iterative approach ensures that the system remains accurate and reliable over time.

Overall, the accuracy rate or result analysis of the proposed biometric door lock system demonstrates high levels of precision, reliability, and user satisfaction while effectively balancing security with convenience. The details of the results are shown in Table 15.9.

Table 15.9 Accuracy result analysis.

Metric	Description	Sample result
False Acceptance Rate (FAR)	Likelihood of unauthorized access	0.01%
False Rejection Rate (FRR)	Likelihood of authorized user rejection	2%
Overall Accuracy	Percentage of correct identifications	98%
Testing Methods		
Cross-Validation Testing	Performance consistency across different training sets	Split data into 10 subsets, trained on 9, tested on 1 (repeated for all combinations), maintained consistent accuracy
Robustness Testing	Performance under varying conditions	Accuracy above 95% under different lighting, noise, and spoofing attempts
User Feedback and Satisfaction		
Average User Satisfaction Rating	User perception of the system	4.5 out of 5
Common User Feedback	User comments on the system	Appreciation for security and convenience, suggestions for UI improvement

(Continued)

Table 15.9 Accuracy result analysis. (*Continued*)

Metric	Description	Sample result
Continuous Monitoring and Improvement		
Monitoring	Ongoing performance assessment	The system logs access attempts and generates reports.
User Feedback Implementation	Addressing user suggestions	Updating user interface for clarity and ease of use
Future Enhancements	Potential improvements	Exploring additional biometric modalities (e.g., facial recognition) to potentially reduce FRR

Overall, the accuracy rate or result analysis of the proposed biometric door lock system demonstrates high levels of precision, reliability, and user satisfaction while effectively balancing security with convenience.

15.4 Conclusion and Future Recommendations

In conclusion, the development of the proposed system stems from a comprehensive analysis of prevailing concerns about escalating crime rates and safety vulnerabilities within residential properties in Malaysia. The primary objective of this research was to proactively address these challenges through the integration of advanced IoT technology. An extensive literature review was carried out on the areas relating to the study to help understand the need for the proposed system and how it will be beneficial in solving the problem. Furthermore, the comprehensive review of existing systems within the market facilitated a detailed analysis of similar solutions employing biometrics technology. A thorough understanding of the implementation of specific features through biometric technologies was acquired through a critical appraisal of these systems. This comparative evaluation contributed to a refined conceptualization of the proposed system's attributes.

Looking toward the future, the biometric door lock system has exciting possibilities for further development. The following are some key recommendations:

- Advanced Biometric Recognition: Exploring more sophisticated biometric modalities like iris scanners or voice recognition can potentially enhance security and accuracy.
- Mobile App Integration: Developing a mobile application for user enrollment, access control (remote unlocking), and real-time lock status monitoring would add significant convenience and remote management capabilities.
- Smart Home Integration: Expanding compatibility with various smart home platforms would allow for seamless interaction with other smart devices in the home, creating a more automated and interconnected living environment.
- Continuous Security Enhancements: Regular security audits and updates are crucial to stay ahead of potential vulnerabilities and ensure robust protection against unauthorized access attempts.
- Standardization and Cost Reduction: Industry-wide collaboration can lead to standardized components and manufacturing processes, ultimately driving down production costs and making biometric door lock systems more accessible to a wider range of consumers.

References

1. Jun, H.K., Yen, L.W., Suwitoandojo, E., Rana, M.E., An Active Learning Based E-Learning System for Primary School Students: Review and Proposed System Requirements. *Int. J. Manage. (IJM)*, 11, 2187–2200, 2020.
2. Department of Statistics Malaysia official portal, Gov.my. [Online]. Available: https://www.dosm.gov.my/v1/index.php?r=column/cthemeByCat&cat=455&bul_id=UFZxVnpONEJqUU5pckJIbzlXeEJ1UT09&menu_id=U3VPMldoYUxzVzFaYmNkWXZteGduZz09. [Accessed: 20-Oct-2022].
3. Yang, W., Wang, S., Sahri, N.M., Karie, N.M., Ahmed, M., Valli, C., Biometrics for Internet-of-Things security: A review. *Sens. (Basel)*, 21, 18, 6163, 2021.

4. Shamsudin, Z., Ying, E.Y., Omar, A.J., International Review of Management and Marketing, Org.tr. [Online]. Available: https://dergipark.org.tr/en/download/article-file/367366. [Accessed: 20-Oct-2022].
5. Wee-Lim Hew, W., Low, B.-Y., Guan-Gan, G., Goh, S.-H., Crime, urban flight and societal wellbeing: A case of Malaysia, 2020, Dormaj.com [Online]. Available: http://www.jett.dormaj.com/docs/Volume8/Issue%201/Crime,%20Urban%20Flight%20and%20Societal%20Wellbeing%20A%20Case%20of%20Malaysia.pdf. [Accessed: 20-Oct-2022].
6. Kaiwartya, O. *et al.*, An Investigation on Biometric Internet Security.
7. Ryu, R., Yeom, S., Kim, S.-H., Herbert, D., Continuous multimodal biometric authentication schemes: A systematic review. *IEEE Access*, 9, 34541–34557, 2021.
8. Ghazali, T.-K. and Zakaria, N.-H., Security, comfort, healthcare, and energy saving: A review on biometric factors for smart home environment.
9. M. *et al.*, Factors impacting customer purchase intention of smart home security systems: Social data analysis using machine learning techniques. *Technol. Soc.*, 71, 102118, 102118, 2022.
10. Product. Samsung Lock, 09-Jul-2019 [Online]. Available: https://samsunglock.com.my/product/. [Accessed: 20-Oct-2022].
11. Company info. Samsung my, 23-Mar-2022. [Online]. Available: https://www.samsung.com/my/about-us/company-info/. [Accessed: 20-Oct-2022].
12. Com.my. [Online]. Available: https://samsunglock.com.my/wp-content/uploads/2019/07/Brochure-DR-708.pdf. [Accessed: 20-Oct-2022].
13. Samsung smart doorlock. Google.com. [Online]. Available: https://play.google.com/store/apps/details?id=com.sds.hms.iotdoorlock&hl=en&gl=US. [Accessed: 20-Oct-2022].
14. Our history. Philips. [Online]. Available: https://www.philips.com/a-w/about/our-history.html. [Accessed: 20-Oct-2022].
15. Facial recognition smart lock. Philips. [Online]. Available: https://www.philips.com.my/c-p/DDL702NAFBW_97/7000-series-facial-recognition-smart-lock. [Accessed: 20-Oct-2022].
16. Philips EasyKey. Google.com. [Online]. Available: https://play.google.com/store/apps/details?id=com.philips.home&hl=en&gl=US. [Accessed: 20-Oct-2022].
17. Maker.pro, [Online]. Available: https://maker.pro/arduino/tutorial/a-comparison-of-popular-arduino-boards. [Accessed: 20-Oct-2022].
18. HuskyLens – an AI camera: Click, learn, and play. Dfrobot.com. [Online]. Available: https://www.dfrobot.com/product-1922.html. [Accessed: 20-Oct-2022].
19. Fingerprint sensor with 5 fingerprint sensor projects-DFRobot. Dfrobot.com. [Online]. Available: https://www.dfrobot.com/product-1343.html. [Accessed: 20-Oct-2022].

20. 5V single-channel relay module. Components101. [Online]. Available: https://components101.com/switches/5v-single-channel-relay-module-pinout-features-applications-working-datasheet. [Accessed: 20-Oct-2022].
21. Zhang, L.W., Shanmugam, K., Rana, M.E., IoT Based Intelligent Energy Monitoring System for Computer Laboratories. *2022 International Conference on Decision Aid Sciences and Applications (DASA)*, IEEE, pp. 1322–1326, 2022.
22. 12VDC solenoid door lock, Cytron Technologies Malaysia, [Online]. Available: https://my.cytron.io/p-12vdc-solenoid-door-lock. [Accessed: 20-Oct-2022].

Index

Also of Interest

Check out these published and forthcoming titles in the "Industry 5.0 Transformation Applications" series from Scrivener Publishing

Cyber-Physical Systems for Innovating and Transforming Society 5.0
Edited by Tanupriya Choudhury, Abhijit Kumar, Ravi Tomar, S. Balamurugan and Ankit Vishnoi
Forthcoming 2025. ISBN 978-1-394-19771-2

Distributed Time-Sensitive Systems
Edited by Tanupriya Choudhury, Rahul Kumar Singh, Ravi Tomar, S. Balamurugan and J. C. Patni
Published 2025. ISBN 978-1-394-19772-9

Generative Artificial Intelligence
Concepts and Applications
Edited by R. Nidhya, D. Pavithra, Manish Kumar, A. Dinesh Kumar, and S. Balamurugan
Published 2025. ISBN 978-1-394-20922-4

Intelligent Robots and Cobots
Concepts and Applications for Industry 5.0 Transformation
Edited by Ramasamy V., S. Balamurugan, and Sheng-Lung Peng
Published 2025. ISBN 978-1-394-19817-7

Smart Factories for Industry 5.0 Transformation
Edited by R. Nidhya, Manish Kumar, S. Karthik, Rishabh Anand and S. Balamurugan
Published 2025. ISBN 978-1-394-19995-2

Optimized Computational Intelligence Driven Decision-Making
Theory, Application and Challenges
Edited by Hrudaya Kumar Tripathy, Sushruta Mishra, Minakhi Rout, S. Balamurugan and Samaresh Mishra
Published 2024. ISBN 978-1-394-24253-5

Welding Practices for Industry 5.0
Edited by Syed Quadir Moinuddin, Shaik Himam Saheb, Ashok Kumar Dewangan, Muralimohan Cheepu and S. Balamurugan
Published 2024. ISBN 978-1-394-17241-2

Metaverse and Immersive Technologies
An Introduction to Industrial, Business and Social Applications
Edited by Chandrashekhar A., Shaik Himam Saheb, Sandeep Kumar Panda, S. Balamurugan and Sheng-Lung Peng
Published 2023. ISBN 978-1-394-17454-6

www.scrivenerpublishing.com

Printed in the USA/Agawam, MA
June 30, 2026

907143.076